THE LORDSHIP OF GALLOWAY

The
LORDSHIP
of
GALLOWAY

Richard Oram

JOHN DONALD
EDINBURGH

First published in 2000 by John Donald,
an imprint of Birlinn Limited
8 Canongate Venture
5 New Street
Edinburgh
EH8 8BH

www.birlinn.co.uk

ISBN 0 85976 541 5

British Library Cataloguing-in-Publication Data
A catalogue record for this book is available from the British Library

Typeset by Textype, Cambridge
Printed and bound in Creative Print and Design, Ebbw Vale

CONTENTS

LIST OF MAPS

LIST OF ILLUSTRATIONS

ACKNOWLEDGEMENTS

In the twelve years that it has taken to get this research to publication stage, a great volume of debt has been accumulated. To begin at the beginning, I would express again my gratitude to Mr David Corner, formerly of the Department of Mediæval History, University of St Andrews, who first suggested the lordship of Galloway as a research topic at the Junior Honours' Garden Party at St John's House in May 1982; to Professor Nicholas Brookes, who steered the PhD through its first years from 1983; and to Professor Donald Watt and Dr Barbara Crawford, who took over its supervision on Nick Brookes' appointment to the Chair of History at Birmingham and who saw it to its belated conclusion in 1988. To them all go my deepest and sincerest thanks for their efforts and encouragement. Thanks are also due to Drs Norman and Simone MacDougall, Dr Chris Given-Wilson, Miss Anne Kettle, Miss Lorna Walker, Dr Colin Martin, Mr James Kenworthy, Dr Nick Dixon, Dr Veronica Smart, Professor Donald Bullough, Professor Christopher Smout and Professor Roy Owen for their freely given advice, support and assistance in the preparation of the thesis from which this book was generated. They corrected me of many errors and misapprehensions and, without them, this book would have been very much the poorer.

For those who suffered in the preparation of the thesis and the book, sorry and thanks for your forbearance. To my contemporaries at St John's House 1983–7 – Christine McGladdery, Seymour House, Glen Scorgie, Lindsay Macgregor, Giles Dove, Ann Johnson, Constance Schummer, Isobel Moreira, Alice and Alicia Correa, Rob Whiteman and Bruce (I've got two degrees – three now!) Gordon, I express my greatest appreciation for their tolerance. To my wife, Justine, who as a flatmate at St Andrews had to endure my changing moods as the thesis moved in fits and starts, then has had to repeat the whole experience fourteen years on, goes my undying thanks and love for all her support and understanding. To Alasdair and Lauren, who have grown up with their father's fixation with boring dead people and piles of rubble in fields – get used to it! There's plenty more where this came from.

In Galloway, I have many debts to repay. To Peter Hill and my many friends and colleagues at the Whithorn excavation go my especial thanks for helping me to see the wood through the trees in 1986 and 1987, and to

Peter a particular thank you for the recipe for vodka strawberries in champagne; to Daphne Brooke must go an especially big thank you, your insights have considerably enriched my research and conversations with you have always made me reconsider many of my basic assumptions; to Bill and Sheila Cormack for their hospitality and encouragement; and to my friends and colleagues on the Whithorn Trust Research Committee.

To the people who helped to bring to an end my dithering over whether or not to re-write the thesis for publication go – I think! – my thanks and appreciation; to Professor Allan Macinnes for telling me to sit down and get on with it; to Geoff Stell, whose input on lordship and architecture and on the role of the Balliols has been invaluable; to Hugh Andrew for agreeing to publish it; and to Dr Alex Woolf for all his efforts in purging the early chapters of heresy and error, and for pointing me in the direction of various tomes on Irish and Welsh history.

A final thanks must go to the late Dr Ronald Cant, who would always tolerate the pretentious ramblings of a research student, was always willing to discuss queries and help unpick knotty problems, and who acted as Devil's Advocate on many doubtful points.

RDO

DEDICATION

To the memory of DMM and MMA, who planted the seed of which this is the fruit, and John, whose own distinctive contribution will never be forgotten.

LIST OF ABBREVIATIONS

SOURCES

AD	*Annals of Durham,* in *Monumenta Germaniae Historica, Scriptores,* xix.
AFM	*Annála Ríoghachta Éireann; Annals of the Kingdom of Ireland by the Four Masters from the Earliest Period to the year 1616,* ed. and trans. J. O'Donvan (Dublin, 1851).
AI	*The Annals of Inisfallen,* ed. and trans. S. Mac Airt (Dublin, 1951).
ALC	*The Annals of Loch Cé,* ed. and trans. W. M. Hennessy (London, 1871).
AMW	*Annals of the Reigns of Malcolm and William, Kings of Scotland,* ed. A. C. Lawrie (Glasgow, 1910).
APS	*The Acts of the Parliaments of Scotland,* eds T. Thompson and C. Innes (Edinburgh, 1814–75).
ASC	*The Anglo-Saxon Chronicle,* trans. G. N. Garmonsway (London, 1972).
AT	'The Annals of Tigernach', ed. W. Stokes, *Review Celtique,* 16–18 (1895–97).
AU	*Annals of Ulster,* ed. and trans. W. M. Hennessy (London, 1887).
Ailred, *de Standardo*	Ailred of Rievaulx, *Relatio Venerabilis Aelredi Abbatis Rievallensis, de Standardo,* in *Chronicles of Stephen* etc., ed. R. Howlett (London, 1884–9).
Ailred, *Epistola*	Ailred of Rievaulx, *Epistola de genealogia regum Anglorum,* in Roger Twysden, *Historiae Anglicanae Scriptores Decem* (London, 1652).
Ailred, *Saints of Hexham*	Ailred of Rievaulx, *Saints of Hexham,*

	in *The Priory of Hexham* (Surtees Society, 1863).
Anderson, *Diplomata*	*Selectus Diplomatum et Numismatum Scotiae Thesaurus*, ed. J. Anderson (Edinburgh, 1739).
Anderson, *Early Sources*	*Early Sources of Scottish History 500–1286*, ed. A. O. Anderson (Edinburgh, 1922).
Anderson, *Scottish Annals*	*Scottish Annals from English Chroniclers 500–1286*, ed. A. O. Anderson (London, 1908).
Annales Cambriae	*Annales Cambriae*, ed. J. Williams ab Ithel (London, 1860).
Annals of Ireland	*Annals of Ireland. Three Fragments by Dubhaltach mac Firbisigh*, ed. J. O'Donovan (Dublin, 1860).
Archbishop Gray's Register	*The Register, or Rolls, of Walter Gray, Lord Archbishop of York*, ed. J. Raine (Surtees Society, 1870).
Archbishop Greenfield's Register	*The Register of William Greenfield, Lord Archbishop of York*, eds A. H. Thompson and W. Brown (Surtees Society, 1931–8).
Archbishop Romeyn's Register	*The Register of John le Romeyn, Lord Archbishop of York*, ed. J. Raine (Surtees Society, 1870).
Bagimond's Roll	'Bagimond's Roll, Statement of the Tenths of the Kingdom of Scotland', ed. A. I. Dunlop, *Miscellany of the Scottish History Society*, vi (1939).
Beauly Chrs	*Charters of the Abbey of Beauly* (Grampian Club, 1877).
Benedict of Peterborough	*Benedict of Peterborough*, ed. W. Stubbs (London, 1867).
Bower, *Scotichronicon*	Walter Bower, *Scotichronicon*, ed. D. E. R. Watt and others (Aberdeen and Edinburgh, 1987–98).
CDI	*Calendar of Documents Relating to Ireland*, ed. H. Sweetman (Dublin, 1875–88).
CDS	*Calendar of Documents Relating to Scotland*, ed. J. Bain, i–iv (Edinburgh, 1881–8); ed. G. G. Simpson and J. D. Galbraith, v [supplementary] (Edinburgh, 1986).

CKS — *Chronicle of the Kings of Scotland*, in *Chronicles of the Picts, Chronicles of the Scots*, ed. W. F. Skene (Edinburgh, 1867).

CPL — *Calendar of Entries in the Papal Registers Relating to Great Britain and Ireland: Papal Letters*, ed. W. H. Bliss and others (London, 1893–).

Cal. Pat. Rolls — *Calendar of Patent Rolls Preserved in the Public Record Office 1216–1509* (London, 1891–1916).

Chron. Fordun — *Johannis de Fordun, Chronica Gentis Scotorum*, ed. W. F. Skene (Edinburgh, 1871–2).

Chron. Guisborough — *Chronicles of Walter of Guisborough*, ed. H. Rothwell (Camden Society, 1957).

Chron. Henry of Huntingdon — *Henrici Archidiaconati Huntendunensis Historia Anglorum*, ed. T. Arnold (London, 1879).

Chron. Holyrood — *A Scottish Chronicle Known as the Chronicle of Holyrood*, ed. M. O. Anderson (Scottish History Society, 1938).

Chron. Lanercost — *Chronicon de Lanercost* (Maitland Club, 1839).

Chron. Majora — Mathew Paris, *Chronica Majora*, ed. H. R. Luard (London, 1872–83).

Chron. Man (Munch) — *The Chronicle of Man and the Sudreys*, ed. P. A. Munch and Rev. Dr Goss (Douglas, 1874).

Chron. Mann — *Chronica Regum Manniae et Insularum. A Facsimile of the Manuscript Codex Julius A. VII in the British Museum* (Douglas, 1924).

Chron. Melrose — *The Chronicle of Melrose from the Cottonian Manuscript, Faustina B. ix in the British Museum*, eds A. O. Anderson and others (London, 1926),

Chron. Rishanger — William Rishanger, *Chronica et Annales*, ed. H. T. Riley (London, 1865).

Chron. Wyntoun — Androw of Wynton, *The Orygynale Cronykil of Scotland*, ed. D. Laing (Edinburgh, 1872–9).

Coupar Angus Charters	*Charters of the Abbey of Coupar Angus*, ed. D. E. Easson (Scottish History Society, 1947).
De Obsessione Dunelmi	'De Obsessione Dunelmi', in *Symeonis Monachi Opera Omnia*, ed. T. Arnold (London, 1882).
De Primo Saxonum Adventu	'De Primo Saxonum Adventu', in *Symeonis Monachi Opera Omnia*, ed. T. Arnold (London, 1882).
Dryburgh Liber	*Liber S. Marie de Dryburgh* (Bannatyne Club, 1847).
Dugdale, *Monasticon Anglicanum*	*Sir William Dugdale's Monasticon Anglicanum*, v (London, 1846).
Dunstable Annals	*Annales Prioratus de Dunstaplia, in Annales Monastici*, ed. H. R. Luard, iii (London, 1866).
ER	*The Exchequer Rolls of Scotland*, eds J. Stuart and others (Edinburgh, 1878–1908).
Finchale Charters	*Charters of Endowment, Inventories and Ancient Rolls of the Priory of Finchale in County Durham* (Surtees Society, 1837).
Flateyiarbók	Flateyiarbók, eds C. R. Unger and G. Vigfusson (Christiania, 1859–68).
Florence of Worcester	Florence of Worcester, *Chronicon ex Chronicis*, 450–1117, ed. B. Thorpe (London, 1848–9).
Flores Historiarum	*Flores Historiarum*, ed. H. R. Luard (London, 1890).
Furness Annals	*Annals of Furness* in *Chronicles of Stephen*, etc., ed. R. Howlett (London, 1884–9).
Glasgow Registrum	*Registrum Episcopatus Glasguensis* (Bannatyne and Maitland Clubs, 1843).
HDE	*Historia Dunelmensis Ecclesiae*, in *Symeonis Monachi Opera Omnia*, ed. T. Arnold (London, 1882).
HR	*Historia Regum, in Symeonis Monachi Opera Omnia*, ed. T. Arnold (London, 1882).
HSC	*Historia de Sancto Cuthberto*, in *Symeonis Monachi Opera Omnia*, ed. T. Arnold (London, 1882).
Heimskringla	*Heimskringla*, ed. Jónsson (Copen-

hagen, 1893–1901).

Highland Papers	*Highland Papers*, ed. J. R. N. Macphail (Scottish History Society, 1914–34).
Histoire des Ducs de Normandie	*Histoire des Ducs de Normandie et des Rois d'Angleterre*, ed. F. Michel (Paris, 1840).
Historians of York	*Historians of the Church of York and Its Archbishops*, ed. J. Raine (London, 1880).
Holm Cultram Register	*Register and Records of Holm Cultram*, eds F. Grainger and W. G. Collingwood (Cumberland and Westmorland Archaeological and Antiquarian Society, 1929).
Holyrood Liber	*Liber Cartarum Sancte Crucis* (Bannatyne Club, 1840).
Inquis. Retorn. Abbrev.	*Inquisitionem ad Capellam Domini Regis Retornatarum, quae in publicis archivis Scotiae adhuc servantur, Abbreviatio*, ed. T. Thomson (1811–16).
John of Hexham	*Historia Regum, continuata per Joannem Hagulstadensem*, in *Symeonis Monachi Opera Omnia*, ed. T. Arnold (London, 1885).
Jordan Fantosme	*Jordan Fantosme's Chronicle*, ed. and trans. R. C. Johnston (Oxford, 1981).
Kelso Liber	*Liber S. Marie de Calchou* (Bannatyne Club, 1846).
Knights of St. John	*The Knights of St John of Jerusalem in Scotland*, eds I. B. Cowan and others (Scottish History Society, 1983).
Lanercost Cartulary	*The Lanercost Cartulary* (Cumbria County Record Office MS DZ/1), ed. J. M. Todd (Surtees Society, 1997).
Lawrie, ESC	*Early Scottish Charters Prior to 1153*, ed. A. C. Lawrie (Glasgow, 1905).
Life of St Malachy	*St Bernard's Life of St Malachy of Armagh*, ed. and trans. H. J. Lawlor (London, 1920).
Lindores Chartulary	*Chartulary of the Abbey of Lindores* (Scottish History Society, 1903).
MGH, Scriptores	*Monumenta Germaniae Historia, Scriptores* (Hanover, 1826–96).
Marianus Scottus	'Mariani Scotti Chronicon', ed. G.

	Waitz, in *MGH Scriptorum*, v, ed. G. Pertz (Hanover, 1844).
Melrose Liber	*Liber S. Marie de Melros* (Bannatyne Club, 1837).
Midlothian Chrs	*Charters of the Hospital of Soltre, of Trinity College, Edinburgh, and other Collegiate Churches in Midlothian* (Bannatyne Club, 1861).
Moray Registrum	*Registrum Episcopatus Moraviensis* (Bannatyne Club, 1837).
Morton Registrum	*Registrum Honoris de Morton* (Bannatyne Club, 1853).
Newbattle Registrum	*Registrum S. Marie de Neubotle* (Bannatyne Club, 1849).
Njal's Saga	*Njal's Saga*, trans. M. Magnusson and H. Pálsson (London, 1960).
North Berwick Carte	*Carte Monialium de Northberwic* (Bannatyne Club, 1847).
Orderic Vitalis	*The Ecclesiastical History of Orderic Vitalis*, ed. and trans. M. Chibnall (Oxford, 1969–80).
Orkneyinga Saga	*Orkneyinga Saga. The History of the Earls of Orkney*, trans. H. Pálsson and P. Edwards (London, 1981).
Oxford Balliol Deeds	*The Oxford Deeds of Balliol College*, ed. H. E. Salter (Oxford Historical Society, 1913).
Paisley Registrum	*Registrum Monasterii de Passelet* (Maitland Club, 1832).
Palgrave, *Docs Hist. Scot.*	*Documents and Records Illustrating the History of Scotland*, ed. F. Palgrave (London, 1837).
RCAHMS	*Royal Commission on the Ancient and Historical Monuments of Scotland.*
RMS	*Registrum Magni Sigilli Regum Scotorum*, ed. J. M. Thomson and others (Edinburgh, 1882–1914).
RRS	*Regesta Regum Scotorum*, eds G. W. S. Barrow and others (1960–).
Ralph de Diceto	*Imagines Historiarum Imagines Historiarum in Radulfi de Diceto Decani Lundoniniensis Opera Historica*, ed. W. Stubbs (London, 1876).
Reginald of Durham	*Reginald Monachi Dunelmensis Libellus de Admirandis Beati Cuth-*

	berti Virtutibus (Surtees Society, 1835).
Richard of Hexham	Richard of Hexham, *De Gestis Regis Stephani et de Bello Standardii*, in *Chronicles of Stephen*, etc., ed. R. Howlett (London, 1884–89).
Rites of Durham	*Rites of Durham, Being a Description or Brief Declaration of All the Ancient Monuments, Rites and Customs Belonging or Being Within the Monastical Church of Durham Before the Suppression. Written 1593* (Surtees Society, 1902).
Robert of Torigni	*The Chronicle of Robert of Torigni*, in *Chronicles of Stephen*, etc., ed. R. Howlett (London, 1884–89).
Roger of Howden	*Chronica Rogeri de Hovedon*, ed. W. Stubbs (London, 1869).
Roger Wendover	Roger Wendover, *Chronica sive Flores Historiarum*, ed. H. G. Hewlett (London, 1886–89).
Rot. Lit. Claus.	*Rotuli Literarum Clausarum*, ed. T. Duffus-Hardy, i (London, 1833).
Rotuli Scotiae	*Rotuli Scotiae in Turri Londiniensi et in Domo Capitulari Westmonasteriensi Asservati*, eds D. Macpherson et al. (London, 1814–19).
St Bees Register	*The Register of the Priory of St. Bees*, ed. J. Wilson (Surtees Society, 1915).
St Bernard, *Letters*	*The Letters of St. Bernard of Clairvaux*, trans. B. Scott James (Stroud, 1998).
SP	*The Scots Peerage*, ed. J. Balfour-Paul (Edinburgh, 1904–14).
Symeon of Durham	*Symeonis Monachi Opera Omnia*, ed. T. Arnold (London, 1882–5).
Walter Daniel	Walter Daniel, *The Life of Ailred of Rievaulx*, ed. and trans. F. M. Powicke (London, 1950).
Watt, *Fasti*	*Fasti Ecclesiae Scoticane Medii Aevi Ad Annum 1638*, ed. D. E. R. Watt (Scottish Record Society, 1969).
Wetheral Register	*Register of the Priory of Wetheral*, ed. J. E. Prescott (Cumberland and Westmorland Archaeological and

	Antiquarian Society, 1897).
Wigtownshire Charters	*Wigtownshire Charters*, ed. R. C. Reid (Scottish History Society, 1960).
William of Malmesbury	*Willelmi Malmesburiensis Monachi de Gestis Regum Anglorum*, ed. W. Stubbs (London, 1887–89).
William of Newburgh	William of Newburgh, *Historiam Rerum Anglicarum*, in *Chronicles of Stephen*, etc., ed. R. Howlett (London, 1884–89).
Vita Godrici	Reginald of Durham, *Libellus de Vita et Miraculis S. Godrici, Heremitae de Finchale*, ed. J. Stevenson (Surtees Society, 1847).

JOURNALS

AHR	*Agricultural History Review*
BIHR	*Bulletin of the Institute of Historical Research*
EHR	*English Historical Review*
JMH	*Journal of Medieval History*
MLN	*Modern Language Notes*
PMLA	*Proceedings of the Modern Language Association*
PPRS	*Publications of the Pipe Roll Society*
PSAS	*Proceedings of the Society of Antiquaries of Scotland*
RCHS	*Records of the Church History Society*
SHR	*Scottish Historical Review*
TCWAAS	*Transactions of the Cumberland and Westmorland Archaeological and Antiquarian Society.*
TDGNHAS	*Transactions of the Dumfriesshire and Galloway Natural History and Antiquarian Society*
TGSI	*Transactions of the Gaelic Society of Inverness*
TRHS	*Transactions of the Royal Historical Society*
TRSE	*Transactions of the Royal Society of Edinburgh*
TSES	*Transactions of the Scottish Ecclesiological Society*

FOREWORD

The origins of this book lie in my St Andrews PhD thesis on the Lordship of Galloway *c*.1000–*c*.1250. Completed in a rush in a bedsit in Birmingham, where I was working as an insurance underwriter, the thesis text was deeply flawed in parts, especially in its analysis of Fergus and Alan. As a consequence, there was no question of publication as a whole, but selected sections were instead reproduced as essays in the *Innes Review, Pictish Art Society Journal, Scottish Historical Review, Transactions of the Dumfriesshire and Galloway Natural History and Antiquarian Society* and *Scandinavian Settlement in Northern Britain*, the volume of essays edited by Barbara Crawford and presented to Bill Nicolaisen. The scale of the flaws was revealed to me with devastating clarity in 1993 by Keith Stringer's outstanding essay, 'Periphery and core in thirteenth-century Scotland: Alan son of Roland, Lord of Galloway and Constable of Scotland', that set a new benchmark not only in the study of medieval Galloway but also in the broader analysis of the relationship between the political and cultural epicentres of the kingdom and the zone of predominantly Gaelic culture that had been presented traditionally as marginalised and increasingly irrelevant in the development of the kingdom. While I do not agree with all of Dr Stringer's analysis and interpretation, the scale of my debt to that piece of work, and to his subsequent work on the *acta* of the lords of Galloway, is very evident in Chapter 4.

Since the completion of my thesis research in 1987–88, a great mass of new work both on Galloway and on the regions that had the greatest bearing on the development and demise of the lordship has appeared in print. Together with my own changing ideas and interpretations, this ensured that a radical re-working of the thesis was necessary. Even Chapters 5 and 7, that first appeared in part as my essays 'A family business?' and 'Dervorgilla, the Balliols and Buittle', have been significantly developed and re-structured to accommodate both much of this new work and my own current research. The consequence of this has been that this present book bears only a superficial resemblance to the thesis from which it grew. Indeed, the volume of my own new research and the stimulating work of scholars such as Keith Stringer, Seán Duffy, Daphne Brooke, Peter Hill and Benjamin Hudson, has produced a significant shift of balance and emphasis within the text. As a result of the major expansion in particular of the discussion of the origins of the lordship – and diocese – Scoto-Galwegian relations in the twelfth century, and of the careers of Fergus and Alan, the decision was taken with great reluctance to drop certain other sections of the original thesis' coverage. The main casualties here have been the studies of the development of the parochial system, and of the monasteries and their estates, that formed the first section of Chapter 6.1 and the whole of 6.2 of the thesis, while large sections of Chapter 7 discussing the ethnic make-up of medieval Galloway, the issue of the mythical Galloway Picts, and the development of burghs and town-based trade in the twelfth and thirteenth centuries, have been omitted here. I hope that at least some of this work will appear subsequently in print.

The study of the monastic church in Galloway in the twelfth and thirteenth centuries has been the subject of two major pieces of fresh research. The first is R. Andrew McDonald's 'Scoto-Norse kings and the reformed religious orders: patterns of monastic patronage in twelfth-century Galloway and Argyll', *Albion*, xxvii (1995), that highlighted the scale of the religious patronage exercised by these Gaelic potentates and compared them with the Canmore kings' own patronage of the new orders. The second is Keith Stringer's magisterial study of 'Reform monasticism and Celtic Scotland: Galloway, *c*.1140–*c*.1240' in E. J. Cowan and R. A. McDonald (eds), Alba (East Linton, 2000). This is essential reading, not only for students of the church in medieval Galloway, but for anyone exploring the interactions of native and newcomer in both secular and spiritual society in twelfth- and thirteenth-century Scotland. Through its examination of the religious attitudes of the lords of Galloway, their use of patronage, and the pattern of relationships forged with the monastic clergy, it has thrown into high relief a hitherto unconsidered dimension of their social life and beliefs, and forces us all to reconsider our use of such phrases as 'conventionally pious' when describing the devotional behaviour of the medieval secular elite.

It is to be hoped that this current explosion of interest in medieval Galloway will continue. Only two decades ago, this was one of the most neglected areas of Scottish historical research and the presentation of the history of the region consisted of the usual suspects presented in the traditional format based on the narrative account of Roger of Howden. Regional studies were unpopular subjects for academic research, other than in terms of exploration of 'border society' or 'frontier theory'. All this has changed, largely through increasing awareness of the need to reconsider many of the basic assumptions upon which our traditional national histories have been based. There has been a move away from compartment-alisation, from the old style of blinkered narrative that considered only the history of the zone that fell within rigidly delineated bounds, towards a freer approach that, while it may have its focus on a particular region, people or person, ranges widely and moves at ease over the national boundaries that have come to mean so much to us today but that either did not exist or mattered little to the medieval mind. It is a lesson that I have learned and from which I have benefited greatly.

INTRODUCTION

The re-organisation of Scottish local government in the mid-1970s had few supporters among the public at large, who were, and remained to be, fiercely loyal to the pattern of shires that had been established in the sixteenth century. It lasted barely twenty years before a further round of re-organisation dismantled many of the administrative entities that had been created in the 1970s. One notable survivor from the first re-organisation was Dumfries and Galloway Region, which had been formed from an amalgamation of the old counties of Dumfries, Kirkcudbright and Wigtown. The creation of this unit had caused little comment at the time, but its second element – Galloway – represented the revival for the first time in 515 years of a political expression for a term that had possessed no reality on the ground since James II annexed the forfeited estates of the Black Douglas family to the Scottish crown. The disappearance of Galloway, other than as a vague geographical notion that meant somewhat loosely the south-western corner of Scotland, was a momentous development in its day. In a single act of royal policy, a political unit that had dominated the region for over 300 years was committed to oblivion.

Since the early twelfth century, Galloway's rulers had enjoyed exceptional independence and power, projecting the might that the wealth and military resources of their domain gave them around the wider world of the Irish Sea and Hebrides, or using its resources to maintain a dominant position within Scotland. Yet its passing has produced no copious literature bewailing the loss of sovereignty or the demise of a culture such as sprang from the forfeiture of the Mhic Domhnaill lordship of the Isles in 1493 – and that was a comparatively recent and short-lived creation. Part of the reason for this may lie in the extent to which Galloway had become integrated into the kingdom by the fifteenth century; although the end of the independent lordship came abruptly in 1234, it marked just one stage in a process of integration that had been moving at an accelerating rate through the twelfth and early thirteenth centuries and was to continue for a further 200 years. It did not entail a sharp break with the past, for there was continuity in the form of the families descended from Alan's daughters, who preserved a direct personal link to the recent and glorious past, and in the institutions of the diocesan church and legal systems that survived with little change. It was not until the traumas of the Bruce–Balliol conflicts of the early fourteenth century that a clearer break with the past occurred, when Galloway's long-standing links with the Church of York were all but severed and when the last of the successor families was eliminated from the pattern of political power and landholding in the region. By the time that David II's protégé, Archibald Douglas, re-united the two portions of Galloway under his rule in 1372, little more than the distinctive native law code that had survived the demise of the political autonomy of the region in the thirteenth century remained to differentiate the lordship from other provinces of medieval Scotland.

Despite the processes of integration, there remained a deep sense of difference and detachment about Galloway. 'Out of Scotland and into Galloway' remained a saying in common currency, and highlighted a sense of separation that may have been born in the geographical remoteness and physical division of the region from the rest of Scotland, but that also reflected a perception of foreignness. And in many ways that perception was justified, for in comparison to the culture and society of much of the rest of Scotland south of the Forth–Clyde line, there was much about Galloway – and Carrick – that was alien. Together with the law codes, the Gaelic structure of society and the survival of a Gaelic-speaking population outwith the burghs, mainly in the upland districts, emphasised the differences between Galloway and the political heartland of the Scottish kingdom to its north. Even as that lingering Gaelic culture withered and died – although it was only in the late seventeenth century that the last pockets of native language disappeared – the perception of separateness survived, fuelled by a growing view of Galloway as a 'problem' zone of political and religious non-comformity. As a centre of covenanting radicalism in the seventeenth century, it was governed by the Edinburgh-based regime as a rebellious subject territory rather than a stable province of the kingdom. With Dumfriesshire and Ayrshire, it became part of the rather vaguely defined disaffected 'Western Districts'.

This long-lived tradition of lack of definition is one of the first problems to be addressed in any study of Galloway. What is the extent of the territory covered by that name? From medieval texts it is clear that the term could be used when dealing with a wider zone of the south-western Scottish mainland, embracing the whole region south and west of Clydesdale and Teviotdale. It was also applied to a much more precise unit that corresponded to either the twelfth- and thirteenth-century lordship of Galloway, which comprised most of the former counties of Wigtownshire and Kirkcudbrightshire, or again with the still smaller bishopric, which was restricted to those areas of the lordship west of the River Urr. The broadest definition of Galloway has a vague geographical character that may have arisen from the general settlement within this zone of Gaelic-speaking Islesmen in the tenth and eleventh centuries. It is used with a certain imprecision to describe an extensive region composed of a number of smaller political units, but with no real political unity or identity in its own right. The narrower definitions relating to the lordship and diocese apply to clearly delineated units, the former representing an enlargement from an original political entity co-terminous with the latter.

The application of the name 'Galloway' in its widest context is generally an early twelfth-century phenomenon in the surviving documentation, but remained in diminishing currency into the later thirteenth century. In the 1130s, David I issued charters in favour of the monks of Dunfermline from 'Strathyrewen in Galwegia',[1] apparently the Irvine valley in Cunninghame. The lands of 'Keresban' (Carsphairn), which were incorporated into the later county of Kirkcudbrightshire, but which, as part of Thomas de Colville's lordship of Dalmellington on the Kyle–Carrick border, lay outwith the medieval lordship, were in 1223 described as lying in Galloway.[2] In the composition known as the *Brevis Descriptio Regni Scotie* of *c*.1296, Annandale, too, is described as part of Galloway. In the same account, however, Ayr is described as 'near Galloway',[3] presumably in reflection of the manner in which the sphere of royal authority had expanded into Carrick, Kyle, Cunninghame and Strathgryffe in the twelfth and thirteenth centuries.

In describing this wider Galloway, the territorial units named in grants of David I and Máel Coluim IV to the Church of Glasgow and the monks of Selkirk and Kelso are highly significant. The earliest of these grants formed part of David I's original endowment of Selkirk Abbey. This included the teind of the royal cain of cheese and half of that of hides from 'Galloway'.[4] This was amplified *c*.1159 by Máel Coluim IV in his great charter of confirmation to Selkirk's successor house, Kelso Abbey. The expanded grant bestowed the right to the teind of crown's annual cain of cattle, pigs and cheese, 'from the four *kadrez* of that (part of) Galloway' which had been held by his grandfather, David, in the lifetime of Alasdair I mac Máel Coluim.[5] No indication of where or what these kadrez were is given in the charter, but in a grant of David I to Glasgow, four territorial divisions that may equate with these are named.[6] These are Strathgryffe, Cunninghame, Kyle and Carrick, which emerge by the later twelfth century as distinct political and ecclesiastical entities, held as lordships from the crown by families such as the Stewarts and Morvilles, or forming rural deaneries of the see of Glasgow. There is, however, no conclusive internal proof that these are the four kadrez of the Kelso grant, or that they were the 'part' of Galloway that formed a portion of David's lordship during the reign of his elder brother. An early thirteenth-century Glasgow document, however, refers to officers of the Earl of Carrick called *kethres*.[7] These men may have had some role in the collection of cain, and the name of their office may reflect a transference of the name used for the fiscal unit on which the render was assessed to the men responsible for its collection.

Contemporary with these references to a wider Galloway are a number of incidental allusions to a more geographically distinct region, the later lordship. In the mid-1130s, Fergus 'of Galloway', made his first surviving attestations of Scottish royal charters,[8] and by the later part of the century his family had come to be associated closely with a region that encompassed the later counties of Wigtown and Kirkcudbrightshire. It is possible that Carrick may swiftly have been subsumed into this territory, but its inclusion within the Glasgow diocese implies that it had come under the political overlordship of David I and that it had later been transferred into the hands of either Gillebrigte mac Fergusa or Donnchad mac Gillebrigta. By the 1190s, Carrick had been assigned to Donnchad as his inheritance following a long, bitter and bloody conflict between Fergus' sons and their families, and any political association with Galloway was severed. To the east, Nithsdale formed another freestanding entity under its dynasty of Gaelic lords, and its territories appear to have embraced the whole of the district known as Desnes Ioan that lay between the rivers Nith and Urr, as well as the valley of the Nith. The lordship of Galloway was, therefore, confined originally to the country west of the River Urr, until the acquisition of Desnes Ioan. It is on this enlarged, but clearly defined political unit, that the chief focus of this present study falls.

Notes

1 *ESC*, nos 84, 85.
2 *Melrose Liber*, no. 195.
3 'Brevis Descriptio Regni Scotie' in *Miscellany of the Maitland Club*, iv, pt i, (Glasgow, 1847), 21–34 at 34. See also *RRS*, i, 38–39.
4 *ESC*, no. 35.
5 *RRS*, i, no. 131.
6 *Glasgow Registrum*, no. 9.
7 Ibid., no. 139.
8 Ibid., nos 3, 9, 10.

1
ORIGINS

When the lordship of Galloway appears in historical record for the first time in the twelfth century, it is as a monolithic political unit. This unitary lordship has exercised a powerful hold over the historiography of Galloway, with the notion of a single political entity spanning the whole region from the Rhinns to the Nith having been projected backwards from the reality of the twelfth into the mythos of earlier centuries. Although the descent of the recorded lords is unknown, it has often been assumed that they represented the continuity of a long-established authority in the Scottish south-west, a kingdom of Galloway and the Gall-Gaidhel which originated in the ninth or tenth centuries with the infiltration of Scandinavian and hybrid Norse–Gaelic colonists into the mainland, where their leaders usurped the political power of the former Northumbrian masters of Galloway. This is, however, at best a simplistic interpretation of the evolution of the political entity which dominated the northern Irish Sea for over a century down to 1234, where the complex interplay of mainland British, Irish and Isles-based powers provided the circumstances for the development of a fiercely independent power which looked to the maritime world of the west rather than to its Scottish hinterland.

SCANDINAVIANS, IRISH AND ISLESMEN

THE SCANDINAVIAN DIASPORA

The chain of events which led to the formation of the lordship of Galloway can be traced back over 200 years to the reverberations felt round the Irish Sea of the expulsion in AD 902 of the Norse from their settlement at Dublin.[1] Although the colony was re-settled around 917 by a Viking warband from Britanny and secured in 919 by a decisive victory over the Irish in which Niall Glúndub, King of Ailech and Tara, was killed,[2] the preceding decade saw the plantation of colonies elsewhere around the northern Irish Sea basin. Irish tradition, for example, records the movements of Ingimundr, a Dublin Norse warlord, who after an abortive attempt to establish a new base in north Wales, occupied the Wirral and attempted to seize Chester.[3] A similar process may be recorded in

Amounderness, where Norse and Norse–Gaelic names occur in some density.[4] It was on the southern limits of this area of Norse settlement that the Cuerdale hoard, deposited c.903, was discovered. Alfred Smyth has linked the deposition of the hoard with political instability at York after the death of King Guthfrith, but the high percentage of Hiberno–Norse material in it points towards an Irish origin, probably Dublin.[5] Amounderness, controlling the western end of the trans-Pennine Ribble–Aire gap, leading through to York, was an important area to be controlled by dynasts aspiring to rule in both York and Dublin. This strategic significance was underscored by its purchase in 934 from the Scandinavians by King Athelstan and its grant to the Church of York.[6] Further evidence for the shockwaves emanating from the expulsion of the Norse from Dublin were felt all the way up the coast from Morecambe Bay to the Solway. The origins of Norse and Norse–Gaelic settlement in Cumbria, where the indigenous Anglian élite fled in the face of Scandinavian incursion, can likewise be dated to the period c.902–c.914.[7] It is as part of this general dispersal of Norsemen around the Irish Sea that the early colonisation of Galloway should probably be seen.

Settlement in Galloway was limited in numbers and extent. The chief body of Dublin Norse, under the leadership of Ragnall, grandson of Imar (Ívarr), headed further north and east and was active over a wide area from central Scotland south to York. Their first major raids penetrated Strathclyde and struck into the heart of the Picto-Scottish kingdom in Strathearn and Strathtay. The invaders plundered Dunkeld in 903 before suffering a defeat in Strathearn in 904 in which Ragnall's brother or cousin, Imar, was slain.[8] A Norse army remained active, however, in south central Scotland, especially within Strathclyde, after that date.[9] There is no firm evidence for Ragnall's movements from c.904 until 910, when, seizing the opportunity presented by Edward the Elder of Wessex's defeat and slaughter of the Danes of York at Tettenhall in 910, Ragnall turned south and occupied the city soon after. As King of York, Ragnall began to settle the Norse army on land seized from the church. This new pressure on the northern rump of Northumbria forced its ruler, Ealdred of Bamburgh, into alliance with the Scots. In c.918, in a hard-fought contest on the Tyne at Corbridge, Ragnall defeated a confederate army of Scots and Northumbrians in a battle that evidently confirmed his mastery over the territory from the Humber to at least the Tyne.

In the aftermath of this victory, Ragnall turned west and re-entered the Irish Sea world. From the rapidity with which he assembled a fleet, won a major naval engagement off Mann, and imposed his rule on the Norse colony at Waterford,[10] he must have found ships available to him west of the Pennines, presumably among the Norse colonists in those areas. Control of the trans-Pennine routes, possibly via the Aire Gap but more probably along the Stainmore route from Teesdale into the Eden Valley, enabled Ragnall and, after his death in 920, his kinsman Sigtryggr (who had re-established the base at Dublin) to exercise rule over a kingdom which spanned the Irish Sea. The Dublin–York axis was maintained down to the middle of the tenth century, foundering in 952 with Óláfr Cuarán's second expulsion from the kingship of York.[11] While that event ended the direct political link between the Ostman cities of Ireland and the kingdom of York, the lines of communication were certainly not severed. Indeed, it was while heading for the Norse colonies in the west along the Stainmore route that Óláfr's successor at York, Eiríkr Bloodaxe, was attacked and killed in 954.[12]

By the middle of the tenth century, the Norse colonies in Cumbria were well established. The existence of a semi-independent Scandinavian lordship in the upper Eden valley in north Westmorland, centred on Penrith, has been postulated in the second half of the 900s, and has highlighted the presence of zones of intensive Norse settlement and lordship down the Solway coastlands.[13] While the origins of this colonisation may have lain in the post-902 diaspora, it has been pointed out that the unsettled military situation down to c.920 would hardly have produced favourable conditions for large-scale settlement. The twenty-five years before the invasion of Cumbria by Edmund of Wessex in 945,[14] however, was a time of comparative stability, marked by what has been interpreted as an episode of *rapprochement* between Cumbrian kings and Norse settlers.[15] It is possibly in similar circumstances, facilitated by Dublin–Norse control of the Northumbrian political and spiritual heartland at York and domination of the Cuthbertine community at Chester-le-Street, that two zones of Scandinavian settlement in Galloway, centred on Whithorn and Kirkcudbright, were established and consolidated.

NORSE GALLOWAY

In the absence of documentary materials from which to construct a coherent narrative history for the Scandinavian colonisation of parts of Galloway, great weight has been placed on the place-name evidence for this process.[16] While traditional historical records can be used to form the most basic of outline discussions of the Scandinavians' roles in the political development of the lordship, they cannot be used to show that they had any lasting impact on the region. Archaeology and place-names, however, emphasise that they cannot be dismissed as an irrelevance and that they settled along the northern shore of the Irish Sea in sufficient numbers to make a significant impression on the place-name record. Indeed, place-names constitute the principal body of evidence for Scandinavian settlement throughout Galloway.

The main distribution of Scandinavian settlement names in Galloway forms two main blocks, one centred on the southern Machars, the other concentrated in the lower Dee valley around Kirkcudbright. The Machars group has attracted particular attention as a consequence of the recent programme of research focused on Whithorn. Their distribution has been considered significant, the names describing an arc round the northern and western, i.e. landward, limits of what was probably the Whithorn estate. This has been taken as indicative of the arrival of the settlers by invitation, as the Norse farms appear to have been slotted into an existing settlement pattern without any disruption,[17] but could equally represent the aggressive takeover of the monastic properties by a Norse warlord. The possibility of a Norse–Gaelic jarl holding court at Whithorn in the early eleventh century suggests that the latter cannot be discounted entirely (see pp. 13–14). The Dee Valley group, however, shows an equally suggestive cluster, with Kirkcudbright lying at the heart of a ring of Norse names. While no modern archaeological work has been undertaken at Kirkcudbright which could confirm or refute the possibility that here, as at Whithorn, a Scandinavian or Norse–Gaelic commercial community was established in the later ninth or tenth centuries, the discovery in the nineteenth century of the burial with grave goods of a Norse warrior in St Cuthbert's Kirkyard in the town, and the finding of a Norse glass linen-smoother, points to at least a passing presence.[18] Furthermore, the strong trading and settlement connections between Dublin and Kirkcudbright in the early thirteenth century may preserve a record of earlier contacts. This clustering of Norse material around two of the most significant foci of political, commercial and religious power in early medieval Galloway is strongly suggestive of a Scandinavian takeover of these power centres.

Overall, the names preserve an essentially coastal distribution, with very few Scandinavian place-names other than for topographical features being found in the interior. This distribution supports the probability that the Norse colonisation of the region was seaborne, probably from areas of primary settlement in Ireland, Mann and the Hebrides, rather than arriving overland from the districts of northern England settled by Danes in the later ninth century. The scattering of Scandinavian naming elements at the eastern extremity of Galloway and in lower Annandale does, however, represent a north-western extension of Danish colonisation. Although Fellows-Jensen has suggested that these belong to the later ninth century, it is likely that they belong to either the eleventh-century expansion of Anglo-Scandinavian York under Earl Siward, or to the early twelfth-century colonisation of the region by settlers from eastern England as part of the English crown's efforts to stabilise southern Cumbria.[19]

The majority of Scandinavian place-names in Galloway are topographical,[20] those containing habitative elements being scarce and confined primarily to the two main zones indicated above. The existing names show no trace of the settlement hierarchy represented by *staðir*, *sætr* or *bolstaðr* farms, as occur in the primary settlement areas in the Scandinavian north and west of Scotland, and their distribution is markedly thinner than that in the Danish-settled zone of south-eastern Dumfriesshire. The principal settlement generic found, mapped by the suffix *-bie* or *-by*, is *býr* or *boer* (farm). Its distribution is restricted, with the exception of one probably Danish example on the west side of the Nith estuary, to the district between the southern Machars and the eastern side of the Dee estuary. Only seven names in this generic survive, but this need not be indicative of the scale of the colonising process, although it is strongly suggestive of a limited movement. It could point alternatively to the already diminishing use of Norse language among a progressively more hybridised Gaelic–Scandinavian population. It is highly significant in this context that no recognisable Scandinavian habitative generics occur in the Rhinns, the one area of Galloway in which Norse–Gaelic rulers are recorded in the later tenth and eleventh centuries (see p. 17).

The origins of the *býrl/boer* settlements in Galloway are still subject to debate. Unlike the Dumfriesshire and Cumbrian examples, the specific element used in name forming in -*by* in Galloway was never a personal name. Personal-name specifics have been interpreted as indicative of land grants to, or seizures of property by, specific individuals and were coined when larger estates were dismembered.[21] The use of appellatival specifics, that is where the specific is not a personal name, interpreted as indicating the complete takeover of the Scandinavian unit, is the norm in Galloway. The implication is that settlers were moving into an already well-ordered settlement pattern and taking over intact the pre-Scandinavian units. The scarcity of personal name forms may be a further indication of the limited scale of the land-take, with insufficient Norse–speakers moving in to encourage the break-up of the original estate.[22] Alternatively, it may be a sign of the decay of Scandinavian cultural norms amongst a population that had already absorbed a significant level of Gaelic mores.

Some additional support for a more widespread Norse, or Norse–Gaelic, settlement can be drawn from the generic *kirkja* (church), especially in its inversion compound form where paired with the name of the dedicatory saint. This occurs when the Scandinavian generic is paired with a non-Scandinavian specific in non-Scandinavian word order, i.e. Kirk-X as opposed to X-Kirk. These so-called 'kirk-compound' place-names have long attracted scholarly debate, with current opinion doubting a direct Scandinavian role in the name-forming process and questioning the chronology of their formation. John MacQueen, for example, proposed a tenth-century context for these names, which would fit the chronology for the dispersal of the Dublin Norse around the Irish Sea after 902.[23] Bill Nicolaisen has suggested an earlier Anglian origin for some of the names but preferred a development in an area of mixed Norse and Gaelic cultures.[24] Daphne Brooke's research into kirk-compounds at first suggested a considerably later date for their formation, but her more recent work has moved towards a tenth- or eleventh-century context for their formation.[25]

A recurring theme within the Scandinavian settlement revealed through place-name studies in Galloway is the clear evidence for the strong influence upon it of Gaelic culture and society. Indeed, it is evident that there is a high degree of hybridity in the place-name record, a situation paralleled in the archaeology, where strong Irish or Isles influences have been identified.[26] The term 'Hiberno–Norse' has been favoured, particularly by archaeologists, to describe this cultural hybridity. However, when viewed from a historical context, this mingled Norse and Gaelic culture points strongly in the direction of one of the most controversial peoples of early medieval north-western Britain, the Gall-Gaidhel.

GALL-GAIDHEL AND GALLOWAY

For many years it was the norm to identify a ninth- or tenth-century Gaelic-speaking element as arriving in Galloway in conjunction with the influx of Norse settlers. This group has been identified as the Gall-Gaidhel, generally though inaccurately represented in modern interpretations as a hybrid race of Norse–Gaelic ancestry who earned a reputation for unbridled ferocity and violent opposition to Christianity.[27] The belief in their settlement in Galloway depended on the linked assumption that the Norse had colonised the Solway region in large numbers in the later ninth century. The Gall-Gaidhel, it was argued, followed in the wake of this movement from areas of primary Norse settlement in Ireland or the Hebrides, or that some were members of the indigenous Gaelic-speaking population of the Rhinns who embraced Norse culture.[28] Later Irish tradition labelled them as apostates, Gaels who had abandoned their native culture and religion in favour of the alien traditions of the Norse. The only description of them is from the probably twelfth-century 'Three Fragments', which survive in a seventeenth-century copy:

> They were a people who had renounced their baptism and they were usually called Northmen, for they had the customs of the Northmen, and had been fostered by them, and though the original Northmen were bad to churches these were worse, in whatever part of Ireland they were.[29]

John MacQueen, unaware of the probable twelfth-century context of the Fragmentary Annals, focused upon this anti-clericalism and compared it with descriptions of twelfth-century Galwegians in the northern English campaigns of David I. The parallels between the ninth- and tenth-century Gall-Gaidhel and the twelfth-century Galwegians persuaded him that they were one and the same people. The twelfth-century date for the Fragmentary Annals' description of the Gall-Gaidhel, placed alongside the contemporary northern English accounts of Galwegian behaviour, and the fact that the term was used of Galloway in this period, point to the identification in the minds of Irish observers of Gall-Gaidhel with Galloway. The description, moreover, must be considered in a twelfth- rather than a tenth-century context and should probably be seen as a thinly-veiled criticism of the religious policies of the contemporary ruler of Galloway, Fergus, possibly part of the wider attack on him by Cistercian commentators.[30]

In view of the categoric statements made in support of a south-west Scottish locus for the lands of the Gall-Gaidhel, it is surprising to find that there is very little concrete evidence to illustrate their origins and activities. Indeed, this lack of evidence persuaded Daphne Brooke originally to question the basis of the arguments that sought to locate them in Galloway.[31] Early Irish sources give them no clear geographical location, but the supposed sphere of activity of their mid-ninth-century leader, Ketil Flatnefr, points to a Hebridean base.[32] It is generally assumed that they were 'wandering bands of mixed Irish and Norse renegades',[33] or 'half Irish half Norse marauders',[34] who preyed on Irish monasteries, and this modern construct of their hybrid nature remains unchallenged. Their 'homeland', however, is less secure. As Ireland was a major target for their attentions, unless they were associated from an early date with the *longphort* settlements of the Norse there, it is unlikely to have been their place of origin. A suggested earlier Norse settlement of the Hebrides from *c*.800 – for which there is currently no concrete evidence – and the survival there of a substantial Gaelic and Gaelicised population, however, has been considered to offer the most obvious breeding ground for such hybridity.[35]

The Western Isles, however, need not preserve a monopoly over the Gall-Gaidhel, for similar conditions could be found elsewhere in north-western maritime Britain and at later periods for the generation of similar crossbreeds. North-western England, indeed, has produced evidence for a substantial influx of Hebridean or Irish Sea Norse in the early tenth century. Alfred Smyth has highlighted the Gall-Gaidhel character of Cumberland society. It was 'half-pagan, half-Christian in religion; and ethnically . . . half-Norse, half-Celtic'.[36] The most striking monuments of this hybrid culture are the Cumberland high crosses, such as that at Gosforth, with its oddly juxtaposed pagan and Christian motifs. Nick Higham developed Smyth's hypothesis and highlighted the strong Gaelic component in the settlement of the region.[37] Similar areas of mixed culture can be identified on the northern side of the Solway in Galloway.

It is only in modern eyes that the equation of Galloway with the land of the Gall-Gaidhel has appeared suspect. The documentary evidence to support that identification is, admittedly, circumstantial and generally late in date, but it establishes that by the twelfth century it was a recognised fact that Galloway was the homeland of these 'Foreign-Gael'. In Irish sources, notably the *Annals of Ulster*, the heads of the Galwegian ruling house in the twelfth and thirteenth centuries are accorded the title *rí Gall-Gaidhel*.[38] Less certainty attaches to the same set of annals' use of that style for an early eleventh-century individual, Suibne mac Cinaedh, whose death is recorded in 1034,[39] for there are no other references to him through which to establish a firm provenance. If any weight can be placed on the historically suspect traditions of Ketil Flatnefr and his associates in the Hebrides, it is possible that Suibne may have been a Hebridean chieftain, but there is no inherent improbability in his being a Galwegian ruler. Independently of the

Irish annal tradition, the early thirteenth-century *Orkneyinga Saga* describes Galloway as *Gaddgedlar*, the Old Norse form of Gall-Gaidhel.[40] The unanswerable question is when did the name become narrowly defined as referring to the south-west of the Scottish mainland?

While chronology remains problematical, the processes of cultural inter-breeding which produced the hybrid society of the Gall-Gaidhel can be seen at work in Galloway. Although purely Scandinavian place-names, as discussed above, are comparatively rare, one element of Gaelic origin, long recognised as commonplace in regions of Norse or mixed Norse–Gaelic settlement, occurs with great frequency. This is the generic *airigh* (a shieling), which represents the adoption of a native Hebridean Gaelic term by the incoming settlers. It occurs widely throughout Mann, Galloway and modern Cumbria, where the common link is the spread of settlement through the Irish Sea, possibly originating in the Isles. In Galloway, its principal distribution is in the south Machars and the Moors districts of Wigtownshire, with one significant territorial occurence in the west Rhinns, and in the central Dee Valley and in the Bengairn Hills to the east of Kirkcudbright, a spread which matches the chief foci of Scandinavian settlement generics. This provides circumstantial evidence for their import as part of the movement of Scandinavian colonists into the region, as is clearly the case in Cumbria where there was no indigenous Gaelic-speaking population, but the earlier presence of Gaelic-speakers in Galloway and Mann raises the possibility of its use in those areas in the pre-Norse period.

The evolution of transhumance pastoralism has been studied in depth, particularly in Mann and Cumbria.[41] The Gaelic origins of the Manx *eary* are well established, and here Eleanor Megaw proposed a pre-Norse origin for the majority of sites that evolved into permanent settlements. The absence of *-sætr* names (the Norse equivalent term) has been taken as indicating that the settlers found a fully developed summer-grazing system in situ and adopted the established Gaelic terminology. Both *sætr* and *airigh* occur in Cumbria, which could indicate that the latter had not entirely replaced its Scandinavian counterpart in the vocabulary of colonists who arrived there from Ireland, Mann or the Isles. The absence of *sætr* from Galloway parallels the Manx situation and may indicate a pre-Norse origin for the shieling system there, but it may also be evidence for a comparatively late settlement of Galloway, by which time the Norse generic had been supplanted by the Gaelic.[42] This is also the case in Iceland, where in the form *ergi*, Gaelic *airigh* largely displaced Norse *sætr* in the settlement vocabulary.

On balance, the above evidence points to a continued influx of colonists to Galloway after the initial settlement period in the late ninth and early tenth centuries. The tenth-century colonisation shows clear signs of having originated in regions where the Scandinavian population had been exposed to considerable Gaelic influences, evident in both their settlement vocabulary and in the saints' cults that they imported to their new

This period centres on the climax of the remarkable career of Óláfr Cuarán, King of the Gall. He has been studied mainly in respect of his role as king of both Dublin and York, his intermittent rule of the former spanning four decades from 941 to 980.[43] His long reign provided the circumstances for the consolidation of the Norse colonies around the Irish Sea, however, it also saw the revival of significant native Irish activity in the maritime affairs of the region of Scandinavian settlement for the first time in about a century and closed with the appearance of new Norse and Danish powers in the same zone. Óláfr's departure for York in 940 to provide military assistance to his cousin, Óláfr Gothfrithsson, in his campaign against Bernicia, coincided with a re-opening of Isles-based raids on the Irish mainland. The *Annals of Ulster* for 941 record a raid on Downpatrick by what were evidently Isles-based Vikings, noting that God avenged this wrong by bringing other 'Foreigners' (? Orcadians) who seized their islands and drove out their king who was subsequently killed in Ireland.[44] It may have been this raid, or the arrival of these aggressive newcomers, which provoked the major naval expedition by Muircertach mac Néill, King of Ailech, from his base in Tír Conaill against the Norse colonies in the Hebrides in the same year.[45]

The 941 raids signalled the beginning of a new trend: the intrusion of naval powers based in the Hebrides and Northern Isles into the Irish Sea basin. It is possible that Eiríkr Bloodaxe, perhaps before his first seizure of the York throne in *c.*947 but certainly in the period 948–52 after his expulsion by Óláfr Cuarán, had used his control of the earldom of Orkney to establish his dominance of the Hebridean colonies.[46] He was, however, unable to use this position to win control of the Ostmen communities of Ireland. After Eiríkr's death in 954, his widow and sons withdrew to Orkney and again used this northern base to project their power briefly into the Hebrides and Ireland.[47]

After the Eiríkssons' departure from Orkney, there is little clear evidence for the political structure of the Western, as opposed to the Northern, Isles until the 980s. There are indications, however, that the late 960s and early 970s had seen the emergence of a powerful kingship in the Hebrides that may have been flexing its muscles further to the south. This may have been one of the factors behind the assembly of a fleet at Chester in 973 by the English king, Edgar.[48] According to the *Anglo-Saxon Chronicle* account of this event, six (un-named) kings came there and submitted to him, and swore 'to be his fellow workers by sea and land' In later Worcester tradition, one of the kings, named 'Maccus', was lord of 'very many islands', a description that is strongly suggestive of a Hebridean base. Who this 'Maccus' was is unknown, but his name may be a garbled form of a Norse name. In this context, the M[agnus?] Haraldsson who raided the monastery of Inishcathy (Scattery Island in the Shannon) in 974, accompanied by 'the Lawmen of the Islands',[49] evidently as part of a wider conflict with the Ostmen of Limerick whose king had taken refuge there, presents himself as a candidate.

Haraldsson appears to have extended his influence south from the Hebrides into the northern Irish Sea basin in the 960s. In 969 and 970, he – named as Macht or Mact – and his younger brother and successor in the kingship, Godred Haraldsson, invaded Anglesey,[50] perhaps establishing lordship over the small but economically important Scandinavian colony established there. The Haraldssons' power was presumably based on control of the increasingly important trade routes that ran north through the Irish Sea and Hebrides from Dublin and Biscay. To secure these routes, they had probably established lordship over the Scandinavian colonies of western Galloway, there being no record of conflict on the Ulster coast that might otherwise have indicated an effort to dominate the western flank of the North Channel bottleneck. There is, likewise, no evidence for conflict with Óláfr Cuarán's Dublin, for whom the security of trade along the western British sealanes may have been more important. Indeed, the fact that Óláfr chose, following his crushing defeat at Tara in 980 by Máel Sechnaill mac Domnaill, to retire to Iona,[51] the re-emergent spiritual heart of the Hebrides, is an indication of his affiliation with the Isles.

The renaissance of Iona's influence along the western seaways is one indication of the spread of Hebridean Norse power in the later tenth century. Although heavily influenced by local Scandinavian culture, as the fine tenth- and early eleventh-century sculptures from the monastic site indicate,[52] this was still an Irish-style community, cultivating Gaelic saints and participating in the wider religious life of Gaelic Scotland and Ireland through its place within the Columban *familia*. The establishment of churches dedicated to Columban saints, particularly to individuals active after the mid-seventh-century decline in the fortunes and prestige of Iona, gives some indication of the revival under Scandinavian patronage. In Galloway, where the strong Northumbrian ties of the local church were hardly conducive to the establishment of the cult of later Columban saints before the tenth century, dedications to Ionan saints may signal a political re-orientation, at least on the part of the Scandinavian colonists.

Dedications to Columban saints, such as Colman at Buittle, Urr and Colmonell in Carrick,[53] Aed mac Bricc at Kirkmabreck, Bride at Blaiket, Cormac at Kirkcormack and Cumméne at Kirkcolm, display a striking correlation in distribution to the main zones of Scandinavian settlement noted above, particularly to the zone around Kirkcudbright. The Cumméne

Six years after the death of Óláfr Cuarán at Iona, the monastery was plundered and the abbot and fifteen senior monks slain.[54] The *Annals of Ulster* linked the attack with an account of a raid by 'Danes' on the shores of Dál Riada, an event that heralded a new phase in the struggle for domination of the Hebridean and Irish Sea zone. In 987, Godred Haraldsson was attacked in Mann by 'Danes' and drove them off with heavy casualties while, in what appears to have been a separate action, the 'Danes' who had attacked Iona the previous Christmas were slaughtered.[55] Continuing disturbances in the Isles culminated in 989 with Godred's death at the hands of the men of Argyll.[56] Barbara Crawford has pointed out the link between the 987 attack on Mann and the account in *Njal's Saga* of Kari Solmundarsson's fight with King Godred and the taking of plunder from the island, and has argued that the term 'Dane' has been used simply to denote 'pirates'.[57] The aggressors in these actions appear to have been Orcadians under the leadership of Sigurd the Stout, Earl of Orkney, who, according to saga tradition, had established his domination of the Hebrides in the 980s, ruling through a vassal earl, Gilli.[58] Until his forced conversion in 995 by Óláfr Tryggvason, King of Norway, Sigurd was aggressively pagan, hence his readiness to target – and shed blood at – the monastery which had become the spiritual focus of the Christianised Hebridean Norse.

Orkney influence, according to saga tradition, extended to Mann. Here, Godred had been succeeded by his son, Ragnall, who was to reign to 1005.[59] Orcadian domination of the western seaways may initially have been less attractive to the Dublin Norse under their new king, Sigtryggr Silkiskegg, younger son of Olafr Cuarán. By the early 990s, the Ostmen cities were showing signs of favouring the new high-status interlopers from Norway and Denmark, Óláfr Tryggvason and Sveinn Haraldsson, both of whom made raids on Mann *c.*995.[60] The late tradition of *Orkneyinga Saga* narrates how Óláfr had married a sister of Óláfr Cuarán of Dublin,[61] an account dismissed by Anderson as romantic and unhistorical[62] but perhaps preserving a memory of an early bid by the king of Dublin to gain control of Mann and extend by proxy his influence over the Irish Sea trade routes. Óláfr also, however, may have been preparing the ground for himself, for it was in the western colonies that he raised the army and fleet with which he sailed for Norway to reclaim his father's throne, stopping off in Orkney to receive Sigurd's submission.[63] Óláfr's success in securing support within the Isles and the Scandinavian colonies around the Irish Sea was evidently a cause for concern in England, which had been on the receiving end of the

Norwegian's attentions since 991. Óláfr Trygvasson withdrew to Norway, where he was killed in 1000. In the same year, Æthelred II staged a major offensive against Cumbria, presumably to neutralise the Scandinavian colonies around the Solway, while his fleet, which had been originally intended to act in concert with his army, operating out of Chester, raided Mann.[64] In the event, the western colonies were to play no significant part in Sveinn Haraldsson's plans for the conquest of England, but were to become caught up instead in a protracted struggle for control of the commercial wealth of the Irish Sea routes and the military wealth it generated.

IRISH RENAISSANCE

So far, the emphasis has been on the Scandinavian element in the Irish Sea zone and its influence upon the development of Galloway. By the 980s and 990s, however, native Irish potentates were to seek to project their authority into the same region. The growing influence in the late tenth and early eleventh centuries of Brian Bóruma, King of Munster, cannot but have been felt across the North Channel in Galloway and in Mann and the Isles. His triumphal visit to Armagh in 1005, 'accompanied by the princes of Ireland', set the seal on his control of the high kingship won from the former Uí Néill high king, Máel Sechnaill mac Domnaill, in 1002.[65] An indication of his perception of his own power at that time can be seen in the *Book of Armagh*, where he was described in unique terms as *Imperator Scotorum*, 'emperor of the Gaels', on the occasion of his gift of twenty-two ounces of gold at the chief altar of the church there, a gift redolent of the symbolic powers of the overlord over his under kings.[66] There is a danger of reading too much into the title, but, bearing in mind the pretentious designations used by the Wessex dynasty to project their claims to the overlordship of mainland Britain, the possibility that Brian was articulating a claim to the political leadership of all *Gaidhel*, in Scotland as well as Ireland, should not be discounted. We should not doubt Brian's ability to project his power far beyond his territorial base in south-western Ireland by sea as well as land, for he effectively controlled the Ostmen cities of Limerick and Waterford and, intermittently from 981 and more or less permanently from 999 to 1013, Dublin. Access to fleets had greatly enhanced Brian's military capacity, as was presumably demonstrated in 1005 when he led a hosting round the coastlands of the north of Ireland through Connaught, Tír Conaill and the lands of the Cenél nEógain before descending on Ulaid, where he made another symbolic demonstration of his overlordship in the church of Downpatrick.[67] From 1002 until the revolt of Dublin and Leinster in 1013, Brian made regular expeditions into the north-east of Ireland, asserting his authority over both the Uí Néill and the lesser kings of Ulaid and Dál nAraide, and, it would seem, exerting his influence beyond Ireland.

Such pressure from Munster was assuredly a contributory factor in the support offered to Sigtryggr Silkiskegg in 1014 from the rulers of the Isles

more at re-establishment of the supremacy over the commercial traffic along the western seaways that Orkney had held in the 990s than the extension of his overlordship over the Irish kingdoms. The sphere of Sigurd's influence through the Isles is quite clearly indicated by the contingents of warriors that he brought to Ireland in spring 1014.

It is in the context of the war of 1014 that some indication comes of a Norse, or Norse-influenced colony in Galloway. According to the late thirteenth-century *Njal's Saga*, in the winter of 1014, following the Battle of Clontarf, the Icelander Kari Solmundarson and his men over-wintered at the court of a certain jarl called Melkólfr, the Scandinavianised form of the Gaelic Máel Coluim.[69] Melkólfr and his court were located at a place called *Hvitsborg* or *Hvitiburg* in the saga, sited somewhat vaguely 'in Scotland'. The identification of *Hvitsborg*, meaning the fort of someone called *Hvítr* (the White) with Whithorn, which is the literal Anglian form of the Latin *Candida Casa*, the White House (*Hwit Aerne*), has been hotly contested but, despite recent proposals that the site in question is represented by the lost Whitburgh in Berwickshire, the issue remains unsettled.[70] Bearing in mind the processes of metamorphosis and linguistic assimilation by which place-names in one language were accommodated into and interpreted in another – as in the case of the name York[71] – the objections against the identification of Hvitsborg with Whithorn further diminish. This may be no more than an attempt to rationalise the Anglian name into a recognisable Scandinavian form.

Attempts to fix its location based on the itinerary of Kari are fundamentally flawed, not least because of the vagueness of the details offered by the saga-writer but particularly because it is clear that his geographical knowledge is based upon the political and economic situation of the thirteenth century, not the early eleventh. The saga narrates how, after Clontarf, Kari and his crew sailed first to Orkney to bring news of the death of Sigurd to the earldom. Thereafter they sailed south to 'Bretland', surely in this context Wales rather than Strathclyde, before sailing back north to their winter-quarters at Hvitsborg. This seems a simple enough route, with a voyage from Wales to Galloway probably being a common occurrence along the Irish Sea trade routes of the time. The complication, however, is the news that they 'sailed up to Beruvik', where they laid up their vessel for the winter, before travelling on to Melkólfr's court 'in Scotland'.

In the past, scholars have debated hard the location of 'Beruvik', with sites from Portyerrock on the Machars coast north of the Isle of Whithorn to unidentified anchorages in Argyll proposed. It is most likely, however, that 'Beruvik' is Berwick-upon-Tweed, hence the effort to find an alternative east coast location for Melkólfr's residence rather than envisage Kari and his crew laying up their vessel then traversing the breadth of the Southern Uplands to Galloway. The probability is, however, that the insertion of Berwick into Kari's itinerary is a red herring, a clear demonstration of the late thirteenth-century gloss on the saga text. Quite simply, Berwick has been added as a demonstration of the saga-writer's knowledge of the contemporary commercial geography of Scotland. Where else would any self-respecting Icelandic trader make landfall in Scotland than at its premier trading port?

If Berwick is discounted as a late interpolation, the objections to Kari and his men finding a friendly berth in Galloway weaken considerably. Still bearing in mind the uncertainty over the identification of Hvitsborg, if Whithorn is intended then there are serious implications for both our understanding of the political structure of Galloway at this time and for the current interpretation of the archaeological evidence from the programme of excavation at the site. The saga hints at the presence in the Machars district of Wigtownshire of a secular power based at what is otherwise regarded as the principal ecclesiastical centre of Galloway.

The origins of such a power lie in the tenth-century Norse colonisation of central and western Galloway. The place-name evidence, discussed above, points to intensive settlement in the southern Machars, while the archaeology points to increasing cultural links with eastern Ireland.[72] The archaeological remains, furthermore, signal an intensification of Hiberno–Norse influences at Whithorn from c.1000 onwards,[73] a development that correlates closely with the spreading power of Norse–Gaelic potentates around the Irish Sea littoral at this time. Peter Hill's excavations at Whithorn revealed what has been interpreted as a planned shift in the non-religious focus of the site in the later tenth century away from the original nucleus at the centre and north-eastern extremity of the ridge occupied by the later medieval cathedral-priory to a new locus considerably to the south-west, centred on a putative market area or other, not necessarily ecclesiastical, core.[74] This he interpreted as the formative period of what he subsequently describes as a 'monastic town'. He identified, too, the further development of this layout in the eleventh century, with the construction of an outer zone of regularly set-out houses of Hiberno–Norse type, their alignment following that of what had become an inner zone of his hypothetical monastic town.[75] This outer settlement zone was strongly industrial and commercial in its character, increasingly so through the eleventh and into the twelfth century. Hill proposed that this had originated as a monastic community supplementing its income through manufacture but which, by the later twelfth century, had become 'an industrious trading centre with specialised craft quarters grouped around a central market place'.[76]

While there is no debating the ecclesiastical continuity of the Whithorn
site through the tenth and eleventh centuries, churned amy... ....
the distribution of the so called Whithorn School sculptu
for the monastic nature of the re planned later tenth and
settlement is unconvincing. Indeed, it is possible that the
the site was a purely secular phenomenon, with the
community remaining focused on its earlier Anglian core t
Perhaps here we have glimpsed the remains of the settlement upon which
the power of Jarl Melkólfr might have been founded. How extensive was
the reach of that power is and must remain unknown, as must the nature of
any relationship with the Ostman dynasties that were intruding their power
into Mann and the Rhinns in the early eleventh century. However he is
interpreted, in Melkólfr we have some indication of the fragmented nature
of secular power in Galloway towards the end of the Viking Age.

The death of Brian Bóruma in 1014 created an opening for influence over
Dublin and the Irish Sea zone which other powers were quick to exploit.
One such figure was Knútr, King of Denmark and England, whose
leadership of the Scandinavian world gave unique influence over the
western colonies and whose control of their commercial arteries gave an
economic edge to political domination (see pp. 30–1). His death in 1035
was followed by a series of upheavals in the Irish Sea region, not all of
which were coincidental on the demise of the dominant figure in British
politics. The removal of his strong hand unleashed a domino effect of
consequential events, several of which had significant impact on the region
of south-western Scotland which became Galloway. One immediate
consequence of the contraction of Anglo-Danish influence was a re-
assertion of Dublin independence, signalled in 1035 by Sigtryggr
Silkiskegg's revival of conflict with the Ostman kings of Waterford, a
dynasty which may itself have been a branch of the Uí Ímair of Dublin,
descended from Óláfr Cuarán. Rivalry between these Ostmen cities had
climaxed in 982, when Sigtryggr's elder brother and predecessor as king of
Dublin, Glúniarainn, in alliance with his half-brother and brother-in-law
the Uí Néill high king, Máel Sechnaill mac Domnaill, had defeated Ímar of
Waterford and his ally or overlord, Domnall Cloen, king of Leinster, killing
Ímar's son, Gilla-Pátraic.[78] In 993, the hostility had been renewed by
Sigtryggr and Ímar's son, Ragnall, and apparently ended with Sigtryggr's
temporary expulsion from Dublin and the killing of Ragnall by the
Leinstermen.[79] Forty-two years later, Sigtryggr killed Ragnall mac Ragnaill,
king of Waterford, in Dublin and triggered the final crisis of his long and
turbulent reign.[80] The following year, it ended in deposition and exile.
    Sigtryggr's fall precipitated a crisis in Dublin that provided a member of
the Waterford dynasty with an opening that he was quick to exploit, no
doubt aided and encouraged by his brother-in-law, Donnchad mac Briain,
king of Munster, who was keen to re-establish the control of the city that

his father had enjoyed. What followed was a seesaw struggle for power in Dublin by representatives of the rival Dublin and Waterford dynasties, itself an extension of the rivalry between their respective patrons, the kings of Leinster and Munster. In 1036, Echmarcach mac Ragnaill, a brother or son of the man killed by Sigtryggr, seized the kingship of Dublin and held the city until his expulsion in 1038 in favour of Ímar mac Arailt, who may have been Sigtryggr's nephew.[81] Ímar, in turn, held the kingship until 1046, when Echmarcach regained control the city, a hold which he was to maintain until his expulsion in 1052 by Diarmait mac Maíl na mBó, king of Leinster.[82]

Echmarcach's ejection from Dublin ended the Waterford dynasty's involvement in the affairs of the city, but not its significant role in Irish Sea politics. It was evidently from a position of established power in the region that he had mounted his bid for the Dublin kingship in 1036. The question is, where was that power based and how had it been achieved? The *Anglo-Saxon Chronicle* offers one clue. In 1031, Knútr had mounted a major expedition into northern England and Scotland and, evidently without battle, had brought the Scottish king, Máel Coluim mac Cinaeda, and two other kings into submission.[83] One of these kings was named Iehmarc, clearly an Anglo-Saxon attempt at rendition of the Irish Echmarcach. His association with Máel Coluim in this context suggests a southern Scottish or northern Irish Sea location for his kingdom. Two possibilities present themselves: Mann and Galloway.

Seán Duffy has outlined the probable domination of Mann by Dublin in the early eleventh century.[84] Sigtryggr Silkiskegg may have based himself there following his flight from Dublin before the advancing power of Brian Bóruma, and maintained a close association with the island and its affairs into the 1020s. While there is no direct evidence for Sigtryggr's possession of the joint kingship of Dublin and Mann, twelfth-century Welsh tradition presented his son, Amlaib or Óláfr, either the individual killed in battle with the Munstermen in 1013 or the one killed in 1034 in England *en route* to Rome, as ruler of a domain which stretched into Galloway.[85] Unsupported though this statement is by any corroborative evidence, it preserves a tradition of Dublin domination of the northern Irish Sea zone during at least part of Sigtryggr's reign. That domination may have been challenged in the past by the Waterford dynasty and Echmarcach was certainly based in Mann following his second expulsion from Dublin in 1052. His control of the island, if he is to be identified with the mac Ragnaill defeated by Murchad mac Diarmata, son of the all-powerful Leinster king, lasted until 1061.[86] This hold on Mann appears well established and it can be safely assumed that he was ruling both Dublin and the island during his second reign in the city. When, though, had control of Mann been achieved? In view of Dublin naval action that followed his overthrow in 1038, with their fleet campaigning in the North Channel/Rathlin Island area, it is possible that Echmarcach was already established in that region before 1036 and had used Mann as a launchpad for his first attempt on Dublin. This may be the power-base that had attracted the attention of Knútr in 1031.

Knútr's interest may also have been drawn by the spread of Echmarcach's power into south-western Scotland. At the time of his death in 1065, Echmarcach was described as *rex innarenn* – king of the Rhinns.[87] It has been plausibly argued that the Rhinns of Galloway constituted the rump of Echmarcach's kingdom, in which he had based himself following his expulsion from Mann in 1061.[88] There is little record of Irish activity in this region in the eleventh century, but there are indications that the Ostmen of Dublin may have sought to control this highly strategic peninsula that commanded the eastern side of the straits that separated the Irish Sea from the Sea of the Hebrides. Sigtryggr Silkiskegg's son, Óláfr, may have added the Rhinns to his Manx-based dominion before 1013, for the somewhat fanciful account in the *Annals of Loch Cé* record that in 1014 at Clontarf, the Dublin host was joined by contingents from Mann and the Rhinns. Echmarcach evidently sought to control a similar power-base, presumably taking advantage of established links between the Scandinavian colonies in western Galloway and those in Mann and Dublin. The chronology for the formation of Echmarcach's maritime domain is unknown, but there are no substantial grounds upon which to argue, as Seán Duffy does, that his control of the Rhinns post-dated his expulsion from Mann by Murchad mac Diarmata in 1061.[89] The spread of the Waterford dynasty from Mann into the Rhinns may well have been the development that attracted Knútr's attention to the north-western peripheries of his realm thirty years earlier.

The spread of Waterford influence in the second quarter of the eleventh century should be seen as part of the developing struggle for power between Donnchad mac Briain, king of Munster, who was seeking to re-establish his family's control of the high-kingship, and Diarmait mac Maíl na mBó, king of Leinster. The Ostmen of Limerick and Waterford were, by this time, simply satellites of the Dál Cais kings of Munster, who could call upon their reserves of heavily armoured warriors and galleys. The slaying of Ragnall mac Ragnaill of Waterford in Dublin in 1035 is probably to be seen in the context of Munster–Leinster rivalry, coloured by the long-standing feud between the Ostmen dynasties. Ragnall's presence in the city is not explained, but might be seen against a backdrop of warfare in the Irish Sea that had not gone all Dublin's way. Certainly, Sigtryggr appears to have lost control of Mann before 1036, for it did not provide him with a refuge after his expulsion from Dublin. While there is no evidence to support the suggestion, it is a distinct possibility that Ragnall mac Ragnaill and Echmarcach mac Ragnaill had established Waterford's maritime supremacy in the 1020s. Here, the maritime war waged between the Ostmen of Dublin and Ulaid hints at the circumstances through which this was achieved. The major naval defeat inflicted on the Dublin fleet by Niall mac Eochaid, King of Ulaid, in 1022, followed by a hosting of the Ulstermen into Fine Gall in

1026,[90] must have severely weakened Sigtryggr's power, while his defeat and capture by the king of Bregha in 1029 brought his authority to a new low. If not actively assisting Niall in 1022 – Ulaid is not otherwise noted as a significant maritime power – than the meic Ragnaill may have capitalised on the eclipse of Dublin's naval power to seize control of Mann. From that base, Ragnall or Echmarcach extended their influence over the lesser Scandinavian colonies along the northern coastlands of the Irish Sea.

MANN IN THE MIDDLE

The man who expelled Echmarcach from Mann in 1061, Murchad mac Diarmata mac Maíl na mBó, had been established by his father as king of Dublin in 1052. He was an active and aggressive figure, who used his control of Dublin to project Leinster power into the maritime world of the Ostmen. The taking of tribute from Mann and the expulsion of its king, who may still have shared the ambitions of his brother-in-law, Donnchad mac Briain, to regain control of the wealth and military resources of the chief Ostman city, marked the beginning of a period where native Irish dynasts sought to assert their control of their maritime hinterland. Murchad's success can be judged by the title King of Leinster and the Foreigners, given to him in his obituary in 1070.[91] On his death, his father stepped into his shoes, resuming personal control of not only Dublin but possibly also exercising the overlordship of Mann at least.[92] There, the kingship was held from before 1066 by one Godred or Gofraid mac Sitriuc,[93] probably the son of Sigtryggr Silkiskegg. Murchad and Diarmait were exercising control of the island through an offshoot of the Uí Ímair, the remnants of whom had been reduced to the status of clients of Leinster. Godred held the kingship until his death c.1070, when he was succeeded by his son, Fingal.[94]

The eleven years of Leinster dominance in Mann does not appear to have ended the Waterford dynasty's aspirations to rule there. It can be suggested that Echmarcach's sons and other kinsmen maintained their association with the Uí Briain, possibly preserving a toehold of power in the Rhinns, for in the aftermath of Diarmait's death in 1072 they re-emerge as contenders for the kingship of Dublin and Mann. The links are clearly established: Donnchad mac Briain had married a sister or niece of Echmarcach, while his second grandson, Tadc mac Toirrdelbach ua Briain, married one of Echmarcach's daughters.[95] Such ties may explain the rapidity with which Munster moved to regain control of Dublin and Mann on Diarmait's death. Toirrdelbach took possession of the city in 1072 and, although granted the kingship by the Ostmen,[96] installed instead one of his meic Ragnaill kinsmen, Gofraid mac Amlaim meic Ragnaill. Gofraid would have been Toirrdelbach's cousin and a nephew of Echmarcach. Furthermore, in 1073, one 'Sitriuc mac Amlaim and two grandsons of Brian [Bóruma]' were killed in the Isle of Mann.[97] This attack on Fingal mac Gofraid should probably be seen as a follow up to the Munster takeover of Dublin, led by a brother of Toirrdelbach's vassal-king and, although there is no evidence for the relationship of the Ui Briain killed, it is possible that they were also grandsons of Ragnall.

After the failure of the Uí Briain attack on Mann in 1073, there is no evidence for further mainland Irish attempts to establish control over the island kingdom for two decades. Fingal mac Gofraid, however, may have been seriously weakened by the invasion, which may also have revealed faultlines in the political structure of an island that had been subject to the rival claims of mutually hostile dynasties for over a century. No more than two years after the Uí Briain attempt, Fingal faced a serious challenge from Gofraid Crobán, a kinsman, adventurer and former mercenary who had made his presence felt in Mann from as early as 1066.[98] Gofraid, founder of the dynasty that was to hold the kingship of Mann until 1265, was a great-grandson of Óláfr Cuarán,[99] but his power seems to have been originally Isles-based rather than Irish. From Gofraid Crobán's reign, the kings of Mann can be seen to exercise lordship over the Hebrides, at least until the challenge mounted to their power by Somairle of Argyll in the mid-twelfth century, and until the extinction of his dynasty in 1265, their power stretched from the Irish Sea to Lewis. Certainly, Gofraid maintained a power-base in the Isles, it being there that Gruffudd ap Cynan, king of Gwynedd, sought him out in c.1094 when gathering aid for his struggle with Hugh of Avranches, earl of Chester, and his brother, Robert of Bellême, earl of Shrewsbury,[100] and it was there, on Islay, that he died in 1095.[101]

Gofraid represents a return to late tenth-century trends; his power was intruded into the region from the Hebrides. He had clearly a deep reservoir of support in the Western Isles, founded presumably upon the ties forged by his ancestor, Óláfr Cuarán, who had died in monastic retirement on Iona in 980.[102] His reign may be seen as an Isles-based attempt to regain control of the southern end of the important trade routes from the south through the Irish Sea, Dublin and Mann, which led ultimately to Orkney and Norway itself. Gofraid clearly intended to control all the elements in this nexus, as is evident from his seizure of the kingship of Dublin in 1091.[103] Although there is no documented evidence for such a move, it is probable that he would have sought control of the Rhinns, thereby safeguarding his domination of the sealanes through the North Channel. Certainly, the church dedications in western Galloway and southern Carrick to saints of the Ionan church may relate to strong Isles' influence in this period, but this cannot be attributed specifically to Gofraid.[104] However, his earlier activity in this region is hinted at in records of an attack launched on Mann in 1087 by the son of the king of Ulaid and two meic Ragnaill dynasts, possibly sons of Gofraid, former king of Dublin, or of Echmarcach himself,[105] mirroring the response from Ulaid in the early eleventh century to Dublin's efforts to dominate the North Channel.

Control of Dublin, Mann and the Isles made Gofraid a power-broker in the politics of western maritime Britain. In its eulogy of the king, for example, the *Chronicle of Mann* claimed that 'the Scots' were so daunted by his power 'that no ship- or boat-builder dared to insert into it more than three bolts'.[106] However this entry is interpreted, the implication is that he maintained a naval supremacy over his neighbours in the northern British mainland. This naval power is underscored by the sixty vessels which Gofraid lent to Gruffudd ap Cynan in 1094, itself an indication of his readiness to project his authority into western Britain. His position, however, did not go unchallenged and the 1087 attack by Ulaid and the Uí Ragnaill, may indicate that there were still elements within his far-flung domain whose loyalties lay elsewhere. Seán Duffy has argued that the attack on Mann should be seen in the context of the developing struggle after 1086 within the Uí Briain kindred for the leadership of the family between the sons of Toirrdelbach ua Briain, and was aimed at preventing Muirchertach mac Toirrdelbach ua Briain from establishing his control over the island by placing a supporter of his rivals for the kingship of Munster, his nephews, the meic Taidc, in power there.[107] It is questionable, however, whether Muirchertach was in any position before 1089, despite his victory at Howth Head over the Ostmen of Dublin in 1087, to attempt to project his authority into Mann where Gofraid Crobán was at the height of his power. From 1087 to 1089, his priority was to secure control of Munster itself. Certainly, the king of Ulaid had marital connections with a rival branch of the Uí Briain descended from Donnchad mac Briain, but for them the meic Taidc were as much the enemy as Muirchertach. Co-operation between Ulaid and the meic Taidc, therefore, seems highly unlikely.

In 1091, Gofraid seized the kingship of Dublin. His possession of the city lasted barely three years and ended with his expulsion in 1094 by Muirchertach ua Briain. The occupation of Dublin represented the climax of Gofraid's steady accumulation of power in the Irish Sea and Isles, but was, in its timing, nothing more than a splendid piece of opportunism which capitalised on the conflict in Ireland which was keeping both Munster and Leinster weakened. His control of the city was evidently prolonged through alliance with Domnall mac Lochlainn, king of Ailech, Muirchertach's chief rival for hegemony in Ireland. In 1094 Mac Lochlainn and Gofraid defeated Muirchertach's first attempt to re-capture the prized city but the Munster king returned once his opponents had disbanded their armies. Driven out of Dublin, Gofraid fell back on his Hebridean power-base, dying there of plague the following year.[108]

Seán Duffy has suggested that Muirchertach succeeded in driving Gofraid not only from Dublin but from Mann as well,[109] heralding an era of unprecedented Munster power in the Isles. This is an ambitious claim, for it is evident that Gofraid was succeeded as king in Mann by his eldest son, Lagmann.[110] The *Chronicle of Mann*, noted for its suspect arithmetic and chronology, credits Lagmann with a seven-year reign that ended between 1096 and 1098 with his death on crusade.[111] Even allowing for the vagaries of the chronicler's calculations, it appears that he had assumed the kingship of Mann before his father's death. Indeed, it can be inferred that Lagmann's reign commenced with his father's departure for Dublin in 1091, a clear indication of the perception of the status of the kingship of that city amongst the *Gall*. Even before the events of 1094, however, Lagmann's rule faced challenge from within his family, his younger brother, Harald, staging a prolonged rebellion which ended with the latter's capture, blinding and castration. According to the Manx chronicle, it was remorse for the mutilation of his brother that led to Lagmann's resignation of the kingdom and departure for the Holy Land. There are indications, however, that more worldly pressures persuaded him to abandon his kingdom.

By 1096, Lagmann was facing mounting hostility to his rule from within the Isles, represented by a noble faction that had formed around his young brother, Óláfr. Perhaps unable to topple Lagmann through their own efforts, this group turned to Ireland for aid and made an approach to Muirchertach ua Briain. The deciding factor in this must have been Muirchertach's recent capture of Dublin and control of its naval power. According to the *Chronicle of Mann*, the chief men of the Isles asked Muirchertach to provide them with a member of his own kin to rule over the Isles until Óláfr reached adulthood,[112] although this is more likely to have been the price for his support imposed by Muirchertach. The man he chose was Domnall mac Taidc, earlier one of his rivals for the kingship of Munster but, more importantly, a grandson of Echmarcach and, since the death of the meic Ragnaill in Mann in 1087, possibly the senior male representative of that line. Domnall's intrusion into Mann, however, was not as easy as the Chronicle implies, for the killing there in 1096 of his brother, Óláfr,[113] indicates that meic Taidc rule was opposed by some, presumably the supporters of Lagmann.

Domnall mac Taidc is credited with a three-year reign over Mann and the Isles, c.1096–98, but it is apparent that the kingdom built up by Gofraid Crobán had begun to disintegrate under his rule. Indeed, it is questionable how extensive his authority was in the northern island territories of the kingdom at any time. Manx tradition records that shortly before the expedition of Magnus Barelegs, king of Norway, into the West in 1098, the king had sent a deputy, Ingimundr, with instructions to seize the kingdom.[114] Based in Lewis, that in the twelfth and thirteenth centuries was to constitute the principal northern portion of the kingdom of Mann and the Isles, he attempted to usurp the kingship but was killed in the process by the chieftains of the Isles. In Mann itself, the factional tensions that had led to the imposition of Domnall erupted into civil war in 1098, a conflict in which Domnall himself evidently played no part and which probably indicates that he had already lost control of the island.[115] How that conflict would have resolved itself is one of Manx history's great 'what ifs?' for the internal struggle for power was swiftly overtaken by external events: the arrival of King Magnus Barelegs in the Isles.

NORTHUMBRIA, WESSEX AND STRATHCLYDE

Despite the western and maritime dimension which dominated the perspectives of the rulers of Galloway in the twelfth and thirteenth centuries and which the preceding discussion of Irish and Norse influences demonstrated had been established as early as the 900s, the traditional presentation of Galloway's history has had a strongly mainland-based bias. Indeed, one of the most restricting of the historiographical straitjackets which has handicapped the development of a clearer narrative for the development of the later lordship has been its presentation as part of the 'making' of the kingdom of the Scots. The narrow limits of Scottish national history, bedevilled by the 'kailyard' approach which saw the development of an unhealthy degree of introspection in research, have served to sever Galloway artificially from its wider maritime – and mainland British – hinterland. The emphasis in the discussion so far has been on the links with Mann, the Isles and Ireland, but equally important for the evolution of the medieval lordship were the region's ancient ties with Northumbria.

STRATHCLYDE AND THE DISMEMBERMENT
OF NORTHUMBRIA 866–1000

The fall of York to the Danes in November 866 and the death at their hands in March 867 of the last independent Northumbrian king has, by tradition, been presented as something of a fullstop in the political history of the northern Anglian kingdoms. The survival of a native dynasty ruling over Bernicia from Bamburgh has been treated somewhat as a rather discreditable coda to the main narrative and presented primarily as a phenomenon of distinctively local, essentially east-coast, significance. From a Scottish perspective, the fall of the ecclesiastical capital has been viewed as signalling the collapse of the kingdom and an end to Northumbrian control over the Southern Uplands. The trend towards constructing national histories for Scotland and England has further marginalised the post-867 history of Northumbria by driving an artificial physical dividing line, the later political frontier line between the medieval kingdoms, through the midst of what was, until the eleventh century, an entity which straddled the Tweed, the Cheviots and the Pennines. While the seizure of York may have ripped the political heart out of Northumbria, and Danish settlement of south-eastern Deira deprived it of its most populous and fertile zone, the Anglian polity continued to function in the extensive territories – too great to be dismissed derisively as the 'rump' – which remained of the old kingdom, over which the Danes set a vassal-king, Egbert.[116]

Pressure was maintained on Northumbria until the death in 877 of

Hálfdan, Danish king of York. In 875 he had sacked Carlisle, Hexham and Lindisfarne, the spiritual centres of what remained of the kingdom – St Cuthbert's community finally abandoning its island monastery and beginning its decade of semi-nomadic existence – and plundered extensively throughout the Southern Uplands zone and into the Forth basin. His raid may have had a greater impact on Northumbrian political society west of the Pennines than the initial onslaught in 866–67, for the account of the peregrinations the monks and the relics which they carried gives little indication of any organised authority in the region. The bleak picture painted by the *History of St Cuthbert*, however, is probably considerably overstated and owes much to the requirement of its author to demonstrate the living martyrdom faced by his predecessors in their efforts to safeguard the precious relics of the saint, for centres of Anglian power continued to function in Cumberland and northern Lancashire down into the opening decades of the tenth century and beyond.

To what extent a recognisably Anglian political or religious structure survived within Galloway is more difficult to determine. The excavations at Whithorn point to the burning of the Northumbrian monastery in the second quarter of the ninth century, but whether this was the result of a raid or accident cannot be established.[117] Reconstruction followed but on a new layout which marked a radical departure from the regimental linearity of the eighth-century Northumbrian community. The underlying economy and material culture of the site, moreover, may also have been transformed, but the excavation results here are decidedly ambiguous.[118] Peter Hill talks in terms of 'a new alliance . . . forged . . . to restore the Northumbrian minster and preserve its endowments', an arrangement which he saw as involving Anglian farmers, the remains of the ecclesiastical community, incoming Scandinavian colonists and a resurgent British elite which re-emerged from the Galwegian hinterland to re-assert its former political and cultural dominance.[119] The archaeology, moreover, has been interpreted as recording a relatively prosperous and stable period through the tenth century, where 'Whithorn participated in the bullion economy of the Irish Sea province . . . but not in its wars'.[120] This has been presented as an 'Anglo-British' phenomenon rather than a consequence of incoming settlement and labelled as a 'picture of independence and prosperity' amidst the turbulence of the time.[121]

British resurgence following the removal of the Anglian yoke is a recurrent theme in most discussions of tenth-century political development in the Humber–Forth zone. The apparent collapse of Northumbrian power in the Southern Uplands is linked in the traditional historiography with a re-expansion of Strathclyde's political and cultural authority to fill the void created.[122] The scenario reconstructed by Hill at Whithorn offers a localised reflection of that phenomenon but his interpretation is coloured by inadequate consideration of the wider political and cultural changes that were occurring around the Irish Sea at this time. Indeed, the apparent peace and prosperity of the Machars in the tenth century would be remarkable, if its hypothetical existence was based on anything broader than the purely archaeological record of a single site. If it can be given any historical setting, then surely it represents nothing more than an extension of the stability noted by Higham in Cumberland and Westmorland in the period down to c.930, a stability that flowed from the dominance of the Dublin–York axis down to the death of King Sigtryggr.

In the absence of any narrative accounts, evidence for a British re-advance within territory formerly dominated by Northumbria has depended heavily upon place-names. These show, at best, a patchy revival, evident most particularly in Annandale and extending into the pre-1974 county of Cumberland where they can be seen to be superimposed over the Anglian settlement pattern.[123] In Galloway, there is no recognisable indication of such stratification and it has proven impossible to distinguish between pre-Northumbrian British names and any coined in the later ninth or tenth centuries.[124] Indeed, with the singular exception of the possibly British-influenced sculptural tradition of the so-called 'Whithorn School', whose distribution is largely limited to the south-east of the Machars district itself,[125] there is no substance with which to support arguments in favour of British social and political dominance within Galloway in the tenth century. If the localisation of south-western sculptural traditions reveals anything, it is the highly fragmented nature of the political structures and cultural patterns of the region.

Belief in a British renaissance within Galloway in the later ninth and tenth centuries hinges on the tradition of the expansion of the power of the kings of Strathclyde in the same period. Maps purporting to show the tenth- or early eleventh-century political structures of the region between the Clyde and Morecambe Bay place a unitary authority – commonly labelled 'Strathclyde–Cumbria' – over the whole zone stretching from the Lennox into the Lake District. Such dynamic growth as this would represent, however, is at odds with the historical evidence for the state of Strathclyde's power in c.900. While the Clyde provided the spine upon which the power of this compact kingdom was built, it also constituted its principal weakness, for it was a highway along which Scandinavian armies were to penetrate with depressing regularity from 871 into the 920s. Faced with the repeated ravaging of their political and economic heartland, it is hard to credit the rulers of Strathclyde with the resources to stage a major and rapid southwards extension of their authority. Despite this, the kings of Strathclyde do seem to have enjoyed something of a revival in their fortunes in the tenth century. What that meant in terms of territorial lordship, however, is less clear.

Before the political upheavals of the 870s, the authority of the Dumbarton-based kings is unlikely to have extended much beyond the river basin from which their kingdom derived its name. Its southern limit probably lay on the watershed between the river-systems of the Clyde and

Annan, represented until 1974 by the boundary between Lanarkshire and Dumfriesshire. A southward shift in the political centre of gravity in the kingdom, possibly triggered by the capture and sack of Dumbarton in 871 and the growth in Scottish power to the north-east, may be signalled by the emergence of Cadzow as a significant centre of royal power.[126] Although Dumbarton may not have been entirely abandoned – fragments of two tenth-century recumbent cross-slabs with Govan School affinities suggest at least ecclesiastical activity on or near the rock – it disappears as a royal centre, probably in recognition of its highly exposed position in relation to Scandinavian attack.[127] It is this shift in the internal dynamics of the kingdom that may have facilitated the expansion beyond the established southern limits of Strathclyde into the river valleys that feed into the head of the Solway.

Evidence on the ground for such a development is not lacking in a broad zone extending from Beattock, down Annandale – or Ystrad Annant as it was known into the twelfth century – into northern Cumberland. Place-names, which constitute the bulk of this evidence, point to new settlement, for it is unlikely that any remnants of the pre-Anglian British elite had maintained their British identity through 260 years of Anglian rule. That new British names are concentrated most heavily in the lower Eden and Irthing valleys, previously the core area of Northumbrian settlement focused on Carlisle, suggests that colonisation was occurring.[128] A further indication of population movement may be seen in the spread of dedications to Strathclyde saints, particularly Kentigern, into Cumberland.[129] This may be placed alongside the situation revealed in the twelfth-century *Inquest of David*, which maps the properties associated with the Church of Glasgow at the time of its reorganisation by the future David I in those parts of Cumbria which he then controlled.[130] In this, five distinct groupings are set out, the first centred on Glasgow, a second in Clydesdale, a third in central Tweeddale, a fourth in Annandale and a final cluster again in Tweeddale. The absence of any Cumberland properties from the list is presumably a reflection of the loss of this district in 1093.[131] The Annandale group probably formed the estate of the former monastery of Hoddam, which heads the list of Dumfriesshire properties, and can be interpreted as the wholesale transfer of the property and rights of an Anglian community to the church most favoured by the kings of Strathclyde in an unequivocal demonstration of the new political realities.

In their distribution, the Glasgow estates are highly revealing. Even allowing for the possibility of alienation or lay appropriation of church properties, it is clear that Glasgow acquired no propertied interests in large tracts of what is considered traditionally to have been part of Strathclyde. With the dubious exception of Edingham to the east of Dalbeattie in Galloway,[132] the Inquest recorded no possessions south and west of a line extending from the Annandale-Nithsdale border to Renfrewshire. This can be interpreted in part by the existence of alternative cult centres, such as

Govan, Paisley and Kilwinning, which attracted the flow of landed endowment, but it also indicates that if the kings of Strathclyde enjoyed any authority within this zone they clearly lacked any personal demesne from which grants could have been made to their favoured saint.

That the districts south and west of this line formed part of the kingdom of Strathclyde has been argued on the grounds that they fell within the see of Glasgow as it was defined in the twelfth century and that they constituted part of the principality controlled by the future King David I during the reign of his elder brother, Alexander I. This latter point is confirmed by charters of David and his grandson, Malcolm IV, which record David's grant to the churches of Glasgow and Kelso of elements of the yearly render of cain (a tribute paid in foodstuffs) due to him from these districts.[133] Significantly, however, the charters do not refer to the land from which these renders were drawn as part of Strathclyde or Cumbria, but as 'that part of Galloway'[134] which David controlled. At best, it would seem, the kings of Strathclyde exercised a loose and probably intermittent overlordship rather than direct lordship of the territory extending from Strathgryfe in what is now Renfrewshire southwards through Cunninghame, Kyle, Carrick and Nithsdale, or at least they did so in the early 1100s. The suggestion, as late as the 1130s, that this territory was part of a wider Galloway, again emphasises the western Norse–Gaelic links of this zone and its separation from the mainland Scottish world of Alba and Strathclyde. In common with Galloway proper, the naming of the discrete territorial units that comprised this region points again to a fragmentation rather than a coalescing of power, offering a parallel to the position evident within Galloway proper in the same period. Colonisation by external agencies, as occurred in Galloway, may likewise have been the determining factor in producing this fragmented political and cultural pattern in the districts fringing the eastern shore of the Firth of Clyde. Fellows-Jensen has pointed to the cluster of Scandinavian settlement names in Cunninghame and Renfrewshire,[135] a group which has been linked to Norse colonisation of the southern Hebrides[136] and, possibly, to attempts to establish control over the Clyde estuary trading nexus. Carrick, too, preserves traces of a Norse–Gaelic settlement in the tenth century, possibly linked to the kingdom of the Rhinns, but here Gaelic rather than Norse was the dominant cultural and linguistic type. Only in Nithsdale are we confronted with a ruling native dynasty, and here, too, it emerges only in the early twelfth century in the person of Dunegal of Strathnith.[137] A scattering of potentially tenth-century British names in lower Nithsdale, centred on what appears to have been the main seat of lordly power at Dumfries, may indicate a western extension of Strathclyde influence from Annandale or the re-emergence of the old elites, but by the twelfth century this, like Carrick, was a thoroughly Gaelicised area.

What emerges from the above is the apparent ephemerality of the power of the kings of Strathclyde throughout much of the western Southern

Upland zone outwith a corridor extending from Upper Clydesdale through Annandale to the Solway plain. This corridor was flanked to the west by territories which may, at times, have acknowledged the overlordship of Strathclyde, but which otherwise fell within the sphere of the western maritime powers and which displayed a strongly Gaelic character liberally laced with pockets of Scandinavian. This hybridity no doubt gave rise to the labelling of this broader south-west as 'Galloway', the land of the Gall–Gaidhel, while the term *Galwalenses*, used by some twelfth-century authorities to describe the inhabitants of this zone, may reflect an attempt to rationalise a hybrid Gaelic–Brythonic or Scandinavian–Brythonic population which emerged in the wake of tenth-century migrations. Rather than comprising a unitary power bloc, Strathclyde–Cumbria was a congeries of minor lordships over which the men labelled as kings of Strathclyde exercised a fluctuating control. Their comparative weakness acted as a magnet to external forces, notably to Alba and Wessex, for both of whom a politically fragmented and unstable Strathclyde constituted a major threat to their security. For the Scots, Strathclyde had been the route by which the Norse entered Fortriu in the early 900s, while for the English it was the opening through which the grandsons of Ívarr had seized control of York. It is as attempts to stabilise this dangerously disunited territory that the tenth- and eleventh-century manoeuverings of Scottish and English kings should be read.

The submission of northern and western British rulers to Athelstan of Wessex at Eamont Bridge in 927 has long been interpreted as a 'border conference' on the southernmost limit of Strathclyde.[138] Nowhere in contemporary record, however, is it presented in such terms and it should perhaps be seen simply as a meeting at a geographically strategic location where the old Roman road south from Carlisle met the roadways from York and Chester. Following swiftly on the heels of his seizure of York on the death of Sigtryggr and expulsion of Gothfrith of Dublin from the city, the meeting shows Athelstan seeking to consolidate his power north of the Humber and to re-define political relationships within the region through which challenges to his new position could be mounted. Significantly, the northern powers with whom he dealt were Causantin mac Aeda, king of Scots, and the Bernician ruler, Ealdred son of Eadwulf, the two men best placed to either wreck or secure the political settlement imposed by Athelstan on the kingdom of York, with no mention being made of the king of Strathclyde.[139] Current historiography favours the conversion of Strathclyde, following the elevation to the throne there of an otherwise unknown brother of Causantin, Domnall mac Aeda, to little more than a satellite of Alba and, even with the native dynasty restored some time before 934, remaining subject to Scottish overlordship or at best firmly allied to its increasingly powerful northern neighbour. This scenario, however, has been shown to be built on a faulty reading of the relevant passage in the Poppleton Manuscript, which refers to the death of Domnall mac Aeda, king of Ailech, and not to the elevation of a brother of Causantin mac Aeda to the kingship of the Britons.[140] Although this indicates that the native lineage continued to reign unbroken within Strathclyde, it does not rule out the probability that they were little more than vassals of Alba. This certainly, appears to be the situation reflected in the events of 934 when, in response to Causantin's dealings with the new Dublin claimant of the throne of York, Óláfr Gothfrithsson, Athelstan staged a major raid by land and sea which defeated the Scots and the men of Strathclyde, penetrated Alba as far north as Dunnottar and which saw the fleet ravage the coastlands of Caithness.[141] While Athelstan secured a fresh submission and Causantin spent Christmas with him in southern England, the Scot was soon negotiating with Óláfr. In 937, along with his Strathclyde vassals, he was the major mainland power to support Óláfr in his bid for York that culminated in the crushing defeat of the Scots at Brunanburh.[142]

Athelstan's victory at Brunanburh, spectacular though it was, evidently had little lasting impact on northern affairs and, following his death in 939, Óláfr staged a fresh, and this time successful, bid for York.[143] Thus began a see-saw struggle for control of York and the country beyond the Humber between the kings of Wessex and a succession of Scandinavian aspirants for the northern kingship, culminating in 954 with the expulsion and death of Eiríkr Bloodaxe and the final annexation of York by Eadred of Wessex.[144] The struggle had seen a significant effort by the kings of Wessex to establish greater security on the northern extremities of their power, King Edmund's invasion of Strathclyde – whence Óláfr Gothfrithsson had fled following his expulsion from York – and his subsequent 'grant' of the kingdom to the Scottish king, Máel Coluim mac Domnaill in 945.[145] A condition of the grant was that Máel Coluim should aid Edmund 'on sea and on land', which suggests that the king of Wessex aimed to end the now well-established connection between Strathclyde and Dublin and close the Clyde and the Solway to Óláfr and his successors. It was this Strathclyde–Dublin axis that had, for a quarter of a century, proven the undoing of English efforts to dominate the North. Presumably born out of fears that Wessex would seek to assert its role as the heir of Northumbria aggressively and regain control over those areas of northern Cumbria and the Southern Uplands which Strathclyde had acquired from the Angles and, possibly, reassert the overlordship of this region which had been exercised by Northumbrian kings down to the 800s, the alliance had been designed to place a buffer between the Britons and the spreading might of the southern British superpower.[146] By ending this unholy alliance, Edmund weakened the York–Dublin axis: when Eiríkr Bloodaxe seized York in 948, it was from the springboard of Orkney – not Dublin – that he launched his attack.[147]

The stability of the Solway region lasted for a quarter of a century until the killing in 971 of the Scottish king, Culen mac Indulf, by Rhydderch of Strathclyde.[148] Whether this stemmed from a feud within the Scottish ruling dynasty,[149] or was the action of an alienated vassal avenging the rape of his daughter, is open to debate, but its consequences revealed the fragility of regional stability. Culen's successor, Cinaed mac Máel Coluim, launched his reign with a major raid against the Britons, possibly ravaging their land as far south as Stainmore.[150] Cinaed's actions appear to have been part of a more general episode of political disturbance on the north-western limits of English power. The gathering in c.973 of a fleet at Chester by Edgar of Wessex, and the attendance on him there of six or eight kings, including Cinaed and Malcolm, 'king of the Cumbrians', should probably be seen in the context of English efforts to impose stability on what was still a vulnerable frontier and neutralise any threat to continued Wessex domination of York and Northumbria.[151] That the assembly of the kings at Chester was not simply a submission to Edgar's overlordship, which is the gloss commonly placed on it by late eleventh- and twelfth-century English chroniclers,[152] is indicated by the territorial concessions that Edgar made to secure a treaty. According to later Durham tradition, Cinaed was conducted to Edgar by the two earls whom the English king had set over Northumbria, Oslac, who ruled from York, and Eadulf Evil-child, ruler beyond the Tees, accompanied by Elfsi, bishop of Chester-le-Street.[153] According to this account, couched in anachronistically 'feudal' language', Cinaed offered his homage to Edgar, in return for which he received Lothian. When stripped of the late eleventh- and early twelfth-century political messages contained in the text, we are left with what appears to be a record of Anglo-Scottish peace achieved at the cost of territorial concessions by Edgar in the remote north of Northumbria, a price that he no doubt considered worth paying for the long term security of his northern frontier. The peace with the Scots survived Cinaed's assassination in 995 and the decade of internecine strife between the Mac Áeda and Mac Domnaill segments of the Mac Ailpín dynasty that followed. The removal of Cinaed's strong hand in Cumbria, however, may have been exploited by other powers with designs on English-dominated territory. For Æthelred II, this zone was a potential entry point for his Norwegian and Danish enemies, a factor which no doubt provoked his military and naval campaign of 1000 into the far north west.[154] The re-newed instability of Northumbria and Cumbria which this signalled was most likely the factor that triggered Scottish raids in the aftermath of the seizure of the Scottish throne by Máel Coluim mac Cinaeda in 1005.

CUMBRIA, SCOTLAND AND ENGLAND, 1000–92

Máel Coluim commenced his reign with an 'inaugural raid' into Northumbria in 1006.[155] This ended with a crushing defeat at Durham at the hands of a Northumbrian force led by Uhtred, son of Earl Waltheof of Northumbria and husband of Ecgfrytha, daughter of Bishop Aldhun of Durham.[156] Uhtred's victory brought a decade of respite for the north from

Scottish attack and restored some prestige to the House of Bamburgh. It may have restored, too, some portion of the land ceded to Cinaed in 973. Although his father was still alive, Uhtred was appointed earl of Northumbria, to which King Æthelred added the earldom of York following his assassination of Earl Ælfhelm in 1006.[157] William Kapelle was probably correct when he suggested that the placing of both earldoms in the hands of one man was a sign of the degree of Æthelred's concerns for English control north of the Humber.[158] In a bid to underpin his authority south of the Tees, Uhtred set aside Ecgfrytha and married Sige, daughter of Styr, a member of the powerful Anglo-Scandinavian York nobility. That this may have been done with Bishop Aldhun's acceptance is suggested by the re-marriage of Ecgfrytha to another influential figure south of the Tees, Kilvert, son of Ligulf, an important Yorkshire thegn.[159] As English resistance began to crumble in the face of the Danish onslaught led by King Svein, Uhtred's loyalty as the king's strong man in the north became vital to Æthelred. To ensure his continued loyalty and to reward past service, Uhtred was given the king's daughter, Ælfgifu, as his third wife. This binding to the House of Wessex may have proven Uhtred's undoing for, in 1016, when Knútr had consolidated his hold over England and forced the ruler of Northumbria into submission, he ordered Uhtred's assassination and replacement at York with his own follower, Eiríkr of Hlaðir.[160]

The de-stabilisation of the Pennine zone that this violent coup produced proved a powerful lure to Máel Coluim mac Cinaeda. Uhtred had been succeeded north of the Tees by his younger brother, Eadulf Cudel, who is portrayed in northern tradition as weak and lacking in capability. Eadulf, though, was in an unenviable position, for it is probable that he faced war on all fronts. While York was under the control of Knútr's supporters, there is no evidence that the country beyond the Tees had submitted to the new king after Uhtred's murder while attempting to reach an accommodation with him. Eadulf, then, may have faced continuing warfare with Knútr's powerful northern supporters. With York now occupied by a hostile Scandinavian earl, he lacked the military resources that had given his brother the ability to check any threats to the Northumbrian heartland. This was demonstrated to devastating effect in 1018, when Máel Coluim and his probable vassal, Ywain, son of Dyfnwal, king of Strathclyde, crushed a Northumbrian army at Carham on the Tweed, an event that was followed by the cession to the Scots of the country north of the river.[161] The defeat was followed by the death of Bishop Aldhun, a key figure in Northumbrian politics, and it appears that Eadulf, too, did not survive for much longer. His successor was Ealdred, the grandson of Bishop Aldhun and son of Earl Uhtred and Ecgfrytha, who evidently continued the resistance to Knútr and his men in York.

Máel Coluim capitalised on this continuing upheaval. Welsh tradition records the violent death of Ywain, son of Dyfnwal, some time after 1015 and, if the Durham tradition which records his presence at Carham is correct, then it is possible that he had been a casualty of the battle.[162] Ywain was the last of his line and it appears that his death saw the consolidation of Scottish power over Strathclyde and the beginning of the absorption of the western Southern Upland zone into the kingdom of the Scots. The process was to take over a century, not being completed until the reign of David I, but Knútr's preoccupation with consolidation of his hold on the English heartlands and in Scandinavia, and the political weakness of Northumbria after 1016–18, provided the Scots with the opportunity to entrench their power within a zone that kings of the English from the time of Edmund had considered vital to the security of their kingdom. It was not until the early 1030s that Knútr was in a position to attempt to redress the shift in the balance of power in the north.[163] Recent arguments have proposed that his primary objective may have been containment of any threat to his authority in Norway from the rulers of Orkney, rather than a rolling back of Máel Coluim mac Cinaeda's power in Cumbria, but his campaign of 1031 which took the submissions of Máel Coluim, Echmarcach, and, possibly, Macbeth, represented a re-affirmation of English power north of the Humber and, more particularly, over the north-west.[164] From 1029–30, Knútr was certainly flexing his muscles in the Irish Sea zone, extending his influence to Dublin, directing campaigns against the Welsh and attempting to install Eiríkr of Hlaðir's son, Håkon, whom he had already made earl of Worcester, as king in the Hebrides. Håkon's drowning in late 1029 or early 1030 whilst sailing to his new territories via Orkney wrecked this plan and may have forced Knútr into more direct action.[165]

Knútr's 1031 campaign appears to have been highly successful. Not only did he secure his dominant position in the Irish Sea region and a treaty with the Scottish king, presumably in return for recognition of his possession of Cumbria, but he appears also to have forced Ealdred into submission. That Knútr now exercised some authority within Northumbria is supported by the record of his grant of property to Bishop Edmund of Durham.[166] This general settlement held until after the deaths of both Máel Coluim in 1034 and Knútr in 1036, but was wrecked in 1038 by the murder of Ealdred. His successor was his half-brother, Eadulf, son of Uhtred and Sige daughter of Styr, who reverted to the defiance of the Anglo-Danish regime in the south maintained by his family down to 1031. Like his earlier namesake, Eadulf faced challenges from all sides, the first significant threat coming from Donnchad mac Crinain, king of Scots. In 1039, Donnchad invaded Northumbria but, like his grandfather Máel Coluim before him, was defeated heavily at Durham.[167] Eadulf followed his success at Durham with a devastating raid into Strathclyde that may have won him temporary control of Cumberland,[168] but was pragmatist enough to realise that Northumbria could not maintain its position indefinitely and, in 1041, attempted to come to terms with the new Anglo-Danish king, Harðaknútr.[169] The king had plans for the country beyond the Humber, and Eadulf figured nowhere in these. On Harðaknútr's instructions, Eadulf was assassinated by the emerging strong man in the north, Siward, earl of York.

Siward, who had been established at York by Knútr in 1033, added Northumbria to his territories after 1041. From then until his death in 1055, Siward dominated the country north of the Humber, to some extent recreating a Northumbrian hegemony over the Southern Uplands and Cumbria. His position had been strengthened by the political upheavals in Scotland in 1040, which had seen the death of Donnchad at the hands of Macbethad mac Findláich and the flight southwards of the close kinsmen of the dead king. The key figures among the exiles were Donnchad's brother, Maldred, who had married Ealdgith, daughter of Earl Uhtred of Northumbria, and Máel Coluim mac Donnchada, eldest son of the late king. Siward, whose control of the region between the Tees and the Tweed had only recently been secured by marriage to Ælfleda, daughter of Earl Ealdred, now sought to project his authority beyond the limits of his earldom. In 1046, he invaded Scotland and succeeded in temporarily installing a rival – possibly Maldred – to Macbethad as king of Scots.[170] Although Macbethad drove out or killed this rival the same year, it appears that Siward held on successfully to some part of his kingdom, possibly in Cumberland, where Maldred's grandson, Dolfin, was to become a major figure at the end of the century.

Insufficient documentary evidence survives from which to build a chronology for the expansion and consolidation of Siward's power west of the Pennines, but some idea can be obtained of the mechanisms employed. A key figure in the political structure of Cumberland in the mid eleventh century was a nobleman named Cospatric, who, between 1041 and 1055 issued a writ in favour of one Thorfinn mac Thore concerning land in Allerdale.[171] The identity of this Cospatric is a matter of some controversy, the two main arguments naming him either as youngest son of Earl Uhtred, or the son of Maldred, who was to become earl of Northumbria briefly between 1068 and 1072, and who subsequently became earl of Dunbar.[172] Alternatively, he may have been the grandson of Bishop Aldhun's daughter, Ecgfrytha, through Sigrida, the daughter of her second marriage to Kilvert, son of Ligulf. Whatever the case, Cospatric descended from one of the noble lineages of eastern Northumbria. The writ discloses that the lands with which it was concerned 'had been Cumbrian' but had been detached from Cumbrian control some time after 1041, possibly as a result of Eadulf's military operations after the defeat of Donnchad at Durham. The loss of what became Cumberland, however, may have resulted from a property transaction arising from the dynastic conflict in Scotland after 1040. The cession of this highly strategic zone to English control, which would have closed off the natural raiding routes into Siward's Northumbrian and York earldoms via the Tyne Gap and Stanemore, may have been the *quid pro quo* for his support for the cause of Maldred and Máel Coluim. It may be significant that Máel Coluim's father, Donnchad, had possibly held the kingship of the Cumbrians during the lifetime of his grandfather, Máel Coluim mac Cinaeda, although the main evidence for this comes from the late fourteenth-century tradition of John of Fordun.[173] Máel Coluim mac Donnchada, therefore, as his father's heir, may have delivered up to Siward, or formalised his seizure of this territory, as the price for the earl's support.

Further evidence for Siward's control of the Carlisle region is largely circumstantial. The scatter of Danish settlement names north-westwards from the Vale of York into the Eden Valley and southern Annandale, discussed above, may represent an eleventh-century development rather than a late ninth- or tenth-century movement. Their spread, certainly, looks like an effort to control the routes from Strathclyde, Galloway and the wider Solway region into the political and economic heart of Siward's power in Yorkshire. A further indication of York-based influence over this area of southern Cumbria in the mid-eleventh century is the rather garbled ecclesiastical record which states that Archbishop Cynsige of York (1051–60) consecrated two bishops 'of Glasgow' during his episcopate.[174] The consecration of these men, named as Magsuea and John, probably post-dates 1055, when Cynsige received his pallium from Rome, and it has been suggested that their appointment was in some way connected with Siward's invasion of Scotland in the previous year.[175] As in 1046, the invasion of 1054 secured control of the country south of the Forth as a base from which Siward's protégé, Máel Coluim mac Donnchada, was subsequently to launch his successful effort to depose Macbethad in 1056–7.[176] This was a somewhat Pyrrhic victory, for in the battle with Macbethad Siward lost his son by his first marriage, Osbeorn, his nephew, Siward, and a significant number of both his own huscarls and of a detachment of King Edward's own bodyguard. Another evidently significant English casualty was Dolfin, Finntur's son, whom Kapelle has identified as Dolfin Thorfinn's son, commander of a contingent from Cumbria.[177] Siward himself died in 1055, and, with his younger son by his second marriage to Ælfleda, Waltheof, probably still under fifteen, the prospect of a continuation of his York-based dynasty collapsed.[178] Siward's successor at York was an outsider, Tosti, son of the powerful Godwin, Earl of Wessex.[179] He lacked Siward's entrenched local position and close relationship with Máel Coluim, and it is likely that any York influence over the Scottish Southern Uplands quickly evaporated on the death of Siward. Under such circumstances, it is improbable that Cynsige could have realistically projected his metropolitan authority into northern Cumbria. This, however, begs the question of a see 'of Glasgow' as opposed to a see 'of Cumbria' at this time, and it is probable that Hugh the Chantor, writer of our source, was basing the political geography of his account on early twelfth-century rather than eleventh-century structures. The twelfth-century partition of the old Cumbrian see into Scottish and English portions, with sees at Glasgow and Carlisle, may offer a partial solution to the problem of where Magsuea and John were based. Siward's control over the Carlisle area was probably more concrete than his influence over Máel Coluim's portion of Cumbria and it is likely that it was in this area, where the bishops could serve as a further prop to the earl of York's power, that their see was fixed.

Analysis of Siward's activities outside his earldom has focused almost exclusively on his king-making role in Scotland. The extension of his power into southern Cumbria, however, may have been related to other concerns, primarily the political developments that were taking place within the Irish Sea zone. As a York-based power, it is likely that Siward's authority had marched with the sphere of influence of the archbishop, who governed a trans-Pennine see that embraced south Westmorland and Lancashire. From the time of his establishment as earl of York around 1033, Siward may have been confronted with the repercussions of the shifting balance of power in the northern Irish Sea, which his patron, Knútr, has set in motion. Knútr, for example, had brought Sigtryggr Silkiskegg into his clientage by 1030, and had used this Dublin alliance to good effect in his invasion of north Wales in 1030. This had seen the possible establishment of a Dublin colony on Anglesey, which may have been Sigtryggr's first destination after his final expulsion from Dublin in 1036.[180] This represented only part of a wider projection of Irish-based power eastwards across the Irish Sea. Perhaps the most significant threat to stability was posed by Echmarcach, with whom Knútr had established some kind of treaty relationship in 1031. His control of Dublin and Waterford, Mann and western Galloway provided him with a formidable power-base, and it is possible that he may have been considered as a potential challenger for control of York itself, where his Uí Ímair ancestors had ruled as kings. The Solway region constituted a vulnerable point of entry through which Echmarcach could have driven, hence Siward's efforts to control the area. Some indication of his success here may lie in the strong links between eastern Galloway and the churches of Durham and York, which are evident in the early twelfth century. The establishment of lasting political control, however, was forestalled by the deaths of both Siward and his adult heir in 1054–55. Within five years of his death, the Northumbrian domain built by Siward had disintegrated.

MÁEL COLUIM CEANN MÓR AND THE CONTROL OF CUMBRIA c.1060–93

However dependent Máel Coluim mac Donnchada had been on Siward down to 1055, there is little evidence after his patron's death for continuing Anglo-Saxon military aid in the struggle against his rivals in Scotland. Having finally defeated and killed Macbethad in 1057 and Lulach mac Gillacomgain in 1058, Máel Coluim mac Donnchada had eliminated for the meanwhile any viable challengers for the Scottish throne. Nevertheless, in 1059, escorted by Archbishop Cynsige and Earl Tosti, Máel Coluim journeyed to the court of Edward the Confessor, possibly to acknowledge the support that he had received over the last two decades through a confirmation of earlier agreements between his ancestors and Edward's predecessors.[181] But Máel Coluim was no complaisant client and, having secured his northern frontier through his growing rapport with his Norse kinsmen in Orkney, was soon looking south with aggressive intent. In 1061, capitalising on the absence of both Tosti, whose description on this occasion as *conjuratus frater* (sworn brother) of the Scottish king emphasises the treaty relationship that may have been established in 1059, and his new spiritual counterpart, Archbishop Aldred, on pilgrimage to Rome, Máel Coluim launched the first Scottish invasion of Northumbria since 1039.[182] This attack has all the hallmarks of a plundering raid to which there was evidently no follow-up, for Máel Coluim's relationship with Tosti appears to have been restored on the latter's return from Rome, but it had demonstrated the vulnerability of the North in the post-Siward years. Yet it may have achieved something more substantial for the Scots, for a body of circumstantial evidence from the mid 1060s and again in relation to his 1070 raid into England hints that its primary objective may have been Cumberland and that Máel Coluim had succeeded in regaining control there as a consequence of this invasion.[183]

What remained of the brief political stability that Siward had imposed through *force majeure* was shattered in 1063–64. In 1063, Tosti had two important northern thegns, Gamell, son of Orm, and Ulf, son of Dolfin, both of whom had kinship ties with both the House of Bamburgh and the family of Siward, murdered in his chamber at York. Gamell, son of Orm, was a nephew of Earl Siward through his mother Ætheldrytha, younger sister of Siward's second wife, and was himself therefore a grandson of Earl Ealdred, and Ulf may have been the son of the Dolfin killed in 1054.[184] Their murder should probably be seen in the context of Tosti's growing unpopularity in both York and Northumbria, possibly connected with growing support for Siward's younger son, Waltheof, who would have been at least in his teens by this date. Both men, however, may also have had Cumberland interests – if Kapelle's identification of Dolfin is correct – and their removal may have been a heavy-handed effort to silence criticism of Tosti's failure to defend his earldom. Kapelle, furthermore, has linked their deaths to the assassination at the king's Christmas court in 1064 of Cospatric, whom he identifies as the youngest son of Earl Uhtred.[185] If this identification is correct, the murder can again be linked both to a potential challenge to Tosti's position, this time from a representative, albeit an aged one, of the House of Bamburgh, and to another major casualty of the loss of Cumberland to the Scots. Such violent removal of potential rivals had been a characteristic of Northumbrian politics throughout the eleventh century, but by striking against both the House of Bamburgh and the House of Siward simultaneously, Tosti succeeded only in uniting local hostility to his rule and in 1065 he was swept from power in a rising which drew its support from both Northumbria beyond the Tees and York.[186]

Máel Coluim's control of Cumberland from 1061 represented a significant shift in the balance of power in the north, but it was nearly a decade until the consequences of that movement manifested themselves. After playing little more than a passive role in the tempestuous affairs of the north which followed the Norman invasion of England in 1066, in 1070 Máel Coluim chose to intervene in Northumbria, where his cousin, Cospatric, son of Maldred, had been established as earl by William the Conqueror.[187] In 1070, invading from Cumberland and initially bypassing his cousin's earldom, he led a campaign through the already harried north of Yorkshire before turning north and ravaging the coastal districts from Cleveland to Wearmouth. In retaliation, Cospatric raided into Cumberland and, from his fortress of Bamburgh, launched harrying attacks against the Scots in Northumbria.[188] Máel Coluim's purpose in 1070 has been the subject of debate, presented variously as a belated effort to aid the northern rebels of 1069, as a mere plundering raid in pursuit of booty and slaves, or as a calculated attempt to terrorise the province into submission.[189] Whichever the case, he had demonstrated with devastating results the extent of his control over Cumberland and the potential which that control gave him to raid or otherwise project his authority into the country east of the Pennines.

No positive gains seem to have fallen to Máel Coluim from the 1070 campaign, but, on the other hand, William of Normandy was in no position in 1070–71 to conduct any counter campaign[190] Indeed, had Máel Coluim not further provoked William through his marriage to Margaret, sister of Edgar Atheling, which finally aligned him firmly with the dispossessed Wessex dynasty, it is likely that William's troubles in Maine and Flanders would have been considered of more pressing urgency than Scottish actions in a zone that lay beyond the effective reach of Norman government. The consequence was a major campaign into Scotland in autumn 1072 that penetrated as far as Abernethy and, without any significant fighting, ended with Máel Coluim's submission to William, paying him homage and handing over hostages, who may have included his elder son of his first marriage, Donnchad.[191] As William returned south, he deprived Cospatric of his earldom,[192] installing in his place Waltheof, son of Siward, to whom he had shown much favour and who was married to his niece, Judith. Ejected once more from his heritage, Cospatric sought allies who could aid him in its recovery. The account of Cospatric's movements from late 1072 offered by the *Historia Regum* has clearly been compressed, but it can be deduced from it that, after attempting to win support from his cousin, Máel Coluim, he crossed to Flanders where a regime hostile to Normandy had been established in 1071 and where, until 1074, Count Robert le Frison was the host of the exiled Edgar Atheling.[193] Cospatric's hopes of restoration through Edgar Atheling were dashed in late 1074 when the pretender made his peace with William.[194] Only now did Cospatric return to Scotland, where Máel Coluim subsequently granted him lands in Lothian that came to form the earldom of Dunbar, held by his descendants into the fifteenth century.[195]

Cospatric's entry into Máel Coluim's service has been linked to a general tightening of Scottish control in Lothian and Cumbria and a strengthening of the new frontier with Norman power in the south.[196] While Cospatric may have regarded this as a temporary arrangement, with recovery of his lands south of the Tweed as his long-term objective, it proved a permanent settlement. The rebellion of Earl Waltheof against his Norman patron that began late in 1074 may have offered him some hope of restoration, but after the ruthless suppression in 1080 of this last major Northumbrian rising against Norman authority and the projection of royal power beyond the Tyne through the construction of Newcastle, that hope was dashed.[197]

While Cospatric and his family may have had no place in Norman plans for Northumbria, it is clear that Máel Coluim had his uses for them. Amongst these uses may have been the government of an extensive territory centred on Carlisle, controlled until 1092 by a certain Dolfin, usually identified as Cospatric's eldest son.[198] Dolfin's relationship with the king of Scots is less clear, Duncan suggesting that he may have retained control of this zone as a rump of the Northumbrian earldom created by Earl Ealdred and subsequently incorporated into Siward's domain. He proposed that it had remained with his family after their expulsion from the eastern portion of their earldom on account of its isolation from the nearest centres of Norman power.[199] This area of Cumberland, however, had clearly been under the control of Máel Coluim in 1070, probably having been detached from Northumbria in 1061, and there are no obvious points in the historical record at which its loss by the Scots is likely to have occurred.[200] Kapelle takes a similar line of a loss of effective control of the Carlisle area to a native potentate, but for him Dolfin is a descendant of the Dolfin, Thorfinn's son, who was killed in 1054.[201] Kapelle's argument, however, is primarily based on the fact that there is no record of military support from this region for Máel Coluim's invasions of Northumbria in 1079 and 1091, whereas he considered the king's actions in 1061 and 1070 to have depended heavily on warriors from this quarter.[202] The account of the 1070 invasion, however, emphasises that Máel Coluim and the Scots passed through Cumberland *en route* to Teesdale, not that he was based in and drew his power from that region.[203] Furthermore, Kapelle founds his argument on the identification of the main components of the invading army in 1070 as 'Galwegians', whereas the sources label them consistently as 'Scots', while an account of events at Hexham in what is probably the 1079 invasion identifies one of its chief components as a contingent from Galloway![204] It is also, as Summerson has highlighted, impossible to square the round of Máel Coluim's apparent eagerness to control this territory down to 1070, his keen awareness of its strategic value and its supposed centrality to his northern English designs with the lack of apparent awareness of, or concern displayed over, its loss until 1091.[205] Furthermore, the entrenched position in western Cumberland of another of Earl Cospatric's sons, Waltheof, who held the lordship of Allerdale early in the twelfth century, would seem to reinforce the hypothesis that the dispossessed House of Bamburgh played a central role in the Scottish network of power in Cumbria.[206]

How extensive Scottish control over Cumbria was, and what territories it embraced by this date, are unresolved questions. Both are problematic issues, for we are handicapped by the lack of contemporary documentary evidence and are reliant on twelfth-century and later material, such as the so-called *Inquest of David* and Fordun's comments concerning Donnchad mac Crinain's position as king of the Cumbrians,[207] from which to attempt an extrapolation back into the eleventh century. The standard view, based on such material, is that Cumbria embraced all the territories incorporated into the medieval dioceses of Glasgow and Carlisle, which, at its most extreme interpretation, has been considered to embrace the whole of what became Galloway.[208] Examination of the *Inquest*, however, indicates that the see of Glasgow was much more circumscribed than is commonly represented, with its sphere restricted largely to Clydesdale, Annandale and Tweeddale. There are no indications that the coastal zone from Renfrew, south through Cunningham, Kyle and Carrick to the Solway, fell under the jurisdiction of the bishops of the Cumbrians and their successors at Glasgow. Indeed, references from the reign of David I indicate that this coastal zone formed a wider 'Galloway' and that portions of it had only recently fallen under David's control, possibly during his period as 'prince of the Cumbrian region' before 1124.[209] This would correspond to the apparent territorial extent of Strathclyde as it emerged in the tenth century, as discussed above. It is unlikely that Mael Coluim's authority extended much beyond this core of territory. This begs the question, however, of the presence of Galwegians in the Scottish army in 1079. Elsewhere, I have suggested that these men may have been mercenaries,[210] but consider now that this notion must be rejected and that the record of Galwegians serving in eleventh-century Scottish armies must be questioned. Our evidence for Galwegians in Máel Coluim's army is derived from a single source, Ailred of Rievaulx's *Saints of Hexham*. While Ailred's family roots in Hexham may have given him access to local traditions of Galwegian involvement in earlier campaigns, his story appears to be grounded in the twelfth-century accounts of David I's campaigns in the region, in which Galwegians figured prominently, and is probably further coloured by his recognised antipathy towards that people.[211] Ailred was an active apologist for David, his efforts to absolve the king from any responsibility for atrocities committed by his armies in 1137–38 and to promote instead an image of a saintly ruler being most evident in *De Standardo* and the eulogies composed on David's death in 1153.[212] Part of Ailred's objective was to create the idea of a holy dynasty descended from Margaret, and the deflecting of blame from her husband, Máel Coluim, onto Galwegians in 1079 may be seen as integral to that aim.

In effect, the reference to Galwegians in his army is an anachronism projected back from the twelfth century.

Máel Coluim's incursions into Northumbria in 1091 demonstrated to William Rufus, the new English king, that the mechanisms set in place in 1080 for the security of the northern frontier were inadequate. In particular, Scottish control of Cumberland enabled raiders to penetrate Northumbria and Yorkshire, turning the flank of the royal fortress at Newcastle and the bishop's castle at Durham. The simplest solution to this problem, as recognised by Siward fifty years earlier, was for English control of Cumberland to be re-established. In 1092, therefore, William Rufus came north with his army, drove out Dolfin, and built a castle at Carlisle as the nucleus of a new network of border lordships on the western flank of his frontier with the Scots.[213] William clearly had no intention of pushing his territorial controls any deeper into Cumbria at this stage and was seeking rather to achieve the stability in the North that had eluded his father and his Anglo-Saxon predecessors. After an abortive attempt at negotiations with William, Máel Coluim resorted once more to raiding, possibly with a view to gaining control of Northumbria through his sons' descent from the West Saxon dynasty. The attempt ended in disaster, for in November 1093 Máel Coluim and Edward, his eldest son by Margaret, were killed in a skirmish with Robert de Mowbray, the Norman earl of Northumberland.[214]

ENGLAND, NORWAY AND THE IRISH SEA 1092–c.1100

The imperative behind the steady expansion through the eleventh century of English power into Cumbria, the Solway region and the Southern Uplands, was security on a flank from which the Wessex-based kings' hegemony of mainland Britain had faced repeated challenge through the tenth century. Norman responses to Máel Coluim's invasions from 1070 onwards demonstrate a clear awareness of the continued reality of that threat from the Scots. William I had, down to 1080, attempted to control Northumbria through successive members of the native lineages that had contended for power in the region since the later tenth century. It had been an expedient forced upon him by the limited reach of his authority in the first decade after the Conquest and was discarded as a solution to the government of the north once he had exhausted the supply of potential candidates for the role and had succeeded in breaking the power of the native nobility of the region. When William II Rufus turned to the problem of Cumberland, he did not face the same difficulties as had confronted his father in the country beyond the Tees, for the crown had established its presence beyond the Tyne in the east, consolidated its hold over Yorkshire and the episcopal lordship of Durham, and had placed the earldom of Northumberland, comprising Northumbria from Tyne to Tweed, in the hands of a Norman earl. This spread of Norman power into north-east England freed William II from dependence on the fickle loyalties of the native potentates. Rather than seek an accommodation with Dolfin, the most powerful regional lord, William was able to establish men of his choosing from the start as the lynchpins of his new frontier's defence.

Adopting a parallel approach to that adopted earlier in Wales,[215] William began to construct a new frontier lordship around which to consolidate his control of the newly acquired territory. It is impossible, however, to construct a firm chronology, or even a clear sequence for the processes through which the Norman power structure in Cumberland was built. Kapelle, for example, has argued that the process probably commenced before 1092 when the king may have granted Ivo Taillebois a block of estates along the southern fringe of Dolfin's lordship, that stretched from east to west through southern Cumberland and northern Westmorland from the Pennines to the sea.[216] Scott has argued that the new royal castle at Carlisle was entrusted to Ivo in or soon after 1092, following the policy adopted in Morgannwg/Glamorgan where the royal steward, Robert fitz Haimo, held the royal castle at Cardiff as the centrepiece of his new lordship, while Barlow considered that Carlisle was given to Ranulf Meschin soon after 1092 and that he had subsequently added Ivo Taillebois' properties to this holding through marriage to Ivo's widow.[217] Kapelle seems unaware of Ranulf's marriage to the widowed Lucy de Bolingbroke and attributes his establishment in Carlisle to Henry I's gratitude for his support in the campaign against his elder brother, Duke Robert of Normandy, and his role in the victory over Robert at Tinchebrai in 1106.[218] This is an unrealistically late date for the establishment of a central figure to whom the defence of the region could be entrusted and seems to depend more on Kapelle's determination to credit Henry I rather than William Rufus with the initiative for the settlement of Cumberland than on a straightforward reading of the evidence. On balance, Scott's and Barlow's analyses present more likely scenarios.

Native power was not wholly expunged from Cumberland in the aftermath of 1092. Waltheof of Allerdale, younger son of Earl Cospatric of Northumbria/Dunbar and, presumably, brother of Dolfin, occupied a key place in the political pattern of the region in the early twelfth century. Waltheof's survival as a regional power, whilst the man identified as his elder brother was expelled, has never been explained satisfactorily, and led Scott, following Kapelle, to question this relationship.[219] It has been proposed that Dolfin, and presumably Waltheof, owed their position in southern Cumbria to Donnchad mac Máel Coluim, who married their sister Octreda. Summerson suggested that, following his release as a hostage in 1087, Donnchad had returned to Scotland where, as heir presumptive to his father, he had assumed control of Cumbria.[220] Following Barlow, Summerson assumed that Donnchad had married Octreda around this time (c.1090) and that he had then established his brother-in-law in Carlisle shortly thereafter.[221] There is, however, no evidence for Donnchad's position – or even his presence – within Scotland after 1087, and, according to the *Anglo-Saxon Chronicle*, it appears that he had chosen to remain at the Norman court after his formal release.[222] In 1094, having sworn fealty to William II and with his military support, Donnchad returned to Scotland and wrested the throne from his uncle, Domnall mac Donnchada. King Domnall's brief first reign is characterised in contemporary sources by a reaction against the English influence that had dominated at his brother's court.[223] At the forefront of such influence stood the House of Bamburgh, which had been a major beneficiary of Máel Coluim's generosity. Mutual interest dictated an alignment between Donnchad and Cospatric's family, and it is more likely that the marriage to Octreda occurred then, in 1094, than earlier. Dolfin may have been dead by that time – he certainly does not feature in any surviving document post-1092 – which would account for the appearance of Waltheof alone in William's peace after 1094. His presence in Cumberland as a landowner should probably be linked to support for Donnchad's short-lived regime, which would have brought his family back into favour with William, and his expulsion from Scotland in the aftermath of Donnchad's temporary accommodation with the Gaelic nobility that had followed the slaughter of the Anglo-Norman force that had put him on the throne. The wheel had now turned full circle, and Waltheof and his family provided William and his successive protégés from among the sons of Máel Coluim and Margaret as kings of Scots with support against Domnall. In 1094, however, Waltheof was little more than a refugee and, until the successful campaign of 1097 that established Edgar mac Máel Coluim on the throne, he was obliged to seek William's favour.[224] It seems likely that it was at this time that Waltheof was granted the lordship of Allerdale for his personal support and as a reward for his service.

Following the successful establishment of Edgar on the Scottish throne, there appears to have been a phase of rapid development in the pattern of lordship within Cumberland and the north-west of England generally. The clearest indication of this is in the successive re-marriages after *c*.1098 of Ivo Taillebois' widow, Lucy de Bolingbroke, firstly to Roger de Roumare, an experienced military figure, then to Ranulf Meschin.[225] This may simply have been an expression of royal concern for the security of the recently established frontier with the Scots, but may be otherwise linked to the appearance of an aggressive new power within the Irish Sea zone that threatened to break the balance of power in the region established by the Norman kings.

According to the *Chronicle of Mann*, probably towards the end of 1097, King Magnus of Norway, grandson of Harald Hardrádi, began to re-assert Norwegian influence in the Western Isles and sent a certain Ingimundr to assume the kingship. After briefly establishing his power in the northern Hebrides, the Islesmen rose against Ingimundr and killed him.[226] In the following year, Magnus himself arrived in the Isles and, according to the Manx account, chose Mann as the seat of his power.[227] It appears that the king aimed to establish Norwegian lordship over the Isles and, possibly, over mainland territories such as Galloway which had received settlement from, and had close political and cultural links with, the main centres of Scandinavian colonisation. The account of his progress shows him moving southwards through the Hebrides, from Lewis, to Skye, Tiree, Mull and Iona, then on again to Islay and Kintyre before arriving in Mann, plundering and receiving submissions as he went.[228] During the southward voyage, he captured King Lagmann, and it was probably as a consequence of this that Lagmann departed from the Isles and joined the First Crusade. Magnus's activities did not stop here, however, for he proceeded to raid Anglesey and north Wales, which brought him for the first time into direct conflict with Norman power. According to saga tradition, in Anglesey he was confronted by a 'Welsh' army commanded by two earls, named as Hugh the Noble and Hugh the Fat.[229] These can be identified as Hugh de Montgomery, Earl of Shrewsbury, and Hugh d'Avranches, Earl of Chester, the chief figures in William Rufus's extension of Norman rule into central and northern Wales. In the resulting battle, Hugh de Montgomery was slain, his death in conflict with 'pirates from oversea' being corroborated by the *Anglo-Saxon Chronicle*.[230] The saga account claims that Magnus proceeded to add Anglesey to his domain, but it is more probable that he was stepping into Gofraid Crobán's shoes as protector of Gruffudd ap Cynan, King of Gwynedd, who had been at war with both earls and had been driven into exile in Dublin.[231] From Anglesey, Magnus headed north. He had already evidently received the submission of the Gall-Gaidhel – he had plundered in both Galloway and Ulster on his voyage south – and received a tribute of cut timber from them.[232] Magnus now, though, sought to consolidate his position and, according to his saga, settled a treaty with the Scottish king, whereby Norwegian possession of all the Hebrides was confirmed.[233] Although there is no supporting evidence from the Scottish side for such a treaty with King Edgar, twelfth- and thirteenth-century Scottish acknowledgement of Norwegian suzerainty in the Isles points to some kind of formal treaty. In one event-filled year, Magnus had effectively halted the expansion of Irish-based power into the Isles, curbed Norman aggression in north Wales and given notice to William and his Scottish protégé that a new Isles-based challenger had arrived in the west.

How much of a threat did Magnus Barelegs represent to Norman power in 1098? His brief appearance in mainland British affairs and the collapse of his schemes for control in Ireland on his death in 1103 have seen his significance played down in most modern analyses of his career. Yet, in the late eleventh century, he appears to have been regarded as a very real threat to Norman security. As the grandson of Harald Hardrádi, who had died in 1066 in his attempt to seize the English throne, and with King Sveyn Estrithson of Denmark's bid to regain his uncle Knútr's English dominion in 1069–70 as an example, Magnus must have appeared to William Rufus as a rival.[234] William of Malmesbury certainly believed that Magnus intended to make a bid for the English throne, and claimed that Harold, son of Harold Godwinsson, the last Anglo-Saxon king, accompanied Magnus on his campaign.[235] Contemporary observers were not to know that the successes of Knútr were never to be repeated. His domination of the Irish Sea gave him a powerful position on the western flank of England, where Norman power was less well developed than on the east. The submission of the Gall-Gaidhel in Galloway, his treaty with the Scottish king, and his re-establishment of Isles-based influence in Gwynedd, were very real threats that had to be confronted and contained. The rapid development of Ranulf Meschin's power in the north-west, stretching from Carlisle south into Lancashire, must surely have been a response to this additional challenge. Despite the concerns of the English in 1098–99, these arrangements were never tested against a Norwegian invasion.

As a threat, the expected challenge from Norway failed to materialise. Magnus spent the winter of 1098–99 in the Isles consolidating his gains of the previous summer. In summer 1099, he returned to Norway and did not re-enter his western domains until 1102. The timing of his campaign may have been intended to capitalise on the weakness of Henry I, but Magnus's primary objective on this occasion appears always to have been Ireland, particularly Dublin.[236] His arrival in Mann with a large fleet, noted by the *Annals of Ulster*, was followed by a possibly successful attempt to seize Dublin, accompanied by demands for the submission of the then dominant political force in Ireland, Muirchertach ua Briain, the same man as had been attempting to extend his influence through Dublin into Mann and the Isles.[237] Negotiations led to a truce, formalised through the marriage of Magnus's nine-year-old son, Siguror, with Muirchertach ua Briain's five-year-old daughter, Bláthmín.[238] While the saga account places this marriage in 1098–99, it has been demonstrated that it fits better into the context of 1102, when Magnus and Muirchertach became allies.[239] An alliance between these two men may appear unlikely in view of their competing ambitions in Dublin and the Isles, but the establishment of Siguror, Muirchertach's new son-in-law, as king over the territories that his father had won would have immeasurably strengthened Munster power in the region, which would in turn have removed the main potential challenger to Norwegian overlordship of the region. It also united Magnus and Muirchertach against the one man in a position to challenge their power in both Ireland and the Isles, Domnall mac Lochlainn, king of Ailech. Muirchertach and Domnall had been at war since 1094, and as recently as 1100 Domnall had raided the country around Dublin, which was then under Uí Briain control. Furthermore, his family exercised considerable influence within the Hebrides: the meic Lochlainn were a very real threat to Magnus's new-won lands. As Magnus intended to return to Norway, there is no question as to where the main benefit of the arrangement would fall.

In spring 1103, the scene seemed set for a confirmation of Munster dominance in Ireland and the extension of that dominance throughout the

Isles and, possibly, into areas of western mainland Scotland. As Magnus sailed north, however, he landed on the Ulster coast to indulge in some last-minute raiding. Although the king of Ulaid was allied with Muirchertach, he was not prepared to ignore the injury and attacked the king's party. In the skirmish, Magnus was cut down and killed.[240] His unexpected death led to the collapse of his grand design and to the evaporation of Muirchertach's dreams. Young Sigurðr did not share his father's enthusiasm for dominion in the west, but was eager to return to Norway to secure his share of the kingdom alongside his brothers. Repudiating Bláthmín, he sailed with what remained of the Norwegian fleet, never to return to his nominal kingdom in the Isles. Behind him he left a vacuum which neither Ua Briain nor Mac Lochlainn were in a position to fill. Although Muirchertach regained control of Dublin and, through it, some degree of domination of the western seas, there was no return to the pre-1098 position. Instead, in the decade after his death, as Magnus Barelegs' sea-kingdom disintegrated, ambitious warlords rose on the flotsam to compete and contend for power, building and losing petty empires. It was in this world that Fergus of Galloway carved a niche for himself.

Notes

1 *AU*, s.a. 901.
2 *AU*, s.a. 918.
3 Smyth, *York and Dublin*, i, 61–62, 78–79; F. T. Wainwright, 'Ingimund's Invasion', in *Scandinavian England*, ed. H. P. R. Finberg (Chichester, 1975), 131–61.
4 F. T. Wainwright, 'The Scandinavians in Lancashire', in *Scandinavian England*, ed. Finberg, 181–227.
5 Smyth, *York and Dublin*, ii, 243–45.
6 Raine, *Historians of York*, ii, 339.
7 F. T. Wainwright, 'The Submission to Edward the Elder', in Finberg (ed.), *Scandinavian England*, 325–44 at 330–31.
8 *AU*, s.a. 903; *CKS*, A, 9.
9 Duald Mac-Firbis, Fragment III, 246.
10 *AU*, s.a. 913 [=914?]
11 *ASC*, E, s.a. 952.
12 Roger Wendover, i, 402.
13 Higham, 'Scandinavians in North Cumbria', 42–48.
14 *ASC*, A, s.a. 945.
15 Higham, 'Scandinavians in North Cumbria', 42.
16 See, for example, Oram, 'Scandinavian settlement in south–west Scotland'.
17 Brooke, *Wild Men*, 67; Hill, 'Whithorn: the Missing Years', in Oram and Stell (eds), *Galloway*, 27–44 at 38.
18 Scott, 'Viking settlement in Galloway'. The warrior burial was in the older graveyard associated with the Anglian minster, not in the later medieval St Andrews kirkyard within the burgh, as is sometimes reported. A somewhat dismissive view of the evidence for Viking activity at Kirkcudbright – and in Galloway generally – has been taken by Professor Edward Cowan, 'Vikings in Galloway'.
19 Fellows-Jensen, *Scandinavian Settlement Names in the North–West*; Kapelle, *Norman Conquest of the North*, 43–44; Scott, 'Strathclyde, 1092–1153', 18–24.

20 Oram, 'Scandinavian settlement in south–west Scotland', 128–29.
21 Fellows-Jensen. *Scandinavian Settlement Names in the North-West* 85–86.
22 There is some evidence from the southern Machars for what may be the parcelling up of a former Anglian estate into smaller properties of Scandinavian holders. Oram, 'Scandinavian settlement in south-west Scotland', 131, 138–39
23 MacQueen, 'Gaelic speakers'.
24 Nicolaisen, *Place-Names*, 108–11.
25 Brooke, 'Kirk-compound place-names'; Brooke, *Wild Men*, 74–75.
26 Hill, *Whithorn*, 48–60, 209–50 passim.
27 *The Fragmentary Annals*, the one medieval text to offer an explanation for the term, simply describes them as Gaels who behaved like Norsemen.
28 MacQueen, 'Gaelic speakers', 26–28.
29 *Annals of Ireland. Three Fragments by Dubhaltach mac Firbisigh*, ed. J. O'Donovan (Dublin, 1860), 138–39.
30 See Chapter 2.
31 Brooke, 'Gall-Gaidhil and Galloway'.
32 Crawford, *Scandinavian Scotland*, 47–48.
33 F. J. Byrne, *Irish Kings and High Kings* (London, 1973), 264.
34 D. O'Corrain, *Ireland Before the Normans* (Dublin, 1972), 70.
35 Smyth, *Warlords and Holymen*, 157; MacQueen, 'Picts in Galloway', 143.
36 Smyth, *Scandinavian York and Dublin*, ii, 265.
37 Higham, 'The Scandinavians in North Cumbria', 37–51.
38 *AU*, s.a. 1200, 1234.
39 Ibid., s.a. 1034.
40 *Orkenyinga Saga* (Taylor), 174 and note.
41 E. Megaw, 'The Manx "Eary" and its significance' in *Man and the Environment in the Isle of Man*, ed. R. Davey (BAR British Series, 54, pt.ii), 327–45; I. D. Whyte, 'Shielings and the Upland Pastoral Economy of the Lake District in Medieval and Early Modern Times', in *The Scandinavians in Cumbria*, eds J. R. Baldwin and I. D.Whyte (Edinburgh, 1985), 103–18.
42 For a more detailed discussion of the Galloway *airigh* names and their development, see Oram, 'Scandinavian settlement in south-west Scotland', 133–35, and Chapter 7.
43 E.g. Smyth, *York and Dublin*, chapter vi.
44 *AU*, s.a. 941.
45 *AFM*, s.a. 939 = 940.
46 Crawford, *Scandinavian Scotland*, 61.
47 *Heimskringla*, Håkon the Good's Saga, c.5.
48 *ASC*, E, s.a. 97; *Florence of Worcester*, s.a. 973.
49 *AFM*. s.a. 972 = 974.
50 Anderson, *Early Sources*, i, 478–79 note 6.
51 *AU*, s.a. 979 = 980; *AT*, 342.
52 Crawford, *Scandinavian Scotland*, 178 and fig. 67.
53 There must be a questionmark over Brooke's identification of the obscure Colman-Elo, the dedicatory saint of these churches (Brooke, *Wild Men*, 75) as part of this group. He was active in Down and Connor in the late sixth century and died in 610 (*AU*, s.a. 610). There may be some confusion with the more famous third abbot of Lindisfarne, who withdrew from Northumbria after the Synod of Whitby, founded the monastery of Inishboffin and died *c*.672–75.
54 *AI*, s.a. 986; *AU*, s.a. 986.
55 *AU*, s.a. 987.
56 *AT*, 346.
57 Crawford, *Scandinavian Scotland*, 66; *Njal's Saga* 183–84, 196.

58 *Njal's Saga*, 182, 341.
59 *AU*, s.a. 1005.
60 Hudson, 'Knutr and Viking Dublin', 320–21; *Heimskringla*, Chapter 30.
61 *Orkneyinga Saga*, c.12.
62 Anderson, *Early Sources*, i, 506 note 2.
63 *Heimskringla*, Olaf Tryggvi's son's Saga, *c.47*; *Flateyiarbók*, i, 229; *Heimskringla*, St Olaf's Saga, *c.96*.
64 *ASC*, E, s.a. 1000.
65 Duffy, *Ireland in the Middle Ages*, 33–34; *AU*, s.a 1004 *recte* 1005.
66 Duffy, *Ireland in the Middle Ages*, 34. Duffy translates the title as 'emperor of the Irish', but the use of this style is more suggestive of a claim to superiority over all the Gaidhil, both in Ireland and in Scotland. The coincidence of the voicing of this claim with Máel Coluim mac Cinaeda's usurpation of the throne of Alba is strongly suggestive of a greater symbolism behind Brian's use of this title.
67 *AU*, s.a. 1005.
68 *ALC*, s.a. 1014.
69 *Njal's Saga*, 353.
70 M'Kerlie, *Lands*, i, 79, Huyshe, *Grey Galloway*, 104; *Wigtownshire Charters*, xi; Robertson, *Story of Galloway*, 38; A. B. Taylor, 'Karl Hundason, King of Scots', *PSAS*, lxxi (1937), 337, 340; Hill, 'Missing Years', 41.
71 Brooke, 'Gall-gaedhil and Galloway', 104.
72 Hill, *Whithorn*, 52–55.
73 Ibid., 55–56, 59–60.
74 Ibid., 55, fig. 2.18.
75 Ibid., 56.
76 Ibid., 56.
77 Craig, 'Pre-Norman sculpture'.
78 *AU*, s.a. 982.
79 *AI*, s.a. 993; *AU*, s.a. 993.
80 *AU*, s.a. 1035.
81 *AT*, s.a. 1038. The Annals of Ulster note the death in 998 of 'Aralt mac Amlaim', along with other Ostmen leaders, in a defeat of the men of Dublin and Leinster by Brian Boru; *AU*, s.a. 998.
82 *AT*, s.a. 1046; Duffy, 'Irishmen and Islesmen', 96.
83 *ASC*, E, s.a. 1031.
84 Duffy, 'Irishmen and Islesmen', 98.
85 *AU*, s.a. 1013, 1034; Duffy, 'Irishmen and Islesmen', 99.
86 *AT*, s.a. 1061.
87 *MGH, Scriptores*, v, 559.
88 Duffy, 'Irishmen and Islesmen', 99–100.
89 Duffy, 'Irishmen and Islesmen', 100.
90 *AU*, s.a. 1022, 1026.
91 *AU*, s.a. 1070.
92 *AU*, s.a. 1072, describes Diarmait as 'king of Leinster and the Foreigners'. *AT* adds the Isles to his territory, which Seán Duffy interprets as meaning at least the Isle of Mann: Duffy, 'Irishmen and Islesmen', 101.
93 *Chron. Mann*, s.a. 1047 = 1066. In the text, Sitriuc has been struck out and replaced with Fingal, the name of Gofraid's son and successor in the kingship.
94 Ibid., 4, s.a. 1051 = 1070.
95 Duffy, 'Irishmen and Islesmen', 105.
96 *AI*, s.a. 1072.
97 *AU*, s.a. 1073.
98 *Chron. Mann*, s.a. 1047 = 1066.

99 Duffy, 'Irishmen and Islesmen', 106.
100 *Life of Gruffudd ap Cynan*, 40, 72.
101 *Chron. Mann*, 6; *AU*, s.a. 1095.
102 *AT*, s.a. 980.
103 *Chron. Mann*, 5; *AT*, s.a. 1091.
104 Brooke, *Wild Men*, 74–76.
105 *AU*, s.a. 1087.
106 Ibid., 5–6.
107 Duffy, 'Irishmen and Islesmen', 104–05 and note 60.
108 *AFM*, s.a. 1095.
109 Duffy, 'Irishmen and Islesmen', 108.
110 *Chron. Mann*, 6.
111 For discussion of its chronology for the reigns of Gofraid and his sons, see Anderson, *Early Sources*, ii, 98 note 1.
112 *Chron. Mann*, s.a. 1075 = 1096–1098.
113 *AFM*, s.a. 1096.
114 *Chron. Mann*, s.a. 1077 = ?1097.
115 Ibid., s.a. 1098.
116 *HDE*.
117 Hill, *Whithorn*, 22.
118 Ibid.., 22, 47, 54.
119 Ibid.., 54.
120 Ibid.
121 Brooke, *Wild Men and Holy Places*, 70–71; Smyth, *Warlords and Holy Men*, chapter 7; MacQuarrie, 'Kings of Strathclyde', 19; Jackson, 'Britons in Southern Scotland', 86.
123 Higham, 'Scandinavians in North Cumbria', 40–41.
124 Brooke, 'Northumbrian settlements in Galloway and Carrick', 314.
125 Hill, *Whithorn*, 54; Craig, 'Pre-Norman sculpture in Galloway'.
126 Govan has been posited as an alternative centre of Strathclyde kingship, but, it was clearly peripheral to the kingdom which emerged in the tenth century, lying close to the area of Norse–Gaelic settlement in Cunningham and Renfrewshire.
127 Alcock and Alcock, 'Excavations at Alt Clut', 99, 117.
128 Higham, 'Scandinavians in North Cumbria', 40.
129 Ibid., fig. 3.2.
130 *Glasgow Registrum*, i, no. 1.
131 Church dedications to Kentigern within the old county of Cumberland point to the probable inclusion of that region within the political–ecclesiastical sphere of Strathclyde. See, Higham, 'Scandinavians in North Cumbria', 40 and fig. 3.2.
132 See pp. 168–9.
133 *Glasgow Registrum*, no. 9; Kelso Liber, p.iv, no. 2.
134 *Kelso Liber*, p. iv.
135 Fellows-Jensen, 'Scandinavians in southern Scotland?'
136 Crawford, *Scandinavian Scotland*, 98.
137 *ESC*, no. LIV.
138 *ASC*, s.a. 926 = 927; Smyth, *Warlords and Holy Men*, 201.
139 The ruler of Strathclyde at this time has been identified with the otherwise unknown Domnall mac Aeda, brother of Causantin, king of Alba, who has been presented as being placed in power in succession to the native king, Dyfnwal *c*.908–916 [MacQuarrie, 'Kings of Strathclyde', 14.]. This idea is now discredited (see below note 140). The twelfth-century chronicler, William of Malmesbury gives the name of the king of the Cumbrians in 926–27 as

'Eogan' (for the British Ywain), and records how he joined with Causantin in giving refuge to Gothfrith following his expulsion from York [William of Malmesbury, *Gesta regum Anglorum*, i, 147.]. Ywain was evidently king of the Cumbrians by 934 when he and Causantin were defeated by Athelstan [*HDE*, i, 76.].

140 B. Hudson, '*Elech* and the Scots in Strathclyde', *Scottish Gaelic Studies*, 15 (1988), 145–49. I am indebted to Alex Woolf for drawing this article to my attention.

141 *HDE*, i, 76; Smyth, *Warlords and Holy Men*, 202–03.

142 *HDE*, i, 76; *ASC*, A, s.a. 937; Smyth, *York and Dublin*, ii, chapters iii and iv.

143 *ASC*, D, s.a. 940 = 939, 941 = 940.

144 *ASC*, D and E, s.a. 954.

145 *ASC*, A, B, C, D, s.a. 945; Smyth, *Warlords and Holy Men*, 222–23.

146 Higham, 'Scandinavians in North Cumbria', 41–43.

147 Crawford, *Scandinavian Scotland*, 61–62.

148 MacQuarrie, 'Kings of Strachclyde', 16; *AU*, s.a. 970=971; *CKS*, D, s.a. 966–71.

149 Smyth, *Warlords and Holy Men*, 223–24.

150 *CKS*, s.a. 971–95.

151 *ASC*, E, s.a. 972; *Annales Cambriae*, s.a. 973; *Chron. Melrose*, s.a. 973.

152 See, for example, *Florence of Worcester*, i, 142–43; *Chron. Henry of Huntingdon* 166; William of Malmesbury, *Gesta regum Anglorum*, i, 165; Symeon of Durham, *De Primo Saxonum Adventu*, 382.

153 Symeon of Durham, *De Primo Saxonum Adventu*, 382.

154 *ASC*, s.a. 1000.

155 *AU*, s.a. 1005 = 1006.

156 Symeon of Durham, *De Obsessione Dunelmie*, 215–16.

157 *ASC*, E, s.a. 1006.

158 Kapelle, *Norman Conquest*, 16.

159 Symeon of Durham, *De Obessione Dunelmi*, 216–17.

160 *ASC*, D and E, s.a. 1016.

161 Symeon of Durham, *De Obessione Dunelmi*, 218; idem, *HDE*, i, 84; idem, *HR*, ii, 155–56.

162 *HR*, ii, 155–56; *Annales Cambriae*, 22.

163 See the discussion of his motives and the timing of his campaigns offered by Benjamin Hudson in 'Knútr and Viking Dublin', *Scandinavian Studies*, 66 (1994), 319–35, and Barbara Crawford, 'The dedication to St Clement at Rodil, Harris', in B. E. Crawford (ed.), *Church, Chronicle and Learning in Medieval and Early Renaissance Scotland* (Edinburgh, 1999), 109–22.

164 Crawford, 'St Clement', 112; Hudson, 'Knútr'; *ASC*, s.a. 1031.

165 Theodoric, *Historia de Antiquitate Regum Norwagiensium*, s.a. 1028–30.

166 *HSC*, 213.

167 *HDE*, i, 90–91.

168 Duncan, *Making of the Kingdom*, 98.

169 *HR*, ii, 198.

170 *MGH*, *Scriptores*, xix, 508; Kapelle, *Norman Conquest*, 42–43.

171 F. E. Harmer, *Anglo-Saxon Writs* (London, 1952), 419–24, 531–36.

172 Kapelle, Norman Conquest, 43–44; Duncan, *Making of the Kingdom*, 98

173 *Chron. Fordun*, i, 175, 176.

174 *Historians of York*, 32.

175 N. Shead, 'The Origins of the Medieval Diocese of Glasgow', *SHR*, xlviii (1969), 220–25 at 220–21.

176 *ASC*, C, D, s.a. 1054; *AU*, s.a 1054; *Chron. Marianus Scottus*, s.a. 1057.

177 Kapelle, *Norman Conquest*, 47. He further proposes (p. 95) that he was the

son of the Thorfinn mac Thore who was the beneficiary of 'Cospatric's Writ'.

178 *ASC*, D, s.a. 1055.

179 Barlow, *Edward the Confessor*, 193.

180 Hudson, 'Knútr', 327–35.

181 *AD*, s.a. 1059; Duncan, *Making of the Kingdom*, 117–18.

182 *HR*, ii, 174–55.

183 Kapelle, *Norman Conquest*, 92–4.

184 Florence of Worcester, i, 222.

185 Kapelle, *Norman Conquest*, 95. Cf. Barlow, *Edward the Confessor*, 235 and n.3.

186 *ASC*, s.a. 1065.

187 For a discussion of the events of the period 1066 to 1070 see D. C. Douglas, *William the Conqueror* (London, 1964), 213–15, 218–22, 225–26; Kapelle, *Norman Conquest*, 106–24.

188 *HR*, ii, 190–2.

189 R. L. G. Ritchie, *The Normans in Scotland* (London, 1954), 26–27; J. le Patourel 'The Normans in Yorkshire', *Northern History*, 6 (1971), 3; Duncan, *Making of the Kingdom*, 118–19.

190 Douglas, *William the Conqueror*, 224–26.

191 *ASC*, D, E, s.a. 1072, *AU*, s.a. 1072.

192 *HR*, ii, 196.

193 Ibid., 199; *ASC*, D, s.a 1075 = 1074; Douglas, *William the Conqueror*, 229.

194 *ASC*, D, s.a 1075 = 1074.

195 *HR*, ii, 199.

196 H. Summerson, *Medieval Carlisle: The City and the Borders from the late Eleventh to the Mid-Sixteenth Century* (Kendal, 1993), i, 48.

197 For a detailed discussion of the events of 1074–80, see Kapelle, *Norman Conquest*, 133–42.

198 For this identification, see for example, *SAEC*, 108, n. 4; Duncan, *Making of the Kingdom*, 120. A similar line is followed by D. P. Kirby, 'Strathclyde and Cumbria: A Survey of the Historical Development to 1092', *TCWAAS*, 72 (1962), 77–94

199 Duncan, *Making of the Kingdom*, 121.

200 The Scottish invasion of Northumbria in 1079 and William Rufus' settlement with Máel Coluim in 1080 had their theatres of operation in the eastern coastal plain.

201 Kapelle, *Norman Conquest*, 151.

202 Ibid., 92–94, 123–24.

203 *HR*, ii, 190–92.

204 Ailred, *Saints of Hexham*, 177–80.

205 Summerson, *Medieval Carlisle*, 47–48.

206 Barrow, 'Lordship and Feudal Settlement in Cumbria', 121; Kirby, 'Strathclyde and Cumbria', 93–94; Kapelle, *Norman Conquest*, 202.

207 *Glasgow Registrum*, no. 1; *Chron. Fordun*, 175, 176.

208 Skene, *Celtic Scotland*, ii, 375.

209 For a discussion of the extent of the term Galloway, see Introduction above. See also Kelso Liber, p. 5, and no. 1; *Glasgow Registrum*, no. 9; *ESC*, 84, 85; *Melrose Liber*, nos 69, 195.

210 Oram, 'Fergus, Galloway and the Scots', 123–24.

211 For discussion of Ailred's, and the general northern English Cistercian and Augustinian hostility towards Fergus and Galloway, see below p. 67.

212 E.g. Ailred, *Epistola*, col. 347–50.

213 *ASC*, E, s.a. 1092.

214 Ibid., s.a. 1093.

215 See, for example, Scott, 'Strathclyde 1092–1153', 13–15.

216 Kapelle, *Norman Conquest*, 147–48.
217 Barlow, *William Rufus*, 298, 321; Scott, 'Strathclyde, 1092–1153', 15, 17.
218 Kapelle, *Norman Conquest*, 200.
219 Scott, 'Strathclyde, 1092–1153', 18.
220 Summerson, *Medieval Carlisle*, 48–49. For Donnchad's release, see Florence of Worcester, ii, 21.
221 Barlow, *William Rufus*, 295.
222 *ASC*, E, s.a. 1093.
223 Ibid.
224 Ibid., s.a 1097.
225 Scott, 'Strathclyde 1092–1153', 19.
226 *Chron. Mann*, s.a. 1077 = ?1097.
227 Ibid., s.a. 1098.
228 *Heimskringla,* Magnus Barelegs' Saga, Chapters 8, 9.
229 Ibid., chapter 10.
230 *ASC*, E, s.a 1097 = 1098.
221 Duffy, 'Irishmen and Islesmen', 110 and n. 82; Barlow, *William Rufus*, 389–90.
232 *Chron. Mann*, s.a. 1098; *Heimskringla*, Magnus Barelegs' Saga, chapter 9.
233 Ibid., chapter 10.
234 Douglas, *William the Conqueror*, 164–66, 213–22.
235 William of Malmesbury, *Gesta Regum*, ii, 376.
236 Duffy, 'Irishmen and Islesmen', 111.
237 *AU*, s.a. 1102; *Chron. Mann*, s.a. 1098 = ?1102; Duffy, 'Irishmen and Islesmen', 111.
238 *Heimskringla*, Magnus Barelegs' Saga, Chapter 11.
239 R. Powers, 'Magnus Barelegs' expeditions to the west', *SHR*, 65 (1986), 107–32; Duffy, 'Irishmen and Islesmen', 112.
240 *Heimskringla*, Magnus Barelegs' Saga, Chapters 23–26; *Chron. Mann*, s.a. 1098 = 1103.

2

FERGUS

Although, as explored in Chapter 1, it is possible to identify independent political units in south-west Scotland in the eleventh century, there is no evidence for a single authority throughout the region before the emergence of Fergus 'of Galloway' in the second quarter of the twelfth century. His ancestry and the source of his power have, since the nineteenth century, been the subjects of endless conjecture. The obscurity of Fergus's origins, which does not stem solely from the lack of any substantial body of *acta* issued by or concerning him but is compounded by his descendants' regular rehearsal of their ancestry back to him and no further, has been clouded further by the inventions of a succession of antiquarian writers in the nineteenth century. Once the layers of conjecture and fabrication have been stripped away, we are left with remarkably few pieces of historical fact from which it is impossible to construct a coherent narrative. In the following chapter, therefore, an attempt shall be made to set Fergus into his political – and geographical – context through a broad exploration of the key episodes in the history of the region which now embraces south-west Scotland, north-west England and the maritime zone of the Irish Sea and Atlantic seaboard of Scotland. This is not intended, nor is it claimed to be, an analysis of his career, but will seek rather to determine, wherever possible, his place in the remarkable era of state building in the first half of the twelfth century.

THE ANCESTRY OF FERGUS: MYTH, FICTION AND LIMITED REALITY

In view of the purported evidence for military service being performed by Galwegians in the armies of Máel Coluim mac Donnchada in the later eleventh century,[1] the subjection of the Solway region to Scottish overlordship at this time has naturally been assumed. Such overlordship was believed to stem from Scottish acquisition of the lands and rights of the former kings of Strathclyde after 1018, reinforced by subsequent recognition of Máel Coluim's control of this territory by the Norman kings of England after 1066. As a result, Fergus has been viewed either as an upstart who carved a position for himself in a region where Scottish royal authority was weak and remote, or as a protégé of the kings of Scots, established as a dependable vassal in a territory that was subject to infiltration by Norman adventurers in the 1090s and earlier 1100s.[2] Early interpretations of his role portrayed him as a replacement for native leaders killed in 1138 at the battle of the Standard.[3] This theory was taken up enthusiastically by the virulently xenophobic P. H. M'Kerlie, whose personal neuroses reached new heights in his account of Fergus's assumed role in the subjection of Galloway to hostile, Scottish overlordship. To M'Kerlie, Fergus was a foreign governor, a non-Galwegian foisted by an unprincipled king upon a people left leaderless by the slaughter of its true rulers at Northallerton.[4] Fergus's lack of any patronymic was seized upon as further evidence that he was a mere adventurer who had ridden to power on David I's shirt-tails. While much of M'Kerlie's denouncement of Fergus's origins and ancestry can be rejected with little consideration, the absence of a patronymic does present some more serious problems and may indeed be suggestive of an underlying truth in the belief that he was a mere parvenu, the first of his line.

More elaborate traditions developed from these basic observations. Fergus came to be depicted as a boyhood friend of the future David I, sharing with him an upbringing at the court of Henry I of England. According to Wentworth Huyshe, Fergus was a 'boon companion' of the boy David and 'favoured guest' at the Norman court. It was there that Huyshe believed Fergus met and fell in love with his future bride, Henry's illegitimate daughter Elizabeth.[5] As a close friend and confidant of David, and son-in-law of the English king, Fergus was destined for greatness. Huyshe concluded that through his close friendship with David, Fergus was granted the lordship of Galloway when his boyhood friend became king of Scots. This supposed upbringing at the Anglo-Norman court and childhood spent with David, however, is mere romantic fiction and is simply a gentler echo of M'Kerlie's belief in Fergus's non-Galwegian origins.

This trend of presentation culminated in the work of J. F. Robertson, whose popular history of the region took up and amplified all of these earlier offerings. He narrates in striking clarity Fergus's training at the English court as a chosen companion of 'Prince David', his chance meeting with King Henry's illegitimate daughter and their subsequent marriage.[6] Robertson's version of events is more detailed than those of his predecessors but this owes more to a fertile imagination than greater scholarship. Most of his work is pure fiction.

Regardless of the standard of scholarship represented by some of these interpretations, they offer one consistent view of the origins and role of Fergus. Their dominant theme is that Fergus was not of native stock or, if he was, had been brought up as a Norman knight in the English court, that he owed his position in Galloway to the favour of his patron, the king of Scots, and that he was David I's appointed governor rather than the natural heir to the lordship. While Fergus can be shown to have had close family ties with the English ruling house, there is nothing to support the theory of his education at their court. This was simply conjecture on Mackenzie's part and is an attempt to explain how Fergus could possibly have met and married the daughter of the English king. Neither he, nor the writers who followed his thesis, gave any thought to the political implications of the marriage, or even considered that it might have been an act of diplomacy. All were caught up with a romantic notion of a love match of childhood sweethearts.

In opposition to the portrayal of Fergus as an alien interloper, there developed a thesis that presented him as the successor to a line of Gall-Gaidhel chieftains, possibly originating in Argyll or the Isles, but with strong links to Galloway. Based primarily upon his descendants' later involvement in Hebridean and Manx politics, and on the supposition that the lords of Galloway bore the surname MacDouall, a variant of the MacDougall patronymic of the principal lineage descended from Somairle mac Gillebrigte, this view presented Fergus as a man of Norse–Celtic stock with strong Argyll and southern Hebridean associations. A whole series of strands are interwoven in this thesis, in some instances forming a circular argument unsupported by outside evidence. The greatest flaw in the construct is the proposition that the names MacDouall and MacDougall represent lines of the same family and were borne by Fergus.[7] On grounds of chronology alone, this is a ludicrous hypothesis, as the founder of the MacDougall lineage was three generations younger than Fergus. Identical problems attend efforts to establish a direct link between the ruling houses of Galloway and Argyll.[8]

Despite the chronological flaws, some more recent scholars have perpetuated the myth of common ancestry and devised increasingly elaborate lines of descent. Radford described Fergus as springing from the 'Norwegian Irish ruling classes' and traced his pedigree back through the Argyll dynasty to the Norse jarls of Orkney.[9] To support his argument, he introduced the supposed evidence of the early thirteenth-century *Roman de Fergus*, identified Fergus of Galloway as the historical original on whom the fictional hero of poem was based, and attempted to link the historical lord of Galloway through the father of the fictional character, one Soumilloit or Somerled, to a suggested ancestor of the Argyll dynasty. Indeed, Radford went so far as to state that 'there is no reason to suspect the writer (of the *Roman de Fergus*) of inventing this parentage for his hero and the name may be accepted'.[10] Radford's argument rested on the identification of the father of the historical Fergus with an equally historical Somairle. His analysis was based on Munch's notes concerning the origins of the twelfth-century lord of Argyll, which suggested descent from a late eleventh-century figure, Somerled, King of the Isles, who died around 1083[11] and whom Radford saw as a possible common ancestor. This man, it has been suggested, was a descendant of Earl 'Gilli' of the Hebrides, son-in-law of Sigurd the Stout, earl of Orkney. From him, Radford suggested, was descended both Fergus of Galloway and Somairle mac Gillebrigte of Argyll.

Such a descent, however, is unknown in any of the genealogies of Somairle, whose lineage is usually traced back to a branch of the Irish kings of Airgialla.[12] At no point in these genealogies does an earlier Somairle appear, which renders Radford's hypothesis redundant.

Over and above the genealogical problems, the value of the *Roman de Fergus* as a trustworthy source for the politics and political geography of early twelfth-century Galloway is a matter for debate. Much weight in the historical arguments was placed on its supposed close connection with the lords of Galloway and its suggested composition at the courts of either Alan, lord of Galloway, or his daughter, Dervorgilla, but the negative and unflattering treatment of both its hero and his father renders this unlikely.[13] In spite of doubts thrown on the validity of attempts at identification of its fictional characters with the historical originals, Dominica Legge persisted in efforts to trace Fergus's parentage.[14] This saw an abandonment of the Radford hypothesis and the advancement of a new prototype for Fergus's father in Sumarlidi Hauldr, *Orkneyinga Saga*'s semi-fictional mid-twelfth-century victim of Svein Asleifarson.[15] He appears, however, to be little more than a thirteenth-century construct, a conflation of several figures including the historical Somairle mac Gillebrigte. Despite these problems, the lingering possibility of composition of the poem for, or by a member of, the household of Alan of Galloway, made a significant impact on the historical debate. The influence of this hypothesis, indeed, can be seen in Duncan's labelling of Fergus as a man 'whose antecedents were probably Norse–Celtic and may have been West Highland.'[16] It is an identification that persists despite the discrediting of that theory.

There is no final agreement on its authorship or the circumstances of the poem's composition, but Roy Owen has produced a compelling argument for its assignation to William Malveisin, Bishop of St Andrews, writing for the court of William the Lion.[17] In his interpretation, the *Roman* is a skilfully crafted poetic exercise, full of literary devices that poke fun at the traditional Arthurian genre and at key figures in the royal court of the early 1200s. A good topographical knowledge of Scotland adds incidental colour and a strong sense of place to the tale, but its realism does not extend into a literary re-working of early twelfth-century political and familial relationships. The weight of the evidence suggests that no store should be placed in the *Roman de Fergus* as a record of the origins of Fergus of Galloway. In no particular can it be shown to relate to his descendants and, beyond the coincidence of names, there are no grounds for accepting it as a source of evidence for his parentage.

THE RISE OF FERGUS

As with the question of his ancestry, obscurity shrouds the processes whereby Fergus assembled the territory to which later generations gave the name, the lordship of Galloway. When he first appears in the surviving sources in 1136, he is already uniquely associated with the region, which suggests that his state-building efforts were already well underway by that date. His supposed involvement with the re-foundation of the see of Whithorn, furthermore, indicates control over both eastern and western portions of what we would recognise as comprising Galloway by the later 1120s (see below). This indicates that the origin of the kingdom or lordship of Galloway probably lies in the turbulent period between the death of Máel Coluim mac Donnchada in 1093 and the consolidation of his son David's power in Southern Uplands Scotland, as protégé of Henry I of England, between c.1108 and c.1112.[18] This would accord well with the re-emergence of the term Gall-Gaidhel and the use of the name as a territorial designation in the second quarter of the twelfth century. Traditional historiography has tended to imply that the Tweed–Solway line had become fixed as a frontier by that time, secured by William II Rufus' plantation of English colonists in the Vale of Eden and fortification of Carlisle on the west and the installation of Ranulf Flambard as bishop of Durham on the east in 1099. That, however, is to project the political geography of the mid-thirteenth century back to the 1090s and lend a spurious solidity to what was still a very nebulous boundary.

As discussed in Chapter 1, Scottish control over the southern portion of Strathclyde probably lacked any substance in the later eleventh century, with the region's main affiliation from the time of Earl Siward lying with York. Máel Coluim mac Donnchada's power, based on recognition by William II of his rights over a region where the Normans themselves lacked anything more than a nominal authority, was probably never more than a distant overlordship recognised by the native nobility and with real power delegated to his kinsman, Dolfin. It has been suggested recently that Norman influence over the wider Solway region had expanded significantly in the aftermath of William II's expulsion of Dolfin and annexation of Carlisle, particularly after 1097 when Edgar mac Máel Coluim had been established on the Scottish throne with Norman aid.[19] As discussed above, the construction of a Norman lordship out of Dolfin's domain around Carlisle may have been the work of Ivo Taillebois, but its consolidation was undertaken by Ranulf Meschin.[20] The extent of Ranulf's holding is unknown, but Jack Scott advanced a strong case for the inclusion within it of lower Annandale, where place-name evidence could be interpreted as recording the settlement of the region by colonists from Lincolnshire.[21] Scott, however, took his argument further, and suggested that beyond Ranulf's lordship, Dunegal, lord of Strathnith, had entered a client relationship with Henry I – he made the comparison with English policy towards the native rulers in Wales – and that Dunegal had possibly acquired Henry's permission to expand to the west of the Nith into Galloway.[22] Scott's argument is based on the later twelfth-century dispute between the bishops of Whithorn and Glasgow over the limits of their jurisdiction, which he saw as stemming from the inclusion within Strathnith, which fell under the spiritual jurisdiction of Glasgow, of portions of Galloway that had formerly pertained to Whithorn. The origins of the dispute, however, seem on the contrary to lie in the expansion of Galloway by Fergus, who extended his territories at the expense of Dunegal's successors and attempted to include them under the jurisdiction of 'his' bishop of Whithorn.[23] Rather than being expansionist powers, Dunegal and his sons appear to have found themselves caught between the developing military might firstly of Ranulf Meschin, then subsequently of David mac Máel Coluim, and the territorially acquisitive Fergus of Galloway.

For Scott, the *quid pro quo* for Fergus's supposed acquiescence to the loss of territory to Dunegal was access to 'Anglo-Norman' aid in his expansion to the west of the Cree. His hypothesis did not stop there, however, for he further proposed that Fergus had been dependent on his father-in-law and overlord, Henry I, for military support in his recovery of the lordship of Kirkcudbright itself.[24] By this reasoning, rather than being a means of binding a powerful regional lord to the Norman court, Fergus's marriage to Henry's daughter becomes the act that created both Fergus and his lordship. Scott was here on decidedly shaky ground, for he based his argument on the proliferation of mottes in the lower Dee valley, which he saw as the product of Fergus's grants of land to the foreign knights who had aided him in his initial conquest. Indeed, he went further and proposed that some had been constructed by adventurers from Cumberland and Annandale *before* Fergus was established in Galloway.[25] This conjecture is based exclusively on comparison of site topography between mottes such as Boreland in Anwoth and the early fortification at Annan, and cannot be confirmed without excavation. The latter, which has been heavily eroded by river action, is identified as the original caput of the de Brus lordship of Annandale, and, unless Robert de Brus took over an already existing centre, cannot be dated earlier than the mid-1110s. Without excavation, the development of some of these sites in the 1090s cannot be entirely ruled out. Such early construction, however, cannot be supported by the surviving documentation, which indicates a probable post-1160 date for the creation of the lordships, such as Anwoth, at whose core such mottes lay.[26] In the absence of any contrary evidence, it can only be argued that while Fergus clearly benefited from his relationship with Henry I, it was not through the efforts of Henry's knights that he built his lordship.

Later twelfth- and thirteenth-century sources point to an original core of power in the lower Dee valley, centred on Kirkcudbright.[27] There, the fortified island in Loch Fergus[28] and the former Anglian minster, provided the political and ecclesiastical focus of a lordship which probably had its eastern limit on the Urr. As its name implies, the River Cree (Gaelic *crích*, a boundary), presumably separated Fergus's territories from the Manx-dominated region to the west. Certainly, the river remained the main line of internal political division within Galloway into the fourteenth century, forming the mutual border of the thirteenth-century sheriffdoms of Dumfries and Wigtown. Eastward expansion may have been limited first by the spread of English influence into the lower portion of the valley systems feeding into the head of the Solway, then its replacement by the power of David mac Máel Coluim. To the west, the almost endemic internal strife in the kingdom of Mann provided a situation ripe for exploitation by an ambitious ruler intent on expanding both the geographical extent and the degree of his power. The processes by which Fergus took control of the Rhinns and Machars are lost to us, but some indication of the means through which he consolidated that grip can be recovered. In the conflict between his sons that erupted in the 1150s, and in the partition of his lordship that followed his overthrow in 1160, Gillebrigte may have drawn his main support from west of the Cree. Why this was the case has never been addressed, but it is an issue that goes straight to the heart of the question of how Fergus assembled his domain.

As Fergus's elder son, Gillebrigte should have succeeded to the patrimonial territory in the east but was passed over in favour of his half-brother, Uhtred. His failure to succeed Fergus has been attributed to bastardy, but, other than admitting the possibility of inheritance under more generous Gaelic tradition that admitted the rights of canonically illegitimate progeny,[29] this fails to explain why Gillebrigte was able to secure a substantial landed inheritance in the west. The fact that a straightforward partition was adopted as the solution to any dispute suggests that Gillebrigte had a case to be answered and was no mere by-blow to be fobbed off with a token gesture. The likelihood is that while his claim to Kirkcudbright could be challenged, his right to western Galloway was more securely founded. Such was the level of support that Gillebrigte enjoyed in this territory in the 1170s and 1180s that it seems most likely to have been based on inheritance and kin connections. The link, however, cannot have been Fergus the interloper, but must descend from his mother. Her identity is unknown, but it is certain that she was not also the mother of Uhtred.[30] It has been implied in the past that she was simply a mistress of Fergus, or a wife under the uncanonical forms of marriage so lambasted later in the twelfth century by Walter Daniel, on the grounds that had Gillebrigte been 'legitimate' in canon law terms he would have succeeded to his father's undivided lordship. That is to assume that 'feudal' law operated in respect of the succession to Fergus. Most medieval authorities imply that Uhtred was the elder brother, reflected in their naming of him first in any joint reference, a line followed by most modern historians.[31] Certainly Uhtred's association with his father as a charter witness, and Gillebrigte's non-appearance in that role, would support suggestions that Uhtred was recognised by Fergus as his preferred heir from the 1130s. In one source, the well-informed chronicle of William of Newburgh, Gillebrigte is described as *natu major*,[32] meaning first born, but lacking the 'feudal' legal connotations of *primogenitus*. In none is he stigmatised as illegitimate. The implication which can be taken from all this is that his mother represented an old ruling line of western Galloway and, whilst she may not have been married to Fergus in line with the standards required by the church, such was her status that her son could not simply be excluded from her heritage.

A political takeover secured by 'marriage' to an heiress was further consolidated through establishment of control over the spiritual heart of the region, Whithorn. There, Fergus succeeded in imposing a cleric from eastern Galloway, perhaps previously the head of the community attached to the old Anglian minster at Kirkcudbright.[33] As one of the major landowners west of the Cree, control of Whithorn would have considerably reinforced Fergus's authority. Fergus, however, had greater plans for the monastery and, in a move that was probably intended to signify the new political unity of Galloway under his rule, he secured York's backing in the revival of Whithorn as an episcopal see with an authority which encompassed the whole of his domain. Both secular and spiritual institutions in the west, therefore, had been harnessed to Fergus's state-building efforts.

The spread of Fergus's power into the country west of the Cree must have been facilitated by the generally disturbed state of the Irish Sea–Hebridean zone in the decade after the death of Magnus Barelegs in 1103. In the scramble for power in Norway that followed, none of his sons could afford to divert their attention to the west and it was not until Håkon IV's expedition in 1263 that a Norwegian king made his presence felt in the Isles. Rival powers sought to fill the vacuum created by the sudden removal of the dominating figure of Magnus, plunging the region into a renewal of the confusion that had reigned after the death of Godred Crobán in 1094. In Mann, Godred's son, Lagmann, seized the throne and ruled until *c*.1110 when he resigned the kingship and departed – to his death – on crusade.[34] His seizure of power did not pass unchallenged, for his brother, Harald, mounted a prolonged rival bid for the throne which resulted eventually in his capture, blinding and castration. Godred's youngest son, Óláfr, who was still a child, was regarded as a further focus of opposition to Lagmann but was removed to safety at the court of Henry I of England.[35]

Lagmann's departure may have been connected with the revival of Uí Briain interest in Mann and the Isles rather than the remorse for the mutilation of Harald to which it is attributed by the *Chronicle of Mann*. This influence had presumably grown considerably since Muirchertach ua Briain, king of Munster, had re-asserted his control over Dublin in 1107 and imprisoned his nephew, Domnall mac Taidc ua Briain,[36] brother of the man who had made a bid for control of Mann after Godred's death. Domnall, as ruler of Dublin, may already have been manoeuvering to re-establish his power in Mann in the immediate aftermath of Magnus's death, but Muirchertach was not prepared to watch passively as his nephew built up an independent power-base from which he could challenge for the Munster kingship. By 1111, Domnall was at liberty and evidently again in conflict with his uncle, for he turned for support to Muirchertach's Uí Néill rivals in a fresh bid for power in the Isles.[37] With northern Irish backing, Domnall staged a successful invasion of the Isles, prompting Muirchertach to occupy Dublin for three months to pre-empt any support for Domnall from there or any bid by Domnall to regain control of the city.

Domnall mac Taidc's reign in the Isles lasted barely three years, during which he may have faced mounting opposition from the Manx nobility. In 1114, he quit his kingdom, lured back to Ireland by the prospect of wresting the kingship of Munster from his sick uncle. In alliance with Toirrdelbach ua Conchobair, king of Connaught, he invaded Thomond in 1115 and was given its kingship by the Connaughtmen but, turning against his erstwhile ally, was attacked and killed by him in the same year.[38] Domnall may already have lost control of Mann before 1114, for the ascription of a forty-year reign to his successor in the Manx kingship, Óláfr Gothfrithsson, would indicate that his reign had commenced in 1112–13.[39]

Óláfr's succession to the kingship of Mann formed part of a major affirmation and expansion of English power into the Irish Sea zone under the direction of Henry I. He had recently commenced the consolidation of English control over the coastal district from Chester to the Solway, with Ranulf Meschin's lordship of Carlisle at its cutting edge.[40] English security in this region had been reinforced after 1097 by the client relationship established by William II over the Scottish king, Edgar mac Máel Coluim. This had been confirmed in 1107 on the accession of Alasdair mac Máel Coluim, to whom Henry married his illegitimate daughter, Sibylla,[41] and further consolidated through the establishment of Henry's greatest protégé, Alasdair's younger brother, David, as 'prince of the Cumbrian region'. This northern consolidation had come swiftly on the heels of his assertion of royal power over the rebellious Montgomery family, who held extensive lordships in the Welsh marches and south-west Wales. It is highly significant in the immediate context that in 1102 the Montgomeries allied themselves with Muirchertach ua Briain, sealing the bond through the marriage of Arnulf de Montgomery, earl of Pembroke, to ua Briain's daughter.[42] Muirchertach's support for the Montgomeries had been ended by Henry's threat of a trade embargo, but the re-emergence of Uí Briain influence in Mann must have revived the spectre of foreign support for dissident elements in England. In 1114, accompanied by his vassal, Alasdair mac Máel Coluim, Henry invaded north Wales and forced the submissions of the rulers of Gwynedd and Powys, the former of whom, Gruffudd ap Cynan, was descended from Sigtryggr Silkiskegg and had long-established connections with the Uí Briain.[43] It is as an extension of this drawing in of English influence around the Irish Sea that Fergus's marriage to Henry's bastard daughter should be seen.

As was discussed above, a tradition developed in late nineteenth-century writings that associated Fergus closely with the household of Henry I of England, proposing an upbringing and education in the Norman cultural milieu of the court circle. This tradition has its basis in suggestions of a marriage to an unknown bastard daughter of Henry, and to a supposed long term friendship with David I that arose from time spent together at the Anglo-Norman court. The latter strand of this tradition can be entirely discounted, springing largely as it does from M'Kerlie's obsessive belief in Fergus's status as an alien protégé of the Scottish king imposed on Galloway in the later 1130s, but there are good grounds for accepting a dynastic link with the family of Henry I. That a marriage alliance occurred is now generally accepted,[44] but it is unlikely to have been the love-match proposed by Huyshe. Instead, it can be seen as a politically motivated union, an act of English foreign policy designed to draw an emergent regional power into the orbit of the English crown.

William Mackenzie made the claim that Fergus was married to 'Elizabeth, youngest natural daughter of Henry I' in his 1841 history of Galloway, developing an idea by George Chalmers in *Caledonia*.[45] The sources cited by Chalmers, however, refer not to any Elizabeth, but to Sibylla, illegitimate daughter of Henry and wife of Alasdair mac Máel Coluim. Balfour Paul could find no evidence for such a marriage, but did point out that the epithet 'cousin' was used to describe the relationship between Henry II of England and Uhtred, son of Fergus.[46] Similarly, the *Complete Peerage*, which dealt at some length with the illegitimate offspring of Henry I, found no evidence for a daughter named Elizabeth or a marriage to the lord of Galloway.[47] Despite their negative findings, however, there is a substantial body of material that demonstrates the existence of such a link with Henry I's family.

The bulk of the evidence for kinship ties between the ruling houses of England and Galloway occurs in relation to Fergus's sons. Roger of Howden referred to Uhtred, son of Fergus, as *consanguineus* of Henry II, related through the king's mother, the Empress Matilda.[48] An incidental reference by Robert of Torigni to the kinship of the king of Mann to Henry II described him as 'consanguineus regis Anglorum ex parte Matildis imperatricis matris suae':[49] cousin, or blood-relation of Henry on his mother's side. Godred of Mann, about whom Robert was writing, was the son of Óláfr, husband of Affrica, daughter of Fergus.[50] This is the only marriage through which Godred could trace kinship with Henry II. The conclusion is inescapable that Fergus was married to an otherwise unrecorded illegitimate daughter of Henry I.

Henry is known with certainty to have had eleven daughters by his five known mistresses. Of the eleven, all can be named and their marriages and careers traced, but a twelfth is known only from an undated letter of Anselm, Archbishop of Canterbury, to the king, in which the archbishop advised against a marriage to William de Warenne, Earl of Surrey, as it would have been within prohibited degrees.[51] The name of the proposed bride is not given, and the possibility must be admitted that she was simply one of the known eleven who married at a later date. The proposed marriage with Earl William must have been under discussion between 1103, when he was restored to royal favour, and 1109, when Anselm died, but cannot be dated any more precisely on the basis of the surviving evidence.

The marriages of Henry I's daughters constituted an important element in English royal policy. Any taint of illegitimacy was amply compensated for by their royal blood, which made them valuable items in the battery of royal patronage. While Henry's bastard sons could be advanced into positions of power as agents and supporters of their father and legitimate siblings – the most notable being Robert, whom Henry created earl of Gloucester in 1122, and Reginald, created earl of Cornwall in 1141 by his half-sister, the Empress Matilda – the daughters' main value was in linking members of the Norman or French nobility with the royal house. A clear policy can be seen in this regard, with marital ties being forged with the ducal house of Brittany, the count of Perche, and the lords of Beaumont, Breteuil, Montmirail and Montmorenci, all men of great importance for the security of the southern and western borders of Normandy. A similar function can be attributed to the marriage of Sibylla to Alasdair mac Máel Coluim, which underscored both the formal dependence of the Scottish king on Henry and the already close ties that existed between their families. The marriage of another daughter to the ruler of Galloway would represent a continuation of this policy, as it provided a link with a man whose territories occupied a key position on the north-western flank of Henry's domain and whose independence – and therefore unpredictability – had increased with the sharp decline in Scottish royal authority after 1093.

Henry's efforts to secure the northern limits of his kingdom and to assert his domination of the Irish Sea zone in the 1110s offers the best context within which such a marriage could have occurred. This accords well with the probable dates of birth of Fergus's two known children of this marriage, Affrica and Uhtred. When Fergus first appeared as a charter witness in 1136, he was accompanied by Uhtred, described by Roger of Howden as 'consanguineus' of Henry's grandson.[52] We can assume that Uhtred was deemed by that date to have achieved 'adult' status, indicating that he was at least twelve to fifteen years old. On this reasoning, it can be suggested that Uhtred was born at latest c.1123–24. Likewise, in 1153 Affrica's son, Godred, was of sufficient maturity to journey to Norway to give his personal homage for the kingdom of Mann, which would suggest that his mother was born no later than c.1122. Fergus's marriage, then, can be placed firmly in the context of Henry I's consolidation of his grip over north-west England.

THE ENGLISH ALLIANCE AND
SCOTTISH DOMINATION

As son-in-law of Henry I, Fergus was drawn into an alliance designed to secure English domination of the Solway. Some indication of his relationship with the English court can be taken from the record of his grant of Galtway in Balmaclellan parish to the Knights Hospitaller.[53] The order had been introduced to England c.1114, soon after its foundation, and enjoyed the patronage of Henry and his barons. Unlike its slightly younger sister order, the Templars, the Hospitallers did not enjoy similar levels of royal or noble patronage in Scotland until the reign of Malcolm IV.[54] It seems unlikely, therefore, that the grant of Galtway belonged to the period of greater Scottish influence over Galloway after 1135, to which time it is usually attributed.[55] In the early fifteenth-century list of properties in which the donation is recorded, moreover, Fergus is given the title 'rex Galwitensium', a style that may reflect Fergus's exalted opinions of his status vis-à-vis the English crown. Fergus's gift, therefore, should not be viewed in association with David I's post-1124 grant of Torphichen in West Lothian to the Hospitallers and should probably be considered as part of the generosity towards the order displayed by Henry I and the Norman court circle.

The balance of power in the north that had been established by Henry I in the early 1100s began to tilt towards David after the drowning of Henry's only legitimate son in 1120. Amongst those who perished with William Atheling was the childless Richard, earl of Chester. Richard's earldom occupied a vital strategic position on the Welsh March and also controlled the ports from which English domination of the northern Irish Sea was projected. Norman interests demanded his speedy replacement. His obvious successor was his cousin, Ranulf Meschin, but his acquisition of the earldom of Chester in conjunction with his lordship of Carlisle would have created a disproportionate concentration of regional power in the hands of one man. Having faced the consequences of one such private empire in the person of Robert de Bellême, Henry was not prepared to permit the development of another. Ranulf, therefore, was obliged to surrender Carlisle on his succession to the earldom, much of his former lordship becoming royal demesne with a new sheriffdom based on the castle at Carlisle.[56] The dominant position of Ranulf was filled by a number of new men, most notably Henry's nephew, Stephen of Blois, who received the lordship of Lancaster. Another beneficiary of the dismemberment of Ranulf's northern lordship may have been Robert de Brus, also a 'new man', who had been established as a major crown tenant in Yorkshire as a reward for his support of Henry in the struggle with his elder brother, Duke Robert of Normandy.[57] De Brus was an early associate of David mac Máel Coluim, and his disappearance from an active role in English royal government between 1114 and 1121 has been linked to involvement in the consolidation of David's power in the Southern Uplands.[58] At some time in this period, he may have been infefted by David in the lordship of Annandale, but, as Scott argued, it is more likely that his establishment there post-dated Ranulf's departure from Carlisle after 1120. Although Robert de Brus was a creation of Henry I, his strongest personal bonds were with David, in whose service he was prominent after 1124. To David, Robert's installation in Annandale probably meant the southward expansion of his influence into what had been the territory of a rival for Henry's favour.

The extension of David's authority to embrace Annandale was only part of a general expansion of his sphere of influence within the Southern Uplands. Analysis of David's state-building operations has, understandably, tended to focus on the better-documented areas of Tweeddale and Teviotdale that emerged as the seat of his power in the years after 1124. He was, however, also active to the west of Strathclyde, where, by entirely unknown processes, he achieved lordship over an ill-defined zone of Gall-Gaidhel territory which may have stretched from Strathgryffe in Renfrewshire to Carrick.[59] Control of this district, remembered in the reign of Máel Coluim mac Henry as 'the four *kadrez* of that Galloway which my grandfather had while King Alexander lived',[60] would have extended David's influence to the Clyde estuary and the limits of Fergus's power to the west and south. To what extent, if any, this development was encouraged by Henry I is unknown, but it would have brought his protégé into direct contact with the western maritime zone over which the English crown was asserting its dominance.

David's growing regional domination was confirmed in 1122 by the death of his brother's queen, Sibylla,[61] which made it virtually certain that David would succeed Alasdair, whose only children were illegitimate. As *tanaiste*, David was able to consolidate his position within the territories already under his control and reinforce his position through attracting ambitious men into his service who looked to David's future as king of Scots for their rewards. It may have been at this point that Robert de Brus aligned himself with David. Fergus cannot have been unaware of the implications for his own position that these developments entailed, or have been blind to the subtle shift in the regional power balance that was taking place. Certainly, David was still Henry's protégé, brother-in-law and vassal, but his dependence on the English king had diminished significantly. When David succeeded to the Scottish throne in 1124, the transformation was complete, for he brought with him into his new kingdom the expanded Cumbria that he had constructed in the previous decade. Fergus's neighbour was no longer just another of Henry's 'new men' but a powerful king and ambitious state-builder in his own right.

The degree of the shift in David's favour was made clear possibly as early as his inauguration at Scone. There, in an undated charter, he gave the lordship of Annandale to Robert de Brus,[62] an act that redrew the map of political affiliations in the region. If Annandale had previously been a creation of Henry I, David had made an unequivocal declaration of his understanding of the political realities of the region and absorbed it into the sphere of his royal authority. This was not a hostile move against his former patron, for David was to enjoy a close, co-operative and essentially vassalic relationship with Henry down to the latter's death in 1135, but it did signal the opening of a new and aggressive phase in the development of the kingdom of the Scots. As a first stage on the road to the creation of a unitary monarchy within the northern British mainland, David was embarking on the process of final integration of Strathclyde and its satellite territories into his realm, a process initiated a century earlier by Máel Coluim mac Cinaeda. In doing so, he was serving notice of his claims to the lordship of all Cumbria as successor to Máel Coluim mac Donnchada. His domination of the region was further confirmed by his creation of lordships in Liddesdale for Ranulf de Soules, upper Eskdale and Ewesdale for Robert Avenel, and lower Eskdale for the de Conisboroughs.[63] These men, whose new possessions lay in what Kapelle termed the 'free zone' between the spheres of effective authority in Scotland and England,[64] now looked to the Scottish crown for lordship.

Where he could, David was clearly moving to eliminate rival powers within what he regarded as the sphere of the king of Scots. His endeavours in this direction are most clearly recognised in Moray and the far north, where intrusive Scottish royal authority was firmly implanted in the period after 1130,[65] but he was equally and probably earlier active in the Clyde estuary area, where he had claimed some form of lordship in the period before 1124. Here, he moved to assert his domination of the territories that extended down the eastern shore of the firth, that lay outwith Strathclyde and that had possibly been settled extensively by Gaelic-speaking colonists from the Isles. His rivals for overlordship of this region may have been Isles-based powers, such as Óláfr of Mann, or northern Irish rulers such as the Uí Néill, who were capable of projecting their authority into the Hebrides and western firths. Indeed, the Uí Néill could claim the leadership of the Gael from long before Brian Bóruma adopted his exalted title at Armagh, and had received recognition of their overlordship from David's distant forebears. When David began to implant further colonial families into the Gall-Gaidhel territories of the Clyde estuary, he was signalling his intention that the king of Scots would be the only monarchical authority in that region. Against such an active projection of David's ambitions, Fergus had only one defence: his shared relationship with Henry I. As son-in-law of the English king, Fergus benefited from the protective ægis of Anglo-Norman power. Its abrupt removal in 1135 left him exposed to the authority of a Scottish monarchy whose power had reached unprecedented heights. However Fergus may have expressed his status, there can be little doubt that from 1135 he was anything other than a satellite of the Scottish crown.

Henry's death on 1 December 1135 triggered a fresh struggle for the domination of Northumbria that saw Norman control of Northumberland, Cumberland and Westmorland challenged and broken by David. His intervention in English affairs has often been presented as a consequence of his obligations towards his niece, Matilda, whom Henry had designated his heir and required the Anglo-Norman baronage to swear to accept, but while familial obligations may have been a consideration, the opportunism in David's actions shows that extension of his own personal authority was the prime consideration.[66] David could do nothing to prevent the seizure of the English throne by Henry's nephew, Stephen of Blois, the husband of David's other niece, also named Matilda. Soon after Stephen's coronation on 22 December 1135, however, David marched into northern England, seized both Newcastle and Carlisle, most northern castles of consequence, and with them control of Northumberland, Cumberland and Westmorland. In February, Stephen came north to Durham, then under siege by the Scots, for a meeting with David. Protracted negotiations led to the understanding that David's son, Henry, would be vested with the earldom of Huntingdon and the lordships of Carlisle and Doncaster. In return, David would withdraw from Durham, relinquish Newcastle and put the question of Henry's right to Northumberland to arbitration.[67] The unresolved question of Northumberland left David with an opportunity to renew hostilities should events not fall out to his satisfaction, but for the meantime Earl Henry stayed at Stephen's court and a brittle façade of stability was maintained in the north.

David's movements after February 1136 are difficult to trace, but in the summer he was at Glasgow for the consecration of Bishop John's cathedral.[68] The ceremony was attended by a substantial gathering of the Scottish political elite and men whose territories fell wholly or in part under the spiritual jurisdiction of the bishopric of Glasgow, and the occasion may have been used by David to take counsel on the deteriorating relationship with Stephen. After Easter 1136, indeed, the agreement between the kings had broken down following the insulting treatment of Earl Henry at Stephen's court.[69] Present at Glasgow were the king's nephew, William fitz Duncan, Malise, earl of Strathearn, and Duncan, earl of Fife, the two latter representing the leadership of the Gaelic nobility of Scotia. They are accompanied by a list of the Gaelic nobility of the south-west, headed by Fergus of Galloway, and including his heir, Uhtred, the two sons of Dunegal of Strathnith, and an impressive body of Gaelic lords from the Lennox and Menteith. Strangely, with the exception of clerical servants, there is a striking absence of Anglo-Norman colonists, an absence that may reflect the discomfort felt by his new tenants-in-chief at the widening breach between David and Stephen. In the following year, that discomfort developed into outright hostility towards David's policies.

The presence of the rulers of the south-western lordships at Glasgow is a clear indication of the increase in David's influence that had followed his establishment of colonial lordships in Annandale, Eskdale and Liddesdale in the aftermath of the contraction of Ranulf Meschin's lordship of Carlisle. The seizure of Carlisle, moreover, gave him a regional authority that Fergus could not ignore: Scottish domination was a reality. The situation, however, is further complicated by Fergus's personal relationship with the Norman dynasty. David's niece was also the half-sister of Fergus's wife and it is possible that Fergus viewed support for the Empress Matilda as both an obligation founded on his relationship with Henry I, and an opportunity to be exploited. The placing of Matilda, half-sister of his wife and aunt of his heir, on the English throne would have immeasurably strengthened his position.

Despite the growing tensions caused by Earl Henry's withdrawal from Stephen's court, an uneasy peace was maintained until early 1137. Immediately after Easter, David summoned his forces and prepared to invade Northumberland. Stephen, however, was well prepared and had ordered his loyal northern barons to muster at Newcastle. Backed by this military threat, Archbishop Thurstan of York travelled to Roxburgh and made a personal appeal to David to withdraw his challenge. Always a careful judge of the situation, David backed down and a fresh truce was settled. In late November 1137, however, David sent messengers to Stephen with a final demand for the cession of Northumberland to Earl Henry, threatening war if Stephen did not accede to his demand.[70] In early January 1138, David, accompanied by a great host that included a large contingent from Galloway, crossed into Northumberland.[71] The army plundered and terrorised its way to the Tyne, the men of Galloway being singled out in chronicle accounts of the campaign as the perpetrators of the worst excesses.[72] Buoyed up by their successes in subduing Northumberland and by William fitz Duncan's easy victory at Clitheroe in Lancashire, the Scots drove south through Teesdale towards York. At Cowton Moor near Northallerton, David's army encountered a hastily assembled army under the nominal leadership of Archbishop Thurstan. Divisions among the Scots and the superior discipline and arms of the English halted David's impetuous advance in the bloody rout known as the Battle of the Standard. In all accounts of that conflict, the Galwegians feature prominently as a major contributory factor in the defeat of the Scots, the repulse of their rash and uncontrolled assault on the armoured mass of the English foot soldiers being held largely to blame for the disintegration of David's ill-disciplined host.

No source records the presence of Fergus at Northallerton, nor mentions his personal involvement in any part of the 1138 campaign, but in the 1139 treaty between David and Stephen which concluded this phase of the war it was stipulated that the son of an 'Earl Fergus' was to be amongst the five hostages given by the Scots as additional security.[73] As there was no contemporary Scottish earl of this name, it is probable that Fergus of Galloway was intended by the chronicler, whose use of the comital style gives a good indication of how Fergus's status was understood in the eyes of northern English observers. That his son was singled out in this way, along with the sons of David's two principal vassals in Lothian, one of them his chief military officer, demonstrates the significance of Fergus's role in the war. It is also an unequivocal sign of his personal importance: Stephen, as another of Henry I's 'new men' cannot have been unaware of Fergus's marital ties with the Norman dynasty and the status of Uhtred as a nephew of his rival for the English crown.

The 1138 campaign had brought Fergus no tangible gain and, while David was soon to break his new treaty with Stephen and extend his power in northern England,[74] there is no indication of further Galwegian involvement in the war in England. This may have been a consequence of the possible diversion of his attention to Mann and the Isles, where his son-in-law's position may have been challenged by Ottar, grandson of Ottar, a Hebridean warlord who in 1142 seized Dublin and who attempted to project his authority across the Irish Sea until his assassination in 1148.[75] There is otherwise no evidence for any breach between Fergus and David, but it is possible that Fergus understood the implications for his own status of David's consolidation of control over Cumberland. Fergus's disquiet was probably intensified in 1140 when Archbishop Thurstan died and David attempted to seize York and install his candidate, Henry Murdac, abbot of Fountains, as archbishop. For Galloway, this brought the possibility of absorption into what looked increasingly like a Scottish archdiocese. King Stephen, however, succeeded in pre-empting David, entering York and securing the election of his kinsman, William FitzHerbert. For the next seven years, possession of the see was bitterly contested between Henry and William, with the Cistercian order throwing its full weight behind the former and eventually engineering the deposition of William in 1147. During this bitter struggle, Fergus appears to have supported the rights of William, flying in the face of both David I's policy and the fulminations of the Cistercians.[76] If David was angered or alarmed by this stance, no record survives of any steps taken by him to neutralise the threat. It was left to the Cistercians to exact a particularly malicious revenge: the libelling of the reputations of both Fergus and his people.[77]

However strained the relationship between David and Fergus may have become, there is no firm evidence for any serious breach between them.[78] The king, on the contrary, moved to bind Fergus's family more firmly to his inner circle of supporters, particularly Uhtred, whose descent from Henry I might have proven useful in consolidating and legitimising David's possession of Cumberland. Probably in the late 1140s, Uhtred was married to Gunnilda, daughter of Waltheof of Allerdale, a distant kinswoman of David's and a cousin of William fitz Duncan, the son of Waltheof's sister, Octreda. Through this marriage, Uhtred became lord of a small estate at Torpenhow in west Cumberland.[79] Small though this property acquisition may have been, it brought Uhtred into direct contact with many of the senior figures of David I's court circle, including both William fitz Duncan, lord of Allerdale and Coupland, and Hugh de Morville, the king's constable, who was lord of North Westmorland. Uhtred's outlook was being drawn to the new horizon of the Scoto-Northumbrian world, and the prospect loomed of Galloway's closer integration into the kingdom once he succeeded his father. The death in June 1152 of David's only son, Earl Henry, followed eleven months later by David himself, however, transformed once again the political balance of northern Britain and lifted this spectre from the horizon. With the new king, David's grandson Máel Coluim mac Henry, not yet in his teens and likely to face dynastic challenges to his position, Fergus was presented with an opportunity to restake his position as an independent regional power.

FERGUS, IRELAND, MANN AND THE ISLES

While Anglo-Scottish affairs predominate in our evidence for Fergus's activities from the 1120s to 1150s, it is evident that he had forged other bonds within the western maritime zone at the beginning of his political career. As Fergus had extended his domain into western Galloway, he had been drawn into the affairs of Ireland and Mann. In following this path, Fergus was moving in the steps of men like Echmarcach mac Ragnaill, who had used their control of the strategic peninsula that all but closed the northern Irish Sea off from the Firth of Clyde and southern Hebrides to establish a dominant role in the politics of the region. It was a dangerous game, for it linked him into the shifting quicksands of Irish politics and exposed him to the influences and authority of the rival contenders for the high-kingship and political leadership of the Gaidhel. Such dalliances were unlikely to endear him to the Scottish crown, which, under David I, had resumed its drive to achieve the dominance of the northern British mainland and the exclusion therefrom of all potential rivals for kingly authority.

Fergus's expansion of his power to embrace western Galloway coincided with a shift in the Irish political scene that might indicate the context within which that development should be viewed. In 1118, Toirrdelbach ua Conchobair, king of Connaught, captured Dublin and assumed the kingship of the Gall for himself.[80] Control of the city provided him with the military and naval might to give substance to his efforts to secure the high-kingship, forces that were soon to be deployed against his rivals. For thirteen years, Connaught maintained its domination of the city, using its resources to keep its opponents in check. One key instance of this occurred in 1121 when, following the death of Bishop Samuel ua hAngliu of Dublin, there were moves to secure his replacement by Cellach, bishop of Armagh, the head of the native Irish Church. Toirrdelbach may have considered such a development as a threat to his authority and supported the Dubliners in their appeal to Canterbury for the consecration of their own choice, Gréne.[81] Toirrdelbach strengthened their appeal with a letter to Henry I, which can be interpreted in no other way than as an explicit recognition of English dominance within the British Isles. Henry's mastery of the Irish Sea world was being acknowledged by the dominant native Irish power.

The consolidation of Fergus's power in western Galloway in the late 1120s and 1130s, reflected in his revival of the episcopal see of Whithorn and the severing of ties to the Manx Church,[82] constitutes a watershed in the development of the political structures of the northern Irish Sea zone. The expansion of his domain had presumably been sanctioned if not encouraged by Henry I, although it had occasioned considerable erosion of the territorial influence of his other Irish Sea protégé, Óláfr of Mann. While no record of any conflict survives, beyond the account of the activities of Bishop Wimund of the Isles offered by William of Newburgh,[83] this cannot have been achieved without confrontation. Manx acceptance of the new status quo, however, was settled with the marriage of Fergus's daughter, Affrica, granddaughter of Henry, to Óláfr. The settled relationship between Galloway and Mann that resulted from the marriage alliance lasted until June 1153 when the ageing Óláfr was murdered in a revival of the internecine rivalry that had torn the island kingdom apart in 1094–1112. Óláfr's nephews, sons of his elder brother, Harald, who had been brought up in Dublin, had gathered an army which contained many Manx exiles and invaded the island to secure a half share of the kingdom which they regarded as theirs by right. Their attack was almost certainly planned to take advantage of a combination of particularly favourable events: the absence of Óláfr's son, Godred, who was in Norway paying homage for the kingdom of Mann; and the death at Carlisle on 24 May of Óláfr's powerful protector, David I. Recognising the weakness of his position, Óláfr attempted to negotiate but was treacherously killed by his nephews, who then proceeded to partition the kingdom.[84] In an immediate follow-up to their coup, the Haraldsons launched an attack on Galloway, 'wishing to subject it to themselves'.[85] This may represent a bid to regain control of the lost Manx domain in western Galloway and reunite the fragmented segments of the eleventh-century kingdom of the Uí Ímair, but was more probably a pre-emptive strike against an anticipated Galwegian invasion in support of Fergus's grandson, Godred. Whatever the case, the invaders were bloodily repulsed, venting their anger on their return to Mann in a massacre of the Galwegians whom they found there.

Support for the Haraldsons in Mann appears to have been limited, probably resting chiefly on the kin of the exiles whom they had gathered around them in Dublin. The shallowness of their base was revealed by the autumn of 1153 when Godred returned from the Norwegian court. News of his arrival in Orkney quickly reached the chieftains of the Isles, who, having gathered to take counsel, acclaimed him as their king. With their backing, he moved south to Mann and, evidently with little opposition, gained control of the island and captured his cousins, one of whom he killed and two he blinded.[86]

The death of David I and Óláfr in quick succession removed the two chief forces for stability in the Hebrides and Irish Sea zone. Their sudden removal revealed the extent to which they had kept a lid on the simmering tensions of the region and had excluded rival powers from influence within it: what appears to have been a long period of peace was followed by an explosion of violence and disorder. From a Scottish perspective, it is the activities of Somairle of Argyll and his nephews that demonstrate most graphically the release of forces that David's domination of northern Britain had held in check. While the conflict that Somairle unleashed quickly transformed itself into a personal campaign of empire building in the Isles, it may have begun as a dynastic challenge on behalf of his brother-in-law and nephews, representatives of a rival line of candidates for the Scottish throne.[87] Conventional historiography identifies this line as the meic Aeda or MacHeths, headed by the man reconciled with Máel Coluim mac Henry in 1157 and subsequently awarded the earldom of Ross.[88] Their challenge had begun in 1124, when one Malcolm or Máel Coluim, described as an illegitimate son of Alasdair mac Máel Coluim, attempted to wrest the throne from his uncle, David.[89] The original Latin accounts of his attempt give him no patronymic other than the reference to his paternity, but the name MacHeth has intruded itself into modern translations through conflation of two individuals – the son of Alasdair and the son of Aed – into a single figure.[90] Defeated in 1124, Máel Coluim mounted a fresh bid in 1130 in association with the ruler of Moray, which had again ended in military defeat.[91] A laconic entry in the *Chronicle of Melrose* records the capture of Máel Coluim in 1134 and his imprisonment in Roxburgh,[92] but a more dramatic triumph evidently lay behind this understated account. The speech that Ailred of Rievaulx put into the mouth of Robert de Brus in his account of the 1138 campaign refers to a major operation organised on behalf of David by Walter Espec following a council at Carlisle. This had involved the collection of a fleet and a prolonged campaign against Máel Coluim and his allies that had resulted in the surrender of the pretender.[93] The assembly at Carlisle followed by a naval campaign, coupled with the reference in the *Chronicle of Holyrood* to the capture at Whithorn twenty-two years later of Máel Coluim's son, Domnall, has suggested to some that western Galloway may have been the scene of the final stages in Máel Coluim's ten-year struggle for his heritage, which had culminated in a challenge to Fergus's control of the region.[94] There is nothing in Ailred's account to suggest that Galloway was the destination of this naval campaign, nor that while the council had met at Carlisle it was there, too, that the fleet had assembled. Indeed, the role of Robert de Brus and Walter Espec in the affair would favour rather a Yorkshire or Cleveland force – Robert controlled the port of Hartlepool – and an eastern Scottish destination. Nevertheless, the association of Máel Coluim with Somairle, whose sister Máel Coluim had married, points to a west Highland and Hebridean dimension to the struggle. Rather than Galloway, however, Argyll and the Mull group of islands, the core of Somairle's power, may have been the target for David's fleet. The western expansion of David's power since the 1110s must have encroached considerably on the territory of Somairle's family. After 1124, David expected to be able to levy cain in Argyll and Kintyre, portions of which income he granted to the monks of Dunfermline and canons of Holyrood.[95] His victory in Moray in 1130 had reinforced his position within the Highlands, emphasised by his grant of the teind of his cain from Argyll of Moray to the monks of Urquhart.[96] David was clearly projecting the authority of the eastern lowlands-based Scottish crown into the west with a forcefulness previously unknown to the local powers: Somairle and Máel Coluim, therefore, were natural allies against David.

The capture of Máel Coluim in 1134 probably ended any involvement that Somairle may have had in this challenge to David's kingship. Certainly, if Ailred is to be trusted, men from Lorn and the Isles fought in David's army at Northallerton in 1138, the list of regional contingents providing a striking illustration of the extended sphere of his lordship within mainland Scotland.[97] Scottish domination of Argyll may have provided the context within which Somairle began to extend his authority into island territories that fell under the lordship of Óláfr of Mann. Down to 1135, Óláfr had moved within the orbit of Henry I and had enjoyed his protection. Óláfr, however, also had links with Stephen through the latter's lordship of Lancaster,[98] and may have aligned with him against Matilda and her allies after 1136. Somairle may, therefore, have capitalised on this falling out amongst the protégés of Henry I to enlarge his own sphere in the Isles. David's occupation of Cumberland after 1136 and seizure of Lancaster as far south as Coupland in 1141, plus Ranulf Meschin's support for David and Matilda from his earldom of Chester,[99] however, had effectively turned the north-eastern sector of the Irish Sea into a Scottish-dominated lake. In such circumstances, it is likely that Óláfr recognised David's superior lordship and abandoned Stephen, a re-alignment that would have ended any Scottish encouragement for Somairle's activities. Any further aggrandisement of Argyll power would only happen without David's sanction.

It is within the context of this period of disturbance in the Isles that the activities of one of the more enigmatic figures of the mid-twelfth century should be placed. Bishop Wimund is known to history largely through William of Newburgh's account of his career.[100] According to William, he had been born in an obscure spot in England and had drifted into religion. He entered the Cistercian order at Furness and in 1134 formed part of the colony of monks sent from there to establish the daughter house of Rushen in Mann. Sometime thereafter, he was elevated to the episcopate, possibly with the seat of his bishopric in Skye rather than Mann.[101] It is unclear whether this represented an attempt by Óláfr to establish a second diocese within his kingdom, possibly serving its northern portion, for accounts of the episcopal succession in the Isles at this time are fragmentary and confused.[102] A northern Hebridean context would fit well with the next stage in his career, for he announced that he was a son of an 'earl of Moray', and gathered around him a force to regain his lost heritage. William's account describes raids on the islands and on the Scottish mainland, including an attack on another bishop from whom he was attempting to exact some form of tribute. This action is commonly located in Galloway and could represent a bid by an Isles-based bishop to regain the position that his predecessors had held in that region before the revival of the see of Whithorn,[103] but the account displays strong similarities to descriptions of the fate of Somairle at the hands of the army of the bishop of Glasgow in 1164 and may represent a conflation of several stories.[104] Despite his defeat, Wimund continued his offensive and eventually forced David to negotiate. To secure peace, David granted him Furness, which he had acquired only in 1141. He enjoyed his position for only a short while, for his supposed subjects captured, blinded and castrated him, treatment which suggests that he may indeed have had some basis for his claims, and was later confined to Byland abbey in Yorkshire, another daughter-house of Furness, established in 1177.[105]

Most of our problems with Wimund revolve around the standard identification of his father with Angus, earl of Moray, who had been defeated and killed in 1130.[106] William of Newburgh, however, does not name Wimund's father, but simply describes him as earl of Moray, and the inference that Angus is the individual intended has been built from William's description of him as 'despoiled of his forefathers' heritage by the king of Scots'.[107] William's reference to Wimund as being born in an obscure spot in England and entering religion at Furness Abbey, however, would seem irreconcilable with any association with Angus and his northern Scottish earldom. Yet, David's eventual landed settlement on Wimund suggests that the king recognised some validity in his claims. Furthermore, is there any significance in the location of the properties supposedly assigned to him by the king? The answer would appear to be yes. The solution may lie in the later thirteenth-century evidence of the genealogy of the lords of Allerdale and Coupland, which styles William fitz Duncan, the nephew of David I and son of Donnchad mac Máel Coluim and Octreda of Allerdale, as earl of Moray.[108] From 1130 until he turned his attentions southwards in 1137, William may have held a lordship of Moray under David I, probably through marriage to a sister or daughter of Earl Angus that produced the later meic Uilleim claimants to the Scottish throne.[109] While this brief northern Scottish career is largely hypothetical, William's Cumberland connections are solid. After the death of his father in 1094, it is probable that William had come with his mother to live with her relatives in Allerdale and he may have remained there until joining the court circle of his uncle, David I. The chronology of Wimund's church career indicates that he had been born before c.1110, which would tally with William's youth in Allerdale. In the Anglo-Scottish wars after 1137, William pursued claims to an extensive lordship in north-western England, most of which pertained to the inheritance of his one recorded wife, Alice de Rumilly, heiress to Craven in western Yorkshire. By the time of his death in c.1151, William controlled a series of properties – Allerdale, Coupland, Skipton and Craven – that extended across the southern limits of David's northern English acquisitions. With this strong Cumberland background and former connections with Moray, therefore, it is possible that William was the father claimed by Wimund.

It is difficult to reconcile this picture of widespread disturbance in the Isles in the 1130s with the traditional presentation of the period, based on the comments of the *Chronicle of Mann*, that the reign of Óláfr had been generally one of peace and tranquillity.[110] It would be closer to reality to say that he had weathered the storms that the uncertain political climate of the times had thrown at him, but by 1153 his kingdom was threatening to disintegrate under the strain. The journey of his son, Godred, to Norway to perform homage for the kingdom, may have been made in an effort to secure Norwegian aid to prop up his declining authority, but his assassination during Godred's absence created a vacuum that threatened to implode as other powers moved to capitalise on this Manx weakness and the coincidental eclipse of Scottish dominance of the western maritime zone. In Ireland in particular, the long struggle for political supremacy between Toirrdelbach ua Conchobair of Connaught and the rising power of Muirchertach mac Lochlainn, king of Cenél nEógain, gained fresh impetus.

In 1154, Ua Conchobair gathered a fleet and launched a plundering raid on Tír Conaill and Inishowen, the heartland of the meic Lochlainn. Muirchertach, however, responded by hiring galleys from the Firth of Clyde powers – Kintyre, Arran, Galloway – and Mann,[111] which confronted the Connaught fleet off the coast of Inishowen. Although Toirrdelbach's commander, Cosnamaig ua Dubdai, was killed, the Connaught fleet was victorious, driving off the mercenary galleys with great slaughter. For Mac Lochlainn, the setback was temporary and in the immediate aftermath of the defeat of his fleet he marched on Dublin and received its submission, securing control of its still impressive naval force.[112] His allies in the battle may have been less resilient. For Fergus, the failure of the naval campaign may have proven the last straw. Coming swift on the heels of the breakdown of his policy of *rapprochement* with the king of Mann and the subsequent devastating raid on Galloway by the Haraldssons, it must have seemed that Fergus's seemingly unshakeable grip on power was at last beginning to slip. Defeat slackened Fergus's hold and ended his ability to hold the mutual jealousies of his sons in check. For Uhtred and Gillebrigte mac Fergusa, the lid had come off the Pandora's box of political power.

THE FALL OF FERGUS 1154–60

The final years of Fergus's long reign are usually viewed from a purely Scottish context.[113] While it was a Scottish king who achieved his overthrow, however, the events that led to this result sprang from a wider background. A significant element in Fergus's troubles stemmed from the rapid deterioration in the political stability of the western maritime region after 1154. Much of this revolved around the conflicting ambitions of his grandson, King Godred, and Somairle of Argyll. At the end of 1153, Somairle had declared his support once again for the rival line of the ruling dynasty in Scotland and backed the bid of his nephews, the sons of the Máel Coluim who had been imprisoned in Roxburgh since 1134, to wrest the throne from Máel Coluim mac Henry.[114] This rising was underway by November 1153, around which time Godred was establishing himself in Mann with the support of the Hebridean chieftains. There are no indications in contemporary Scottish or English sources that Somairle and his nephews succeeded in making any significant headway, the *Chronicle of Holyrood* alone noting the death in trial by combat of a certain Arthur, who had planned to betray the young king of Scots, but does not provide any indication of his relationship to the rebels.[115] The failure of the meic Máel Coluim cause to attract significant support within Scotland, coupled with the blow to Manx power which resulted from the defeat of the fleet assembled to aid Muirchertach mac Lochlainn, may have persuaded Somairle to reconsider his options.

Our knowledge of western affairs in the mid- and later 1150s is dependent primarily upon the *Chronicle of Mann*, whose notoriously suspect chronology is even more confused than usual at this point. The conventional scheme outlines a bid by Godred in 1155 or 1156 for the Dublin kingship, the failure of Muirchertach mac Lochlainn to eject him from the city by military means, and the subsequent securing of Godred's control there. On his return to Mann, Godred provoked a rebellion amongst the Hebridean chieftains, who turned to Somairle with a request that he send his son, Dubgall, Godred's nephew, to be their king. Won over by this offer, Somairle abandoned his support for the meic Máel Coluim, who were forced into desperate measures which culminated, according to the traditional interpretations, in an attack on Galloway, defeat there and the capture at Whithorn of Domnall mac Máel Coluim, who was then imprisoned with his father in Roxburgh. In the interim, Somairle had launched an attack on Mann, defeated Godred and forced him into a settlement whereby the kingdom was divided between Godred and Dubgall. Two years later, the settlement broke down and Somairle again attacked Mann. Driven from his kingdom, Godred fled to Norway to seek aid.[116] Presented thus, the narrative appears to flow simply and easily, but recent reappraisal of the sources and comparison with Irish records has highlighted possible flaws within the chronology.

The most significant problem concerns the dating of the event that started the traditional narrative, Godred's occupation of Dublin. According to the *Chronicle of Mann*, the Dublin aristocracy – who had earlier supported Ottar and then the Haraldssons – approached Godred with an offer of the kingship.[117] This was a direct challenge to Muirchertach mac Lochlainn, who had controlled the city since 1154, and whose ally Godred had been in the naval war of that year. Irish annals for 1156, however, make no mention of such an event, nor of any major hosting by Muirchertach and subsequent military confrontation. Indeed, it is not until 1162 that accounts that tally with the Manx version of events occur. Both the *Annals of Ulster* and the *Annals of the Four Masters* corroborate some of the details of the Manx account of Muirchertach's campaign against Dublin, but place these events in 1162, six years after the date offered by the *Chronicle of Mann*, and do not name the leader of the Dublin resistance.[118] This appears to bring into question the sequence and dating of the events that follow from this action in the conventional narrative, for if the Manx occupation of Dublin is re-dated to 1162, as Seán Duffy suggests it should, then Godred cannot have been the aggressor as he was currently in exile in Norway and did not return until 1164.[119] This suggests that a similar sequence of events in 1155–56 has failed to be recorded in any surviving Irish source, or that Godred's occupation of Dublin did not occur and that a later Isles-based occupation – presumably by Somairle – has wrongly been attributed to him, or that separate actions in 1155–56 and 1162 have been conflated into a single event.

In view of the place given to the account of the Dublin campaign in the Manx record of Godred's reign, the first or third of the above options is to be preferred. Despite the good gloss that the chronicle puts on the operation, what follows suggests that it had been a dismal failure that undermined Godred's standing amongst the chieftains of the Isles. It has been suggested that Somairle's attack on Mann, which follows on immediately from the Dublin episode in the *Chronicle of Mann* account, stemmed from an alliance or association between Somairle and Muirchertach mac Lochlainn that dated from at least 1154.[120] This analysis is based on the suggestion that Somairle had been involved in the 1154 naval hosting assembled by Muirchertach and hinges on the identification of the ships hired from 'the shores of Scotland' as being an Argyll and Hebridean force.[121] There is nothing in the *Annals of the Four Masters* account to support this proposition. Indeed, rather than being allies, Muirchertach and Somairle were potential rivals for influence in the Isles, as revealed in Muirchertach's blocking in 1164 of Somairle's attempt to persuade Flaithbertach ua Brolcháin, comarb of Coluim Cille, to assume the abbacy of Iona and, presumably, return the highly symbolic relics of Coluim Cille to that community, over which Somairle exercised great influence.[122] This may have been a bid by Somairle to establish his credentials as leader of the Gaidhel, or more plausibly a step towards securing the re-location of the see of the Isles to the reinvigorated community that lay firmly within the sphere of his authority. A further indication of rivalry between Cenél nEógain and Argyll is established by the source of instigation for Somairle's attack on Godred. According to the *Chronicle of Mann*, Godred's tyrannies against his nobles in the aftermath of his failed attempt on Dublin prompted them to turn to Somairle, with one, Thorfinn, son of Ottar, requesting that Dubgall mac Somairle be set over them as king in Godred's place.[123] This Thorfinn, whom the chronicle describes as 'more powerful than the rest', was descended from the Earl Ottar, ruler of half of Mann whose death is recorded in 1098, and was probably a kinsman of the man who had ruled Dublin from 1142 to 1148.[124] The timing of his approach to Somairle, immediately following the end of Godred's Dublin adventure, makes it unlikely that he was Muirchertach's agent, for his claimed objective was to obtain another Uí Ímair dynast – Óláfr's grandson, Dubgall – to supplant his uncle. This looks more like a bid to find a viable candidate with the right credentials for the Dublin kingship, who could draw on the support of the dominant power in Argyll and the Hebrides and who already stood as a rival to Muirchertach mac Lochlainn. Thorfinn should probably be seen as a member of that 'clique of aristocrats with a foot in both camps' identified by Seán Duffy,[125] for whom the failure of the attempts from 1142 to 1156 to re-establish a joint Dublin–Manx kingship had brought no reconciliation to rule of Dublin by a native Irish power. Such men clearly now looked to Somairle, through his son, Dubgall, to provide them with the leadership and support necessary to end Muirchertach's overlordship. The degree of Somairle's success in this may be gauged by the support from Dublin that he drew for his ill-fated rebellion against Máel Coluim mac Henry in 1164.[126]

Early in 1157, Somairle made his move against Godred.[127] A naval battle off Mann on the night of 5–6 January ended inconclusively, and on 6 January negotiations led to a partition of the islands between Godred and Somairle. The deal held until 1158, when Somairle attacked Mann again and this time succeeded in defeating and driving out Godred.[128] While the mid-thirteenth-century Manx account indicates that Godred fled directly to Norway – the course taken in the thirteenth century by exiled kings of Mann – it is clear that he attempted to find allies against Somairle closer to hand. Significantly, however, he did not seek aid from Galloway. Before the end of September 1158, Godred had arrived in western England, possibly by way of Wales. He was evidently in dire straits, for the sheriffs of Worcester and Gloucester were pardoned at the exchequer for payments made to provide the refugee with arms and equipment.[129] His decision to seek the aid of Henry II may have been prompted by the recent flexing of Angevin muscles in Gwynedd, during which an English fleet had featured prominently if ingloriously,[130] and by his kinship with the English king. Henry, however, failed to offer him any assistance, for in August 1158 he departed for France to begin his recovery of lost Norman possessions there.[131] Unsuccessful in England, Godred turned to Scotland and was present at a great gathering of Máel Coluim mac Henry's court at Roxburgh early in 1159.[132] Here, he was equally unsuccessful, for at the end of May, the Scottish king began his journey to France to participate in Henry II's campaign to Toulouse. Only now did Godred travel on to Norway, where he was present in February 1161 fighting at Oslo in the army of King Ingi.[133]

Where in this tangle did Fergus stand? Apart from the association with Mann in Muirchertach's 1154 fleet, there is no direct evidence for Galwegian involvement in the spiralling conflicts of the Irish Sea and Hebrides other than the *Chronicle of Holyrood's* cryptic reference to the capture of Domnall mac Máel Coluim at Whithorn in 1156. This has commonly been presented as the consequence of a failed military operation, with Somairle's nephews attempting to provide themselves with a mainland base following their uncle's abandonment of their cause to pursue his own ambitions in Mann and Ireland.[134] It has been suggested, indeed, that Domnall was mounting a challenge to Fergus's possession of western Galloway.[135] The annal account is laconic even by the standards of the Holyrood chronicle and provides no indication of the circumstances of Domnall's capture. It is unlikely, however, that the traditional interpretation offered above is correct, and that a significant military operation in Galloway would have entirely slipped the notice of contemporary observers. His arrest at Whithorn, the spiritual and pilgrimage centre of the region, rather than at one of the seats of secular power, may point to his presence in Galloway in some other role than invader. Furthermore, it is unclear who was responsible for his capture and surrender to the king of Scots. One reconstruction of the events behind Domnall's capture conjectures that it stemmed from the divisions within Galloway, with Fergus favouring alliance with the pretender while his sons actively opposed him and succeeded in forcing him to abandon his dangerous scheme.[136] What is clear, however, is that his taking preceded Somairle's first attack on Mann rather than followed it, as is traditionally proposed, which may indicate that Fergus was flirting with an Argyll alliance in the mid 1150s. It is possible, therefore, that Domnall had been attempting to win over Fergus when news of Somairle's alliance with Thorfinn and imminent move against Fergus's grandson, Godred, became known. Somairle's ambitions for his son, therefore, sealed the fate of his nephew.

If Fergus was the agent responsible for Domnall's capture, then in 1156 he was evidently still at peace with Máel Coluim mac Henry and, presumably, opposed to Somairle. His relationship with the Scots may have depended on their continuing domination of the Solway region through possession of Carlisle and Cumberland rather than any sense of loyalty to David I's grandson. This, however, was to change within a few months when Henry II laid claim to the territories ceded to the Scots during the war with Stephen. In summer 1157, Máel Coluim surrendered Cumberland and Northumberland to Henry and, travelling to meet with Henry at Chester, became his vassal.[137] This transformed again the political geography of the Solway region and may have been viewed by Fergus as marking a restoration of the pre-1135 status quo, under which he had stood in a direct personal relationship with the English king. To Fergus, furthermore, the events of 1157 may have seemed a stark demonstration of Scottish weakness that was begging to be exploited.

While there is no clear evidence for any form of alliance between Fergus and Somairle, it is probable that Fergus recognised the potential benefits to himself from association with the rising power of the western seaboard. Certainly, there is no tradition in Scottish or Manx sources of any activity on his part in support of his grandson, Godred. On the other hand, the possession by Iona Abbey of a group of parish churches and chapels in the lower Dee valley in Galloway may signal the re-alignment of Fergus with Somairle. Iona's possession of these churches has been dated to the eleventh century,[138] but the grant of parochial churches in this fashion is a phenomenon of twelfth century and later Scottish alms-giving rather than of an earlier period. A grant of this kind by Fergus to Iona, a monastery linked closely to Somairle, hints at an underlying political re-alignment. It is at best, however, only circumstantial evidence for the forging of a Galloway–Argyll alliance.

The final episodes in Fergus's career are reduced to a few tantalising and quite obviously garbled fragments. These have, traditionally, been strung together in an effort to create a coherent narrative of events, and, at a basic level, have generally resulted in the production of a simple portrayal of an ageing father clinging to power in the face of challenges from his increasingly impatient sons, and involving himself in a disastrous foreign war in a bid to win unity at home and so re-build his fading prestige. Behind the simple narrative, however, it is possible to trace a more complex situation of mounting family tensions and political rivalries, to which the increasing political and cultural influence of the Scottish crown added stronger colour. It is unfortunate that the principal narrative source for this crucial period in the history of Galloway is the hostile account offered as incidental detail in Walter Daniel's *Life of Ailred of Rievaulx*, which paints the domestic political scene in simple black and white terms as the merest backdrop for the glorious success of his heroic subject in restoring tranquillity to a troubled land. Leaving aside the eulogising of Ailred and the anti-Galwegian tone of his account, however, Walter Daniel constitutes the most detailed record of the political turmoil in the lordship in the mid-1150s.[139] He describes how Ailred

found the petty king of that land incensed against his sons, and the sons raging against the father and each other . . . The king of Scotland could not subdue, nor the bishop pacify their mutual hatreds, rancour and tyranny. Sons were against father, father against sons, brother against brother, daily polluting the unhappy little land with bloodshed.[140]

Walter goes on to claim that through Ailred's efforts peace was restored, with the father – clearly Fergus – being prevailed upon to renounce his lordship and retire into a monastery, leaving the sons to rule jointly in amity. It is a bare-bones narrative concerned more with the vilification of Fergus and his family than with the background to the civil strife in Galloway, but it does appear to reflect faithfully the divisions within the ruling dynasty that were to weaken the lordship for nearly three decades.

The outline picture of irreconcilable internecine strife painted by Walter Daniel is re-drawn in graphic detail in the accounts of the continuing feud between Uhtred and Gillebrigte that culminated in the former's violent death in 1174. Less sensationally, however, there are hints throughout the 1150s of division and mounting tension within the lordly family, with Uhtred in particular moving towards a relationship with the Scottish crown which threatened a closeness, if not subservience, which ran counter to the line pursued by Fergus. By the 1150s, Uhtred was a mature adult, married and with a growing family, but apparently possessed no independent landholding from which to support himself other than the property in Cumberland which had come to him as his wife's dowry. Approaching forty, he must have viewed his father's longevity with mounting unease, and may have used the opening into the Scoto-Northumbrian ruling elite brought by his marriage to a kinswoman of David I to compensate for his political impotence in Galloway. Uhtred's standing as a landholder in Cumberland, albeit on a small scale, opened new social and cultural horizons to him, and through it he continued to attach himself to the court and policies of King David in spite of the breach between Fergus and the king in 1147. Evidence for this link is slender and circumstantial, but his independent presence in attendance on David can be traced from soon after 1140.[141] More significant, however, is his presence at Roxburgh in early 1159, where he witnessed Máel Coluim mac Henry's great charter to the monks of Kelso.[142] His high positioning in the list of witnesses, where he is the first secular dignitary named after the earls, indicates that he held a prominent role amongst the circle of nobles then attendant on the king, the majority of whom were drawn from the colonial nobility of south-eastern Scotland or the Gaelic aristocracy from beyond the Forth. Uhtred stands out in stark isolation among such company, and it is difficult to avoid the conclusion that his attendance at court was in some way linked to the situation in Galloway.

The reasons for Uhtred's appearance at Roxburgh in 1159, where he met with his nephew, Godred, are unknown. While his independent presence there may indicate that the decisive breach with Fergus had already occurred, it is equally possible that he was representing his ageing father at a major assembly of Máel Coluim's principal vassals, at which important business concerning his family, i.e. the position of Godred, and the implications of the king's impending absence from the kingdom would have been discussed. Whatever the case, Uhtred evidently distanced himself from his father in the following months.

Traditional accounts of the downfall of Fergus in 1160 link his name to dissident elements within Scotland, in particular to the so-called 'Revolt of the Earls' that greeted Máel Coluim on his return from Toulouse.[143] These accounts are based on a conventional reading of annal entries in the Holyrood and Melrose chronicles. The first of these states baldly that 'King Malcolm led an army three times into Galloway, and thence, having defeated his federate enemies, he returned with peace and without loss'.[144] There is no link made with any action by the earls, which receives no notice in the Holyrood chronicle. In the Melrose account, however, we are provided with more detail. This narrates how in 1160 'Malcolm, king of Scots, came from the army of Toulouse, and when he had come to the city which is called Perth, Earl Ferteth and six other earls, enraged against the king because he had gone to Toulouse, besieged the city and wished to take the king captive, but their presumption in no way prevailed.' This account is followed by the statement that, 'King Malcolm went into Galloway on three occasions with a great army, and at last subdued them.'[145] The 'them' in the Melrose account has normally been taken to refer back to the earls in the preceding section, while the 'federate enemies' of Holyrood has been interpreted as a reference to Fergus and his comital allies, but it has never been explained satisfactorily why the earls of Scotia should have fled to Galloway from Perth rather than seeking the security and resources of their own territories. The failure of any other contemporary account to make any mention of what would have been a major political and military incident has, moreover, seen the significance of the encounter between the king and his earls downgraded from a 'revolt' to an 'orchestrated protest'.[146] Daphne Brooke, furthermore, has dismissed the link between the Perth incident and the royal campaign into Galloway, other than as a demonstration of the unity of the political community behind the king.[147]

All that can be agreed with certainty from the above is that Máel Coluim successfully invaded Galloway in 1160 and defeated Fergus and his ally or allies. The use of the term 'federate enemies', suggests that Fergus's accomplices in his rebellion were not his sons, who would surely have been named as such. It is possible that the reference is to Fergus and Somairle, who certainly re-entered the king's peace shortly afterwards. The Chronicle of Holyrood makes it clear that Fergus had been defeated and disgraced, for, following on directly from its reference to the invasion, it records that 'Fergus, prince of Galloway, received the habit of a canon in the church of the Holy Rood of Edinburgh, and he gave to them the vill which is called Dunrod.'[148] What prompted the invasion is unknown, but Brooke has conjectured that raids into adjoining Nithsdale and Clydesdale, and the seizure of portions of the territory between the Nith and the Urr, may have occurred in 1159.[149] That his fall may have been the consequence of something grander than cattle raids, however, might be indicated by the dating clause attached to a charter of Máel Coluim issued at the king's Christmas court at Perth in 1160. This places the issue of the charter in the Christmas 'next after the agreement of the king and Somerled'.[150] The year had clearly seen the rigorous reassertion of Scottish royal authority after the weakness of the period 1153–59 and the settling of a whole range of problems of quite long standing: Somairle may have been in defiance of Máel Coluim's authority continuously since 1153. The fall of Fergus, whose power was already considerably weakened by dissension within his own family, may have been the easy route towards bringing Somairle to terms. The defeat of an important ally and the re-advance of Scottish power in the Solway region that followed offered a real threat to Somairle's recently established control of Mann. It was not the first, nor would it be the last time that involvement in the stormy waters of the Irish Sea and the Isles would bring ruin to a lord of Galloway.

The Scottish invasion of Galloway and overthrow of Fergus provided a striking demonstration of the extent to which the pattern of authority in, and the political geography of, northern mainland Britain had been transformed in the period 1100–60. Set in the midst of a major period of dynamic state building within the British Isles, the career of Fergus provides a powerful illustration of the mechanisms at work within that process.[151] Although a state-builder himself, Fergus ultimately proved to be a casualty of the expansion of the more successful and politically mature kingdoms of England and Scotland, and their growing rivalry for the domination of the British Isles or, more particularly, of the petty states of the maritime west. His power had been advanced at first by Henry I, for whom he was a useful agent in consolidating his hold on the Irish Sea littoral and lending stability to his northern frontier, and behind whom Fergus could shelter from the progressive expansion of Scottish ambitions in the 1120s and early 1130s. The removal of the powerful figure of Henry and his replacement as the dominant force in British politics not by his successor as king of England but by the aggressive, ambitious and opportunistic king of Scots, brought Fergus into a new dependency. However Fergus may have viewed his personal status and relationship vis-à-vis King David, it was inevitable that Scottish domination of Galloway would bring the lordship into closer dependence on and, probably, absorption into, Scotland. This process was being accelerated by the bonds with the Anglo-Norman ruling elite that had been forged during the period of English domination. Fergus may have attempted to throw that process into reverse after 1153, possibly through revival of his English links, but more likely through association with Somairle. Such an alignment, however, failed to recognise the extent to which the power of the Scottish monarchy had spread throughout what had been Cumbria. From being a remote, eastern lowlands-based power the Scottish crown had extended its effective sphere to the landward limits of

Fergus's domain. Galloway was no longer a remote fastness from which the king of Scots could be defied. Domination of Galloway was now vital for the security of the whole south and west of the enlarged kingdom and the dangerous liaisons of its ruler with the maverick powers of the Irish Sea and Isles posed a threat that had to be neutralised. The new political realities of the mid-twelfth century dictated that Galloway could not survive outwith the Scottish realm. It was the unpredictability of Fergus that sealed his fate.

Notes

1 E.g., Ailred, *Saints of Hexham*, 178–80.
2 Scott, 'Strathclyde, 1092–1153'.
3 W. Mackenzie, *The History of Galloway from the Earliest Period to the Present Time* (Kirkcudbright, 1841), i, 167–68; Ailred, *De Standardo*, 197.
4 M'Kerlie, *Land and Their Owners*, i, 109–11.
5 Huyshe, Grey Galloway, 107–08.
6 Robertson, *Story of Galloway*, 41.
7 A. Agnew, *A History of the Hereditary Sheriffs of Galloway* (Edinburgh, 1864), 613; J. Kevan MacDowall, *Carrick Gallovidian* (Ayr, 1947), 34; J. M. McGill, 'A genealogical survey of the ancient lords of Galloway', *Scottish Genealogist*, ii (1955), 3–6.
8 Oram, thesis, 33–35.
9 Radford, 'Excavations at Whithorn, 1949', 99–100.
10 Ibid., 99.
11 Notes by P.A.Munch in *Chron. Mann* (Munch), 167–68.
12 Sellar, 'Origins and ancestry of Somerled'.
13 *Fergus*, ed. E. Martin (Halle, 1872); K. Webster, 'Galloway and the Romances', *Modern Language Notes*, lv (1940), 363–66; M. D. Legge, 'Some notes on the Roman de Fergus', *TDGNHAS*, xxvii (1948–49), 164; J. Greenberg, 'Guillaume le Clerc and Alan of Galloway', Proceedings of the *Modern Language Association*, lxvi (1951), 524–33; B. Schmolke-Hasselmann, 'Der arthurische Versroman, et "Le Roman de Fergus": technique narrative et intention politique', in *An Arthurian Tapestry: Essays in Memory of Lewis Thorpe*, ed. K. Varty (Glasgow, 1981), 342–53.
14 M. D. Legge, 'The father of Fergus of Galloway', *SHR*, xliii (1964), 86–87.
15 *Orkneyinga Saga*, 208–09.
16 Duncan, *Making of the Kingdom*, 163.
17 Owen, *William the Lion*, Chapter 6.
18 For David's relationship with Henry in respect of 'Cumbria' see Kapelle, *Norman Conquest of the North*, Chapter 7.
19 Scott, 'Strathclyde 1092–1153'.
20 Ibid., 18–19.
21 Ibid., 19–21.
22 Ibid., 24.
23 For a detailed discussion of this dispute, see below Chapter 6.
24 Scott, 'Strathclyde 1092–1153', 25.
25 Ibid., 25–26.
26 For discussion of the dating of the mottes, see below Chapter 8.
27 See below, p. 221.
28 See below, p. 221.
29 See, W. D. H. Sellar, 'Marriage, concubinage and divorce in Gaelic Scotland', *TGSI*, li (1978–80).
30 But see Brooke, *Wild Men*, 80.

31 *Scots Peerage*, iv, 136–37 and note 1; Duncan, *Making of the Kingdom,* 181. Compare this with Barrow, 'Lordship and feudal settlement in Cumbria', 128.
32 William of Newburgh, 186.
33 See below Chapter 3 for a detailed discussion of this matter.
34 *Chron. Mann*, 6, where his reign is erroneously implied to have commenced *c.*1095. See also Anderson, *Early Sources*, ii, 98.
35 *Chron. Mann*, 9.
36 *AFM* s.a. 1107.
37 Duffy, 'Irishmen and Islesmen', 114–15.
38 Anderson, *Early Sources*, 143 and note 2.
39 *Chron. Mann*, 10.
40 Kapelle, *Norman Conquest of the North*, 199–200.
41 *SAEC*, 128–29.
42 Duffy, 'Irish–Welsh relations', 100.
43 Anderson, *Early Sources*, 144; Thornton, 'Genealogy of Gruffudd ap Cynan', 87–90; Duffy, *Ireland in the Middle Ages*, 44.
44 See e.g. C. Given-Wilson and A. Curteis, *The Royal Bastards of Medieval England* (London, 1984), 71.
45 Mackenzie, *History of Galloway*, i, 70; Chalmers, *Caledonia*, i, 366 and note.
46 *Scots Peerage*, iv, 136.
47 *The Complete Peerage*, eds G. E. Cockayne and others, xi (London, 1949), Appendix D, 105–21.
48 Roger of Howden, ii, 105; Benedict of Peterborough, i, 80.
49 *The Chronicle of Robert of Torigny, in Chronicles of Stephen etc.*, ed. R. Howlett (London, 1889), iv, 229.
50 *Chron. Mann* (Munch), 60.
51 Epistolae S. Anselmi, *Patrologia Latina*, ed. J-P. Migne, ii (Paris, 1854), no. lxxxiv.
52 *Glasgow Registrum*, no.3.
53 Dugdale, *Monasticon Anglicanum*, vi, 838. For the identification of Galloway, see Brooke, 'Fergus', 55 and appendix B.
54 *Knights of St John*, xxvii–xxviii.
55 E.g., Stringer, 'Records', no. 1.
56 Kapelle, *Norman Conquest of the North*, 200–201, 206; Scott, 'Strathclyde 1092–1153', 29.
57 Kapelle, *Norman Conquest of the North*, 198.
58 Ibid., 206; Scott, 'Strathclyde 1092–1153', 29–30.
59 *RRS*, i, 38–39.
60 *Kelso Liber*, v.
61 Symeon of Durham, *Historia Regum*, ii, 265.
62 *APS*, i, 82.
63 Kapelle, *Norman Conquest of the North*, 206; Barrow, 'Lordship and feudal settlement in Cumbria', 126, 131–32.
64 Kapelle, *Norman Conquest of the North*, especially 130–33, 142, 144–46, 147–48.
65 E.g. Oram, 'David I and the Scottish conquest and colonisation of Moray'.
66 Stringer, *Stephen*, 28–37.
67 *Chron. Melrose*, 33; Richard of Hexham, 146.
68 *Glasgow Registrum*, no. 3.
69 *Richard of Hexham*, 146.
70 *Ibid.*, 150–151.
71 *John of Hexham*, 289.
72 Ailred, *De Standardo*, 187–88; *Richard of Hexham*, 152–53, 155–56, 156–59.
73 *Richard of Hexham*, 177–78. The other hostages were the sons of Gospatric,

Earl of Dunbar, Hugh de Morville, Malise, Earl of Strathearn, and an Earl Mac—.

74 Stringer, *Stephen*, 32–37.

75 Duffy, 'Irishmen and Islesmen', 121–23.

76 Brooke, *Wild Men*, 90–91. For a detailed discussion of these events, see Chapter 6 below.

77 Ibid., 95–99.

78 The fifteenth-century Holyrood tradition concerning the foundation of the priory cell at Traill by Fergus, narrates how he regained David's peace after having incurred royal offence through unspecified but serious challenges to the king's will. 'Historia Fundacionis Prioratus Insule de Traile', *Bannatyne Miscellany*, ii (Edinburgh, 1836), 19–20. While this most probably represents a garbling of the events of 1160, when Fergus was forced to submit to Máel Coluim IV, the linkage with David I might preserve the memory of an earlier quarrel.

79 *Holyrood Liber*, no. 24.

80 *AT*, s.a. 1118.

81 Flanagan, *Irish Society*, 30–31; Duffy, 'Irishmen and Islesmen', 117–18

82 See below, Chapter 6.

83 William of Newburgh, *Historia Rerum Anglicarum*, 73–76. For a discussion of the Wimund episode, see below pp. 71–3.

84 *Chron. Mann*, 11–12.

85 Ibid., 12.

86 *Chron. Mann*, s.a. 1153.

87 McDonald, *Kingdom of the Isles*, 49–51.

88 E.g. *RRS*, i, 3, 7–8, no. 179; Duncan, *Making of the Kingdom*, 166–67; *Chron. Holyrood*, 38. Geoffrey Barrow changed his opinion expressed in *RRS*, i, and subsequently identified the meic Aeda as descendants of an earlier earl of Ross rather than of a bastard son of Alasdair mac Máel Coluim: see, *RRS*, ii, 13 and Barrow, *Kingship and Unity*, 51.

89 Orderic Vitalis, *Historia Ecclesiastica*, viii, 20.

90 Compare, for example, Marjorie Chibnall's translation of the text with the Latin original. This convention of adding MacHeth appears to originate with Anderson, who inserted [MacHeth] after Malcolm in his 1908 translation of the passage from Orderic: *SAEC*, 158.

91 Orderic Vitalis, *Historia Ecclesiastica*, viii, 20; *Chron. Robert of Torigny*, 118.

92 *Chron. Melrose*, s.a. 1134.

93 Ailred of Rievaulx, *De Standardo*, 193–94.

94 *Chron. Holyrood*, 128; Scott, 'Strathclyde 1092–1153', 34.

95 *RRS*, i, no. 118 and discussion on p. 40; *ESC*, no. 153. See also Duncan and Brown, 'Argyll and the Isles', 195.

96 *ESC*, no. 240.

97 Ailred of Rievaulx, *De Standardo*, 191. Note that I have rejected my original suggestion that Galwegians were possibly present in David's armies as mercenaries: Oram, 'Fergus', 123–24; cf. MacDonald, *Kingdom of the Isles*, 48–49.

98 In 1134, for example, he established a colony of monks from Furness Abbey, Stephen's own foundation, at Rushen in Mann (*Chron. Mann*, s.a. 1134) and, some time after that date gave Furness the right to elect the bishops of the Isles.

99 Stringer, *Stephen*, 33, 35.

100 William of Newburgh, *Historia Rerum Anglicarum*, 73–76.

101 Raine, *Historians of York*, ii, 372.

102 See Watt, *Fasti*, p. 197–200.

103 Scott, 'Strathclyde 1092–1153', 37. Skene, *Celtic Scotland*, i, 464 and note 64.

104 I am indebted to Alex Woolf for drawing my attention to the similarities between William of Newburgh's account and the *Carmen de Morte Sumerledi*, in Anderson, *Early Sources*, ii, 256–8.

105 For a discussion of mutilation of political enemies, see J. Gillingham, 'Killing and mutilating political enemies in the British Isles from the late twelfth to the early fourteenth century', in B. Smith (ed.), *Britain and Ireland 900–1300* (Cambridge, 1999). Archie Duncan dates his rebellion to 1142 in *Making of the the Kingdom*, 166, but William of Newburgh's account suggests that it had been underway for some considerable time before he came to terms.

106 For Angus, see *ASC*, D, s.a 1080 = 1130; *AU*, s.a. 1130; *Chron. Robert de Torigni*, s.a. 1130; *Chron. Melrose*, s.a. 1130. For Wimund's identification as Angus's son, see Duncan, *Making of the Kingdom*, 166; Barrow, *Kingship and Unity*, 51.

107 William of Newburgh, *Historia Rerum Anglicarum*, 74.

108 *RRS*, ii, 12.

109 Oram, 'David I and Moray', 9–10.

110 *Chron. Mann*, s.a. 1102; Duncan and Brown, 'Argyll and the Isles', 196; McDonald, *Kingdom of the Isles*, 49.

111 *AFM*, s.a. 1154. The annal speaks also of the hiring of ships from the shores of Scotland, presumably meaning Argyll, since the Stewarts had only recently started their career as major Clyde estuary lords.

112 Duffy, 'Irishmen and Islesmen', 125.

113 See, for example, Brooke, *Wild Men*, 92–95.

114 *Chron. Holyrood*, 124–25.

115 Ibid., 126.

116 *Chron. Mann*, s.a. 1144 = ?1154–56; ibid., s.a. ?1156; *Chron. Holyrood*, 128; *Chron. Melrose*, s.a. 1156. For discussion of these events see, Duncan and Brown, 'Argyll and the Isles', 196; Duffy, 'Irishmen and Islesmen', 126–28; McDonald, *Kingdom of the Isles*, 52–58.

117 *Chron. Mann*, s.a. 1144 = 1154–56.

118 *AU*, s.a. 1162; *AFM*, ii, 1147. For discussion of these events, see Duffy, 'Irishmen and Islesmen', 127–28.

119 Duffy, 'Irishmen and Islesmen', 127; *Chron. Mann*, s.a. 1164.

120 McDonald, *Kingdom of the Isles*, 56.

121 *AFM*, s.a. 1154; McDonald, *Kingdom of the Isles*, 55.

122 *AU*, s.a. 1164; McDonald, *Kingdom of the Isles*, 205–206; MacQuarrie, 'Kings, lords and abbots', 355–56.

123 *Chron. Mann*, s.a. 1144.

124 *Chron. Mann*, s.a. 1098; *AFM*, s.a. 1142; Duffy, 'Irishmen and Islesmen', 121–23.

125 Duffy, 'Irishmen and Islesmen', 126.

126 *AU*, s.a. 1164.

127 *The Chronicle of Mann* dates the encounter to the night of 5–6 January 1156. January 1156, in the Julian calendar that ran from New Year's Day on 25 March, would be January 1157 by modern reckoning.

128 *Chron. Mann*, s.a. 1158.

129 *Pipe Roll 4 Henry II*, 155, 168.

130 Warren, *Henry II*, 69–70.

131 Ibid., 71.

132 *RRS*, i, no. 131. Interestingly, Uhtred, son of Fergus, was also present at this assembly, where he stood first in order of precedence amongst the laymen after Godred and the Scottish earls.

133 *Heimskringla*, Håkon Broad-shoulder, c. 17.

134 McDonald, *Kingdom of the Isles*, 52.

135 Scott, 'Strathclyde 1092–1153', 25 and note 50.

136 Scott, 'Origins of Dundrennan and Soulseat', 40.

137 *Chron. Holyrood*, 131; *Chron. Melrose*, s.a. 1157.

138 E.g. Brooke, *Wild Men*, 75.

139 Walter Daniel misdates this visit of Ailred's to Galloway to 1163, by which time Fergus had been overthrown. The situation he describes clearly pre-dates 1160. From independent sources, Ailred is known to have visited Scotland in 1159, and it is most probable that his visitation of Rievaulx's daughter-house at Dundrennan, which provided the opportunity for his intervention in Galwegian affairs as recorded by Walter, occurred in that year. Scott, however, suggests an earlier visit took place in 1156: Scott, 'Origins of Dundrennan and Soulseat'.

140 Walter Daniel, *Life of Ailred*, 45–46.

141 *Kelso Liber*, ii, no. 375.

142 *RRS*, i, no. 131.

143 E.g. Duncan, *Making of the Kingdom*, 163–64; Barrow, *Kingship and Unity*, 47–48; Oram, Thesis, 91–93.

144 *Chron. Holyrood*, 136–37.

145 *Chron. Melrose*, s.a. 1160.

146 Lynch, *Scotland*, 85–86.

147 Brooke, 'Fergus', 51–55.

148 *Chron. Holyrood*, 137.

149 Brooke, 'Fergus', 54–55.

150 *RRS*, i, no. 175.

151 For discussion of this key theme of state building, see Davies, *Domination and Conquest*, and Frame, *Political Development of the British Isles*.

3

DIVISION AND RECOVERY

THE LORDSHIP DIVIDED:
UHTRED AND GILLEBRIGTE, 1161–74

The overthrow of Fergus removed the nexus that had bound Galloway together as a unitary territory. It had been his personal creation and, in common with the personal empires built by his contemporaries, Óláfr Gothfrithsson and Somairle mac Gillebrigte, it threatened to prove an impermanent feature on the political map of twelfth-century Britain. Fergus's demise and the tensions between his heirs saw the re-opening of the internal divisions which he had so recently welded together. This was aided by the intervention of Máel Coluim IV, for whom the break up of Fergus's dominion offered an opportunity to extend his authority into a highly strategic and volatile region where the activities of both English and Irish kings had so recently threatened Scottish interests. His actions, of course, had consequences far beyond Galloway, represented most tellingly by the sudden disappearance of the lordship and its rulers as significant players in the politics of the Irish Sea and Hebridean zones. After Fergus, indeed, it is only the obits of the lords of Galloway that are noticed in Irish chronicles until the remarkable career of his great-grandson, Alan, who re-staked his family's place as the dominant military and naval power in the region after forty years of withdrawal. The partition of Galloway into two territorial lordships, one at least held by a man who had already formed close political and familial bonds with the Scottish crown, and the effective severance of the links with Mann and Ireland which had been forged by Fergus, represented a major advance for the Scots on their path to domination of the northern British mainland and isles. To some extent, moreover, it compensated for the loss of Scottish control over Cumbria and re-affirmed the spread of Scottish interests into the Irish Sea zone.

While partition favoured the Scots, it had not been on the agenda of either of Fergus's sons, both of whom had been seeking the lordship over all Galloway and superiority over the other. The animosity between Uhtred and Gillebrigte was deep-seated and was clearly centred upon matters of inheritance and seniority. What was at issue was lordship, not property, for both sought seniority over the other and, with that position, the social leadership of their father's domain, not physical possession of the other's lands.[1] Howden is careful to stress this point: Gillebrigte did not resent Uhtred's inheritance of their father's estates east of the Cree, it was the fact that he held them as his social equal, free from his overlordship. A divided lordship was a deeply unsatisfactory compromise that left both aggrieved and bitterly resentful of an arrangement that, in their opinions, cheated them of their birthright. While personally unsatisfactory, it offered some resolution of the tensions raised by clearly conflicting modes of inheritance and succession, with Uhtred benefiting from the newly favoured 'feudal' laws of primogeniture and receiving recognition of his rights within Gaelic tradition.

The rival regional power-bases that may have been established by Uhtred and Gillebrigte as early as the mid-1150s, during the three-cornered struggle with Fergus,[2] clearly formed the basis of the 1160–61 Scottish-brokered partition. Uhtred's lordship lay east of the Cree and it is evident that he had received the original core of his father's dominion in the lower Dee valley, focused on Kirkcudbright.[3] Although it is nowhere stated explicitly, it can be assumed that Gillebrigte's portion comprised the lands west of the Cree. Details of the government of Galloway during this thirteen-year period to Uhtred's death are scanty, but it appears from the events of 1174 that Máel Coluim IV and subsequently William had imposed royal agents in a supervisorial role within both segments of the lordship. Lower Nithsdale, whose native lord, Radulf, disappears from the sources around this time, played an important role in this system. Radulf last appears in a royal charter datable to between late March and early December 1165, issued at Jedburgh;[4] he witnessed no surviving charter of William. There is no indication that he had any direct successor, and the crown may have assumed control of his remaining lands despite the potential claims of his kinsmen in upper Nithsdale.[5] This brought Dumfries, at the lowest fording point on the Nith, into royal hands and guaranteed the crown a stronghold on the fringes of Galloway that also possessed direct sea access to the Solway.[6]

The dismemberment of Radulf's domain may have commenced as early as 1160, extended over several years and have preceded his death, for he had evidently lost control of the territory between the Nith and the Urr before 1165. It is nowhere stated, but it is possible that he had been implicated in the actions that had brought the downfall of Fergus. The date at which Desnes Ioan was confirmed in the possession of the lords of Galloway cannot be fixed precisely, but Uhtred's grants of the church of Urr to Holyrood Abbey and of property in Troqueer to St Peter's Hospital, York, can be dated no later than 1164.[7] Uhtred may possibly have gained recognition of his control of the district in that year, confirming an earlier acquisition by his father or himself, but that is purely speculative. Irrespective of the circumstances through which Uhtred acquired Desnes Ioan, the region remained distinct from his lands west of the Urr in that it was burdened with dues to the Scottish crown that derived from its former status as part of David I's principality of Cumbria. The distinction was emphasised in ecclesiastical terms by the maintenance of the diocesan boundary between Glasgow and Whithorn on the Urr. A further mark of distinction between Desnes Ioan and the remainder of Uhtred's domain was the fashion in which he disposed of it. While he also alienated some land and property rights to aristocratic colonists and non-Galwegian monasteries west of the Urr, Desnes Ioan was parcelled out with great rapidity in a programme of intensive settlement.[8]

The concession of control over Desnes Ioan may have been a sign of Uhtred's favour with Máel Coluim IV, but it is clear that despite the evidently good relationship which had existed between them before 1160, the king had acted to impose a more rigorous overlordship on Galloway than had been exercised by previous kings of Scots. The establishment of a supervisory system within Galloway was just one manifestation of this tighter control. That Máel Coluim considered Galloway to have been integrated into his realm is also demonstrated by the few pieces of royal legislation from his reign that touch upon the region. The clearest indication of this is in the extension of the king's peace to Galloway, indicated in a brieve directed to Uhtred and Gillebrigte in Galloway and Radulf and Domnall in Nithsdale. This stated that the men of the canons of Holyrood going to and from their land at Dunrod had been taken under firm royal protection.[9] The language of the brieve implies that Malcolm was confident of his authority over Galloway, and that through his conquest of 1160 and subsequent imposition of royal officers he could enforce and maintain his peace in the interests of his dependants. The king's peace could be maintained only within the sphere of effective royal government. In Máel Coluim's mind, Galloway lay firmly within that sphere.

Gillebrigte, too, may have benefited from the crown's inability to absorb all the lands over which it was beginning to assert more rigorous lordship in the mid-twelfth century. It is only with the benefit of hindsight that we can see how disastrously his relationship with the Scottish crown was to end, but in 1160–61, Gillebrigte was an unknown quantity that the king needed to court and to bring firmly within his circle. As with Uhtred, the principal mechanism for binding Gillebrigte into the Scottish polity may have been marriage. The identity of Gillebrigte's wife is unknown, but there is a body of circumstantial evidence which suggests that she may have been a daughter or sister of Donnchad II, earl of Fife, the greatest of the Gaelic magnates of Scotland and a key political figure in the reigns of Máel Coluim IV and William the Lion. In particular, the generosity of Gillebrigte's son, Donnchad, to the nunnery at North Berwick founded by Earl Donnchad I of Fife c.1150, might indicate a family interest in what would be otherwise a remote and obscure community from the context of Carrick.[10] Furthermore, there is the introduction of the name Donnchad into the Carrick family and the close relationship maintained between the Carricks and other Fife families, culminating with the marriage of Countess Marjory to the Fife knight, Adam de Kilconquhar. Kinship between the Fifes and Carricks may have added a further dimension, moreover, to Isabel, countess of Buchan's involvement in the inauguration of Robert Bruce as king in 1306. If the Carrick–Fife marriage occurred, the possible identity of the bride indicates the level of Scottish concern over the integration of Galloway into the kingdom. A marital tie with the greatest native comital house might also have provided the context for the award to Gillebrigte of extensive new lands. As with Uhtred, the grant of land which, at least nominally, had formed part of the Scottish realm in the later eleventh and earlier twelfth centuries, would have served to bring Gillebrigte into a direct 'feudal' relationship with the crown. It is at this time that Carrick may have passed into his hands, for the leading Carrick kindred of Kennedy was to be named among the native forces ranged against Roland, son of Uhtred, in 1185, and the district was to be established by the crown after c.1190 as a separate lordship for Gillebrigte's son, Donnchad. Carrick, though, had been named as one of the regions of that part of greater Galloway controlled by David I and which fell within the diocese of Glasgow, which might indicate that it was added to the lordship in the 1160s.[11]

Gillebrigte and Uhtred's relationship with the Scottish crown after 1161 appears straightforward. According to Fordun, Uhtred had been held hostage by the king after Fergus's surrender,[12] but this is borne out by no earlier source and would appear at odds with the closeness to the Scottish court displayed by him in the 1150s. There are, instead, indications that Máel Coluim was attempting to build on this earlier relationship and aimed to draw the brothers more firmly into the royal orbit. Between c.1161 and 1172, both men witnessed a handful of important royal acta, all issued at significant gatherings of the Scottish ruling elites at the royal court. Uhtred appeared at Edinburgh and Jedburgh,[13] Gillebrigte at Edinburgh,[14] and both brothers jointly at Lochmaben to witness the confirmation of Bruce tenure of Annandale by King William.[15] Only in the last instance can any of these appearances be linked directly to south-western politics, the others pertaining to ecclesiastical subjects which only affected the brothers insofar as they held lands which fell under the jurisdiction of the bishop of Glasgow. Their presence at these gatherings should probably be interpreted in simple terms as the paying court of vassals to their overlord.

Uhtred's more regular presence at court dated back to Fergus's lifetime and the evident favour displayed towards him by David I. This may have made him more receptive to the influences of continental Frankish culture that were pervading Scotland in the mid-twelfth century. Certainly, he enthusiastically embraced many of the attributes of the new culture: the foundation and endowment of monasteries (notably Lincluden nunnery and the abbeys of Holyrood and Holm Cultram); the introduction of colonists holding land for knight service; and the use of parchment to record his acts.[16] Gillebrigte's two appearances at court after 1161 and the scarcity of evidence for acts of infeftment – beyond the reference to him as 'my lord' by Roger de Skelbrooke, a south Yorkshire knight who held the lands of Greenan on the Doon in Carrick in the time of Donnchad mac Gillebrigta[17] – monastic foundation or endowment on his part stands in sharp contrast and, as stressed by Stringer, appears to bear out his 'traditional reputation as an arch-conservative' who was either unwilling or unable to adapt to the rapidly changing world with which he was confronted.[18] The loss of the cartularies of the Wigtownshire monasteries of Soulseat and Whithorn offers a partial explanation for this contrast between the brothers, but his failure to make any gift to non-Galwegian houses, in stark contrast to Uhtred, is more difficult to explain. This difference in outlook probably reflects the contrasting roles developed by Fergus for his two sons. Uhtred, as the grandson of Henry I, was introduced to Anglo-Norman social and cultural traditions in his youth, if not through his mother's influence from childhood. His association with Holm Cultram originated with his marital ties to the Allerdale family, on the fringes of whose territory the abbey lay. The Allerdale link cemented Uhtred's openness to foreign cultural influences: his kin connections through them not only tied him into the wider family circle of the Scottish royal house but also forged links with the Cumbrian aristocracy which provided him with many of the colonists whom he introduced on to his lands. The clearest evidence for the difference in outlook that this engendered may be seen in the witness lists to Uhtred's *acta*, where, while men of clearly Gaelic lineage continued to dominate his following, a new colonial aristocracy was of increasing importance as his career as lord of Galloway progressed.[19] By way of contrast, if the men who witnessed the charters of Donnchad of Carrick can be taken as being largely representative of his father Gillebrigte's followers, then it is clear that his following remained of strongly Gaelic character.[20] Uhtred's royal Norman blood secured him the precedence in his father's eyes and won him access to the court of the king of Scots and a good marriage during his father's lifetime, while Gillebrigte, despite his mother's probably illustrious ancestry, was all but passed over until after 1160: for Fergus, he had no place in the developing relationship between Galloway and the two dominant mainland British powers. This exclusion from the glittering world which was unfolding beyond the frontiers of Galloway may, more than any other factor, have triggered the deep cultural conservatism which Gillebrigte displayed throughout his life.

Evidence for the intensity of Scottish royal intervention in the affairs of Galloway during this period is scanty, with much being extrapolated backwards from the comments made by Roger of Howden in respect of the 1174 rebellion. The Scottish connections of many of the colonists introduced by Uhtred onto his lands are discussed in detail in Chapter 6, together with evidence for the tighter supervision of the south-west by royal agents. This apart, however, there is little to support arguments in favour of intrusive Scottish overlordship. One indication of a shift caused by

Galloway's new political affiliations, however, can be seen in King William's intervention in the proprietary control of the churches and chapels in the Dee valley upstream from Kirkcudbright, discussed in Chapter 2. In c.1172–74, these were stripped from Iona's possession and granted instead to Holyrood.[21] The royal charter recording this act presents it in terms of a direct gift by the king – which would be a dramatic expression of the degree of power exercised by the crown within Galloway – but in Bishop John's general confirmation of the properties and rights of Holyrood within Whithorn diocese, dated c.1200–09, the grant of these churches to Holyrood is attributed to Uhtred.[22] It has been suggested that this was a considered act of deprivation, or was an act of ingratiation by Uhtred in an effort to win William's favour.[23] It should, perhaps, be seen more in the context of the politics of the western Highlands and Islands than Galloway and may have been linked to the renewed involvement of external powers in the affairs of the Isles.

The initial grant of these churches to Iona may have arisen from Fergus's renewed involvement in Manx and Hebridean politics after 1153. The marriage of Affrica to Óláfr of Mann, within whose kingdom Iona lay, may have provided the link. Furthermore, in 1153, together with his Manx son-in-law, Fergus had fought in alliance with Muirchertach mac Lochlainn, King of Ailech, whose people, the Cenél nEógain, were associated intimately with Iona and were patrons of the abbot of Derry, the leading figure in the community of Colum-Cille. By the 1170s, Muirchertach was dead and the high kingship had passed from meic Lochlainn control into the hands of Ruaidrí ua Conchobair, King of Connacht. Cenél nEógain power, however, was still formidable and its influence was widespread. Its links with Mann were particularly important. There, Muirchertach mac Lochlainn's granddaughter, Findguala, since about 1170–72, had been the concubine of Godred Olafsson, the nephew of Uhtred and Gillebrigte, who had returned from exile in Norway in 1164 to regain his kingdom on the death of Somairle.[24] Through this link, meic Lochlainn influence may have been considerably expanded in the Isles, where they had no doubt already been reviving their interests since the disintegration of Somairle's personal empire after his death, for Godred had re-established control over the northern Hebrides, including Skye.[25] Such a revival of interest in so sensitive a zone by a family with a history of support for pretenders to the Scottish throne must have been of grave concern to the Scots. Enmity between the descendants of Máel Coluim Ceann Mór and the Cenél nEógain appears to have been of long standing and, as will be discussed below, was to continue into the thirteenth century with Cenél nEógain provision of refuge and support for William's rivals for the Scottish throne, the meic Uilleim. There is no record of meic Uilleim activity as early as 1170–72, but this act of deprivation against a community so intimately associated with the meic Lochlainn might point to Cenél nEógain involvement in the disturbances in the Isles which can be glimpsed in contemporary records.[26]

REACTION AND REBELLION:
GILLEBRIGTE AND ROLAND 1174–85

In 1173 the Scottish king, William the Lion, involved himself in the festering quarrel between Henry II and his sons. His involvement must be seen as largely opportunist, driven by the hope that he might thereby regain for himself his lost patrimony in Northumberland, which had been stripped from him in 1157. William planned a full-scale military campaign, summoning his vassals to fulfil their service obligations. Uhtred and Gillebrigte responded with a substantial force of Galwegian warriors, which under their joint leadership marched to join the king in his offensive in Northumberland. Early in July 1174, William is reported to have divided his army to ravage the lands of Odinel d'Umrafville, the major landholder and supporter of Henry II in the region, sending his main force eastwards into the Northumbrian coastal plain, the Galwegians westwards and taking his own retinue to attack William de Vescy's stronghold at Alnwick.[27] On 14 July, the king, attended by only a small force, was surprised outside the castle and taken prisoner.[28] This unlooked for disaster for the Scots provided the Galwegians with the opportunity they required to break the stranglehold which Máel Coluim IV and his brother had fixed on the lordship and immediately on receiving news of William's capture the brothers abandoned the expedition and returned post-haste to Galloway.[29]

From this point, chronicle entries relating to the central events of the rebellion that followed their desertion become more detailed. The chief sources for the rebellion of 1174 and the events of the next decade in Galloway are the chronicles of Roger of Howden, who served in November 1174 as one of Henry II's two emissaries to Galloway.[30] As a consequence of his eyewitness value for the short period of his embassy and the background to it, historians have tended to accept his testimony without question. The possible hyperbole of Roger's account has been recognised,[31] but the authority of his knowledge of local affairs has never been doubted. When it is remembered that the rebellion in Galloway began after the capture of William in mid-July 1174, that Howden did not arrive in Galloway until late November 1174 and that of his two chronicles, the *Gesta* (better known under the name of the *Chronicle of Benedict of Peterborough*) was not compiled until 1192–93 and the *Chronica* until between 1192–93 and 1201–02,[32] there seems little reason to accept his account in anything other than general terms. There is, moreover, no evidence that Roger had any further personal contact with Galloway after his mission in winter 1174–75, although he remained a clerk in Henry II's service and would no doubt have been aware of the main shifts in English policy towards the lordship in the period 1174–86. While constituting the most detailed account of events in the lordship in the decade after 1174, it is essential that Roger no longer be treated as an unimpeachable authority for all things Galwegian. It is the generalities of his narrative rather than the assumptions that have been built upon it which should be stressed.

Howden's account implies that both brothers rose in rebellion immediately on their return to Galloway in late July 1174 and that their first targets were the visible symbols of Scottish domination introduced since 1160.

> But Uhtred, son of Fergus, and his brother Gilbert, when they heard that their lord the king of Scotland was captured, immediately returned with their Galwegians to their own lands, and at once they expelled from Galloway all the bailiffs and wardens whom the king of Scotland had set over them; and all the English and French whom they could seize they slaughtered; and all the fortifications and castles which the king of Scotland had established in their land they besieged, took and levelled, and slaughtered everyone captured inside them.[33]

The fourteenth-century chronicler, John of Fordun, claimed that the rising was the work of Gillebrigte alone and that Uhtred 'a true Scot, and could not be shaken' remained loyal to King William,[34] but this is quite clearly his post-Wars of Independence Anglophobia speaking, and Gillebrigte certainly fits the stereotypical mould of the treacherous betrayer of one's natural lord, as presented in later medieval Scottish historiographical tradition, whom the perfidious English would employ. Having thus freed their territory from Scottish controls, the brothers sent a joint deputation to Henry II, asking him to take the overlordship of Galloway for himself.[35]

The motivation for this appeal to Henry was quite simple. The English king was a distant figure, preoccupied with his territories in France and southern England and who, since 1157, had taken little direct interest in the affairs of the northern part of his realm. Such remoteness was preferable to the interventionist policies of kings of Scots who had advanced their political/military presence to the threshold of Uhtred and Gillebrigte's domains and established their servants within Galloway itself. Henry was, moreover, blood-kin through his mother, Matilda, with Uhtred. If it was the brothers' assumption that Henry would be unable to resist the opportunity of a bloodless extension of his own sphere of titular over lordship but too involved in his difficulties with the king of France and his brood of rebellious sons, they were to be proven sadly mistaken. Annexation of Galloway to the sphere of his direct lordship was certainly attractive to Henry, as evidenced by his sending of an embassy to evaluate the situation. A consummate diplomat and legalist, Henry was not prepared to become embroiled in a political quagmire from which nothing but discredit to his reputation might emerge; nevertheless the promise of territorial gain and the winning of a new vassal in a highly strategic location at the northern end of the Irish Sea zone was not to be dismissed lightly. Certainly, it would have offered strong reinforcement to English royal authority in Ireland, where Henry had been forced to intervene in person in

1171 to curtail the ambitions of the colonial lords, and would have restored English domination of the Irish Sea to the level of Henry I's reign. Furthermore, it would have significantly weakened Scottish power in the region, an important consideration for Henry who had not yet secured a peace settlement with his royal prisoner. The upshot, therefore, was the dispatch of a mission headed by Roger of Howden and Robert de Vaux, sheriff of Cumberland, to explore the issues. In the interim, however, the rivalries between Uhtred and Gillebrigte that had been held in check under Scottish overlordship had re-emerged and were to come rapidly to a bloody conclusion.

Howden provides us with what appears to be a summarised account drawn from what may have been his formal report to Henry.[36] After recounting how the brothers had been at odds over the issue of superiority, he states that Gillebrigte took counsel from his men and that it was decided that Uhtred should be captured and killed.[37] It appears to be Howden's assumption that Uhtred's death was the objective, but his description of how he eventually met his end suggests that it was the capture and mutilation of a political rival in good Norse–Gaelic tradition that was intended. Uhtred, we are told, was captured in 'insulam de', the island of Dee, which is probably Threave Island, where pre-Douglas remains were identified during the excavation of the fourteenth-century castle.[38] His captor was his nephew Máel Coluim mac Gillebrigte,[39] who acted in accord with his father's design and sent in his 'butchers', who blinded and castrated Uhtred and cut out his tongue.[40] They did not, however, kill him and he evidently survived the ordeal, only to die shortly after from his injuries.

A second near-contemporary source, the *Historia Rerum Anglicarum* of William of Newburgh, adds further detail to the generalised Howden narrative. According to him, hostility between the brothers had emerged quite soon after their return to Galloway and culminated in the death of Uhtred at the hands of Gillebrigte's followers. Uhtred's death was followed by an invasion of his lands by Gillebrigte and his cronies, in the course of which many of Uhtred's men had been slaughtered. It was, however, no walkover, but met a stiff campaign of resistance led by Uhtred's heir, his eldest son, Roland, who received the backing of his murdered father's friends and vassals.[41] William's account is commonly passed over in favour of the supposedly better testimony of Roger of Howden, but his brief comments begin to unravel some of the difficulties within the Howden narrative. The former supporters of Uhtred who were targeted by Gillebrigte in the *Historia Rerum Anglicarum*'s account and who supported Roland against his uncle should probably be identified with the colonising tenants introduced into Desnes Ioan primarily. These could certainly be equated with the 'English and French' of the Howden account. It seems likely, moreover, that Howden has conflated the rebellion of Uhtred and Gillebrigte of July and August 1174 and the subsequent joint appeal to

Henry II, and the assault on the foreign dependants of Uhtred carried out between Uhtred's murder and Howden's own arrival in Galloway in late November 1174, into a single event. According to John of Fordun's fourteenth-century account, the rebellion had been in progress for two months before Uhtred's murder on 22 September,[42] which would leave two further months for Gillebrigte to consolidate his position before the arrival of Henry II's envoys in Galloway.

All the contemporary accounts of the events of autumn 1174 are in agreement as to the root of the quarrel between Uhtred and Gillebrigte, pointing to the division of the Galwegian inheritance in 1161 and the issue of seniority.[43] According to Howden:

> Uhtred and Gillebrigte, sons of Fergus, were quarrelling over which of them should be the (over)lord of the other and have lordship over the Galwegians; and had great enmity between them, so that each lay in wait for the other to slay him.[44]

William of Newburgh adds:

> Gilbert, the elder, grieved that he had been defrauded of the entirety of his father's right, and ever hated his brother in his heart, although fear of the king restrained an outburst of the wrath he had conceived.

As has been pointed out recently, despite the claim in the 'official' Howden version that it was the aim of both brothers to kill the other and the particularly gruesome gloss given to the event by William of Newburgh, it is evident that Uhtred's death came about as a consequence of a mutilation which was the primary intention of his attackers.[45] Blinding and castration of political opponents was a common action in the twelfth century, employed across Europe from Byzantium to Ireland. Indeed, it was the fate accorded to many usurpers and pretenders, including in Scotland Domnall III and Wimund.[46]

Uhtred's death was followed by a brutal campaign directed against his remaining supporters in eastern Galloway. This had been largely concluded by the time that Roger of Howden and Robert de Vaux arrived in the lordship and met Gillebrigte on 23 November. Appalled by the manner in which their king's cousin had met his death at the hands of Gillebrigte's men, Howden and Vaux refused to make any binding settlement, despite the added inducement of an annual tribute of 500 cattle and 500 pigs and a one-off payment of 2000 silver merks, until they had apprised Henry of the dramatic turn of events and received his judgement of the situation. Events, moreover, were rapidly overtaking the unfolding rebellion in Galloway, for by the time that his envoys reached him in France, Henry II had already reached a settlement with the captive William the Lion.[47] On 8 December 1174 at Valognes in Normandy, William, who had been held in the royal fortress at Falaise since his capture in July, agreed to what has since become known as the Treaty of Falaise. By its terms, the Scottish king became the liege man of the king of England 'for Scotland and for all his other lands',[48] it being implicit that Galloway was included among these. Equally bound by the advantageous terms of the treaty, Henry was provided with a face-saving formula for ending direct negotiations with a fratricide and instead began to take steps to bring him to account.

On 11 December William, newly released from captivity, was permitted to return to England. There he was to remain until the English administration had received sufficient guarantees of the surrender of the Scottish fortresses stipulated in the treaty. Two months later, on 15 February 1175, William was released from this looser custody and permitted to return to his kingdom.[49] In early August, with Gillebrigte still in revolt, William and his younger brother, Earl David, returned to England for the ratification of the Treaty of Falaise at York. As the agreement expressly stated that William became Henry's vassal for both Scotland and Galloway, it is clear that by 10 August 1175 the English king had no plans to detach the lordship from the territories under Scottish overlordship.[50] Following ratification of the treaty, William was permitted to return to Scotland to raise an army to bring Gillebrigte to book for his rebellion and for the murder of Uhtred. Presumably faced with the continuing opposition of his nephew, Roland, and recognising that his bid to escape from Scottish overlordship had been wrecked by the settlement between William and Henry, Gillebrigte came to terms at some time in 1176.[51]

In the autumn of 1176, William escorted Gillebrigte into England, and around 9 October at Feckenham the lord of Galloway made his peace with Henry, paid him homage and fealty against all men, accepted a fine of 1,000 marks of silver and, as security for the peace, gave his son and heir, Donnchad, as a hostage.[52] Since Henry had already confirmed William's overlordship of Galloway in August 1175, Gillebrigte's performance of homage and fealty without any saving clause in respect of the intervening lordship of the Scottish king should probably be viewed in the light of his policy of receiving the direct homage and fealty of all of William's chief vassals, as set out in the Treaty of Falaise. Certainly, Roger of Howden considered Gillebrigte to have remained a vassal of William, despite this personal submission to Henry. Gillebrigte, however, may have viewed things differently, for, on his return to Galloway, he ordered that all men holding land in the lordship through King William were to leave, any who remained being threatened with death.[53] This was clearly intended to cut the ground from beneath the feet of Uhtred's sons, who could be expected to look to the colonial families introduced by their father, and to the king of Scots, for support in their struggle to secure their patrimony. Whether Henry had intended it or not, Gillebrigte clearly meant to end Scottish overlordship of Galloway.

The extent of Gillebrigte's dominion within Galloway after the settlement of 1176 is debatable. Uhtred's eldest son, Roland, was a young man (*adolescens*)[54] at the time of his father's death and had not sat tamely by and allowed himself to be disinherited. He had been associated with his father in the government of eastern Galloway for a number of years, being referred to in documents from the mid-1160s, witnessing charters and attending the Scottish court.[55] Only William of Newburgh mentions Roland in chronicle accounts of the events of 1174–76, referring to his strenuous resistance to Gillebrigte and the aid that he enjoyed from his father's friends and supporters. It has often been assumed that Gillebrigte gained control of the entire re-united lordship following his submission to Henry, but the evidence of William of Newburgh and aspects of the settlement reached between Roland and Henry in 1186 argue against this. Roland may have succeeded to his father's lands through inheritance – not re-conquest – possibly gaining admission to his patrimony as part of the 1176 compact.[56] However, a more proactive policy may also have been pursued on Roland's part, with portions of his inheritance being granted away to buy military support in the struggle to regain his heritage. This may lie behind the apparent disposal of the Allerdale lands of Torpenhow, which were in the hands of William the Lion's chamberlain, Philip de Valognes, by 1178.[57] The de Valognes' possession of land as vassals of Roland's Balliol descendants in Kirkpatrick Irongray on the northern limit of Desnes Ioan, from which Isobel de Valognes granted the fifteen poundlands of Dalquhairn to the Church of Glasgow in 1250,[58] probably represents the reward for such service. It was certainly mainly in Desnes Ioan that Roland infefted the majority of the colonial families who provided him with service in his struggle with Gillebrigte.[59] However this evidence is read, the dating of Roland's re-grant of land in Kirkgunzeon to the monks of Holm Cultram can be placed within a range from c.1176 to March 1185, and probably before 1185 to allow time for this to be confirmed by papal bull dated 2 May 1185,[60] suggests that he had control of part of his father's lands before Gillebrigte's death. It is implicit from the wording of the charter that the monks had lost possession of the property, presumably abandoning it in the chaòs which erupted in 1174, and that it had lain in Roland's hands for some time before he made this full and detailed restitution.

By force of circumstance, if not from personal inclination, Roland was thrust into a closer relationship with the king of Scots than any previous member of the Galloway dynasty. The favourable settlement that Gillebrigte had obtained from Henry II, together with the ties with the crown established by Uhtred, ensured that Roland had little option other than to turn to William the Lion for council and aid. Certainly, it was in the period 1174–85 that Roland formed his relationships with the narrow circle of supporters who would come to provide his inner curial circle in the period after 1185. The primary link, through the Scottish court, was with the de Morvilles, lords of Lauderdale and Cunninghame and constables of the kings of Scots. The head of that family in Scotland at this time was Richard de Morville, younger brother of Hugh de Morville, lord of North Westmorland. He held the office of constable from 1162 to 1189 and was among the most eminent of William the Lion's *curiales*. Probably soon after 1176, Richard arranged the marriage of his daughter, Helen, to Roland. The marriage itself is a sure indication that Roland was no mere landless exile hanging around the fringes of the royal court, but was clearly deemed a suitable match for the daughter of one of the greatest of the Anglo-Norman nobility in Scotland. The de Morville connection provided Roland with a new circle of dependants on whom he could draw. Through it, he strengthened his existing kinship bond with the family of Cospatric of Workington, whose elder son, Thomas, was a tenant of William de Lancaster, lord of Kendal, brother-in-law of Richard de Morville.[61] Thomas's younger brother, Gilbert, was to become one of Roland's intimates. Through the de Morvilles, Roland also forged ties with the de Vieuxpont family, who were to become his tenants for Sorbie in the Machars after 1185.[62] A final link with the de Morvilles is represented by Roger Masculus, member of a family who were tenants in the lordship of Lauderdale, who received a moiety of the lands of Colvend from Roland.[63] With such powerful backing, consolidated by his ties to the de Berkeley and de Valognes families, which both provided King William with chamberlains, Roland could be assured of Scottish support against his uncle. The *quid pro quo*, however, was recognition of his greater dependence on the Scottish crown.

Gillebrigte's actions in 1176 may have been a response to the continued division of Galloway that Roland's successes entailed and may have been fuelled by his recognition of the increased dependency of his nephew on King William and the bonds that he was forming with families like the de Morvilles. The silence of the sources indicates that an uneasy peace held until the 1180s, but in 1183–84 warfare again erupted as Gillebrigte broke his undertakings made in 1176 and ravaged lands under Scottish lordship (in eastern Galloway?), slaughtering King William's vassals.[64] Our sources do not specify where these lands and men were located, but the territories of Roland, in which he was establishing new colonial families, seem the most likely location. William was unable to negotiate peace and, without securing the permission of Henry II as required by the Treaty of Falaise, had raised an army to crush him. This he disbanded in June 1184 on receiving news of Henry's return from Normandy, without having moved against Galloway. Infuriating to William though this defiance on Gillebrigte's part may have been, the Scottish king had more pressing matters to discuss with Henry and no moves were made to end this fresh outbreak of rebellion. On Gillebrigte's sudden death on 1 January 1185, he was still in rebellion, 'the enemy of his lord, the king of Scots'.[65]

THE LORDSHIP RE-UNITED:
ROLAND 1185–1200

Gillebrigte's death, with his heir Donnchad a hostage in England, left Roland's enemies leaderless. According to Howden, he quickly seized advantage of the situation, assembled an army and invaded his uncle's lands, killing all those who resisted him.[66] His intention, as later became evident, was to eliminate those among the native leadership who could be expected to back Donnchad's claims, to seize their lands and wealth for his own uses, and forcibly to re-unite the lordship to what it had been in his grandfather's days. To secure his takeover, he ordered construction of a network of garrisoned strongpoints from which to dominate the land. Fordun, expanding upon the brief notice given in the *Chronicle of Melrose*, states that Roland had the connivance of William the Lion in all he planned.[67] This is not unlikely, for Roland's personal relationship with the king had been strengthened in the decade since 1176 and he was clearly high in royal favour, as is evident in the advantageous marriage that he had obtained. The extent of William's involvement, however, was revealed only gradually, although his failure to comply with Henry II's infuriated commands to invade Galloway and bring Roland to heel can have left the English king with little doubt of his complicity in the events.

Roland's invasion was no walk-over and met with stiff resistance from the men whom Fordun regarded as the principal supporters of Gillebrigte and 'the instigators and whole cause of all the hostile feeling and war', namely one Gillepadraig, Henry Kennedy, and a certain Samuel.[68] Little can be said of these men other than that the first two represent Gaelic leadership, Kennedy probably being head of the Carrick kindred of that name.[69] His prominence among Gillebrigte's supporters strengthens the probability that Carrick was included within the lordship of Galloway at that time. On 4 July 1185, Roland confronted these men in battle and eliminated them. This did not end the conflict, for a renegade named Gillecolm who had been terrorising parts of Lothian for some time, no doubt seeing the potential offered by a situation where the remnants of the western Galwegian leadership were not as yet prepared to accept Roland's lordship, set himself up as ruler of Gillebrigte's former territories. Roland was forced to stage a second conquest of the area, defeating and slaying Gillecolm on 30 September in a battle that also claimed the life of his own younger brother.[70] The greatest challenge to his control of the territory west of the Cree, however, was yet to be faced.

Henry II was not prepared to accept a *fait accompli* that disinherited the son of a useful vassal, flew in the face of the settlement which he had imposed a decade before, and deprived him of influence over a vitally strategic zone on the north-western periphery of his realm. It was not until May 1186, however, that he was free to move against Roland. King

William, his brother Earl David, and his leading magnates were summoned to Henry's court at Oxford, ostensibly to discuss the pressing matter of the Scottish king's marriage. In a clear sign that he entertained no illusions as to where William's sympathies lay, Henry detained him in England to await his bride-to-be, Ermengarde de Beaumont, while hostages were taken from the Scottish nobles who, no doubt reminded of their personal submissions to the English crown under the Treaty of Falaise, were then sent back to Scotland with instructions to subdue Roland unless he agreed to submit himself to the judgement of Henry's court. Henry's position, outlined by Howden, was that Roland had acted against the explicit orders of both his justiciars and himself, had invaded Gillebrigte's lands and seized them for himself.[71] Howden claims that in response to this threat Roland collected his forces and prepared to resist any invasion by the Scottish lords, though how seriously he took the risk of conflict with an army that contained many of his wife's kin is open to question. Provoked thus further, Henry assembled an army at Carlisle, from where he sent William and Earl David to bring the recalcitrant Roland to him. After protracted negotiations, perhaps deliberately drawn out by William, who was well aware of Henry's growing anxieties in the summer of 1186 over the activities of his son, Geoffrey, and his need to secure a speedy settlement in Galloway and return south, Roland obtained a safe conduct which met his terms and, escorted by William, he presented himself at Carlisle.

With Geoffrey of Brittany's plotting with Philip II of France preying on his mind, Henry displayed a remarkable willingness to compromise. After all, the only alternative was a protracted military campaign that would have kept Henry from dealing with his son's treachery. Roland's grip on Galloway, secured in the year that had passed since his defeat of Gillepadraig and his associates, would not easily be shaken loose. Uhtred's son, moreover, did have unresolved grievances against the family of Gillebrigte for the murder of his father, a man whom Roland would no doubt have reminded Henry was his kinsman. Consequently, Roland was permitted to retain his patrimony, while his right to Gillebrigte's lands, challenged by his cousin, Donnchad, were to be put to the arbitration of the English court, to which Roland would be summoned. This having been settled, Roland gave oaths to observe the terms, gave his three sons as hostages, and swore fealty to Henry on William's instructions.[72] The importance which Henry placed in this settlement can be seen in the elaborate safeguards which he ordained for its preservation: King William, Earl David and the Scottish magnates swore to enforce Roland's adherence to its terms, while Bishop Jocelin of Glasgow, the see of Galloway then being vacant through the recent death of Bishop Christian, threatened excommunication should he breach his oaths.

Henry cannot have been entirely unsatisfied with the agreement he had extracted at Carlisle. He may have been unable to force Roland's withdrawal from Gillebrigte's lands, but he had gained the personal submission of this upstart protégé of the Scottish king and recognition of his right as overlord to adjudicate in the disputed succession to western Galloway. Circumstances, however, were to prevent Henry from further involvement in the issue, for, despite the unexpected death of Geoffrey of Brittany in August 1186, his relationship with Philip II had continued to deteriorate and reached crisis point in May 1187. From then until his death two years later, the great Angevin was wholly preoccupied with the defence of his continental domain and containing the rebellion of his remaining sons.[73] Deprived of Henry's active support, Donnchad, or Duncan fitz Gilbert as he styled himself in reflection of his upbringing at the Angevin court, was in no position to press his case.

While the temporary settlement that had left Roland in control of all Galloway was clearly advantageous to the Scots, William was no doubt conscious of the very public oaths that had been taken to ensure that justice was done. Henry, however, was too embroiled in his domestic and foreign crises to instruct any court to proceed with the arbitration, and William, as the English king's vassal, was powerless to act in a case that Henry had reserved to himself. As a consequence, the final settlement of the issue had to await Richard I's abrogation of his rights of overlordship of Scotland by the Quitclaim of Canterbury in December 1189. William was now free to settle what he no doubt saw as a domestic issue. By 1190, there can have been little question in men's minds as to what the outcome would be. Roland had proven his loyalty and value to William in the intervening years, providing him with active military support in the second major political challenge to his position mounted by the meic Uilleim line, and serving him as a senior officer of state. In the summer of 1187, he led his army in support of the king in the campaign in Moray and Ross against Domnall meic Uilleim, grandson of the brief-reigned King Donnchad mac Máel Coluim (1094). At 'Mam Garvia', probably near Garve on the route west from Dingwall, Roland brought the pretender to battle, defeated and killed him.[74] From about that time, and certainly by 1190, Roland also held the office of justiciar, being so styled in three royal *acta*.[75] The implication is that William had created a third Scottish justiciarship in addition to those of Scotia and Lothian, probably to facilitate the imposition of royal peace and justice in a wide region that had been disturbed by protracted conflict since 1174. Evidence for the function of this office is sparse, but its sphere of operation can be seen to have embraced the sheriffdoms of Ayr, Dumfries and Lanark, but probably not also Galloway itself, where the native law code remained in force.[76] Roland, then, was a man of proven loyalty to William and one whom the king was unlikely to alienate intentionally.

Roland's readiness to accept the judgement of the king of Scots on an issue which touched him so personally is an indication both of his closeness to William and of the profound change in domestic political circumstances over the previous thirty years, that had seen Galloway drawn under the dominating force of the Scottish crown. No record survives of the court in which the claims of Roland and Duncan were settled, or of the terms of its judgement. Fordun merely records that Roland was confirmed in what was his by hereditary right, and also in the lands that he had won by conquest. For his part, Duncan swore to accept the decision as binding and abjured any claim to Galloway on his or his descendants' behalf. In return for this renunciation and in compensation for his more general disinheritance, William detached Carrick, possibly a continuing focus for opposition to Roland under the leadership of the Kennedies, from the remainder of Galloway and granted it to Duncan.[77] This act created for Roland a unitary lordship that extended from the Rhinns to the Nith, embracing both the former domain of Fergus and the territories added under Uhtred in the 1160s. It was a momentous development, for it established the largest territorial lordship in southern Scotland, indeed, a bloc probably greater in physical extent, wealth and reserves of manpower than the earldoms north of the Forth. Furthermore, despite the role that the king of Scots had played in brokering the deal that placed this huge agglomeration of territory in the hands of one man, the relationship between the Scottish crown and the lord of Galloway remained uncomfortably ambiguous. While Roland may have acknowledged William's overlordship, there was no attempt made at this stage to convert this newly constituted lordship of Galloway into a feu held of the Scottish crown and thereby tie Roland into 'feudal' dependency on William. The reservoir of power that the reunited lordship represented had enabled Fergus to project his influence far beyond the limits of his domain and had drawn him into the unstable world of Manx, Irish and Hebridean politics. It had, moreover, given him a freedom that had made him the target of foreign diplomacy, entangling him in the network of alliances built up by Henry I. Certainly, the radically changed political geography of southern Scotland would have curtailed that freedom of manoeuvre to a considerable degree, in that William's power had now spread to the very borders of Galloway, but Roland's current alignment with Scottish interests rested solely on very personal bonds. For William, the judgement in favour of Roland was still a considerable gamble.

One question often overlooked in discussion of the settlement is why did Duncan submit to a situation that represented nothing more than disinheritance? The easy answer would be to point to the degree of favour which Roland enjoyed with the king of Scots, but that alone does not explain his acquiescence, for, if Duncan was a grandson of Donnchad II, earl of Fife, he too would have enjoyed powerful backing from within the political community. It has been suggested that, despite his oaths to accept that the king's judgement settled the issue for once and for all, Duncan's family nursed a bitter grudge against the Galloways and their successors that would later manifest itself as one dimension in the Bruce–Balliol conflict of the later thirteenth and fourteenth centuries. Yet, it is clear that the relationship between the cousins and between Roland's son, Alan, and

Duncan, was good if not exactly close in the aftermath of the settlement. Roland, for example, witnessed Duncan's grant of Maybole and Beath to the monks of Melrose datable 1189–March 1198.[78] Their interests may have clashed in the 1200s, when both Duncan and his Galloway cousins pursued lands in Ulster (see below, Chapter 4), but there is no sign of outright hostility. The inducement that may have secured Duncan's agreement to Scottish terms appears to have been an earldom. Although it has been suggested that Duncan only received the title of earl of Carrick c.1225–30,[79] he is thus designated in charters datable to c.1200,[80] which might indicate that he and his kinsmen had held out for a settlement that established Duncan's social superiority over his cousin albeit at the cost of the core of his paternal inheritance in western Galloway.

The legitimisation of Roland's takeover of Gillebrigte's land was marked with a highly symbolic act. While there is little indication of a widespread policy of infeftment of knights on properties in the west of Galloway, he proclaimed his lordship through foreign colonisation of another form. On 21 January 1191/2, Roland founded Glenluce Abbey in the heart of the district west of the Cree and colonised it with monks from his grandfather's foundation at Dundrennan.[81] Although the foundation charter of the new community has not survived, sixteenth-century evidence recording the feuing of the abbey's lands indicates that Roland endowed it with a substantial landed estate that encompassed much of the post-Reformation parishes of Old and New Luce.[82] Large portions of Gillebrigte's former demesne, it would appear, were being alienated to furnish the economic base necessary for the support of a Cistercian community that was the daughter-house of the monastery linked most closely to Fergus and Uhtred. Here, Roland was setting a very public and permanent seal on his victory over his uncle's family, disposing of the propertied base that had sustained their lordship beyond any hope of future recovery.[83] It can be surmised that the soul's weal of Uhtred featured prominently in the masses that this act of politicised piety purchased.

There can be no doubt that the Galloway–Carrick settlement of c.1190 marked a significant advance in the levels of control exercised by the Scottish crown over the descendants of Fergus. It also brought the Scottish crown once more closely into contact with the shifting politics of the northern Irish Sea and southern Hebridean world, restoring links and lines of influence that had been effectively severed in the mid-1170s. It was a vastly different scene that confronted William the Lion in the west in the 1190s than that which he had known before 1174. In particular, two major developments had transformed the political structures of the region, both of which had profound implications for the interests of both the Scottish crown and the rulers of Galloway and Carrick. The first dated from 1177, when the adventurer, John de Courcy, a knight with strong Cumberland connections,[84] had headed north from English-controlled Dublin into eastern Ulaid. There, in the years down to 1182, he had carved out a personal empire for himself and had sufficiently impressed his mark on the political structures of the region by *c.*1180 for Godred Óláfsson, king of Mann, Fergus's grandson, to seek an alliance with him and seal the agreement with de Courcy's marriage to Godred's daughter, Affrica.[85] This marriage may have established links between de Courcy and Galloway, where Gillebrigte cannot have been a disinterested observer of the spread of English power into Ulaid. Certainly, Gillebrigte's son, Donnchad, gave military support to de Courcy in the 1190s and campaigned in person in Ulaid in 1197 in an effort to gain possession of lands awarded to him by his ally in the Bann valley.[86] The Manx marriage had undoubtedly been intended to provide de Courcy, whose relationship with the English crown in respect of his conquests was not regularised until the mid-1180s, with an effective ally against the Gaelic forces ranged against him in Ulaid and the districts to the west of the Bann. Chief amongst de Courcy's opponents outwith Ulaid were the Cenél nEógain and their north County Londonderry-based Uí Catháin dependants. The Cenél nEógain had been allied with Godred in the later 1160s and early 1170s: Godred's long-standing concubine and, from 1177, wife, Findguala, was a grand-daughter of Muircertach mac Lochlainn; but in 1177 the kingship of the Cenél nEógain had been seized by the meic Lochlainn's cousins and long-term rivals, the Uí Néill, in the person of Áed Méith ua Néill. Godred's alliance with de Courcy, therefore, may have been more a reaction to the Uí Néill seizure of power than a rejection of the meic Lochlainn link. That the internal politics of the Cenél nEógain may have had some bearing on the marriage alliance is possibly borne out by the attack on Mann in 1182 staged by Raonall mac Echmarcacha, who may have been an ua Catháin dynast.[87] The conflict in northern Ireland was spilling over into the Irish Sea and Hebridean zone.

The second major development had been occasioned by the death in 1187 of Roland and Duncan's cousin, Godred Óláfsson.[88] According to thirteenth-century Manx tradition, post-dating Óláfr Godredsson's suc-cessful challenge for the kingship, Godred's preferred heir had been Óláfr, the legitimised son of his marriage to Findguala, who was about thirteen at the time of his father's death. The Manx, however, preferred his illegitimate elder half-brother, Rognvald, whom Godred had evidently placed in power over the Hebridean portion of his kingdom, an arrange-ment that suggests that he may, in any case, have been the acknowledged heir. Although there is no direct evidence for any diplomatic relationship between the two men, Rognvald appears to have developed close links with his cousin, Roland, and, through him, with the king of Scots. This would have represented a significant re-alignment of interests, since Mann had fallen into the orbit of the English crown since the late 1150s. For William, who, despite the victory over the meic Uilleim at Mam Garvia in 1187, still faced dynastic challenge from within the north and west of the kingdom, the forging of new links with the dominant maritime power of the western seaways would have been a major gain.

William's concerns for the greater security of the south-western flank of his kingdom may have been linked to the most recent meic Uilleim incursion. Most traditional analyses of meic Uilleim activity emphasise their primarily northern mainland reserves of support and sphere of activity,[89] but more recent re-appraisals of their careers have emphasised the support that they evidently drew from north and west Ireland and the Hebrides.[90] It is possible that Domnall meic Uilleim's insurrection, that started c.1179–81 and was launched from outwith the kingdom,[91] had found its origins in the disturbances in the north of Ireland after 1177 and received fresh impetus in 1187 from a spill-over of violence from the upheavals among the Cenél nEógain recorded in that year.[92] Indeed, the slackening of the native offensives against John de Courcy from 1181 may signal the diversion of military resources towards this new venture. It was not just the MacWilliam threat, however, that the king sought to contain in the west. The internecine bickering of the successor lordships that had emerged from the fragmented ruin of Somairle's kingdom after 1164 was a matter of great concern, for it had brought about the general destabilisation of the wider Argyll, Firth of Clyde and southern Hebridean zone. The latest incidence of this was in 1192, when Somairle's sons Aongus and Raonall had clashed.[93] The Scots had capitalised on the divisions within the Somairle family, the Stewarts in particular continuing their expansion into the north-western districts of the Clyde estuary that had triggered Somairle's final rising in 1164. Stewart expansionism, however, may have been becoming a matter of concern to King William, for the extension of their lordship into Bute moved them into territory which was technically under Norwegian jurisdiction and a part of the kingdom of the Isles.[94] Shortly after his defeat by his brother, Aongus, Raonall mac Somairle may have sought an alliance with Alan FitzWalter, head of the Stewart family,[95] a league that may have threatened to draw the Scots into a wider conflict in the Isles. This, together with Duncan of Carrick's current involvement in de Courcy's wars in Ulaid, may have spurred King William into action. Among many other considerations, the need to assert crown authority in the Clyde estuary probably underlay his speedy acceptance of Roland's succession to the de Morville lordship in 1196, for this placed a confirmed supporter of the king in control of the strategic lordship of Cunningham. Furthermore, the construction of a new royal castle at the mouth of the River Ayr in 1197, the westernmost outpost of crown authority in the kingdom, signalled to all parties involved that William intended to curb the independent activities of his frontier lords.

While the new royal castle and burgh established at Dumfries by c.1186 and castle at Ayr constructed in 1197 brought the symbols of Scottish royal power to the borders of Galloway, however, the crown still lacked an immediate presence anywhere within the region to the south and west of the rivers Doon and Nith. Within that territory, the authority of the Scottish crown rested primarily on the personal relationship between William, Roland and Duncan, reinforced by the primary ties of lordship which existed between the crown and several of Roland's tenants and by the growing spiritual bonds between Galloway and monasteries that identified closely with the kings of Scots and their magnates. William used these various ties as means of strengthening his domination of the region, particularly through the re-assertion of rights of legal jurisdiction and fiscal rights which pertained to overlordship. From the start, Roland was involved closely in these developments, operating clearly as a royal agent. As early as May 1187, in a court at Lanark, Roland was supporting the king of Scots' rights to cain from Galloway and setting out arrangements for its collection and the punishment of defaulters.[96] The confirmation or re-affirmation of fiscal rights in Desnes Ioan and Carrick may have been the primary subject of his judgement, but clarification of the vague rights pertaining to the king of Scots within the broad zone south and west of Clydesdale, into which the crown had but recently expanded its administrative sphere, was also desirable. It is in a similar fiscal context that a judgement of the royal court at Dumfries should be interpreted. This concerned punishment for breaking the king's peace[97] and surely represented the symbolic re-assertion of royal authority in a region that had defied the king's will for over a decade. The date of this ruling is unknown, but Duncan has suggested that the scale of the punishments, clearly aimed at substantial landholders rather than the lower orders, indicates a connection with the 1186 settlement.[98] This seems unlikely, for in 1186 William was not at liberty to make such a ruling, since settlement of the Galloway question had been reserved by Henry II for judgement in his court. Rather, it may represent part of the c.1190 general settlement of the case between Roland and Duncan, and was designed as a warning to those who failed to abide by its terms. Further royal legislation affecting Galloway is alluded to but does not survive.[99]

The closer integration of Galloway into the Scottish sphere, which was signalled by the above developments, moved onto a new plane in 1196. Roland's marriage to Helen de Morville was central to this process. In 1189, Roland's father-in-law, Richard, had died and been succeeded as constable by his son, William. Through the deaths of William's nearer male relatives, Helen had become her brother's sole heir for the lands and titles of the de Morville family in Scotland and England. His death sometime after 31 July 1196[100] saw, on the payment of a relief in the order of 700 marks, this huge inheritance pass into the hands of Helen and her husband.[101] In right of his wife, Roland assumed the office of constable of the king of Scots and took sasine of the lordships of Lauderdale and Cunningham.

The union of the de Morville heritage with the lordship of Galloway confirmed, *prima facie*, the trend towards integration into the kingdom of the Scots that had become increasingly evident since the time of Uhtred. For Roland, his upbringing and the political circumstances that had prevailed throughout his adulthood had closed him off from the western maritime world that had been the natural environment of his grandfather and forbears. Nevertheless, his family links within the region were clearly important to both him and King William, and may have played a key part in royal policies in the northern mainland in the late 1190s. While he is not named in any of the records of Scottish military operations in Moray, Ross and Caithness in 1196–97, it is most likely that Roland, as constable, would have played an important role in the campaigns. It was probably through the medium of Roland that King William drew King Rognvald into his plans to contain the threat from Orkney posed by Earl Harald Maddadson, which saw a short-lived attempt to deprive the imprisoned Harald of his mainland earldom of Caithness and its award to Rognvald.[102] Roland, however, did not pursue an active career in this maritime world and there is no indication of any wider interest on his part in the affairs of Mann and the Isles, probably a further manifestation of his alienation from his Gaelic roots. This effective withdrawal of active Galwegian involvement in the political affairs of the western sealanes is confirmed by the silence of the Irish chronicles with regard to the domestic affairs of Galloway at this time. Quite clearly, Roland had taken his inheritance and turned its face away from the regions that had provided its genesis. The value placed by him on his status within the kingdom of the Scots is underscored by his rapid adoption of the style 'constable of the king of Scots' in his charters in preference to any other title.[103] For Roland, high – if largely honorific – office in the service of the king of Scots represented the pinnacle of his career. Despite this, there is no sign of any increase in his attendance at King William's court, rather the years after 1196 saw a decline in the frequency with which he appeared, perhaps a consequence of his increasing age. Furthermore, litigation surrounding Helen's inheritance in England may have forced his focus towards the English courts.

Helen's inheritance was to prove the death of Roland. In November 1200 he accompanied King William south to Lincoln, where the Scots king swore fealty to King John for his English lands. Roland was, presumably, in attendance in his capacity as constable and a chief baron of Scotland to make supporting oaths and also to give his personal oaths of homage and fealty for the de Morville lands to the new English king. The journey south, however, presented an opportunity for him to advance other business in connection with that inheritance, for, following the ceremony at Lincoln, Roland travelled on to Northampton, where he initiated a lawsuit concerning Helen's estate at Bozeat in Northamptonshire.[104] He pledged 500 marks to have the recognisance of twelve free men of the vill to answer questions concerning the seisin of Richard de Morville in the manor and to determine the reasons for his disseisin. On 19 December, however, Roland died at Northampton and was buried in the abbey of St Andrew in the same town,[105] the suit still unsettled.

Notes

1 *Benedict of Peterborough*, i, 79.

2 Scott, 'Dundrennan and Soulseat', 40.

3 It is with property in this region that most of his charters are concerned. See, e.g. *Holyrood Liber*, nos 23, 24, 49, 73.

4 *RRS*, i, no. 265.

5 Jack Scott's suggestion that Dumfries may already have been a royal burgh and castle before 1165 has much to commend it: Scott, 'Galloway in the 1100s', 133.

6 For discussion of the development of the crown's position in lower Nithsdale, see Chapter 7 below, especially pp. 196–7.

7 Stringer, 'Records', nos 3, 6. As Keith Stringer has pointed out, Urr was confirmed to the canons by Pope Alexander III on 29 July 1164, rendering my earlier suggested date of *c*.1165–70 for the acquisition of Desnes Ioan (Oram, 'Fergus, Galloway and the Scots', 126–27) untenable.

8 For a detailed discussion of this colonial process, see below, Chapter 7.

9 *RRS*, i, no. 230.

10 For Donnchad of Carrick's acts in favour of the nuns, see *North Berwick Carte*, nos 1, 13, 14, 28.

11 For discussion of the brothers' disposal of property in Carrick and Desnes Ioan, see Chapter 6.

12 *Chron. Fordun*, i, 256.

13 *RRS*, i, nos 159, 265.

14 Ibid., no. 254.

15 *RRS*, ii, no. 80.

16 R. A. McDonald, 'Scoto-Norse kings and the reformed religious orders: patterns of monastic patronage in twelfth-century Galloway and Argyll', *Albion*, xxvii (1995); Stringer, 'Records'.

17 *Melrose Liber*, no. 31.

18 Stringer, 'Records', 205.

19 Stringer, 'Records', nos 3, 6, 9,10, 12.

20 See, for example, *Melrose Liber*, nos 29, 30, 32, 36, 192.

21 *RRS*, ii, no. 141.

22 *Holyrood Liber*, no. 49.

23 *RRS*, ii, no. 141 and comment; MacQuarrie, 'Kings, lords and abbots', 356–57.

24 *Chron. Mann*, s.a. 1164 and 1176. According to the Chronicle, Godred and Findguala were canonically married on the instructions of Cardinal Vivian. Their son, Óláfr, was about three years old at that time.

25 McDonald, *Kingdom of the Isles*, 70–71.

26 *AU*, s.a. 1170. For a discussion of Orcadian activity in the western maritime zone after *c*.1165, see P. Topping, 'Harald Maddadson, Earl of Orkney and Caithness, 1139–1206', *SHR*, lxii (1983), 105–20 at 110–12.

27 *Jordan Fantosme's Chronicle*, ed. R. C. Johnston (Oxford, 1981), 126.

28 *Chron. Howden*, ii, 60.

29 *Benedict of Peterborough*, 67–68.

30 *Benedict of Peterborough*, 80.

31 Tabraham, 'Norman settlement in Galloway', 120.

32 D. Corner, 'The *Gesta Regis Henrici Secundi* and *Chronica* of Roger, Parson of Howden', *BIHR*, lvi, no. 134 (1983), 126–44.

33 *Benedict of Peterborough*, 67–68.

34 *Chron. Fordun*, i, 266.

35 *Chron. Howden*, ii, 105; *Benedict of Peterborough*, i, 126.

36 Scott, 'Galloway in the 1100s', 131.

37 *Benedict of Peterborough*, i, 79.

38 Barrow, *Scotland and its Neighbours*, 75 and note 34, and Scott, 'Galloway in the 1100s', 131, assume that the island in question must be St Mary's Isle, the peninsula to the south of Kirkcudbright. This, as 'insulam Trail', however, had been granted to the canons of Holyrood by Fergus (*Holyrood Liber*, no. 27) and was to become the location of their priory cell, from which the promontory derived its alternative name of St Mary's Isle. The most likely location is Threave Island, where earlier remains were noted but not excavated during work in the mid-1970s: Good and Tabraham, 'Excavations at Threave Castle'.

39 In his *Chronica*, Roger of Howden first names the perpetrator of the act as Máel Coluim (*Chron. Howden*, ii, 69) but subsequently names him as Donnchad, the son who was given as a hostage for the peace in 1176 (ibid., 105, 299). It has been suggested that Máel Coluim was an illegitimate son (*Scots Peerage*, ii, 421), hence Henry II's demand that the legitimate son and heir be given as hostage. As Donnchad did not die until 1250, it is likely that he was a minor in 1176 and probably played no personal part in the events that led to his uncle's death (*Scots Peerage*, ii, 422–23).

40 *Benedict of Peterborough*, i, 80.

41 William Newburgh, *Historia Rerum Anglicarum*, in Chronicles of Stephen etc., ed. R. Howlett, i (London, 1884), 186–87.

42 *Chron. Fordun*, i, 266.

43 *Benedict of Peterborough*, 79–80; William of Newburgh, 186–87.

44 *Benedict of Peterborough*, 79.

45 Scott, 'Galloway in the 1100s', 131.

46 William of Newburgh, 76. For a recent discussion of the function and context of such mutilation, see Gillingham, 'Killing and mutilation'.

47 *Benedict of Peterborough*, 80; Ralph de Diceto, *Imagines Historiarum*, i, 396.

48 *Benedict of Peterborough*, 94–99.

49 *Chron. Holyrood*, 156–57.

50 *Benedict of Peterborough*, I, 94–99.

51 Fordun, who gives the only account of William's campaign and Gillebrigte's submission, dates these events to 1175, following William's release from captivity. The contemporary record of events at York in August 1175 clearly contradict that scenario, and it is likely that Fordun has mis-dated the campaign which followed the ratification of the treaty. His details of the submission, however, evidently brokered by a mission of Scottish bishops and earls, is probably close to fact. *Chron. Fordun*, i, 266.

52 *Roger of Howden*, ii, 105; *Benedict of Peterborough*, i, 126.

53 *Benedict of Peterborough*, I, 126.

54 *William of Newburgh*, 187.

55 *Holyrood Liber*, no. 24; *RRS*, ii, no. 80; *CDS*, ii, no. 1606 (4); *Holm Cultram Register*, no. 120.

56 Duncan, *Making of the Kingdom*, 183.

57 Stringer, 'Records', no. 10 and comment.

58 *Glasgow Registrum*, nos 199, 200.

59 For a discussion of Roland's 'Anglo-Norman' supporters and their lands in Galloway, see p. 201–4.

60 Stringer, 'Records', no. 15 and comment.

61 Ibid., no. 18 and comment.

62 Reid, 'De Veteripont'.

63 *St Bees Register*, no. 60.

64 *Benedict of Peterborough*, I, 313.

65 Ibid., 336.

66 Ibid., 339.

67 *Chron. Melrose*, 45; *Chron. Fordun*, I, 269.
68 *Chron. Fordun*, I, 269.
69 Duncan, *Making of the Kingdom*, 183, suggests on no firm grounds that this Gillepadraig was a son of Dunegal of Nithsdale.
70 *Chron. Melrose*, 45.
71 *Benedict of Peterborough*, I, 348.
72 *Roger of Howden*, ii, 309; *Benedict of Peterborough*, i, 348–49.
73 Warren, *Henry II*, 614–26.
74 *Benedict of Peterborough*, ii, 7–9.
75 *RRS*, ii, nos 309, 400, 406.
76 Duncan, *Making of the Kingdom*, 203–04.
77 *Chron. Fordun*, i, 270.
78 *Melrose Liber*, no. 30.
79 *Scots Peerage*, ii, 423.
80 For example, if *Melrose Liber*, no. 32 contains the original charter wording, then Duncan is styled earl before the death of William de Morville in 1196; no. 192, dated to 1202–06 by the abbacy of William, abbot of Melrose.
81 Stringer, 'Records', no. 24.
82 *Wigtownshire Charters*, nos 37–39, 47, 53, 60-61, 65.
83 For the similar dismantling of the demesne estates of the rulers of Moray in the twelfth century, see Oram, 'David I'.
84 For the most recent discussion of de Courcy's background, see S. Duffy, 'The first Ulster plantation: John de Courcy and the Men of Cumbria', in T. B. Barry, R. Frame and K. Simms (eds), *Colony and Frontier in Medieval Ireland: Essays Presented to J. F. Lydon* (London, 1995), 1–27.
85 *Chron. Mann*, s.a. 1204.
86 *Chron. Howden*, s.a. 1197.
87 *Chron. Mann*, s.a. 1172 = ?1182.
88 Ibid., s.a. 1187–88.
89 *RRS*, ii, 11–13; Barrow, *Kingship and Unity*, 51–52; Duncan, *Making of the Kingdom*, 193–94; R. A. McDonald, ' "Treachery in the remotest territories of Scotland:" northern resistance to the Canmore dynasty, 1130–1230', *Canadian Journal of History*, xxxiii (1999), 161–92.
90 See especially Stringer, 'Periphery and Core'.
91 *Benedict of Peterborough*, i, 277–78. See discussion of the events of 1179–81 in *RRS*, ii, 11.
92 *AU*, s.a. 1187.
93 *Chron. Mann*, s.a. 1192.
94 For a general discussion of this matter see N. Murray, 'Swerving from the path of justice: Alexander II's relations with Argyll and the Western Isles, 1214–49', in R. D. Oram (ed.), *Scotland in the Reign of Alexander II* (forthcoming).
95 Ibid. This putative alliance may have produced the grant by Raonall to Paisley Abbey of a penny from every house that contained a hearth within his territories (*Paisley Registrum*, 125).
96 *APS*, I, 378, c.xxiii.
97 Ibid., c.xii.
98 Duncan, *Making of the Kingdom*, 185–86.
99 *RRS*, ii, no. 406.
100 *Chron. Bower*, vol. 4, 413 and note.
101 *Chron. Fordun*, I, 278.
102 *Icelandic Annals*, s.a. 1198; *Chron. Howden*, s.a. 1196.
103 See Stringer, 'Records of the lords of Galloway', nos 26–29.
104 *CDS*, i, no. 294.
105 *Chron. Howden*, iv, 145; Stringer, 'Early lords of Lauderdale', 45–46, 52.

4

ZENITH AND NADIR:
ALAN 1200–34

The effectiveness of Roland's control of Galloway and the strength of the settlement imposed with Duncan of Carrick was demonstrated clearly on Roland's death: no disturbance unsettled the transition of power to the new lord, Alan. Before 1200, Alan had rarely emerged from behind the shadow of his father. His sole independent appearance was at King William's Christmas court at Forfar in 1199, where he witnessed one royal act.[1] For historians, this has rendered him something of an unknown quantity until he began to carve a career for himself that made an impact on contemporary observers. It should not be doubted that Roland had groomed Alan for the power that would be his on his accession to the lordship, for he certainly worked to advance the career of his younger son, Thomas. There is, however, little material evidence for Alan's formative years, and the references to an Alan, son of Roland, as a landholder in the Thames valley in the 1190s, often taken in the past to record the business of the lord of Galloway's son, have been shown to refer to a namesake who was a tenant of the honour of Wallingford.[2] Even when stripped of this spurious evidence for early activity in England, however, Alan's de Morville heritage in southern Scotland and the English Midlands, together with the traditional links between his family and the English crown, pointed towards a political career in both kingdoms. His first marriage, to an un-named sister or daughter of Roger de Lacy, constable of Chester and lord of Clitheroe in Lancashire and Pontefract in Yorkshire,[3] emphasised this outlook. Although the date of this marriage cannot be established more precisely than post-1194 (when Roger de Lacy inherited the honour of Pontefract) and before c.1206, since the marriage produced at least two children before the widowed Alan re-married in 1209, and more probably before 1203–04 when Roger was conducting the defence of Château Gaillard in Normandy, it is possible that it had been amongst the business conducted by Roland on his last journey into England in November–December 1200. Roger, indeed, had been in Scotland in October 1200 as part of the deputation sent by King John to arrange William the Lion's journey to Lincoln, had presumably returned south as part of William's escort, and was a witness to the conference and homage-giving ceremony at Lincoln on 21–22 November.[4] While this must remain purely conjecture, it is possible that Roland had identified in Roger de Lacy, a fast-rising star in John's service, a potentially useful ally for his family as it extended and consolidated its new landed interests in England.

Alan's first de Lacy wife brought him a substantial marriage portion in south-east Yorkshire centred on Kippax near Leeds.[5] The acquisition of this property, however, did not signal Alan's active entry into the English landholding elite, and it is not until *c*.1205 that his presence in England – settling business concerning Kippax with Roger de Lacy – can be established.[6] Instead, his Scottish inheritance and his duties as constable dominated Alan's affairs down to 1209. Indeed, Alan may have faced something of a baptism of fire, for in the early winter of 1201 and the spring of 1202 major royal expeditions by land and sea were mounted against Harald Maddadson, earl of Caithness and Orkney, who had again been defying King William and who may have been involved in treasonable dealings with King John.[7] Amidst this flurry of military business, however, Alan was stamping his mark on the management of his inheritance. Among his first acts was the settlement of a long-running dispute with the monks of Kelso concerning revenues from Galloway due to the monks but unpaid since the time of Uhtred. In exchange for the monks' rights and the arrears of payment, Alan granted them five ploughgates of land at Oxton in Lauderdale.[8] This was a pious rather than a political act, for it was intended to gain absolution for the souls of Uhtred and Roland for the withholding of revenues due to the Church. Similar motivation may have lain behind a sequence of acts by Alan and his mother concerning the monks of Melrose, probably contemporary with the Kelso agreement, where property at Harehope in Eddleston parish in Peeblesshire was settled on the monks in compensation for lands in Cunninghame bequeathed to them by William de Morville but evidently retained by his successors.[9] The majority of this business involved de Morville properties, over which Alan appears to have exercised a form of joint lordship with his mother, to whom at least nominal possession would have reverted on the death of Roland. He was, however, equally active within his Galloway inheritance, confirming his ancestors' grants to the church, settling property on the parish churches of Kirkcudbright and Kelton, and confirming the possessions of his tenants.[10] Throughout this period, he was also establishing his role as constable and, while he can hardly be described as an assiduous attender of the royal court, from *c*.January 1201 until 1209, he witnessed a series of royal acts at locations spread from Aberdeen and Kincardine in the north to Roxburgh and Selkirk in the south.[11] Overall, it is a picture of quiet, business-like activity, in striking contrast to the upheavals of his father's time.

While Alan was easing into his new position in the Anglo-Scottish landholding elite, his younger brother, Thomas, was already carving a niche for himself in the militarised society of Angevin England. What won him his place in John's favour were the military and naval resources at his disposal, drawn presumably from lands in Galloway settled on him by his father. To the beleaguered John, his Galloway cousin was a valuable source of manpower to be employed in the struggle to preserve the crumbling Angevin empire in France. Thomas first appears in English records in January 1204–05, when he received a gift of twenty marks from King John with which to provide himself with armour.[12] This was followed in March of the same year with the grant to him of 100 marks of land in the honour of Richmond, presumably as reward for the galleys that Thomas had brought into John's service.[13] Additional grants appear to have accompanied this recorded award: in April 1205 a royal writ instructing the enfeoffment of Roger de Turreville in his land at 'Banbrugh' (probably Banbury, Oxfordshire, rather than Bamburgh, Northumberland) ordained that if Thomas of Galloway had been previously given seisin there he was to be provided with an alternative holding.[14] This royal benevolence should be seen in the light of John's ordering of the defences of England in expectation of a French invasion following the fall of Normandy on the surrender of Rouen in June 1204 and preparation for a campaign to Poitou in the summer of 1205.[15] In the face of baronial reluctance to support this expedition, John was forced to abandon his grandiose plans and remained in England in 1205, sending instead smaller forces to Poitou and La Rochelle.[16] Thomas may have participated in this limited operation, or his services were retained by the king, for in November 1205 John instructed that he be given seisin of all the lands that had been Hugh de Ferrers', in right of his wife, within the bailliary of the sheriff of Hereford.[17] Comprising the honour of Richard's Castle, this was a significant landholding and is a clear indication of the good graces in which Thomas stood.

In the summer of 1206, Thomas was again active in John's service. On this occasion, he accompanied the king on his campaign in Poitou, receiving from him a loan of twenty marks towards his expenses.[18] Thomas's good service was recognised: in 1206–07, he was discharged at the exchequer of his assessment under the king's seventh scutage on his lands in Herefordshire, Worcestershire and Berkshire.[19] But a landholding comprising properties seized by the king from men who had fallen from grace lacked long-term security, as Thomas found in June 1207 when he was commanded to surrender Richard's Castle and its subsidiary castles of Stapleton and Ham to the king's steward, William de Cantilupe, who was further commanded in August to take possession of all the 'plain land', cattle and stock, that had earlier been given to Thomas.[20] The reasons for this deprivation are not stated, but Thomas was evidently not in disgrace with John, for close on the heels of the loss of Richard's Castle, he successfully offered 1000 marks to the king for the wardship of the heir or heiress of another West Country lord, Hugh de Say, and received delivery of the Worcestershire lands of Roger de Amundeville.[21] Thomas, however, did not complete the deal concerning the de Say wardship, for greater prospects drew him back to Scotland in c.1208–09. There, before the end of 1209, he had married Isabella, Countess of Atholl in her own right, and through her had acquired the lordship of that earldom.[22] This was a highly advantageous marriage for the constable's younger brother, but, contracted in the same year that the widowed Alan received as his second wife Margaret, eldest daughter of Earl David of Huntingdon and niece of the king,[23] it is an uncompromising declaration of the power and influence of the Galloway family.

Thomas's return to Scotland had occurred at a critical moment. As King William's health deteriorated in the closing years of his reign, predatory forces had begun to circle and King John, ever the opportunist, had sought to capitalise on William's weakening grip on power. In April 1209, John summoned William to a conference at Newcastle, presumably to discuss the relationship between their kingdoms and the question of overlordship, which had lain dormant since the Quitclaim of Canterbury in 1189. Nothing was settled on that occasion, but at a second meeting, at Norham in July 1209, William's resistance crumbled in the face of John's bluster and the threat of invasion by the large English army encamped across the Tweed. In return for the promise of peace between them, William, in an act that symbolised his submission to John's superior lordship, handed over two of his daughters for the English king to arrange their marriages, promised a cash payment of £13,000, and surrendered the sons of some of his leading men as hostages.[24] The double marriage of the Galloway brothers should be viewed in the context of this crisis year and possibly represented an act of insurance by William designed to safeguard the loyalty of two men with strong personal links with the English crown and whose military resources and experience would have considerably strengthened William's hand. The memory of 1174 must have remained strong in William's mind.

William's thoughts, however, were soon being drawn in other directions. In 1210, the domestic conflicts of Norway had spilled over into the Hebrides, with leading figures of the so-called Birchleg faction – supporters of King Inge Bardsson – launching a plundering raid into the islands which saw widespread devastation, including the ransacking of Iona – and forced the submission of King Rognvald Godredsson and his son, Godred.[25] This raid coincided with John's invasion of Ireland in June 1210 in pursuit of his vendetta against the de Briouze family and their supporters, and aimed primarily against Hugh de Lacy (who in 1204 had invaded and wrested from the control of John de Courcy the eastern portion of Ulaid which de Courcy had conquered between 1177 and 1182), who was harbouring Matilda de Briouze and her sons.[26] John had originally recognised de Lacy's position, despite the illegality of his actions, and in May 1205, after Hugh had seen off an attempt by de Courcy to regain his lands with the assistance of his brother-in-law, King Rognvald,[27] had created him earl of Ulster. By 1210, however, de Lacy's involvement in the de Briouze affair had settled John's will against him. John's forceful intervention in Ireland produced shockwaves around the Irish Sea and Hebrides, further de-stabilising this already disturbed zone. To King William, the raid and hostage-taking led by John's mercenary captain, Falkes de Breauté, on Mann, whither Hugh de Lacy, Matilda de Briouze and her sons had first fled,[28] must have signalled a rigorous re-assertion of the overlordship over the island kingdom formerly exercised by Henry II. John's authority was now extending along Scotland's western flank, threatening the balance of power in the region that had been maintained since the 1180s and throwing into turmoil a zone from which the authority of the kings of Scots had faced repeated challenge throughout the twelfth century. The reality of John's domination of the British Isles and the effectiveness of his overlordship of William was now revealed. From Mann, the fugitives had fled to mainland Scotland, where most, excluding de Lacy, were captured by Duncan of Carrick, formerly an ally of de Lacy's enemy, John de Courcy, who, no doubt with the agreement of William, promptly delivered them to King John.[29]

As with de Courcy's original de-stabilisation of the region after 1177, the shockwaves of John's violent intervention in Ireland reverberated around the western maritime zone. The appearance in 1211 of the next generation of meic Uilleim pretenders in the person of Gofraid mac Domnaill, whose father had died at Roland's hands in 1187, should probably be linked to the Irish situation.[30] Gofraid had been based in Ireland until the summer of 1211, probably enjoying the protection of Áed Méith ua Néill, and had been able to draw on Irish military support for his venture.[31] William's response in 1211 had been to mount two major military expeditions into Ross, the second led by himself. The Galloway brothers served prominently in this campaign, Thomas, as leader of the army of Atholl, being joint commander of a force that succeeded in defeating the main enemy army.[32] Gofraid, however, remained at large and continued to pose a serious challenge to William's position in the north. Indeed, the continuing warfare in Moray and Ross, linked as it was with the Gaelic Irish reaction to John's activities in Ulster, may have driven William to renew the treaty made with John in 1209 and secure military assistance from him.[33]

The 1212 Anglo-Scottish alliance, described as 'a treaty of mutual security'[34] produced a new response in the efforts of both kings to stabilise the western maritime zone. A key role in the negotiations appears to have been played by Alan of Galloway, who acted as the sole Scottish oath-taker swearing to uphold the treaty terms on behalf of King William.[35] During these negotiations, John made to Alan a massive grant of property in Ireland – 160 knights' fees according to Bower – for his service and the service of ten knights, for which Alan, with King William's agreement, performed homage to John at Norham.[36] The purpose behind the grant was soon to become clear: the military resources of the lord of Galloway were to be used to resolve the problems of both the kings of England and Scotland that stemmed from the hostility of Áed Méith ua Néill, and through Alan's efforts resistance to royal authority on the peripheries of both kingdoms was to be crushed. Decisive action followed swiftly on the heels of the agreement. In 1212, Thomas of Galloway, in alliance with the sons of Raonall mac Somairle, with a fleet of seventy-six galleys, ravaged Derry and, joining with the Uí Domnaill king of Cenél Conaill, the enemy of the Uí Neill and Cenél nEógain, plundered Áed's heartland in Inishowen.[37] Thomas and Ruaidrí mac Raonaill, the eponymous founder of the MacRuaidrí dynasty of mercenary captains, returned in 1214 and again plundered Derry, but on this occasion, with the support of the English from Ulster, he constructed a castle at Coleraine from which to dominate the country west of the Bann.[38] Stringer has suggested that these attacks were directed against areas from which the meic Uilleim had drawn support, and it is perhaps significant in this context that Gofraid seems to have been unable to replace his losses of 1211 with fresh Irish warriors, which evidently contributed to his desertion and betrayal by his erstwhile supporters in Ross.[39] There may have been an element of retaliation in the Irish support for the bid for the Scottish throne made in 1214–15 by Gofraid's younger brother, Domnall Bán mac Domnaill, timed to coincide with the perceived weakness of the Scots on the death of King William, but the swift defeat of this attempt in Ross might indicate that Thomas's raids had significantly reduced Áed Méith ua Néill's ability to lend substantial aid.[40] Records of the slaughter in 1216 of the Cenél Fergusa, one of the kindreds of Inishowen, by Muiredach, son of the 'mormaer' of Lennox, might refer to reprisals by the Scots for this most recent meic Uilleim incursion.[41]

Galloway activity in north and west Ulster went beyond mere plundering raids. It was King John's intention that the territory extending from what is now north Antrim, through the Bann valley to Lough Foyle, should be brought into the sphere of English administration and that those Gaelic Irish chieftains who had opposed him and supported his enemies should be deprived of their lands and replaced with dependable 'feudal' vassals. The Galloway brothers and their cousin, Duncan of Carrick, featured prominently in those plans. Duncan had been active in Ulster since the later 1190s, when John de Courcy had granted him a block of lands in the Bann valley near Coleraine. His possession of these does not appear to have been confirmed after Hugh de Lacy's takeover of the de Courcy lordship, nor did John confirm the grant on the expulsion of de Lacy in 1210, although later reference to his tenure of lands at 'Balgeithelauche', thought to be Ballygelagh near Portstewart to the north of Coleraine, suggests that he had possibly succeeded in retaining some portion of his original holding.[42] As a reward for his capture of Matilda de Briouze and her family in 1210, John awarded Duncan a substantial block of land – some fifty carucates – in the district from 'Wulvricheforde' (Larne) to Glenarm, while some unspecified lands were also given to an un-named nephew of Duncan.[43] This was a minor landholding in comparison to the huge award made to Alan in 1212. A letter to King John from John de Grey, bishop of Norwich and royal justiciar in Ireland, reveals the extent of the grant. Assessed at 140 knights' fees (which tallies closely with Bower's 160), this encompassed the whole of 'Dalrethe', that is, Dál Riata (equating today with north Antrim), Rathlin Island, the cantred of 'Kymlalmerathe', the lands of Twescard and Larne to the east of the Bann, and beyond the river the cantreds of 'Kunnoche', (Ciannachta), the land of the Uí Catháin, and 'Tirkehike' (Tirkeeran). Twenty fees nearest to the castle of Kilsantan, identified as the motte at Mount Sandal, were reserved to the crown.[44] This award has been described as 'pure speculation', as most of these properties lay in the hands of Áed Méith ua Néill and his allies,[45] but Alan clearly considered this a genuine and attainable award and sent a delegation headed by his uncle, Fergus, son of Uhtred, to take seisin. In July 1213, John, who was seeking to retain Thomas's services for the planned royal expedition to Poitou, gave Thomas his first landed interest in Ireland. This has been considered the most speculative of all the awards to the Galloways, for it comprised Ua Néill's lands in Derry in the heart of Cenél nEógain territory.[46] In view of Thomas's activities in that area in 1212, however, it may have been thought perfectly attainable by contemporary observers. Four days after this initial award, Thomas received six fees out of the ten retained by the king on either side of the Bann around Coleraine,[47] still very much frontier land, but more easily controlled – or acquired – than the territories further west. For all three beneficiaries, however, physical possession of these lands was to require active and long-term commitment to English interests.

For Alan and Thomas, their interests in the north of Ireland and the adjacent sea areas were to become of central importance in the 1220s, but in the years after 1212 they represented only part of a wider military and naval commitment on John's behalf. In late June 1212, William had met with John in northern England during the English king's attempted intimidation of his restive northern barons, travelling in his company from Carlisle to Durham.[48] William appears to have been attended by the Galloway brothers, Thomas evidently accompanying John subsequently, at least as far as York, while John later referred specifically to business that he had discussed in person with Alan, possibly at Carlisle.[49] John was now in regular communication with Alan,[50] possibly, as suggested by Stringer, in a bid to use the lord of Galloway's resources as a means of holding the northern English lords in check, but also for the finalisation of the business set in train in June.[51] John had been planning to campaign in France in summer 1212, and it is probable that he had, with King William's agreement, secured Alan and Thomas's service for this expedition. While he was in the north, however, Llewelyn of Gwynedd had risen in revolt and was soon seriously threatening the English position in northern Wales. After at first proposing to send only a small-scale punitive expedition to deal with the revolt, in mid-July John abruptly changed his plans, cancelled the French expedition and determined to turn the full weight of his host against Llewelyn.[52] Writing to Alan on 20 July, John asked him to send 'one thousand of his best and most active Galwegians' to Chester for the muster of the royal host on 19 August. It was requested that Alan maintain these warriors at his own cost, but if that were not acceptable, John would pay them from their arrival at Carlisle.[53] Alan clearly refused to pay these men out of his own pocket, most probably because he, and presumably King William, feared that this might be used by John in future as recognition of English rights to military service from Galloway, but he did lead his force south in person.[54] On the eve of the Welsh campaign, however, John was advised of a plot against his life by his disaffected barons and, cancelling the expedition, prepared to deal with the treachery at home.[55]

Despite the climate of fear and suspicion in England after the cancellation of the 1212 campaign, John was determined in 1213 to again direct an expedition against the French. Alan and Thomas were both involved in John's plans for an expedition to Poitou in that year and were in receipt of a flow of royal favours. Alan received remissions of debts due at the exchequer over the settlement of the Bozeat dispute initiated by his father in 1200, small grants of land, and an extension of his rights within his Irish properties.[56] This was the occasion of John's grant of land in the Bann valley, but in addition to these he received money payments, and remissions for one of his men.[57] Again, baronial opposition forced John to abandon his expedition, but not before his fleet had won a striking victory over the French at Damme.

The cancellation of the 1213 Poitou campaign marked an unconscious turning point in the relationship between John and the Galloways, who returned to their Scottish and Ulster concerns. Thomas's attack on Derry in 1214 and his building of the castle at Coleraine should probably be considered as a determined effort to put into effect the awards made to him by John in the previous year.[58] Indeed, the absence of any evidence for Alan's activities on the British mainland in 1214 might indicate that he and Thomas were now directing their energies towards turning their titles to their Irish lands into something more concrete. It is also possible that both men were distancing themselves from events in England, where the crisis between John and his barons was sliding rapidly towards open conflict.

Anglo-Scottish relations deteriorated rapidly on the death on 4 December 1214 of William the Lion. The new Scottish king, Alexander II, had little cause to trust John and was already associated closely with the baronial opposition to him in northern England.[59] Thomas, who as earl of Atholl had been present at Alexander's inauguration at Scone on 5 December, and Alan, who was presumably also present, but was otherwise certainly in Alexander's company for the Christmas festivities at Forfar, from where they proceeded to Edinburgh for a parliament on 6 January 1215 at which Alan's possession of the constableship was confirmed, figured prominently in the young king's plans.[60] At this stage, Alexander may have intended simply to capitalise on John's difficulties and extract some concessions from him regarding the northern English counties rather than involve himself actively with John's enemies amongst the English baronage. Negotiation rather than military intervention was to be preferred, and, as Stringer, has highlighted, few men were better placed than Alan of Galloway to conduct this diplomacy. John, for his part, clearly still looked to Alan for military support should his difficulties in England slide into open conflict and directed a flow of favours towards both him and Thomas. On the same day that the barons voiced their defiance of the king, John instructed payment to him of 300 marks of prests.[61] Alan, however, clearly did not commit himself militarily to John's cause and was involved deeply in the negotiations that led to the drawing up of Magna Carta. He was with the king at Windsor on 3 June,[62] and the naming of Alan as one of the men on whose advice John supposedly granted the great charter, and the inclusion within it of a clause (number fifty-nine) that promised specifically to address Alexander II's grievances, must indicate the nature of his dealings with the English king.[63] John, however, was still manoeuvring to secure Alan's military backing, and on 27 June granted a confirmation to him of all his Irish lands with a reduced service obligation of only ten knights.[64] A confirmation of Thomas's possessions followed, assessed at two knights' service, and on 30 June he was given the keepership of the royal castle of Antrim.[65] Thomas, like his brother, however, was evidently still in southern England, John instructing payment for his maintenance in July.[66] His efforts to secure the support of Alan and Thomas, however, proved to be in vain, for when John renounced the June settlement in September 1215, both men immediately demonstrated their allegiance to Alexander II, who entered the English civil war on the side of the rebels.[67]

Alan's role in the war has been analysed in detail by Keith Stringer and only a summary of his account will be offered here.[68] By early 1216, Alan was active in the field against John, with Galwegian warriors serving in Alexander II's armies in northern England in 1216 and 1217. Alan's involvement was not purely disinterested, for he used the occupation of Cumberland and Westmorland as an opportunity to realise the claims that he had inherited through his de Morville mother to Hugh de Morville's lordship of Westmorland. It is probably safe to argue that Alan was Alexander's principal agent in the campaign which drove John's key agent in the north, Robert de Vieuxpont, from the region, and Alan's established family and tenurial links with members of the Cumberland and Westmorland nobility facilitated the process of political integration of the area into Alexander's domain. Charter evidence shows the extent of Alan's network in the region, which in itself emphasises the effectiveness of his control there down to 1217.[69] This new lordship, however, was short lived, and on the restoration of peace with England that had followed on the heels of John's death and the quick re-unification of the English polity around his young son, Henry III, Scottish control of the occupied zone of northern England was swiftly relinquished. In September 1217, Henry III's government wrote to Alan requiring him to render up Carlisle castle,[70] and Robert de Vieuxpont was shortly thereafter restored to his position in Cumberland and Westmorland.

Although peace between Alexander II and Henry III had been concluded before the end of 1217, when Alexander had travelled to Northampton to do homage for the earldom of Huntingdon,[71] neither Alan nor Thomas formally re-entered the English king's peace and did homage for their English and Irish lands until 1220 and 1219 respectively.[72] The reasons for this delay appear to be bound up in the politics of the government of minority for Henry III, the principal figure in which, the regent, Earl William Marshal, was a sympathiser of Hugh de Lacy's and known to favour his restoration as earl of Ulster. A restoration of Earl Hugh would have raised questions over the status of the lands awarded to Alan and Thomas by John, part of which at least had been carved from the earldom. Alan's failure to perform homage, then, was a consequence of this uncertainty and may have been prolonged while he attempted to reach an accommodation with the de Lacy interest.[73] That the attitude of William marshal was central to this situation appears to be borne out by the speed with which the issue was settled after his death in May 1219. Alan had performed a holding operation since the end of the war in 1217. Soon after the peace between Alexander II and Henry III's government, Alan had written to Henry reminding him of both his and Thomas's kinship with him and acknowledging the lands and gifts that they had received from John. He had, however, pointed out that they had as yet had little benefit from their lands in Ireland, and sent two of his familiar clerks, William, prior of Traill, and Thomas of Kent, to discuss the situation.[74] Here, then, is corroboration that it was concerns over the Irish lands that lay at the heart of the issue. The marshal does not appear to have been prepared to provide the assurances sought by the Galloways, who were simply expected to perform the required homage. Safe conducts were issued to Thomas in December 1218 and to Alan in March 1219 for them to come to perform homage,[75] but neither appeared. Thomas received a further safe conduct in May 1219, and had performed homage by 19 June, by which date the marshal had been dead for a month, when instructions were issued for the restoration of his Irish lands.[76] Moves towards a general settlement of the Ulster situation may have followed swiftly. In October 1219, Duncan of Carrick, who claimed to have remained loyal to John throughout the recent war, was restored to his lands in Larne and Glenarm, and in April 1220, in expectation of Alan's imminent performance of homage, instructions were issued for the restoration of his Irish properties.[77] In June 1220, Alan was at York for the negotiations between Alexander and Henry that led to the settlement of many of the outstanding grievances that still lingered from John's reign, and the agreement of a marriage contract between Alexander and one of Henry's sisters.[78] Alan's long delayed performance of homage was given on this occasion, instructions being issued on 16 June for the restoration of his lands at Whissendine and in Ulster.[79] Relations with the English crown at last normalised, the Galloways were determined to give some substance to their notional lordship in Ireland.

By 1221, the Galloways were again active in Ireland and the western seaways, this time as part of Alexander II's campaigns in the west, that were themselves possibly linked to a renewed English offensive in western Ireland. The 1221 royal campaign had been a major undertaking, comprising levies from Lothian and Galloway.[80] The massing of forces in the Clyde estuary ports, presumably for transportation by the Galloway fleet,[81] has been linked traditionally to a campaign against the meic Somairle kindreds in Argyll and the southern Hebrides, but wider considerations appear to have been at stake. Alexander's own part of the expedition was apparently dispersed by bad weather and he was forced to abandon his enterprise, but Thomas evidently conducted a successful naval operation in the Isles. There, he defeated a fleet that had been collected by Diarmait ua Conchobair, grandson of the mid-twelfth-century Irish high king, Tairdelbach ua Conchobair, King of Connacht, in support of a bid for his grandfather's kingship against his kinsman, Henry III's ally Cathal Crobderg ua Conchobair. Diarmait and one of his key backers, Maél Ruanaid ua Dubdai, king of the Uí Amalgada, perished in the defeat. From this, it would seem that Alexander's aim had been to curb the activities of the meic Somairle, whose provision of mercenary service to Gaelic Irish dynasts may have been of grave concern to the English administration. Certainly, when Alexander mustered a second force in 1222, in which Earl Thomas again served, accompanied by another south-western lord, Fergus of Glencairn, his principal target was Ruaidrí mac Raonaill, Thomas's ally in 1212 and 1214 against the Cenél nEógain, whose career as a mercenary captain is well known, and who may have been involved in earlier meic Uilleim risings.[82] The resources of the Galloways were once again being employed in the service of both kingdoms, in continuation of the policy evident from 1212.

To what extent these maritime operations were supported by active efforts to further the Galloways' interests in Ireland is unknown. Thomas had probably been restored to the keepership of Antrim castle following his performance of homage in 1219, but in July 1222, presumably as part of Henry III's resumption of his demesne, he was ordered – temporarily it was to prove – to surrender his charge to the Irish justiciar.[83] How this affected his tenure of Kilsantan is unknown, but it is possible that the Galloways' position in Ulster had been unintentionally undermined by this effort aimed at restoring royal finances. The fatal blow, however, came in 1223, when Hugh de Lacy, in alliance with Áed Méith ua Néill, began his effort to regain control of Ulster. An attempt by Henry's government at compromise with Hugh failed in the early summer of 1223, and warnings of a planned invasion of Ireland by Hugh soon reached the ears of the government.[84] In July 1223, Thomas was ordered to defend Antrim against attack by de Lacy and instructed to go there in person if he was not already in Ireland.[85] By the end of the year, Hugh and his Gaelic Irish allies were rampaging through Ulster, spreading panic through the largely powerless Dublin-based administration. The situation changed in April 1224, when William Marshal, earl of Pembroke, was appointed to the Irish justiciarate with the express intention that he end de Lacy's activities. Through 1223–24, de Lacy had been spectacularly successful: Thomas's castle at Coleraine had been captured and destroyed; eastern Ulster was effectively overrun; and Carrickfergus, the key to the earldom, was under siege.[86] Pembroke's relief of Carrickfergus and defeat of Hugh's kinsmen in Meath by August 1224 signalled defeat for de Lacy, but suggestions that Pembroke was negotiating with him in the autumn provoked a panicked response from the Galloway brothers and their cousin, Duncan of Carrick. In August 1224, Duncan, apparently to no good effect, was seeking restoration of his lands at Ballygelagh or Ballygally, which de Lacy had seized and granted to one of his supporters, the tone of Duncan's letters and the mandate from the English chancery suggesting that it was felt that Pembroke was not doing all that he might to restore seisin.[87] Alan, who was distracted to some extent by an unfolding crisis in the kingdom of Mann and the Isles in which he was to become involved, had massed his fleet in the late summer and was preparing to cross to Ireland when news reached him of some agreement between Pembroke and de Lacy. Fearing for his Irish properties, he now wrote to Henry to request that they, and those of his brother, Thomas, be placed under the king's protection.[88] Rumours that de Lacy was preparing to submit to Pembroke and place himself at the king's mercy must have seemed to confirm the Galloways' suspicions that their Irish properties were no longer secure.

It is only at this juncture that Alan took steps to tighten his control over his Ulster lands. In April 1225, Pembroke was instructed not to interfere in Alan's leasing of his properties, or his introduction of tenants on to them.[89] It is unlikely that he was particularly successful in any colonising venture, for the continuing uncertainty over the tenurial position within the earldom of Ulster must surely have acted as a deterrent to would-be colonists. Even the specific exclusion of the lands of Alan and Thomas from those granted in May 1226 to Hugh de Lacy's brother, Walter, lord of Meath, under the agreement whereby he would control the earldom for three years before its restoration to Hugh, must have appeared a hollow victory.[90] When, in 1227, Hugh broke the agreement and took possession of his earldom, the English government took no action against him. This may have marked the end of the Galloways' involvement in Ulster, for, as McNeill has suggested, it is unlikely that the earl would have tolerated the survival within the earldom of two potential power blocks held by men who had been his enemies since c.1210 which could have rivalled his own position.[91] Certainly, so long as he maintained his alliance with the Uí Néill, there was little prospect of Thomas being able to re-assert his authority in the Bann valley, and when Coleraine castle was re-built in 1228 it was by Hugh.[92] Alan, though, managed to salvage something from the wreckage, his marriage in 1229 to Hugh's daughter, Rose, having the appearance of a match arranged as part of a wider settlement.[93] Indeed, so far as the English administration was concerned, at the end of October 1229 both Alan and Thomas were still considered tenants-in-chief in Ireland and as such were summoned to perform military service in Henry III's French war in 1230, which would imply that some landed interest had survived the debâcle of the previous five years.[94] This apart, though, the great adventure embarked upon with such high expectations in 1212 had ended with barely a whimper and little to show for all the effort and financial outlay expended in its pursuit.[95]

The failure of the Galloways, especially Alan, to make any serious military effort to defend their Ulster territories, stemmed from their already heavy commitment to warfare in the Isles after 1224. As Keith Stringer has highlighted, this policy made strategic sense up to a point, for a powerful position in the Isles would have enabled him to dominate Ulster with greater effect.[96] Despite the personal dynastic considerations that underlay Alan's involvement in this conflict, it should also be seen in the light of wider Scottish policy towards the domination of the Western Isles. Certainly, until Alan's activities finally threatened the security of the kingdom itself, he appears to have enjoyed Alexander II's full backing in a venture that could have greatly extended Scottish influence in the west.

At the root of the conflict in the Isles that erupted in 1223–24 lay the succession to the Manx kingship on the death of Godred Óláfsson in 1187. His successor was his eldest son, Rognvald, who was apparently illegitimate, rather than his certainly legitimate youngest son, Óláfr.[97] Rognvald's earlier position as ruler over the northern portion of his father's kingdom gave him authority in a region from which the Scots had experienced repeated threat in the twelfth century, and as a consequence he was actively courted by William the Lion. His good relationship with the Scots saw him being employed in Caithness against Harald Maddadson, whose ambitions in the Isles may have been as much a threat to Rognvald as to King William. Rognvald was also courted by the English of Ulster, John de Courcy being his brother-in-law, for his naval power was vital in the prosecution of the war of conquest against the Cenél nEógain. In 1204, on his expulsion from Ulster, de Courcy fled to Mann and in the following year attempted to regain his domain with the aid of a large fleet provided by his brother-in-law.[98] The failure of that attempt may have prompted Rognvald's acceptance of English protection in 1205, and it is surely significant in the context of the unfolding pattern of Anglo-Scottish relations that, following the ravaging of Mann in 1210 by Falkes de Breauté as part of English operations against Hugh de Lacy, in May 1212, just as Alan and Thomas of Galloway were entering John's service, so too did Rognvald.[99] In the Anglo-Scottish war of 1216–17, Rognvald, in view of his established pro-Scottish and Galloway connections, may have adhered to the Scots, for in 1218 his homage was demanded by the English government, which also demanded reparations for the excesses committed by his men in Ireland, where the colony had remained loyal to John.[100] Although he had submitted and performed homage by 1219, it is probable that the English government lacked any confidence in his loyalty thereafter, which was to tell decisively against him in the 1220s.

According to the *Chronicle of Mann*, shortly before *c*.1208, Rognvald conceded a share in the government of the Isles to his half-brother, Óláfr, granting him the rule of Lewis, which the chronicler described as mountainous, rocky and incapable of bearing agriculture.[101] After living there 'pauperem' for some time, Óláfr approached his brother with a demand for a more equitable share of the kingdom, but Rognvald had seized him and handed him over to King William, who kept him incarcerated. Released on William's death in 1214, he returned to Mann but immediately departed on pilgrimage to Compostella. On his return from Spain, Óláfr was reconciled with his brother and restored to possession of Lewis. At this time he appears to have married a daughter of Ruaidrí mac Raonaill, lord of Kintyre and Garmoran, the sister of Rognvald's wife. In *c*.1222, however, Óláfr put aside his wife on the grounds of her consanguinity with his former concubine, but more plausibly because of the recent Scottish campaigns against Ruaidrí and his expulsion from Kintyre by Alexander II. Indeed, Óláfr's almost immediate re-marriage to a daughter of Alexander's principal lieutenant in the north, Ferchar, earl of Ross, confirms that his repudiation of his wife was a political manoeuvre. The chronicle account suggests that this act lay at the root of the final break in the relationship between the brothers. In 1223, Rognvald's son, Godred, who was ruler of Skye, invaded Lewis intending to kill Óláfr, but on his return to Skye was surprised and captured instead by his uncle and his supporters, who blinded and castrated him. The conflict between the brothers had now escalated into war.

This was the situation in which Alan had become enmeshed just as Hugh de Lacy launched his war in Ulster. The civil conflict in the Isles presented the Scots with a dilemma. Rognvald, who had been aligned with the Scots as recently as the war of 1216–17, despite his possible marital links with the notorious schemer Ruaidrí mac Raonaill, had proven a good ally in the past. He was, furthermore, a vassal of Henry III, who would have been unlikely to permit him to be overthrown were the Scots to commit themselves to his rival. Óláfr, on the other hand, whose long imprisonment by the Scots might have given him little cause for any pro-Scottish sentiment, had recently severed his links with Ruaidrí and allied himself through marriage with one of Alexander II's closest supporters. It was rumoured, however, that Óláfr had appealed to his nominal overlord, Håkon IV of Norway, who was threatening to send a fleet westwards in summer 1224.[102] It is possible that Alexander let himself be guided in the decision on whom to support by Alan, who had probably co-operated closely with Rognvald since the 1200s. Alan, certainly, appears to have immediately committed himself – and by extension King Alexander – to

Rognvald's cause, and it is likely that his galleys in 1224, which he described as sailing from island to island, were directed chiefly against Óláfr.[103]

The *Chronicle of Mann* suggests that in the summer after the mutilation of Godred Rognvaldson (possibly the summer of 1224), Óláfr, who had established his mastery over the northern islands of the kingdom and taken hostages from the Hebridean chiefs, came to Mann and forced his brother to partition the kingdom.[104] This involved recognition on Rognvald's part of his brother's control of the northern half of the kingdom, which left him with only Mann itself and the title of king. He was not, however, prepared to accept this diminution of his power and, on Óláfr's return to his portion of the kingdom, turned to Alan of Galloway for aid. In 1225, Alan mounted a joint expedition with Rognvald into northern Hebridean waters, but the Manx were unwilling to fight against Óláfr and the Islesmen, and nothing was achieved.[105] Part of the Manx reluctance to fight in 1225 may have arisen from concern for the future, for Rognvald was already elderly by the standards of the day – he had been on the throne for thirty-eight years – and his adult male heir had been ruled out of the succession by his mutilation in 1223. It was highly probable, therefore, that Óláfr was regarded as Rognvald's obvious heir, and the Manx nobility were unlikely to wish to antagonise their future master. Alan now clearly sought to capitalise on Rognvald's weakness with an arrangement that, if it had succeeded, would have greatly enhanced his own dynastic position and significantly advanced Scottish influence in the Irish Sea region. In 1226, under guise of travelling to meet with Henry III, Rognvald sailed to Galloway and, in act that trumpeted his dependence on Galwegian support, acceded to the marriage of his daughter to Alan's bastard son, Thomas.[106] Thomas was clearly being established as his new father-in-law's successor, but the prospect apparently appalled the Manxmen, for Thomas can have been little more than a child and it would have been obvious to them that real power in the kingdom would probably have belonged to Alan.[107] When news of the deal broke, they repudiated their allegiance to Rognvald and handed rule of the kingdom over to his brother. Alan's scheme had misfired catastrophically.

Alan's motivation in 1226 has been analysed in detail by Keith Stringer, who has pointed to Alan's need to find an alternative power base for Thomas, whose bastardy excluded him from succession to his father's sprawling mainland British and Irish domain.[108] Although it is possible that Alan's only recorded legitimate son, also confusingly named Thomas, was still alive at this date, his only certainly living legitimate progeny were his three daughters. Under Gaelic custom, the succession of the illegitimate Thomas was to be preferred to a female succession and, barring the birth of another male heir – for which Alan clearly still hoped – the prospect loomed one way or another of a partition of his composite lordship. Thomas clearly would not be permitted to succeed to Cunninghame, Lauderdale or the Anglo-Irish inheritance, which under feudal law would pass intact to any legitimate male heir or be partitioned between the legitimate heiresses. He could, however, have succeeded to Galloway itself, which was not held as a feu from the crown, although King Alexander's acceptance of such an arrangement when there were legitimate heiresses could not be guaranteed. To exclude Thomas from any share in the succession without making alternative provision for him, however, ran the risk of future challenge. The kingship of Mann offered a way out of this impasse that would, in Stringer's words, help 'to protect the future unity and stability of [Alan's] ancestral Scottish lands'.

At this point, Alan still enjoyed the support of Alexander II, who may have given his approval to the proposed marriage when the constable attended the royal court at Stirling at the end of March 1226.[109] Certainly, it must have seemed to the king that he could only benefit from the scheme, for it would establish a dependable client-king in Mann who could significantly advance Alexander's efforts to control the unstable politics of Argyll and the Isles and over whom he could exercise great influence by dangling the carrot of possible succession to Alan's paternal inheritance.[110] The reaction of the Manx to the marriage and its obvious implications cannot have been lost on the king, but Alan was not prepared to abandon his plans. In 1228, seizing the opportunity presented by Óláfr's absence from Mann on a circuit of the northern part of his kingdom, Alan, his brother, Thomas, and Rognvald, descended on the island and systematically ravaged its southern half. This was no mere raid but an attempted conquest of Mann in which Rognvald appears to have been a secondary figure, for it was Alan rather than Rognvald who established his men in control of the island. Success, however, was short lived, for on Óláfr's return from the Hebrides, the Galwegians were swiftly driven from the island. Support for Rognvald had clearly failed to materialise. By this date, Óláfr's possession of the kingdom was being recognised generally – the English government and Irish administration were dealing with him as king of Mann by 1228[111] – and Alan's persistence with his schemes now threatened to strain Anglo-Scottish relations. It is perhaps significant that Earl Thomas did not participate in his brother's continued efforts in Mann and the Isles after 1228, when he must have been made only too aware of the lack of any support for Rognvald and his allies within the kingdom, and in 1229 was to serve instead in Henry III's French wars. It is unlikely that Alexander II now harboured any illusions as to the probable outcome of the conflict.

Alan, too, may have lost his earlier enthusiasm for the war, for, in early January 1229, Rognvald, with only five ships, made a final bid to regain his heritage.[112] Sailing from Galloway, he arrived unexpectedly at Peel, where he succeeded in burning all the galleys of his brother and the Manx nobility. Remaining off the island, he opened negotiations in an attempt to regain some share of his former kingdom, which might indicate that Alan had abandoned him after the failure of the 1228 invasion. Finding that he still had some residual support, he resolved to fight, but in the battle at Tinwald on 14 February, he was defeated and killed. Under normal circumstances, this final disaster might have been expected to draw a line under the whole episode, but it seems instead to have spurred Alan to yet greater efforts. His search for allies may have led him to seek an accommodation with Hugh de Lacy, if his marriage to Hugh's daughter, Rose, can be dated to 1229 rather than 1219.[113] Hugh, certainly, would have been a valuable ally, but it was amongst the meic Somairle that Alan found his most active support.

The already tortuous politics of the kingdom of the Isles were further complicated by the efforts of various descendants of Somairle to establish their claims to kingship in the Hebrides.[114] Two of the meic Somairle, Donnchad mac Dubgaill meic Somairle, and his brother, Dubgall Screech, who controlled Lorn, Mull and the adjacent island districts, proved willing allies, and, under their combined assault, Óláfr now found himself forced onto the defensive.[115] Early in 1230, the pressure on him was such that Óláfr was driven from his kingdom and fled to Norway to appeal to his nominal overlord, King Håkon, for aid.[116] Although Håkon had been king since 1217, it was only in 1228 that the last of the uprisings associated with the prolonged episodes of civil war that had divided Norway since the mid-twelfth century had been put down. In association with his uncle Jarl Skúli, Håkon was actively re-asserting royal authority throughout Norway and had ambitions to resuscitate Norwegian overlordship of the western colonies from Iceland to the Hebrides. Óláfr was surely aware of the recent political developments in Norway, and he probably gambled on the fact that while Håkon would be keen to gain recognition of his overlordship of the king of Mann and would be likely to support him against any further encroachment on his kingdom by the king of Scots or his vassals, he would be unlikely to lead an expedition west in person so soon after the end of the civil unrest in Norway. On his arrival at Bergen, however, he found that news of the disturbances in the west had already reached the king's ears the previous summer and that Alan, described in the saga account of these events as 'the greatest warrior', was recognised as the chief perpetrator of hostilities.[117] Håkon, determined to exploit the situation in the Isles to his own advantage, was already intriguing with another of the meic Somairle, Gilleasbuig mac Dubgaill, known to the Norwegians as Uspak Håkon, who was evidently a brother of Donnchad and Dubhgall Screech, and in late 1229 had appointed him king in the Isles and had promised to send him west in the spring with a naval force.[118] Furthermore, Óláfr found another unwelcome surprise waiting for him at Bergen in the person of Godred Dond, a son of his half-brother, Rognvald, who had perhaps been the bearer of the news of the events of 1228–29. What was discussed between them is unknown, but it appears that Håkon may have set the price for his support for Óláfr at a division of power in the kingdom between uncle and nephew.

In spring 1230, Óláfr and Godred Dond returned with Gilleasbuig's fleet, which comprised twelve galleys from Norway, reinforced by a further twenty from Orkney. Initial operations in the northern Hebrides met with considerable success: Donnchad and Dubgall Screech were defeated and the latter was captured. Dubgall, however, soon escaped from his captors, and may have brought word of the scale and movements of the enemy force to King Alexander. The king was clearly alarmed by the news, for by 28 May, leaving the settlement of another meic Uilleim incursion in the north to his military deputies,[119] he was at Ayr, where, accompanied by some of the key figures of his military establishment, he met with Alan of Galloway, no doubt to discuss the impending crisis.[120] In the interim, having dealt with Alan's allies, Gilleasbuig headed south and entered the Firth of Clyde, where his targets were the Stewarts, whose spread into Bute constituted an occupation of territory that was notionally under Norwegian overlordship. Rothesay castle was assaulted and captured, but Gilleasbuig was wounded in the attack and the fortunes of the expedition began to decline thereafter. While in the firth, news was brought that Alan had assembled a great fleet for the invasion of Mann, but had diverted it northwards to intercept and crush the Norwegian force. Rather than risk battle, Gilleasbuig and Óláfr withdrew round Kintyre into the comparative shelter of the Isles, where Gilleasbuig died from the wounds he had received at Rothesay. Óláfr now took over command of the expedition and turned it to his own purposes. Eluding Alan's galleys, he sailed for Mann and, having dispersed a force raised against him there by a certain Torcuil mac Niaill, evidently an Islesman allied with the Galwegians, was able to resume his kingship.[121] With the Norwegians over-wintering in Mann, Óláfr was obliged to honour his agreement to divide the kingdom with Godred Dond, and assigned to him rule over the northern Hebrides. In the spring, the Norwegians sailed north with Godred to establish him on Lewis, on the way raiding Kintyre, where they were confronted by a Scottish force and only driven off after heavy casualties had been inflicted on both sides.[122] In Lewis, the Norwegians attacked Torcuil mac Niaill's son, Diarmid, who had evidently been established in power there, drove him out and installed Godred. Alan, on this occasion, was nowhere to be seen, and the summer brought no renewal of his offensive against Mann, where Óláfr was to rule unchallenged until his death in 1237. The Hebridean adventure was over.

Keith Stringer was surely correct when he attributed the ending of Galwegian military intervention in the affairs of the kingdom of Mann to Alexander II,[123] but his evaluation of Alan's achievements to that point is perhaps overly negative. In Stringer's assessment, Alexander held Alan personally responsible, directly or indirectly, for the disturbances in the north and the naval war in the west in 1230–31, regardless of any royal sanction that he had given to Alan's plans. Furthermore, it had taken the involvement in that latter conflict of forces sent by the Norwegian crown to finally waken the king to the threat to the security of his kingdom that Alan's ventures posed. This turning against Alan is presented as the product of a cumulative process that commenced with the inconclusive campaign of 1228, with it being neither the nature nor scale of his ambitions that had settled Alexander against him, but rather his incapability of realising them. Yet, in 1229–30 Alan appeared to have done exactly that, for Óláfr, regardless of the gloss put on the events of that period by either the Manx chronicler or the saga-writers, had been driven out of both Mann and the Isles and fled into exile, and Alan had, as the events of late summer 1230 and spring 1231 demonstrated, established some form of control over both segments of the kingdom, and had brought the meic Dubgaill, the dominant lineage of the meic Somairle, into alliance with him. That is quite an achievement.

To what extent the meic Uilleim attempt of *c.*1228–30 was a direct consequence of these events can never be determined. It is probable that the disturbances in the Isles linked to Alan's campaigns provided a fertile recruiting ground for the pretender, exactly the opposite result to what the king may have hoped for in the long term from his constable's operations, but the possible source of much of Gilleasbuig's military manpower points to different stimuli. It has been suggested that in the early 1220s, Alexander had been prepared to co-operate with the policies of Alan and Thomas in the maritime west, for they offered the prospect of an end to the regular challenges to the monopoly on royal power exercised by his segment of the Canmore dynasty that had entered the kingdom through this zone and drawn military support from it.[124] Alexander, however, had taken the initiative in this policy, it being royal campaigns in 1221–22 that had succeeded in expelling Ruaidrí mac Raonaill, who may have been involved in the meic Uilleim rising of 1214–15, from Kintyre, a territory that may technically have lain outside the kingdom of the Scots since King Edgar's cession of the Isles to Magnus Barelegs at the end of the eleventh century. Alexander's pursuit of Ruaidrí had not ended here, however, for although there do not appear to have been subsequent naval operations directed specifically against him, the king's policies in the northern and western Highlands in the 1220s appear to have had him firmly in mind. Geoffrey Barrow has highlighted Alexander II's efforts to control the Great Glen and the passes from it through into Strathspey, through which the meic Uilleim had penetrated in the past.[125] Indeed, Gilleasbuig meic Uilleim had made short work of some of these arrangements in the 1228–30 rising, burning Alan of Galloway's Lauderdale vassal, Thomas of Thirlstane, in his timber castle at Abertarff at the southern end of Loch Ness, and burning and plundering around Inverness.[126] Thomas of Thirlstane's lordship of Abertarff represented part of a network of new crown tenancies that spread westwards from Strathspey, with lordships being established on the east side of Loch Ness at Boleskine for Gilbert Durward and Stratherrick for Walter Bisset, while to the west of the loch Alan Durward received Urquhart and John Bisset a complex of lordships extending through the Aird into the mouths of Strathconon and Strathfarrar.[127] While these colonial lordships quite clearly control a series of key points along the Great Glen and would have policed north–south movement along it, they are also designed to command the east–west routes that feed into the glen. Alexander's creation of the lordship of Lochaber in c.1229–30, which he granted in conjunction with Badenoch to his principal military lieutenants in the north, the Comyn family, completed a mechanism for crown dominance of the central and west Highlands. The passes that run west from the lordships of Lochaber, Abertarff, Urquhart and the Aird lead towards Ardnamurchan, Moidart, Sunart, Arisaig, Knoydart, Glenelg and Kintail and on to the Small Isles and Skye. In the 1220s, the west coast between Ardnamurchan and Loch Duich, together with the Small Isles and the Uists, comprised the lordship of Garmoran, the centre of power of Ruaidrí mac Raonaill. For the king, the campaigns in the Clyde estuary in 1221–22 had been merely the opening round in a concerted effort to break the power of the most independently minded of the meic Somairle, and in 1229–30, the offensive was reaching a climax as royal power established itself at the head of Loch Linnhe on the very threshold of Ruaidrí's lordship. It was not Alan of Galloway that brought Ruaidrí into alliance with the meic Uilleim, it was Alexander II through his relentless pursuit of the Hebridean warlord.

The above does not challenge Stringer's conclusion that it was Alexander II who ended Alan's warfare in the Isles, but it does suggest that other motivations lay behind the ending of hostilities. Alexander can hardly have been taken by surprise at the intervention of Norway in what was, after all, a region that fell under the overlordship of the Norwegian crown. After all, rumours of a Norwegian campaign into the Isles in support of Hugh de Lacy had abounded at the Scottish court as long ago as 1224. Yet, with the exception of some minor plundering raids in the early 1200s, there had been no active intervention in the Hebrides on the part of a Norwegian king or his representatives since the death of Magnus Barelegs over a century earlier, and the Stewarts in Bute and the king himself in Kintyre had encroached on Norwegian territory with apparent impunity. Alexander, who was clearly well aware of the political situation in Norway before 1228, had probably gambled that Håkon IV was in no position to intervene in person in the western colonies. That gamble had failed, and the flexing of Norwegian muscles in the Isles that resulted threatened the security of all that Alexander had gained over the preceding decade. We should not doubt the seriousness of the crisis that this represented in 1230–31, but it was a crisis for which the Scots were in some degree prepared. Certainly, as English chroniclers observed, it had been a significant confrontation that had inflicted heavy losses, some personal humiliations, and had only been repulsed through a concerted military and naval operation on the part of the Scottish king and his vassals,[128] but it had been driven off and with no more than short-term consequences for the territorial advances of the Scottish crown in the West.

Why, then, did Alexander halt his offensive in 1231? The answer is probably that he had achieved all his objectives in his campaign against Ruaidrí mac Raonaill. It is not clear whether Ruaidrí had been killed along with Gilleasbuig meic Uilleim in 1230, but after the suppression of this final meic Uilleim insurrection there is no indication of any activity on his part in either the mainland or Isles. The establishment of the Comyns in Lochaber and Badenoch, and of the network of lordships along the length of the Great Glen, together with the creation of a new earldom of Ross for Ferchar mac an t-Sagairt in c.1226,[129] effectively neutralised the threat from the mainland – and island – territories of the lordship of Garmoran. Alan of Galloway's agreement with Hugh de Lacy, sealed by his marriage to Hugh's daughter, and perhaps won only through the concession of territory in Ulster, had helped to close off the other end of the Irish–Isles axis from which the meic Uilleim had drawn much support over the years, for Hugh's ally was Áed Méith ua Néill of Cenél nEógain. It is perhaps significant that the ending of Irish involvement in the conflicts in the west Highlands coincided with the Ulster–Galloway treaty and Áed's death in 1230. After that, the Cenél nEógain were riven by inter-dynastic rivalry over the kingship between representatives of the Uí Néill and meic Lochlainn, a conflict fuelled by the machinations of Hugh de Lacy and his ally, Maurice fitz Gerald, that ended only in 1238 when their candidate, Brian ua Néill, secured the kingship.[130] Alexander, then, had achieved his war aims and was now intent on consolidation of what he had won.

Alexander's withdrawal of support for Alan's schemes may also have been the product of a marked shift in the composition and outlook of the circle of advisors around the king. The first, and very personal, blow for Alan was the death in 1231 of his brother, Earl Thomas, who was killed in unknown circumstances by Patrick, son of Constantine of Goswick, a knight of the Earl of Dunbar.[131] The brothers had been close collaborators in their western campaigns since 1212, and Thomas's clear affinity with the Norse–Gaelic maritime world, that continued to dominate his career after his acquisition of landlocked Atholl, must have rendered him an enthusiastic ally for Alan's designs and a firm advocate of aggressive royal action in the west. Although Thomas can hardly be classed as one of the king's closest councillors, his position as earl of Atholl had placed him within the upper circle of the governing elite, and he had served both William the Lion and Alexander loyally. The loss of Thomas coincided with the return to favour of the Stewart family after a prolonged period in the political wilderness that had commenced as far back as 1197.[132] Stewart expansion westwards had ceased abruptly c.1200, probably as a consequence of royal unease over Alan fitz Walter's alliance with Raonall mac Somhairle in the late 1190s. Alan fitz Walter was still in disgrace at the time of his death in 1204, having incurred the wrath of King William by using the absence from Scotland in November 1200 of both the king and Roland of Galloway to secretly arrange the marriage of his daughter,

Avelina, to Duncan, Earl of Carrick.[133] The marriage was a clear signal of Alan fitz Walter's ambitions in the Firth of Clyde and beyond, for it allied him with a man who was already pursuing expansionist policies across the troubled waters of the northern Irish Sea. The degree of William's displeasure with fitz Walter for this deception is evident from both the number of pledges taken from him for his good behaviour – twenty-four, an unprecedented number – and from his disappearance as a witness to royal *acta*. From *c*.1198 until his death in 1204, Alan fitz Walter witnessed no surviving royal charters. His son, Walter II fitz Alan, was evidently a minor in 1204, and may not have come of age until after 1214.[134] This had the consequence of prolonging the political eclipse of the Stewarts, and by the time that Walter fitz Alan was of age to establish his position within the king's council, that council was already dominated by the Galloway brothers and their allies. The Stewarts, with their lordships of Renfrew, Cowal, Bute and northern Kyle, were rivals of the Galloways for domination of the outer Firth of Clyde and southern Argyll areas. Through the 1210s and 1220s, they had been obliged to watch as the king, in association with Alan and Thomas of Galloway, had established a crown presence at Dumbarton, in Cowal and in Kintyre, all areas of traditional Stewart interest, and pursue policies in the Isles that had threatened the territories and interests of the Stewarts and their allies, the earls of Carrick and Lennox, in southern Argyll and the Clyde estuary. In 1231, however, that powerlessness ended when Walter was made justiciar of Scotia, the principal deputy of the crown in the territory north of the Forth.[135] In this role, he and his political associates could dominate the royal council and secure a shift towards policies that ran closer to his family tradition. Alan's influence on policy making in respect of the west was over.

From 1231, royal policy in the west of the kingdom was directed more towards consolidation of the advances made since the early 1220s, and it was not until several years after Walter fitz Alan's death in 1241, by which time Alexander's influence over the mhic Somhairle had begun to decline, that the crown again began to pursue a more proactively aggressive policy in the region.[136] Alan of Galloway's ambitions in Mann and the Isles no longer meshed with those of both the king and his justiciar, who, after all, had been the one man whose territories and castles had suffered at the hands of the Norwegians. Walter fitz Alan, certainly, had no cause to look favourably on Alan of Galloway after the siege and sack of Rothesay, and the Stewarts appear to have been virulent in their denunciation of both him and his policies, something that became embedded in later Stewart tradition.[137] In place of Alan's dreams of Hebridean dominion, the Steward and his allies, principally Earl Máeldomhnaigh of Lennox, were entrusted by Alexander with the task of securing Scottish lordship in the Clyde estuary islands, Kintyre, Cowal and southern Argyll, principally through the development of their existing links with the mhic Dubhgaill and with

Domhnall mac Raonaill, Lord of Islay, brother of Ruaidrí. Aggressive campaigning in Atlantic waters was not to be resumed until the last weeks of Alexander II's life in 1249.

By the end of 1231, Alan had been isolated and abandoned. Most bitter for him to swallow must have been Alexander's rejection of the policy that he had so enthusiastically backed for a decade, particularly since Alan had gained nothing from his years of warfare and, indeed, had lost much. In the face of such blows, the virtual absence of Alan from historical record after 1230 could be read as a turning in onto his own estates and a withdrawal from active political life. Yet there are signs that he may have been seeking to regain influence in Scotland and re-establish his connections with the English crown. In 1233, amongst his last recorded acts, Alan arranged the marriage of his youngest daughter, Dervorgilla, to John Balliol of Barnard Castle, and of his sister, Ada, to Walter Bisset, lord of Aboyne.[138] The Bisset marriage may be particularly significant, for it established a link between Alan and a rapidly rising family that had, in effect, been 'created' by Alexander II and who stood prominently in royal service. Walter's nephew, John, held the lordship of the Aird to the west of Inverness and, it would seem, had acquired some interest in the lordship of Arran, where he died in 1257.[139] The date at which this interest was acquired is unknown, but it is possible that it may have been part of the consolidation of crown authority in the Clyde estuary in the 1230s. The Bissets were associated closely with another rising family, the Durwards, lords of Lundie in Angus, half of the lands of the earldom of Mar, of Urquhart and Stratherrick, and of Atholl, in the person of Alan Durward, earl from c. 1233.[140] Both the Bissets and the Durwards had established their positions as part of the colonial establishment along the frontier of royal power in the north and west Highlands in the 1220s, and had expanded their authority with crown encouragement at the expense of Gaelic lineages, especially the mhic Raonaill in Garmoran. These men had benefited greatly from Alexander II's more aggressive policy before 1231 and may have represented something of a hawkish element in the royal council. After their disgrace in 1242, moreover, the Bissets were to demonstrate that they had well-developed links with the maritime west, moving easily in an Ulster and Hebridean milieu.[141] If the Bisset marriage can be interpreted in this way, then it is possible that only two years after the failure of his war policy in the Isles, Alan was manoeuvring once more for a return to the aggressive expansionism that had characterised Scottish royal policy in the 1220s. Alan's death on 2 February 1234,[142] however, ensured that there was to be no revival of the policy of military expansion for a further fifteen years, and drew down the curtain on one of the most dynamic episodes in the making of the medieval kingdom.

The judgement of history has often been harsh on Alan, who has been portrayed as an irresponsible adventurer who used his position as ruler of a territory that may have acknowledged the overlordship of the king of Scots, but which was not integrated into the 'feudal' structure of the kingdom, to pursue personal ambitions that were barely compatible with the interests of his nominal master. As a consequence, when the opportunity arose on Alan's death with no legitimate male heir to succeed him, to end the ill-defined relationship between the Scottish crown and the lordship of Galloway, Alexander II moved swiftly and decisively. Prima facie, the limited evidence for an active role in the political life of a kingdom in which he was the holder of one of the highest offices in the land – the constableship – and where he was a leading feudatory of the crown, and the ambivalence of his position in Anglo-Scottish politics, has enabled his commitment to the interests of, and loyalty towards, the king of Scots to be questioned.[143] Yet, as Stringer has pointed out, in no way can Alan's relations with the Scottish crown be characterised as antagonistic or unco-operative.[144] On the contrary, he maintained stability within his hereditary lands – from which the Scots had faced repeated challenge throughout the twelfth century – gave service and aid to the crown when required, and preserved the close alignment with Scottish interests that his father, Roland, had established in the later 1170s. Furthermore, the involvement in Anglo-Irish affairs after 1212, that has been designated a key instance of Alan's lack of commitment to Scottish interests, can be shown to have developed with the full agreement and encouragement of the Scottish king, who saw it as an opportunity to stabilise a zone from which his enemies had drawn regular military aid. Even the wars that Alan waged in pursuit of the Manx throne for his bastard son, while indubitably driven by personal and family concerns, can be shown to have formed part of a wider policy initiated and led by the king of Scots. Far from being out of sympathy with Scottish interests, Alan's activities throughout his career marched in step with the policies of William the Lion and Alexander II.

The close alignment of Galwegian with Scottish royal interest throughout the careers of Alan and his father was part of a general process of integration of the lordship into the kingdom. While Galloway was still clearly a distinct entity in 1234, and one in which the native magnates, at least, had a strong sense of self-identity, as events subsequent to Alan's death demonstrated, they had begun to think and operate within a wider Scottish context.[145] Keith Stringer has outlined the complex range of regulatory mechanism – 'honouring him with high office in the royal household and marriage to a royal bride; stressing his direct tenurial dependence on the crown for the lordships of Lauderdale and Cunning-hame; enmeshing prominent members of his retinue in a network of royal governance and control' – through which the Scottish crown governed its relationship with Alan and extended its influence over the ruling elites of the lordship,[146] but similar devices had been utilised with good effect since the time of Fergus. Under Alan, however, the cumulative effect of these devices developed at an accelerating pace, and the process was set to continue as a consequence of the marriages that he had arranged for his daughters with prominent members of the northern English and Anglo-Scottish nobility. What had changed, however, was the general socio-political and cultural framework within which Alan had operated. While the Scottish – and, for that matter, English – crowns had been remote overlords for most of the twelfth century, by the 1190s they had established a direct and permanent presence in the regions that bordered Galloway. Scottish royal authority was reaching its thirteenth-century zenith under its most ruthlessly effective state-builder since the days of David I. In Argyll, the central and west Highlands, Ross, Sutherland and Caithness, as well as in Galloway, Alexander II was driving home a policy of domination and integration through a complex interplay of colonialist aggression and accommodation with the native powers. The regulatory mechanisms employed in respect of Alan were deployed to good effect against the mhic Dubhgaill or the mhic an t-Sagairt, while the new colonial nobility of the Highlands, in common with central figures in Alan's household, were bound to the crown through not only bonds of tenure but through their appointment to offices in the royal household and administration. As Stringer has so aptly expressed it, this was a merging of the local with the national and national with the local, rather than a manifestation of the core establishing its domination of the periphery. By the time of Alan's death, it was impossible to separate Scottish national interests from local Galwegian concerns.

Notes

1 *RRS*, ii, no. 41.
2 E.g. in Oram, thesis, 124–25. For Alan, son of Roland, tenant of the honour Wallingford, see Stringer, 'Alan of Galloway', 83 and note 3.
3 K. J. Stringer, 'A new wife for Alan of Galloway', *TDGNHAS*, xlix (1972), 49–55.
4 *Chron. Howden*, iv, 140, 141.
5 Stringer, 'New wife', 50–54.
6 Stringer, 'Records', no. 32.
7 Bower, *Scotichronicon*, vol. 4, 427; Topping, 'Harald Maddadson', 119.
8 Ibid., no. 30.
9 *Melrose Liber*, i, nos 82, 83, 84; for discussion, see Stringer, 'Records', nos 37, 38. For consideration of the motives behind the acts, see K. J. Stringer, 'Reform Monasticism and Celtic Scotland: Galloway, *c*.1140–*c*.1240', in E. J. Cowan and R. A. McDonald (eds), *Alba: Celtic Scotland in the Middle Ages* (East Linton, 2000), 127–65 at 144.
10 Stringer, 'Records', nos 31, 33, 34, 35.
11 *RRS*, ii, nos 337, 428–30, 432, 438, 460, 497.
12 *CDS*, i, no. 357.
13 Ibid., nos 358, 359, 360.
14 Ibid., no. 362.
15 Warren, *King John*, 110–13.
16 Ibid., 11–16.
17 *CDS*, i, no. 370.
18 Ibid., no. 382.
19 Ibid., nos 382, 395, 397.

20 Ibid., nos 402, 404.
21 Ibid., nos 405, 409. Thomas agreed to pay sixty marks in two instalments at Michaelmas 1207 and Easter 1208 as a down payment, to be followed by annual payments as fixed by Roger de Lacy, constable of Chester. After the initial payments, however, Thomas defaulted on the agreement: CDS, i, nos 426, 432, 442, 481, 497.
22 The earliest surviving occurrence of Thomas as earl is in William the Lion's confirmation of Alan of Galloway's grants of property to the churches of Kirkcudbright and Kelton, issued at Stirling, 7 January 1210 (RRS, ii, no. 489).
23 Chron. Melrose, s.a. 1209.
24 Ibid.; Roger of Wendover, Flores Historiarum, s.a 1209.
25 Eirspennill's Håkon, Guthorm and Ingi's Saga, c. 18, Ingi Bard's son's Saga, 192–94; Icelandic Annals, s.a. 1210.
26 Chron. Melrose, s.a. 1210; T. E. McNeill, Anglo–Norman Ulster. The History and Archaeology of an Irish Barony 1177–1400 (Edinburgh, 1980), 6–7; Warren, King John, 184–87, 193–97.
27 Chron. Mann, s.a. 1205.
28 Chron. Mann, s.a. 1210.
29 CDS, i, no. 480; Histoire des Ducs de Normandie, 112–14.
30 McDonald, 'Treachery', 179, 184.
31 Bower, Scotichronicon, vol. 4, 467; Memorials of St Edmund's Abbey, ed. T. Arnold (London, 1890–96), ii, 20; Memoriale Fratris Walteri de Coventria, ed. W. Stubbs (London, 1872–73), ii, 206; Stringer, 'Periphery and core', 87. A re-expansion of Cenél nEógain influence into the Isles in the later twelfth century is indicated by the establishment of Domnall ua Brolchain as prior of Iona (AU, s.a. 1203). Following his death in 1203, the northern Irish clergy, headed by the comarb of Columcille, attacked Iona and drove out Cellach and the community that he had established there on the death of Domnall. Following this, the abbot of Derry, Amalgaid ua Feargail, assumed the abbacy of Iona (AU, s.a. 1204). In ecclesiastical terms, this is a clear statement of continuing – and aggressive – Cenél nEógain authority in what had earlier been the core of Somairle's domain. This must have been a matter of grave concern to the king of Scots.
32 RRS, ii, no. 501 (which establishes Alan's presence at Forres in autumn 1211 in the royal army); Bower, Scotichronicon, vol. 4, 465–67.
33 Memorials of St Edmund's Abbey, ii, 20; Memoriale Walteri de Coventria, ii, 206; Stringer, 'Periphery and core'.
34 Duncan, Making of the Kingdom, 196.
35 Bower, Scotichronicon, vol. 4, 469.
36 Ibid., 463.
37 AU, s.a. 1212; ALC, s.a. 1212.
38 AU, s.a. 1214.
39 Stringer, 'Periphery and core', 88.
40 Chron. Melrose, s.a. 1215.
41 AU, s.a. 1216.
42 R. Greeves, 'The Galloway lands in Ulster', TDGNHAS, xxxvi (1957–58), 115–21 at 115–16; CDS, i, no. 879. An alternative identification is Ballygally between Larne and Glenarm, where Duncan held other lands by royal grant.
43 These were specifically excluded from the grant made to Alan (CDS, i, no. 573). For their composition, see CDS, i, no. 737. For the nephew of Duncan of Carrick, see CDS, i, no. 578.
44 CDS, i, no. 573 [misdated by Bain to May 1213]; Greeve, 'Galloway lands in Ulster', 117; McNeill, Anglo-Norman Ulster, 15; Stringer, 'Periphery and

core', 87–88.

45 McNeill, *Anglo-Norman Ulster*, 15.

46 *CDS*, i, no. 585; McNeill, *Anglo-Norman Ulster*, 15.

47 *CDS*, i, no. 586.

48 *RRS*, ii, 105.

49 Stringer, 'Periphery and core', 88 and notes.

50 E.g., the letters sent by John dated 15 and 20 July 1212, *CDS*, i, nos 527, 529.

51 Stringer, 'Periphery and core', 88.

52 Warren, *King John*, 199–200.

53 *CDS*, i, no. 529.

54 Stringer, 'Periphery and core', 88; *CDS*, i, nos 533, 540.

55 Roger of Wendover, *Flores Historiarum*, ii, 61; Warren, *King John*, 200.

56 *CDS*, i, nos 580, 583, 584.

57 Ibid., nos 577, 582, 585, 586. Thomas was probably at the muster of the royal host at Portsmouth, to which the Bishop of Winchester was instructed to bring Thomas's son, who was one of the Scottish hostages (*CDS*, i, no. 574). For Thomas to have had a son old enough to have served as a hostage under either the 1209 or 1212 treaties between William and John, the boy must either have been a child of a first marriage, pre-dating the marriage with Isabella of Atholl, or a bastard. One of Alan's daughters by his de Lacy first wife also served as a hostage, her death being recorded on 13 June 1213 (*CDS*, i, no. 574).

58 *AU*, s.a. 1214.

59 Stringer, 'Periphery and core', 88–89.

60 Ibid., 89; Bower, *Scotichronicon*, vol. 5, p.81.

61 *CDS*, i, no. 621.

62 Ibid., no. 628.

63 Stringer, 'Periphery and core', 89.

64 *CDS*, i, no. 625. McNeill has suggested that the reduction is an attempt by John to persuade Alan to take up his award seriously (*Anglo-Norman Ulster*, 15), but it is clearly linked to the continuing crisis in England after June 1215.

65 *CDS*, i, nos 626, 627.

66 Ibid., 631.

67 Stringer, 'Periphery and core', 89.

68 Ibid., 89–92.

69 See, for example, Stringer, 'Records', no. 53; *Lanercost Cartulary*, no. 28.

70 *CDS*, i, no. 673.

71 *Chron. Melrose*, s.a. 1217.

72 *CDS*, i, nos 722, 763.

73 Stringer, 'Periphery and core', 92–93.

74 *CDS*, i, no. 754 (misdated by Bain to before April 1220).

75 Ibid., nos 702, 717.

76 Ibid., nos 720, 721.

77 Ibid., nos 737, 755.

78 *Annals of Dunstable*, 58; *CDS*, i, no. 762.

79 *CDS*, i, nos 763, 764.

80 Bower, *Scotichronicon*, vol. 5 p. 105.

81 Thomas's charter of confirmation to the monks of Newbattle of a gift by one of his tenants, Adam, son of Edulph, witnessed by the abbot and convent of Kilwinning, was probably issued at this time. It points to the presence of Thomas and some of his tenants from Lothian, probably for the muster of the royal host at nearby Irvine or Ayr. *Newbattle Registrum*, no. 27.

82 Bower, *Scotichronicon*, vol. 5, p. 107; McDonald, *Kingdom of the Isles*, 83–84.

83 *CDS*, i, no. 830; for the resumption of the demesne, see D. A. Carpenter, *The*

Minority of Henry III (London, 1990), 281–89. For Thomas of Galloway and Fergus of Glencairn in the 1222 campaign, see *Dryburgh Liber*, no. 84.

84 Carpenter, *Minority*, 306–07.
85 *CDS*, i, no. 857.
86 *AU*, s.a 1222; McNeill, *Anglo–Norman Ulster*, 18; G. H. Orpen, *Ireland Under the Normans 1169–1216* (Oxford, 1911), ii, 44–45. Thomas's losses were recognised by the English government, who awarded him 100 marks from the Dublin exchequer in December 1225, *CDS*, i, no. 922.
87 *CDI*, i, nos 1161, 1201, 1224,
88 *CDS*, i, no. 890. Thomas wrote in like fashion, *CDS*, i, no. 891.
89 *CDS*, i, no. 905.
90 *CDI*, i, nos 1371, 1372
91 McNeill, *Anglo-Norman Ulster*, 21–22.
92 *AU*, s.a 1228.
93 *Chron. Lanercost*, s.a. 1229; cf., Stringer, 'Periphery and core', 93.
94 *CDS*, i, no. 1050.
95 In January 1227, Thomas was still seeking payment of the 100 marks promised to him in compensation for his losses in 1223–24, *CDI*, i, no. 1473.
96 Stringer, 'Periphery and core', 94.
97 *Chron. Mann*, s.a 1187 and 1188.
98 Ibid., sa. 1204, 1205.
99 McDonald, *Kingdom of the Isles*, 87.
100 Ibid., 88–89.
101 *Chron. Mann*, 'Liber adhuc ad edificationem legentium de gestis reginaldi et olaui fratrum' etc.
102 *CDS*, i, no. 852, misdated to 1223 by Bain.
103 Ibid., i, no. 890.
104 *Chron. Mann*, s.a. ?1224.
105 Ibid., s.a. 1225.
106 Ibid., s.a. 1226.
107 As Thomas was still alive in 1296, it is unlikely that he was little more than a young teenager at the time of his marriage.
108 Stringer, 'Periphery and core', 95–97.
109 *Moray Registrum*, no. 29.
110 Stringer, 'Periphery and core', 96–97.
111 *CDS*, i, no. 1001; v, no. 9.
112 *Chron. Mann*, s.a. 1228.
113 *Chron. Lanercost*, s.a. 1229.
114 For the most recent general discussion of this, see McDonald, *Kingdom of the Isles*, 88–94.
115 The loyalty of the mhic Dubhgaill to their Norwegian overlord had been called into question as early as 1224, *Eirspennill's Håkon Håkon's Saga*, c. 165.
116 *Chron. Mann*, following on from the events s.a. 1228–29.
117 *Eirspennill's Håkon Håkon's Saga*, cc. 164–65.
118 Ibid., cc. 167–68.
119 *Chron. Lanercost*, s.a. 1230. Walter Bower places the start of this rising in 1228 and its conclusion in 1229, Bower, *Scotichronicon*, vol. 5, 143, 145.
120 *Paisley Registrum*, 48.
121 *Eirspennill's Håkon Håkon's Saga*, cc. 167–69; *Chron. Mann*, s.a. 1230; *Chron. Lanercost*, s.a 1230.
122 *Eirspennill's Håkon Håkon's Saga*, c. 169.
123 Stringer, 'Periphery and core', 97.
124 Ibid., 94–95.
125 G. W. S. Barrow, 'Badenoch and Strathspey, 1130–1312. 1 Secular and

Political', *Northern Scotland*, viii (1988), 1–15 at 4–6.
126 Bower, *Scotichronicon*, vol. 5, 143.
127 *Moray Registrum*, nos 21, 28, 51, 71, 73, 74, 83; *Beauly Chrs*, 18–37.
128 *Annals of Dunstable*, s.a. 1231.
129 McDonald, 'Treachery in the remotest territories of Scotland', 184–85.
130 Duffy, *Ireland in the Middle Ages*, 115–17.
131 *Chron. Melrose*, s.a. 1231; *CDS*, i, no. 1894.
132 Murray, 'Swerving from the path of justice'.
133 *Chron. Howden*, iv, 145.
134 *RRS*, ii, 34–35
135 Bower, *Scotichronicon*, vol. 5, 145.
136 *Chron. Melrose*, s.a. 1241; Murray, 'Swerving from the path of justice'.
137 See discussion in Bower, *Scotichronicon*, vol. 5, 261–63.
138 *Chron. Melrose*, s.a. 1233.
139 *AU*, s.a. 1257.
140 For a discussion of the rise of the Durwards, see R. D. Oram, 'Accommodation, adaptation and integration: the earls and earldom of Mar *c*.1130 to *c*.1300', in S. I. Boardman (ed.), *Native Kindreds* (forthcoming).
141 See the general discussion in Duncan, *Making of the Kingdom*, 544–45; McNeill, *Anglo-Norman Ulster*, 22, 27; Greeves, 'Galloway lands in Ulster', 120–21.
142 *Chron. Lanercost*, s.a 1233.
143 See especially, Duncan, *Making of the Kingdom*, 529.
144 Stringer, 'Periphery and core', 85.
145 Ibid., 102.
146 Ibid., 101.

5

THE HEIRS OF ALAN: DE QUINCY, DE FORZ AND BALLIOL

REBELLION AND SUPPRESSION

Tension within Galloway mounted rapidly in the months after Alan's death as the issue of the succession began to unfold. It is unknown when Alan's legitimate son by Margaret of Huntingdon, Thomas, had died, but Alan's recent re-marriage indicated that he had believed he would father the son who would succeed to the great agglomeration of properties that he had amassed, and no alternative scheme had been worked out to address the possibility of his death without a direct – legitimate – male heir. In spite of his subsequent position among the native nobility as the favoured successor, it is improbable that Alan's bastard son, Thomas, had been intended to inherit the lordship: although the marriage to King Rognvald's daughter had produced no tangible results, Alan had otherwise made only some small-scale landed provision for Thomas within Galloway.[1] Thomas did, belatedly and evidently once the preferred options of the native magnates had been rejected by Alexander II, gain some credit in the eyes of at least a significant segment of the Gaelic clergy and nobility of the lordship. While in the past this has presented as a clash of traditions, with Thomas being the preferred candidate under native custom that did not debar from inheritance on the grounds of illegitimacy, while Alexander II, presented as 'determined to uphold feudal law', was set on introducing 'feudal' principles and, treating Galloway as a feu, divide the lordship between the husbands of the legitimate heiresses,[2] it appears rather to have been a last resort employed to stave off the threat of partition. That this was not an 'anti-feudal' or anti-Scottish reaction is evident from the earlier request that Alexander take Galloway intact under his direct lordship. He can hardly have been considered to be more in tune with their culture and society than the alternatives on offer in the shape of the husbands of Alan's daughters.

Thomas emerges from the accounts of the rising made in his name as very much a passive figure, manipulated by other interests. He appears to have been a convenient vehicle through which to answer the desire on the part of the Galwegian nobility to retain the integrity of the lordship, and so avoid the partition which female succession would entail. There had evidently been some expectation on their part that Alan's daughters would be passed over in favour of one of the surviving male representatives of the lordly house. According to Matthew Paris, they proposed to the king that the heritage should fall to Thomas, who had evidently been reared in the Gaelic tradition, or, if succession by an illegitimate line was unacceptable, to Patrick, Alan's nephew, whose father had epitomised that same tradition. Failing that, one of the more distant male relatives, presumably the head of the MacDowell kindred, was offered as an alternative.[3] As a last resort, the Galwegians invited the king to take possession of the lordship for himself, thus keeping the land united under one lord. The appeal was in vain and the division of the inheritance between Alan's three daughters was ordered.[4]

Alexander II's motives in 1234 were hardly dictated by concern for the interests of the women whom he was being asked to dispossess. There was no question under the feudal tradition by then established in the kingdom that the legitimate heiresses to Lauderdale and Cunningham be set aside for anyone else, king, illegitimate son, or legitimate male collateral. The position in Galloway itself, which technically lay outwith the sphere of Scots legal tradition and was not held as a feu from the crown, was more questionable, but Alan himself had evidently sought to avoid the alternative of dividing his inheritance into two blocks under different heirs by countenancing the succession of Thomas to the lordship. Keith Stringer has suggested that Alan's adventures in Mann and the Isles in 1230–31 presented compelling reasons for ensuring that no one man should fall heir to the military potential of Galloway.[5] While this may have been one consideration in his decision in favour of partition, it seems more probable that the division of Galloway should be seen in the same context as Alexander's near-contemporary settlement of inheritance disputes else-where within the kingdom. Royal domination of the peripheries of Scotland had come a long way since the crisis-ridden reign of William the Lion and Alexander II could, with confidence, impose a partition that would finally end the threat to Scottish security represented by the existence of such a semi-autonomous and militarily powerful lordship. The legal niceties of the decision to treat Galloway as a feu were irrelevant to a king who had embarked on a policy of aggressive expansion of his realm. By simply treating Galloway as a feu, he resolved any ambiguity in respect of the succession. Alexander needed no more reason for his actions than the political necessities of his monarchy. The break-up of Alan's domain, however, had not been a foregone conclusion, nor was it simply the act of a king 'determined to uphold feudal law'.[6] The Galloway succession issue was just one of a series of major disputes concerning magnate inheritances in Scotland at this time, albeit the only one which resulted in armed insurrection in a bid to overturn the king's decision. As the succession to the earldoms of Buchan and Mar in the period c.1210–c.1220 highlight, inheritance law in Scotland was in a state of flux with both 'feudal' and Gaelic traditions operating in uneasy conjunction.[7] In Mar, where succession was disputed between two segments of the comital family and where uncanonical marriages and the resultant illegitimacy of heirs was imputed of both parties, the crown was successful in establishing the principle of legitimate male primogeniture but at the price of conceding a substantial lordship carved out of the earldom demesne for the unsuccessful claimants. There was, thus, no clear legal precedent and the views of clerical observers such as Matthew Paris or the Melrose chronicler that partition between the heiresses was the just solution is no more than an articulation of church doctrine concerning canonical marriage and the rights of legitimate heirs. Political expediency and family interests rather than any adherence to a preferred legal principle lay behind Alexander's decision. After all, not only would partition check the formidable military potential of the lordship but it would place that power in the hands of men linked closely with the king and his government and therefore likely to be more amenable to his interests: Christina and Dervorgilla were cousins of the king, and Helen's husband, Roger de Quincy, was head of a family long prominent in royal service and who, with his father, Earl Saher, had been a close associate of the king during the Magna Carta crisis in England and the subsequent Anglo-Scottish war. The rejection of Gaelic succession law, however, where illegitimacy was no bar to inheritance, drove the Galwegians into open rebellion in support of the rights of Thomas.

The rebellion of 1235 is portrayed generally as a spontaneous rising on the part of the people against an unpopular and innovatory judgement on the part of the king of Scots. The three main contemporary sources that chronicle the rising, however, contain within their narratives hints of deeper motives and outside forces at work. The briefest description, that of the *Chronicle of Lanercost*, presents the rising as a bid to remove Galloway from the subjection of the Scottish king with the aim of setting Thomas up as 'lord or (for all intents) king'. It mentions attacks on royal land on the frontiers of Galloway, presumably in Kyle and Nithsdale, and names the chief supporter of Thomas as the otherwise unknown 'Gilleroth',[8] evidently a powerful figure among the Gaelic nobility of the lordship, possibly even a member of the MacDowell kindred. Matthew Paris and the *Chronicle of Melrose* – in view of the abbey's close association with Alexander II and its involvement in the aftermath of the rising clearly a partisan report – give more detailed accounts of the action, the latter incorporating a Cistercian narrative presumably obtained from Dundrennan or Glenluce. Paris speaks of an alliance of Galwegian, Manx and Irish interests, brought together by the efforts of Hugh de Lacy, earl of Ulster, father of Alan's last wife, with the avowed intent of winning the inheritance for Thomas or one of his male relatives, preferably Patrick of Atholl.[9] De Lacy is not mentioned subsequently, probably as a consequence of his growing involvement in the war of succession which he and Maurice fitz Gerald had stirred up in Tír Eógain between the Uí Néill and meic Lochlainn, nor does he appear in any other account, but all three sources agree that Ireland was a source of foreign support for Thomas's cause, providing men and a temporary refuge when required. Indeed, in the second phase of the rebellion, Thomas returned from Ireland in the company of 'a king's son,'[10] quite possibly one of de Lacy's Uí Néill allies, with his military retinue, presumably a reflection of the west Ulster interest in the outcome of the rising. Hugh de Lacy's motives in assembling such support for the bastard son of his late son-in-law were probably complex, at the very least bound up in the lingering uncertainty over control of the Galloway lands in Ulster, but more probably linked to securing significant and long term military and naval aid for his ambitions in Tír Eógain where, following the death of his erstwhile ally, Áed Méith ua Néill, Hugh planned to expand his domain and influence. There must also have been the worrying question of the replacement of the lordship of Alan, with whom he had recently reached a settlement, with the extension of Scottish royal influence into a zone of vital interest to Hugh, a move made even more threatening by the imminent marriage of the sister of the Scottish king to Gilbert Marshal, earl of Pembroke and lord of Leinster, brother of Richard Marshal, in whose death at the Curragh in Kildare de Lacy had been implicated.[11] The identity of the Irish and Isles supporters of Thomas and his male kin is unknown, but the close association of his uncle with Ruaidrí mac Raonaill, lord of Garmoran, and with the Ua Domnaill of Tír Conaill provides some clues. Both kindreds had, in the past, joined in Thomas of Atholl's attacks on the Uí Néill and, though the Uí Domnaill were subsequently to ally with King Brian ua Néill against de Lacy and his associates,[12] the old alignments may still have held strong in 1235.

A detailed account of the suppression of the revolt is given in the *Chronicle of Melrose*. According to it, Alexander invaded Galloway in mid-July, determined to bring the affair to a swift and decisive conclusion. This was soon achieved when the Galwegians ambushed the royal army that was in difficulties in the marshy terrain, but Ferchar, earl of Ross, who had been bringing up the rear of the Scottish force, fell on the attackers and routed them. The following day the Galwegian leadership yielded to the king, but Thomas and Gilleroth escaped to Ireland. Believing the question to be settled, Alexander withdrew and was at Berwick by 1 August for the marriage of his younger sister to Gilbert Marshal, leaving Walter Comyn, earl of Menteith, to complete the pacification. His sister's marriage, however, may simply have been a convenient excuse for Alexander to absent himself from the mopping up operations, for these clearly involved attacks on the chief centres of the church in Galloway, which had emerged as one of the principal opponents of the king's policies. Tongland Abbey, Alan's own foundation, and Glenluce, whose abbot was deposed in the aftermath of the rebellion, were ransacked by Comyn's men. The pro-Comyn Melrose chronicler, however, acts as an apologist for Earl Walter, presenting the attacks as the actions of elements of the army who acted *ultra vires*, outwith his control, and who were subsequently brought to book for their crimes. The return of Thomas and Gilleroth from Ireland with a mercenary force in the midst of these disturbances caused panic among the Scots, who fled rather than fight. Gilleroth, however, evidently reckoned that Thomas's cause was lost and, in a bid to preserve his influence in the native political community and, presumably, to stake his place in the new apparatus of power in the lordship, entered negotiations with another of Alan and Thomas's former associates, Patrick, earl of Dunbar, who was leading the new royal army against the rebels. Abandoned by his chief native supporter, Thomas threw himself on Alexander's mercy and was imprisoned in Edinburgh Castle.[13] Melrose presents his incarceration as of short duration, but he was eventually handed over to his half-sister, Dervorgilla, and, in the words of the *Chronicle of Lanercost*, 'shut up until decrepit old age in the confines of Barnard Castle'.[14]

Thomas played no further active part in the history of Galloway and remained in Balliol custody until 18 March 1286, when the question of his release was among business discussed at Alexander III's last council meeting.[15] The king's death that night ended moves towards the release of the unfortunate Thomas, for ten years later he was brought out of imprisonment in Barnard Castle by Edward I. On 6 March 1296 the king had him released and, in a rather optimistic move, armed him with a charter of liberties and despatched him towards Galloway. Edward's purpose was clear: Thomas was to be used as an alternative focus for Galwegian loyalty in an attempt to undermine the power of the Balliols in the lordship. How effective he would have been is questionable for it is unlikely that he would have received much support after sixty years of absence during which time Dervorgilla and her family had established themselves at the heart of the political life of the lordship. The strength of Galwegian loyalty to the son of Alan may never have been put to the test, however, for Thomas had reached only as far as Carlisle before the outbreak of hostilities between his nephew, John Balliol, and the English king.[16] On the collapse of Scottish resistance in July 1296, however, he was restored at last to liberty, and on 30 August Edward I instructed delivery to him of the lands that his father had once given him.[17] It is the last mention of this pathetic figure in historical record.

The collapse of Galwegian opposition in 1235 and the subsequent imprisonment of Thomas marked the end of any serious challenge to Scottish rule in the region until the end of the thirteenth century. The victory was absolute and left Alexander II free to impose the most favourable settlement for Scottish royal interests. Apart from the bastard, Thomas, the only viable claimant was Patrick of Atholl, the under-age son of Earl Thomas, but he was under the dominance of his mother's Comyn kinsmen and thus firmly associated with crown interests. His death in 1242 without issue, before he was even formally of age, removed any potential future claim from that direction. Determined to end the ambiguities of its status and the threats to his interests posed by a united Galloway, Alexander re-affirmed his original intention of dividing the lordship between the heiresses.

The traditional narratives, which take a largely monarchocentric approach to the whole episode, draw a line under the affair with Thomas's surrender to the king. There appears, however, to have been a more protracted process of consolidation than these narratives would allow, extending down to 1237. Linked to this are indications of Scottish actions in the Irish Sea area and in Ulster, with both Patrick, earl of Dunbar, and Walter, earl of Menteith, the two men whom Alexander had charged with the pacification of Galloway, standing accused by Henry III of involvement in the piratical activities of the English outlaws, William and Robert Marsh, in the Irish Sea.[18] Although both men swore on oath in 1244 that they had taken no part in the attacks on Ireland,[19] it must be suspected that, just as had happened with regard to the behaviour of the Scottish army in Galloway in 1235, Alexander had turned a blind eye to a military operation of which he must have approved but which, for diplomatic reasons, he could not officially sanction. Here, then, may have been Alexander's revenge against those among the Anglo-Irish and native Irish communities who had instigated or been implicated in Thomas's insurrection.

THE DIVIDED INHERITANCE

It is a positive reflection of Alan's outward-looking policies that of the families to which he allied himself through his daughters' marriages, only one had any previous substantial landed interest in Scotland. To these three women and their husbands fell a share in the great Galloway inheritance, a decision made, *prima facie*, in accordance with feudal legal principles but, in reality, dictated by the political necessity of the Scottish crown to enforce a partition of a power block which lent its rulers an uncomfortable independence of the crown. The traditional view of this partition was summarised by R. C. Reid, who considered that:

> When Alan [of Galloway] died in 1234, Galloway was divided into three parts for his three daughters. It has been generally assumed that the three divisions were definite units and not scattered groupings. [Helen], the eldest daughter, married Roger de Quenci and her share must have been the most westerly and may have covered most of Wigtownshire. Dervorgilla received the eastern portion, probably from Nith to Fleet. Between these must have been the portion of Christina who married the earl of Albemarle. But there may have been odd estates or particles of land outwith the clear-cut divisions; thus the Balliols owned lands in Glasserton and the heirs of [Helen] held land in Troqueer, Girthon and elsewhere.[20]

The theme is of delineation into discrete blocks – reduced to two after 1246 when Christina died and her properties fell largely to Dervorgilla[21] – with the caput of Dervorgilla and the Balliols at Buittle, and that of Helen at

Cruggleton.[22] Geoffrey Barrow has gone further and claimed that Dervorgilla 'eventually acquired the entire lordship of Galloway because of her sisters' childlessness.'[23] This suggested Balliol domination of Galloway, however, was a late thirteenth-century phenomenon, for analysis of Dervorgilla's position within the succession and the landholding of her eldest sister's family establish beyond doubt that the pre-eminent power down to the early 1260s was Roger de Quincy.

Alan had six children by the first two of his three marriages. By his first marriage, to an un-named lady of the Pontefract Lacy family, he had two daughters, of whom only Helen survived him.[24] His marriage in 1209 to Margaret, daughter of Earl David of Huntingdon, produced three children, a son who pre-deceased his father and two daughters, Christina and Dervorgilla (see family tree).[25] The order of the marriages of Alan's daughters and the status of their husbands is an indication of their order of seniority. Before 1234 Helen married one of the greatest Anglo-Scottish landholders of the day, Roger de Quincy, who succeeded to his father's estates in 1219, and in 1235, following the death of his mother, became second earl of Winchester.[26] No date is recorded for the marriage of Christina, but it occurred before Alan's death. The status of her husband, William III de Forz, heir to the earldom of Aumale and its estates spread across northern England from Cockermouth in Cumberland to Holderness on the Humber,[27] underscores her seniority over Dervorgilla.

Dervorgilla was the last to marry, her father only arranging her match in 1233 to John Balliol, lord of Barnard Castle and Bywell on Tyne in England and of Bailleul-en-Vimeu in Picardy.[28] Although the Balliols were prominent members of the English baronage and had risen through loyal service to the English crown, John was socially the inferior of his wife's brothers-in-law and hardly the elevated match that might be expected had Dervorgilla been the senior heiress.[29] It would appear, rather, that she was simply another daughter for whom a match had to be found. As the most junior of the heiresses, therefore, how did she acquire the social and territorial pre-eminence that she is accorded by tradition? The answer to that question is gradually and, perhaps, opportunistically.

Reid's hypothesis has a compelling logic to it. It draws support from the precedent for this form of division in the twelfth century when the lordship was partitioned between Gillebrigte and Uhtred. While it is nowhere stated that the lordship was divided into separate blocks for those bitter enemies, there is circumstantial evidence for Gillebrigte's control west of the Cree and Uhtred's to its east. But the 1234 partition was more complex, for there were three claims to answer and the division had to satisfy the 'feudal' legal system within which the husbands of the heiresses operated. When the result is pieced together from the remaining fragments, it becomes clear that the supposed post-1246 division into two discrete lordships is illusory. On the contrary, Alan's demesne was divided systematically between his daughters, but with Helen's, and *de facto* through her Roger de Quincy's, seniority recognised.[30]

The chief evidence for the dismantling of the monolithic lordship of Alan is an inquest post mortem of August 1296 into the heritage of Elena de la Zouche, youngest of Helen's three daughters by Roger de Quincy.[31] Jury returns from Wigtownshire found that she held one third of Craichlaw in Kirkcowan parish,[32] an estate in which there was no Balliol involvement, which indicates that the remainder was held by Elena's sisters, Margaret de Ferrers, countess of Derby, and Elizabeth Comyn, countess of Buchan. The return from Dumfriesshire found that she held one third of Girthon and Senwick, one sixth of Troqueer and Drumflat, and one merkland in Kelton. Margaret and Elizabeth held the remainder of both Girthon and Senwick, but in Troqueer and Drumflat the de Quincys possessed only half of the estate. Here, the moiety was held by Dervorgilla. In Kelton, the arrangement was more heavily fragmented. Although this scatter of property does not represent an equal third of the de Quincy heritage in Galloway, it reveals the existence of a significant block of de Quincy lands between the Dee and the Fleet.

Further properties were held by the Ferrers and Comyn co-parceners in the de Quincy heritage. The 1266 Exchequer accounts record that the sheriffship of Wigtown was held by Alexander Comyn, Earl of Buchan, husband of the second daughter of Helen and Roger de Quincy. He also had the keepership of two parts of the Galloway properties of the late Roger,[33] presumably until the process of partition of the de Quincy heritage had been settled. Control of the sheriffdom underscored his territorial influence west of the Cree, where Cruggleton Castle was his caput.[34] That this property was the chief seat of the lordship in western Galloway is confirmed by its descent to the eldest of Alan's daughters and by the fact that the attendant estate was neither split into thirds for Christina and Dervorgilla, nor after 1264 for the other de Quincy heiresses. Kirkcudbright also fell to Roger through Helen, and was in his hands by 1237.[35] The lords of Galloway had a 'house' there in the late twelfth century,[36] and an earlier role as caput is confirmed in the *Brevis Descriptio Regni Scotie*, a traveller's guide to late thirteenth-century Scotland. This describes Kirkcudbright as the property of William de Ferrers,[37] the son of Roger's eldest daughter, Margaret. Its descent intact to him argues strongly that this was the chief place not just of eastern Galloway, but of the former lordship itself.

Little detail survives of Dervorgilla's landholding and much must be extrapolated from mid-fourteenth-century sources. One consequence of this is that her original heritage cannot be differentiated from Christina's properties acquired after 1246. The only reference to the fate of her sister's heritage is a letter of May 1304 of John, earl of Buchan, complaining that property received from John Balliol 'in recompense of the earl's right in the Galloway lands of the said king, of which he had much more than his purparty' had been seized by Edward I's deputies.[38] The hub of the Balliol lordship in Galloway was, by tradition, Buittle in the Urr valley.[39] This emerged as Dervorgilla's caput in the later thirteenth century, probably after the death of her husband in 1268,[40] but lay peripheral to the bulk of her demesne. *Arsbotl* or *Insula Arsa*, otherwise Burned Island in Loch Ken,[41] was more probably her original administrative seat. With it, Dervorgilla gained possession of at least a portion of Kells, regarded by her grandson, Edward Balliol, as part of his patrimony,[42] plus land in Balmaghie, Parton and Crossmichael.[43] To its east, she held a portion of Kirkpatrick-Durham,[44] while at the extreme south-east of Galloway, her family held Preston under Criffel in Kirkbean parish.[45] Lochkindeloch, granted in the twelfth century to the fitz Troites but which had reverted to their superiors, was also in Dervorgilla's demesne until 1273 when it formed the core estate of her greatest display of piety, Sweetheart Abbey.[46] In Wigtownshire her inheritance was less compact. In the Rhinns she had property in Kirkcolm,[47] and also Milmain in Stoneykirk parish:[48] in the Machars, Kidsdale in Glasserton.[49] Property in the burgh of Wigtown is inferred by the attribution of the foundation of the friary there to Dervorgilla,[50] and there are indications that the Balliols possessed land and rights in the parish of Wigtown and the adjoining parish of Kirkinner. Presentations to these parishes and the grant of Kirkinner to the bishopric of Whithorn by Edward I were made by right of his possession of the heritage resigned in 1296 by John Balliol.[51] A final recognisable portion of Balliol demesne was four quarterlands at Outon to the north of Whithorn.[52]

Superiorities, too, were partitioned between the heiresses. The evidence is patchy, but a network of de Quincy superiorities can be identified east of the Cree. The northern Glenken was under Comyn superiority;[53] Colvend, granted by Robert I in *c*.1327–28 to his nephew Alexander Bruce, formerly pertained to John Comyn, Earl of Buchan, William de Ferrers and Alan de la Zouche, evidently through reversionary rights arising from superiority.[54] Greater documentary survival gives Dervorgilla's overlordship a more widespread distribution. East of the Urr lay Kirkgunzeon, for which the monks of Holm Cultram paid an annual rent of £10 to the Balliols,[55] with to its north Kirkpatrick, held in chief of the lordship of Buittle in *c*.1304.[56] In the Machars, the Vieuxponts acknowledged Balliol superiority of Sorbie in 1251[57] and further west the Marshal lords of Toskerton/Stoneykirk, prominent in Dervorgilla's following in the 1270s, were probably Balliol vassals.[58] Bertram de Cardoness, Lord of Anwoth, who was a regular witness to Balliol documents,[59] may also have been her vassal but there are dangers in following this line, as is demonstrated with regard to the de Campanias. Radulf de Campania, who held Borgue in the time of Alan,[60] was associated with Roger de Quincy after 1234,[61] as was his kinsman, Robert de Campania, lord of Castleton of Borgue.[62] In 1282, however, Radulf's grandson, Robert, quitclaimed Borgue to Dervorgilla, from whom he had held the lands in chief.[63] The inference is that Radulf had associated himself with the politically influential Earl Roger although he held his estate of the Balliols. How many lesser noble families, tenants of the de Quincy heirs, followed a similar course with regard to Dervorgilla after 1264 can never be established.

Roger de Quincy's succession to the social leadership of the Galwegian community after 1235 had far-reaching consequences for the lordship and its people. Alexander II's support for the 'feudal' solution to the inheritance question had been more than just a matter of legal principles, for it had provided him with the opening through which he could intrude men more responsive to his will into one of the last regions of mainland Scotland in which the authority of the crown operated under severe limitations. As predominantly eastern Scottish or northern English landholders in their own right, de Quincy, de Forz and Balliol forced a radical re-alignment of Galloway's traditional political perspectives. This can be seen most clearly in the abrupt disappearance of Galloway's rulers as key players in the tortuous affairs of northern and eastern Ireland, Mann and the Hebrides, leaving a void into which the Stewarts and, to a lesser extent, the Bissets, were to step. While individual Gaelic families within Galloway may have maintained their traditional maritime links, Roger de Quincy's horizons were fixed firmly on the British mainland: the role of the lords of Galloway as power-brokers in the northern Irish Sea zone had died with Alan.

TOWARDS A NEW LORDSHIP

Rather than stability, the period of just over a decade after the failure of Thomas's revolt saw protracted upheaval. The tripartite partition itself was a transient arrangement, lasting barely a decade before the failure of the de Forz line in 1246, but the division of Christina's Galloway heritage – as opposed to her Chester-Huntingdon properties – between her surviving sisters, had already been preceded in 1242 by the re-absorption of the lands of the Atholl segment of the Galloway family on the death of Earl Thomas's only legitimate son, Patrick. In addition to the earldom of Atholl, his in right of his mother, Patrick had been heir to his father's lands in Lothian, Cunninghame and Ulster. As part of the great Comyn nexus of power, Patrick's death was a bitter blow to a family that was already experiencing a slackening of its grip on Scottish political life as Alexander II directed his patronage towards other magnate families, principally the Durwards and the Bissets. Rightly or wrongly, the supposedly suspicious death of the young man, burned to death while sleeping with his companions in a barn at Haddington in 1242, has been linked to the rivalry between these magnate families.

Immediately after the event, the Comyn interest in Scotland, articulated in the *Chronicle of Melrose*, pointed the finger of accusation at Patrick's uncle-by-marriage, Walter Bisset, lord of Aboyne, and his nephew, John Bisset.[63] Although there are suggestions that personal enmity that had arisen from Patrick's besting of one of the Bissets in a tournament at Haddington had provoked a brutal reprisal,[64] a view quickly emerged that control of property lay behind the whole episode. The Lanercost chronicler claimed that Patrick had in fact been murdered, 'because he was expected to become a great lord of a certain heritage', and that he had been warned of his danger in a letter from the wife of the murderer.[65] Although he does not name the lady, he cannot have been ignorant of the fact that Walter Bisset was married to Ada, sister of Alan and Thomas of Galloway, Patrick's aunt. The implication is that the Bissets coveted some portion of Thomas's paternal inheritance. Certainly, the Bisset family was emerging as an important player in the crown's schemes for domination in the western Highlands and Hebrides, where Earl Thomas had forged alliances in the early 1200s, and was building up a significant presence in the Clyde estuary. There, Thomas's Cunninghame lands may have represented a useful and substantial acquisition, while his Antrim interests would have provided a firm base in the tangled politics of northern Ireland and the Isles. There is, however, not one shred of evidence to support the claim that Patrick's tragic death was the result of a Machiavellian plot hatched by his Bisset kin with the aim of securing this attractive heritage.

The hysterical reaction of the Comyns and their associates to Patrick's demise was a symptom of the anxiety that a succession of blows to their political hegemony had produced.[66] Patrick's heritage may not have been the cause of his death but it was certainly the cause of the violence that it provoked. In 1242, King Alexander initially saw no reason to take action against the Bissets, who stood high in his favour and were important recipients of his patronage, and it can be assumed that the components of his heritage would have been divided between the respective heirs, of whom Walter Bisset was one. The Comyns' actions in 1242–43, therefore, stemmed not only from the loss of their grip on Patrick's extensive landed influence but was compounded by the fact that a significant portion of that power-base was gravitating into the hands of one of their major territorial rivals. The accusations against Walter and his nephew, then, were designed to block this and force the king to summon a magnate assembly in which the Comyns and their allies could be sure of swinging conservative opinion firmly against the upstart Bissets. Despite the king's continued support for Walter and his kin, noble opinion aligned with the Comyns, the Bissets were driven into exile, and Patrick's paternal inheritance fell into the politically neutral hands of his Galloway cousins. That there was justice in their cause is implicit from Henry III's admission of the Bissets to some portion of the former Galloway lands – and also Duncan of Carrick's landholding – in Antrim, including the island of Rathlin,[67] presumably following the escheat of the earldom of Ulster to the English crown on the death of Hugh de Lacy in 1243. In Scotland, however, by the time that the Bissets were re-admitted to the king's peace in 1249 the Galloway-Atholl properties had been firmly absorbed by the de Quincy and Balliol families.

This further erosion of the male branches of the lordly family evidently elicited no reaction within Galloway, where Patrick may have been heir to few lands, despite the place that he had held in the Gaelic nobility's efforts to preserve the integrity of the lordship. This facade of passivity, however, was shattered in 1247 by a rising, reported by Matthew Paris as directed against Roger de Quincy, the man who had for all intents succeeded to the political and social leadership once exercised by Alan. As the only one of Alan's sons-in-law to have had a significant landed interest in Scotland before 1234, Roger had evidently sought to integrate his wife's heritage fully with his existing landholding and to extend to it the effective administration which his family had developed to manage their far-flung properties.[68] Matthew Paris implies that it was Roger's rigorous exploitation of his rights of lordship in Helen's inheritance, riding roughshod over Gaelic custom in the process, which provoked rebellion.[69] Attacked in one of his castles, the earl fought his way to safety on horseback and immediately sought the aid of the king. With royal support, Roger quelled the rising and was restored to power. Thus presented, the rising was purely a spontaneous and domestic affair, but it took place against a background of wider disturbances in the northern Irish Sea area, but especially within the outer Firth of Clyde zone where Alexander II was tightening his grip preparatory to his final move against the Isles.

The immediate background to these disturbances can be traced to the crisis of 1231 and crown efforts to build up its power in this unstable zone. Royal attention was fixed in particular upon the lordship of Donnchad mac Dubgaill, 'king' of Argyll, and a series of royal grants in mid-Argyll from the early 1240s can be seen as a move towards containment of this unpredictable power.[70] The Stewarts, too, were encouraged by Alexander to resume their expansion through the Clyde islands and in Cowal and Knapdale. Here, the target may have been Domnall mac Raonaill, Thomas earl of Atholl's ally in Antrim in the 1210s, who was the dominant power in Kintyre and Islay. His possible association with his brother, Ruaidrí, in the provision of mercenary assistance to the meic Uilleim down to 1230–31 would have given Alexander sufficient cause to move against him,[71] likewise his possible involvement in the 1235 rising in Galloway. More serious for the king, however, was Domnall's activity in Ireland, where he was fighting in alliance with the Uí Néill and Uí Domnaill kings of Tír Eógain and Tír Conaill against the English justiciar in Ireland (until 1245), Maurice FitzGerald. It was there in 1247 that Domnall might have been killed by FitzGerald's men.[72] Although FitzGerald was, in essence, fighting a private war of conquest in Tír Conaill, which Hugh de Lacy had granted him, his position in the English administration in Ireland made the involvement of one of the Scottish king's at least nominal vassals in the native resistance to him a source of further friction with the notoriously sensitive Henry III. Relations with Henry had deteriorated sharply after 1242, the crisis being fuelled by information provided to Henry by the exiled Bissets which suggested that Alexander had entered into negotiations with Henry's chief foe, Louis IX of France.[73] This had brought the kings to the brink of war. A raid in 1243 against the Bisset-held lands in Ulster by Patrick of Atholl's bastard brother, Alan,[74] had further soured relations. He, like his cousin Thomas, was a product of the Norse–Gaelic world of the Irish Sea and the Isles, being described in Alexander II's reply to Henry's demands for his handing over to him as 'a vagabond and foreigner [who] was seeking better means of support as he came and went between England, Ireland and Norway'.[75] This description hardly accords with his status thirty years later, when he took part in the Scottish campaign against Mann. At that time, he was a man of authority in Galloway, and at his death in c.1284 is revealed as a figure of financial substance in the lordship.[76] Once again, Alexander was quite obviously washing his hands of any involvement in, or responsibility for, operations that placed diplomatic strain on his relations with Henry III. Alan's intervention again in c.1248 threatened a further crisis, coming close on the heels of meic Somairle involvement in the wars against FitzGerald, possibly even representing an action related to that conflict. On this occasion, he had attacked and taken John Bisset's castle of 'Dunaverdun', possibly Doonavernon in County Antrim or Dunaverty in Kintyre, killing Bisset's men, seizing supplies, and possibly capturing Bisset himself.[77] Bisset, however, evidently came into Alexander's peace soon after, thus neutralising the diplomatic fallout of a further attack on one of Henry's vassals in the lordship of Ireland.

The 1247 rising in Galloway may have been not entirely unrelated to these bush-fires along the fault lines between Scottish and English influence in the western seaboard. For the king, it must have proven an unwelcome reminder of the fragility of his hold over Galloway, where he was still dependent on the loyalty and service of men such as Roger de Quincy, and more particularly upon their ability to hold their unwilling vassals in check. Alexander may have exacted a price for the earl's failure to maintain the peace. Although no details survive of any settlement imposed in 1247, it is possible that the king took this opportunity to extend the shrieval framework of south-western Scotland into Galloway, adding the region east of the Cree to the sheriffdom of Dumfries and establishing a new sheriffdom of Wigtown in the country to its west. By the time of Roger's death eighteen years later, Galloway had been integrated fully into the system of royal administration.

Like his father-in-law, Roger had only three daughters to succeed him, with the inevitable consequence of the further partition of the Galloway inheritance. His daughters had, like their mother and aunts before them, been married into eminent noble families, only one of which was an established feature of the Scottish political landscape. The eldest, Margaret, was married to William de Ferrers, earl of Derby, whose propertied interests in the north Midlands of England coincided with the chief concentration of de Quincy's English lands. His youngest daughter, too, was married to a prominent Midlands nobleman, Alan la Zouche, lord of Ashby in Leicestershire.[78] Both marriages reflected Earl Roger's English interests and the lines that sprang from them were to pursue chiefly English careers, although both families maintained their interests in Galloway and Scotland until their forfeiture as adherents to the English crown in the early fourteenth century. The marriage of his second daughter, Elizabeth or Isabel, however, was a product of both the secondary position held by Scotland in his political and territorial interests but also of his social eminence in mid-thirteenth-century Scotland. She was married to Alexander Comyn, Earl of Buchan, half-brother to Walter Comyn, earl of Menteith, Alexander II's deputy in Galloway in 1235, the dominant magnate figure in the kingdom. Through her, the Comyns were able to project their already extensive network of landed power and political alliances into the south-west.

Comyn influence in south-western Scotland had developed steadily after 1234: by 1258, John Comyn I of Badenoch, holder of a substantial estate centred on Dalswinton in Nithsdale, held the justiciarship of Galloway;[79] from c.1263 his cousin, Alexander, earl of Buchan, held the sheriffship of Wigtown.[80] Comyn regional dominance was completed when their political associate, Aymer Maxwell, who also held the justiciarship of Galloway from c.1264, secured the sheriffship of Dumfries.[81] Control of these offices, however, merely underpinned the regional dominance that stemmed from Elizabeth de Quincy's heritage. Although she was not the eldest heiress, her husband's centrality to Scottish political life and the inactivity in Scottish affairs of her brothers-in-law, William de Ferrers and Alan la Zouche, ensured his advancement as the crown's agent in Galloway. This position had developed in advance of Roger's death in April 1264, with Earl Alexander presumably stepping into the shoes of the ageing constable who had played no prominent part in Scottish affairs since 1247. Indeed, despite his hereditary position as the king's chief military officer, Roger took no part in Alexander II's 1249 expedition against Ewen mac Dubhgaill of Lorn, was of no consequence in the factional struggles which scarred Scottish political life during the minority of Alexander III – he had acted as intermediary on behalf of Henry III in 1257 – and age ensured that he did not participate in either the planning for or military actions in the 1263–64 campaign in the Isles. The Comyns and their political associates, however, held a central place in Alexander III's response to King Håkon IV of Norway's 1263 expedition, and the appointment of Earl Alexander to the sheriffship of Wigtown in that same year must be seen in the context of the military preparations to resist the Norwegians.[82]

The advancement of Comyn interests in Galloway was a clear expression of royal policy towards a region where crown authority was not yet bedded firmly. To the king, domination of Galloway by a family already established as leaders of the Scottish political community and as the crown's most loyal servants, and who possessed close ties with several leading south-western families, such as Maxwell, Randolph and Soulis, offered the best prospect of consolidating his hold on the region. Furthermore, as the leading member of a family which, although fully integrated into Gaelic Scottish noble society and with a network of lands and alliances spread throughout the central and western Highlands, was rooted strongly in lowland Scottish society, Alexander could be expected to complete the re-alignment of Galloway's political perspectives. The absenteeism of Earl Roger after 1247 must surely have hindered a process that required strong local leadership, and the prospect of a continuation of this situation with his succession by another inevitable absentee, William de Ferrers, Earl of Derby, husband of Roger's eldest daughter, was unacceptable. The influence of Alexander Comyn in Scottish government, and his importance to the crown as an agent for control in Galloway, is emphasised by his emergence in the period 1264–66 as keeper of two parts of the de Quincy heritage there, in advance of the settlement of an inheritance in which his wife was a major beneficiary. Clearly, what mattered to Alexander III was that Comyn had the stature and authority to ensure that the transition of power following de Quincy's death did not degenerate into confusion and rebellion, as had occurred in 1235 and 1247.

There is, however, another facet to the domination secured for Earl Alexander: the growing hostility among the Scottish political elite to the intrusion of 'new' families into the confined pool of aristocratic power and property. This had made itself manifest in the late 1250s in the dispute which had arisen over the control of the earldom of Menteith following the death of Walter Comyn, where there had been considerable resentment amongst the Scottish nobility that his widow, Countess Isabel, had married the minor and 'low-born' English knight, John Russell.[83] The hostility to Russell's intrusion resulted in concerted action by crown and magnates to secure the transfer of the earldom from Countess Isabel and her new husband to one of their own number, Walter Stewart. As Alan Young describes it, 'this was another episode which . . . illustrates a very conservative aristocratic elite acting in unison to protect itself from new or low-born intruders.'[84] Further episodes, such as the crown's purchase of Bathgate and Ratho from the junior line of the English de Bohuns, to whom it had descended, indicate that the progressive haemorrhage of property and titles from Scottish-based families to absentee lords was a perceived problem.[85]

The issue of the constableship of Scotland, which would have descended through Margaret de Quincy to her husband, William de Ferrers, was another instance of this problem. Here, one of the most senior royal offices in the kingdom was passing from one absentee lord who had, at least, been an established figure in Scottish government and society, to another who had no such standing and who lacked the resources to establish such a position. It may not, immediately, have been a major political issue, for, as a primarily military office, there had been little call after 1263–64 for its active functioning. In 1275, however, a situation had arisen which highlighted the problem starkly. This was the arrival in Mann in September 1275 of Godred, evidently a bastard son of the last Manx king, Magnus, who had died in 1265 and on whose death the kingdom had passed into Scottish hands. Scottish control of Mann was bitterly resented by the Manx, who rallied behind Godred and acclaimed him as their king.[86] The Scottish military response to this rising was swift and overwhelming, with a large force assembling in Galloway under the leadership of John de Vescy, John Comyn of Badenoch, justiciar of Galloway, and Alan son of Thomas, together with contingents from the Isles led by Alasdair, son of Ewen mac Dubhgaill of Lorn, and Alan mac Ruaidri, lord of Garmoran.[87] The ease with which the rising was suppressed should not distract attention from the threat which it posed to Scottish royal authority and the scale of the military operation mounted to quell it. This was an action in which the constable should have figured prominently, providing the unifying leadership for a complex military operation launched, furthermore, from a territory in which he himself was a significant landholder. Undoubtedly, it brought into sharp focus the risks inherent in the continuing tenure of this office by a foreign and absentee lord. It is surely no accident, therefore, that at this juncture King Alexander intervened and in c.1275 Countess Margaret was induced to resign her right to the office in favour of her brother-in-law, Alexander Comyn.[88] It was a transference that confirmed the Comyns' position as the dominant power in Galloway, a role that they were to maintain until the 1300s.

BALLIOL HEGEMONY

The Comyns' control of the chief political offices in Galloway from the 1260s was not backed by control of a dominant landholding. While they had gained possession of the chief seat of de Quincy lordship in Wigtownshire and the attendant headship of the political elite in Galloway, their Ferrers and Zouche co-parceners had secured their share of the landed inheritance, if not of the political influence attendant upon that position. This fragmentation of the de Quincy heritage handed Dervorgilla Balliol territorial dominance in Galloway, particularly in its eastern half.

The dissolution of a unitary power in the region is underscored by the disappearance of the title of 'lord of Galloway'. Even for Alan that style was secondary to the honorific 'Constable of Scotland', and did not feature in the legend on his seal.[89] For both him and the Anglo-Scottish aristocratic community through which he strutted the constableship was his principal title, hence its transmission to Roger de Quincy. If the title of lord of Galloway did not lapse, it would likewise have passed to Roger, for titles descend with land and both Kirkcudbright and Cruggleton, the lordly capita, were in his hands. Indeed, from an aside made by the English chronicler Matthew Paris, referring to Galloway 'which is known to belong to the earl's right,'[90] Roger's regional superiority was an accepted fact. Dervorgilla, however, is regularly accorded the honorific 'Lady of Galloway' by modern writers.[91] Balliol territorial dominance after 1264 is often presented as a continuation of Alan's lordship,[92] and the application of this title to Dervorgilla is used as convenient shorthand to reflect that position. There is, however, no precedent for its use in the thirteenth century, although it occurs from the later fourteenth century.[93] Dervorgilla's personal seal establishes that she had no pretensions to the title:[94] the obverse reads DERVORGILLA DE BALLI[defaced] FIL' ALANI DE GALEWAD', and the reverse DERVORGULLA DE GALEWAD' DOMINA DE BALLIOLO. The reference to her ancestry comes closest to an articulation of a claim to the lordly title, and was her preferred style; it is the form employed in her most significant surviving charter, the foundation charter of Sweetheart Abbey.[95] In general, she is styled Dervorgilla de Balliol or simply as the wife or widow of John Balliol.[96] In her widowhood, she made greater, but not exclusive, use of the form Dervorgilla de Galloway, Lady of Balliol.[97]

Although Dervorgilla's acquisition of the larger share of Christina's inheritance and the sub-division of the de Quincy heritage had given her *de facto* social domination, it did not give *de jure* rights to the title 'Lady of Galloway'. Nor does social and territorial dominance indicate her headship of the Galloway kin. While they are never styled kenkynnol in any source, the failure of the senior male line in 1234 had brought that status to the senior cadet line, the MacDowells. This status is particularly evident after 1296, and especially after 1306, when the Balliols – and Comyns – ceased to offer any political leadership. Instead, it was the MacDowells who led resistance to Robert Bruce down to 1312, and who re-emerged after 1332 as kingmakers in Galloway. They provided essential support to Edward Balliol, whose cause collapsed after their defection in 1353.[98] It was the support and recognition of the MacDowells that conferred effective, if not titular, lordship on the Balliols.

Other than the brief chronicle reference to his intervention in the Whithorn election in 1253, there is little to indicate that John – or Dervorgilla – were active in Galwegian politics after 1235 (see Chapter 7). This episode occurred in the midst of Balliol's one prolonged period of residence in Scotland, as co-representative of Henry III in the Comyn-dominated regency council for the boy king, Alexander III,[99] and should perhaps be seen as no more than a self-interested and isolated voice of dissent on that council against a partisan nomination which further strengthened the growing power of the Comyns in western Galloway. Despite his role in government, John used the opportunity afforded by his time in Scotland to set Dervorgilla's estates in good order. Building operations at Buittle symbolise his intentions, with development of the site constituting a visual assertion of the authority of a couple who, from 1247, were superiors of half of the former lordship.[100] The estates were to be rigorously exploited as a source of revenue, and John extended his notorious money lending and speculation activities into Galloway.[101]

The meagreness of evidence for Balliol activity in Galloway must be set beside the fact that by *c.*1260 John and Dervorgilla together possessed an estate that spanned three kingdoms and in which the Galloway lands were a minor component. This position had developed in stages, the first in 1237 when her maternal uncle, John, earl of Chester and Huntingdon, died childless. Before the end of the year Dervorgilla was granted seisin of the royal manors of Torksey in Lincolnshire, Lothingland in Suffolk, and the farm of the port of Yarmouth until the partition of Earl John's estates had been arranged.[102] These brought an annual income of a little under £150,[103] more than the revenues of many barons, but still of lesser value than Dervorgilla's due share of the Chester heritage, which she eventually received in early 1244.[104] Two years later she fell heir to the Yorkshire and Northamptonshire lands of her elder sister Christina, the senior heiress in the partitioned earldom of Chester,[105] and in 1253 she petitioned for and eventually received her share of the dower lands of her uncle's widow.[106] Earl John had also been earl of Huntingdon, and further properties and rights from that earldom fell to Dervorgilla. The deaths of Christina and of John's widow brought possession of the castle and manor of Fotheringhay in Northamptonshire, with its satellite properties of Nassington and Yarewell, Tottenham in Middlesex and Kempston in Bedfordshire.[107] Despite the protracted and expensive litigation involved in the recovery of this inheritance, Dervorgilla and her de Quincy nieces launched further suits over land in Cumberland and Westmorland associated with the de Morville portion of her Galloway heritage.[108] Her Scottish heritage outwith Galloway was scarcely less impressive. Her paternal inheritance brought one-third of Lauderdale and Cunninghame. This included rights in Lauder itself,[109] perhaps an indication that the caput of this lesser lordship had fallen to her rather than to Helen de Quincy. In Cunninghame, she held Largs, one-third of Dreghorn, and portions of Kilmarnock, Bondington and Hartshaw.[110] The Huntingdon inheritance brought her one-third of the Garioch in Aberdeenshire, plus land in Dundee, Fife and Lothian.[111]

Such far-flung possessions do not necessarily imply a life of constant mobility. Dervorgilla's properties from the Chester–Huntingdon inheritance had long been possessed by absentee lords, and a finely tuned administration had evolved to facilitate the flow of revenue to distant masters. The Balliol household, moreover, was amply provided with clerks and lawyers who managed their master's business affairs, obviating the need for the Balliols to engage in perpetual travel. Dervorgilla, indeed, was preoccupied from 1237 to *c.*1251–52 with her English properties. With the exception of the period 1251–55, there is little evidence for her regular presence in Scotland, let alone Galloway, until after John's death in 1268. Even then, as she retained personal control of the English estates that pertained to her Galloway and Chester–Huntingdon heritage, and in addition controlled her terce of the Balliol lands, her southern properties continued to command her main interest.

Major acts of piety, such as the foundation of her friaries at Dumfries and Wigtown, demanded Dervorgilla's presence in Galloway.[112] Her chief act, the foundation of Sweetheart Abbey in April 1273, must surely have seen her personal attendance,[113] the main body of secular witnesses to the foundation charter representing the core of her Galloway curia rather than a mobile retinue. Even by the 1280s, when Buittle was without question the centre of Balliol power in south-west Scotland, Galloway was not Dervorgilla's sole or principal concern. In March 1281, when Edward I sent his representative to meet Dervorgilla in person to take a recognisance of her settlement of various lands in England on her son, the meeting took place at Dryburgh Abbey,[114] near her Lauder properties. This recognisance, however, points to one reason for the increasing exploitation of her Galloway heritage, for it detailed the infeftment by her of John in all the estates she had received from the Chester settlement and some of the English lands of the Huntingdon inheritance, excluding Fotheringay and Kempston. If this were matched by a similar act in relation to her Scottish lands from the Huntingdon inheritance, it would have reduced her landed estates to a core in eastern Galloway with outlying blocks in Cunninghame and Lauderdale and a substantially contracted demesne in the eastern Midlands of England. It is following this rundown in her maternal inheritance that Galloway acquired a new significance for Dervorgilla, marked by the growing importance of Buittle, where she had the statutes of Balliol College, Oxford, drawn up in August 1282.[115] Specifically Galloway business, such as the quitclaim to her of the de Campania lordship of Borgue, was also completed at that date.[116] Further sojourns in Scotland were undertaken in late December 1284, when Edward I issued letters of protection to Dervorgilla, and in September 1285 when the protection noted that she had appointed attorneys to act in her absence until Michaelmas (29 September) 1286.[117] She was not, however, in residence at Buittle by late autumn 1286 when the Bruces raided the south-west in the aftermath of the death of Alexander III.[118]

The exact motivation behind the Bruces' seizure of the royal castles at Dumfries, Kirkcudbright and Wigtown, burning at Whithorn, and widespread depredations,[119] remains a matter of debate. What is clear, however, is that Buittle was by 1286 regarded as the focus of Balliol power in Galloway. As such, it was the symbolic seat of authority of the family whom the Bruces regarded as their chief potential rivals in any future contest for the Scottish throne should the child queen, Margaret of Norway, die. This is underscored by the peculiar declaration that the Bruces forced Patrick McCuffock, possibly Dervorgilla's steward, to proclaim in the bailey of the castle.[120] The text is fragmentary, but it seems to call for the expulsion of foreign interests from Scotland. If this was directed against

Dervorgilla's family and their retinue of English servants and administrators, it was singularly unsuccessful.

There is no evidence for Dervorgilla's return to Scotland after her 1285–86 sojourn. By then very elderly by the standards of the time, the rigours of long-distance travel ended her lifelong mobility. Age, however, did not blunt her determination to maintain her rights in her carefully garnered heritage, and it is fitting that at the end of her life she was contesting the abbot of Lindores' right to the patronage of the church of Whissendine, which pertained to her father's de Morville inheritance in Leicestershire.[121] Her death on 28 January 1289/90 at the Balliol caput of Barnard Castle in Teesdale[122] marked the end of an era, severing the final direct link – with the exception of the long-forgotten Thomas – with the lordship of Alan. While she had secured the continuity and integrity of her inheritance, which was now re-merged with the Balliol lordship, her tenacious grip on her patrimony had ensured that her son, John Balliol II, had remained a remote figure, excluded from any active involvement in the government of his mother's domain. While his lineage may have provided him with a reservoir of traditional loyalty that he and his kinsmen were to tap in the years ahead, he had been denied the opportunity to forge the close personal bonds upon which Gaelic lordship depended. In 1290, the Balliol lordship was the largest landed edifice in Galloway, but the opening of a more turbulent phase in the history of the south-west quickly revealed how shallowly rooted that structure had become.

Notes

1 This subsequently found its way into the hands of the Balliols, who had custody of Thomas after 1235. Shortly before 1296, agreement was reached between King John Balliol and John Comyn, earl of Buchan, over, amongst other properties, shares in Thomas's lands; CDS, no. 1541. They were restored to Thomas by Edward I of England on 30 August 1296: CDS, V, no. 162.
2 Barrow, *Kingship and Unity*, 114.
3 *Chron. Melrose*, s.a. 1234; cf. Matthew Paris, *Chron. Majora*, iii, 364–65.
4 *Chron. Melrose*, s.a 1235.
5 Stringer, 'Periphery and core', 96–97.
6 Barrow, *Kingship and Unity*, 114.
7 Oram, 'Earls and earldom of Mar'.
8 *Chron. Lanercost*, 42.
9 Matthew Paris, *Chron. Majora*, iii, 364–66.
10 *Chron. Fordun*, ii, 286.
11 Orpen, *Ireland under the Normans*, iii, 62–63.
12 Duffy, *Ireland in the Middle Ages*, 116–17.
13 *Chron. Melrose*, 84–85.
14 *Chron. Lanercost*, 42.
15 Ibid., 116
16 CDS, ii, nos 728, 729; *Rotuli Scotiae*, i, 22.
17 CDS, v, no. 162.
18 Duncan, *Making of the Kingdom*, 535–36.
19 *Cal. Pat. Rolls*, Henry III. 1232–1247, p. 447.
20 Reid, *Wigtownshire Charters*, p. xxxix.

21 But see, Matthew Paris, *Chron. Majora*, iv, 563; Reid, *Wigtownshire Charters*, p. xxxix.
22 Huyshe, *Dervorgilla*, 25, 27; A. M. T. Maxwell-Irving, 'The castles of Buittle', *TDGNHAS*, 3rd series, lxvi (1991), 59; Ewart, *Cruggleton Castle*, 9.
23 Barrow, *Kingship and Unity*, 115.
24 *CDS*, i, no. 574; Stringer, 'A new wife', 49–55.
25 *CDS*, ii, no. 169; Anderson, *Early Sources*, ii, 506; *Chron. Melrose*, 144; K. J. Stringer, 'A new wife'.
26 *CDS*, ii, no. 169; *Scots Peerage*, iv, 142.
27 Stringer, *Earl David*, 187. There is no substance to the statement in *Scots Peerage*, iv, 142, that Christina's marriage occurred in 1236.
28 *Chron. Melrose*, 143.
29 For an assessment of the Balliol position in 1234 see Stringer, *Earl David*, 186–87.
30 For a detailed discussion of the landed settlement, see Oram, 'Dervorgilla'.
31 *CDS*, ii, no. 824.
32 Brooke, 'Northumbrian settlements', 314, 320 for identification of this property.
33 *ER*, i, (Edinburgh, 1878), 22.
34 *CDS*, ii, no. 616 for its possession in 1292 by his son, Earl John.
35 *CDI*, i, nos 2380, 2424.
36 Reid, *Wigtownshire Charters*, no. 129.
37 'Brevis Descriptio Regni Scotie', in *Miscellany of the Maitland Club*, iv, pt i, (Maitland Club, 1847), 21–34 at 34.
38 *CDS*, ii, no. 1541.
39 *Rotuli Scotiae*, i, 273.
40 Oram, 'Dervorgilla', 174–76.
41 Brooke, 'The Glenkens', 43.
42 *CDS*, iii, no. 1578 (3); but see *Rotuli Scotiae*, i, 273, where the land in Kells is named more specifically as Kenmure.
43 Ibid., nos 1578 (1), 1578 (3)
44 *RRS*, vi, no. 235.
45 *CDS*, ii, no. 1338.
46 *RRS*, vi, no. 235.
47 Cowan, *Parishes*, 119.
48 *RMS*, i, app. i, no. 20.
49 *CDS*, ii, no. 1338; *Rotuli Scotiae*, i, 273.
50 Cowan and Easson, *Medieval Religious Houses*, 121; *Chron. Wyntoun*, Bk VIII, Chap. 8, lines 1515–16.
51 Stevenson, *Documents*, ii, no. DXX; *CDS*, ii, nos 1023, 1772.
52 *RMS*, i, app. i, no. 20.
53 Brooke, 'The Glenkens 1275–1456', 44.
54 *RMS*, i, app. ii, no. 319.
55 *Holm Cultram Register*, nos 120, 121, 141d.
56 *CDS*, ii, no. 1630.
57 *CDS*, i, no. 1808.
58 E.g. *RRS*, vi, no. 235.
59 Ibid.; *Glasgow Registrum*, i, no. 230; *CDS*, ii, no. 212.
60 *Dryburgh Liber*, no. 64.
61 *Midlothian Charters*, no. 21.
62 *Lindores Cart.*, no. cxiii.
63 *CDS*, ii, no. 212.
64 *Chron. Melrose*, 90.
65 Matthew Paris, *Chron. Majora*, iv, 200–02; Duncan, *Making of the Kingdom*, 544.

66 *Chron. Lanercost*, 49–50.
67 Young, *The Comyns*, 41–43.
68 Duncan, *Making of the Kingdom*, 544–45; for the lands of John Bisset in Ireland, see, *CDS*, ii, no. 163. These included Rathlin, granted to Alan by John *c*.1212–13, see *CDI*, i, no. 42.
69 For a detailed analysis of Roger de Quincy's administrative machinery see G. G. Simpson, 'An Anglo-Scottish baron of the thirteenth century: the acts of Roger de Quincy, earl of Winchester and constable of Scotland' (unpublished Edinburgh University PhD thesis, 1965).
70 Matthew Paris, *Chron. Majora*, iv, 563.
71 See, for example, *Highland Papers*, ii, 121–24; McDonald, *Kingdom of the Isles*, 97–98; Murray, 'Alexander II and the western seaboard'.
72 McDonald, *Kingdom of the Isles*, 94–95.
73 Duffy, *Ireland in the Middle Ages*, 117; Duffy, 'Bruce brothers', 68; cf. McDonald, *Kingdom of the Isles*, 94.
74 Bower, *Scotichronicon*, vol. 5, 185; Duncan, *Making of the Kingdom*, 535–36.
75 Bower, *Scotichronicon*, vol. 5, 187
76 Ibid.
77 *Oxford Balliol Deeds*, nos 601, 602.
78 *CDI*, ii, no. 2; McNeill, *Anglo-Norman Ulster*, 22; cf. Duncan, *Making of the Kingdom*, 550, for the traditional Scottish identification of this castle with Dunaverty in Kintyre.
79 *Chron. Wyntoun*, ii, 314–16.
80 *CDS*, i, no. 2155.
81 *ER*, i, 22.
82 *ER*, i, 16; Young, *The Comyns*, 69.
83 Young, *The Comyns*, 77–78.
84 *Chron. Fordun*, ii, 293.
85 Young, *The Comyns*, 74.
86 Duncan, *Making of the Kingdom*, 587.
87 McDonald, *Kingdom of the Isles*, 137.
88 *Furness Annals*, 570–71; Duncan, *Making of the Kingdom*, 582.
89 *CDS*, ii, no. 92.
90 This is evident in the style employed in his charters, where he is most commonly presented as Constable. See Stringer, 'Periphery and core', 103–11, and on his personal seal 108.
91 Anderson, *Scottish Annals*, 367, extract from Matthew Paris, *Chronica Majora*.
92 E.g. Huyshe, *Dervorgilla*; Brooke, *Wild Men*, 140–41.
93 Barrow, *Kingship and Unity*, 115.
94 E.g. *Chron. Rishanger*, 21, where John Balliol of Barnard Castle, Dervorgilla's husband, is described as lord of Galloway.
95 *Oxford Balliol Deeds*, facsimile between pages 276–77; a clearer reproduction of the seal is in Brooke, *Wild Men*, 141
96 *RRS*, vi, no. 235.
97 *CDS*, i, nos 1353, 1375, 1381, 1398, 1449, 1485, 1488, 1510, 1513, 1535, 1537, 1543, 1562, 1566, 1569, 1616, 1633, 1635, 1686, 1697, 1715, 1760, 1914, 2214, 2330, 2333 etc.; *Glasgow Registrum*, i, no. 230.
98 *Oxford Balliol Deeds*, 277–83; *CDS*, ii, nos 212, 214.
99 Oram 'A family business?', 111–45 at 139–40; Oram, 'Dervorgilla, the Balliols and Buittle'.
100 Anderson, *Scottish Annals*, 368 n. 2, 370; Young, *The Comyns*, 53.
101 A silver penny of Henry III, minted in 1247, was recovered towards the end of the 1998 season from the foundation trench of a substantial and evidently

high-status stone structure in the bailey at Buittle. Its level of wear suggests deposition *c*.1250. Personal communication from Mr. A. Penman, director of the Botel Bailey Excavation.

102 *Oxford Balliol Deeds*, no. 592.

103 *CDS*, i, no. 1380; R. Stewart-Brown, 'The end of the Norman earldom of Chester', *EHR*, xxxv (1920), 26–54, at 38.

104 *CDS*, i, nos 1510, 1513.

105 *CDS*, i, nos 1616, 1633.

106 *CDS*, i, nos 1686, 1697; Stewart-Brown, 'Earldom of Chester', 44.

107 *CDS*, i, no. 1914.

108 *CDS*, ii, nos. 189, 405, 410, 736.

109 *CDS*, i, no. 2333; *CDS*, ii, no. 172.

110 *Dryburgh Liber*, nos 9–13; *RRS*, v, no. 95; *RMS*, i, no. 18.

111 *Glasgow Registrum*, no. 230; *RMS*, i, app. ii, nos 4, 42, 46.

112 For a discussion of the Huntingdon estates in Scotland, see Stringer, *Earl David*; for her foundation of a friary in Dundee, see *Chron. Wyntoun*, Bk VIII, Chap. 8, l. 1514

113 That her generous patronage of the church stemmed from deeply held personal beliefs is suggested by the surviving evidence of her personal library of devotional works, several of which – possibly by her bequest – came into the hands of the monks of Sweetheart. These included texts by Jerome and Hugh of Saint-Victor, and possibly a copy of Gregory's *Dialogues*. She may also have commissioned for Sweetheart the splendid four-volume Bible, of which three volumes survive, now in Princeton. See, J. Higgitt, 'Manuscripts and libraries in the diocese of Glasgow before the Reformation', in R. Fawcett (ed.), *Medieval Art and Architecture in the Diocese of Glasgow, British Archae-ological Association Conference Transactions*, xxiii (1998), 102–10 at 103, 105–06, 107.

114 *RRS*, vi, no. 235.

115 *CDS*, ii, no. 189.

116 *Oxford Deeds*, no. 564.

117 *CDS*, ii, no. 212

118 *CDS*, ii, nos 263, 274.

119 Barrow, *Robert Bruce*, 17.

120 *ER*, i, 39; Palgrave, *Docs Hist. Scot.*, i, no. 6; *Reg. Romeyn*, i, 8–9.

121 Palgrave, *Docs Hist. Scot.*, i, no. 6.

122 *CDS*, ii, no. 380.

123 *Chron. Lanercost*, 134; *CDS*, ii, no. 405. The belief that Dervorgilla died at her manor of Kempston in Bedfordshire appears to stem from a misreading of the calendared entry in *CDS*, ii, no. 405, which arranges for an inquest into the extent of the lands of Dervorgilla there following her death on 28 January.

6

A SPIRITUAL COUNTERPART: THE MEDIEVAL DIOCESE OF WHITHORN c.1100–c.1300

Despite its traditional position as the location of Scotland's first recorded church, little is known of the ecclesiastical history of Galloway until the twelfth century other than what can be inferred through archaeology and place-name studies. The major programme of excavations that began at Whithorn in 1984 has confirmed the continued existence – and, indeed, vibrancy – of activity at this centre throughout the undocumented period from the early ninth century to the 1120s, although whether or not this was primarily ecclesiastical in nature has yet to be established. The scale of the work at Whithorn, however, coupled with its twelfth-century and later status as the focus of the spiritual life of a territorial diocese which stretched from the North Channel to the River Urr, has given the site a rather spurious centrality in all discussion of the Church in medieval Galloway. In-built to current analysis of the material evidence from the excavations is the otherwise unsupported proposal that this clearly wealthy and well-ordered community continued to function as the seat of a bishopric throughout the ninth, tenth and eleventh centuries.

The Davidian reform of the Scottish Church had two main strands: the foundation of monasteries of the reformed continental orders and the re-structuring of the diocesan system.[1] While the supposed decadence of the native Church may have been over-stressed by reformist clergy introduced by David and his successors, in a propaganda offensive designed to highlight their self-perceived superior religiosity and spirituality, there are indications that all was not well in the exisiting structure. In particular, few sees enjoyed anything like a regular episcopal succession and chronicle sources indicate protracted vacancies in even the most senior bishoprics of Alba.[2] At Whithorn, no bishop is recorded between the last notice of Heathored, c.833, and the appearance of Gilla-Aldan in c.1128.[3] The continuity of ecclesiastical life attested by the excavations demands that this apparent hiatus be treated with caution[4] but the absence from northern English and Irish sources of any mention of bishops at Whithorn argues strongly against continuity in the succession. The survival of the monastery is no sure indicator of the survival of the bishopric, as the case of

Whithorn's sister see at Hexham illustrates. The bishopric there failed in the early ninth century,[5] but the community survived until 1113, when it was refounded as an Augustinian priory.[6] Opposition from Durham, which claimed possession of Hexham from the 880s, ensured that its local episcopal rival was never revived.

Past analysis of the status of the pre-twelfth-century Church in Galloway has tended to regard the see under Gilla-Aldan (c.1128–51) as the reconstitution of its ninth-century precursor.[7] Whithorn's twelfth-century role as a spiritual focus also encouraged the related notion that it always functioned as the episcopal centre for a territorial diocese of Galloway, as we today would understand that term, throughout the undocumented era. This, in turn, has been regarded as implying that the territorial limits of the twelfth-century diocese reflected the ecclesiastical – and political – status quo that prevailed throughout the eleventh century at least. This view is unsupportable, not least since it is apparent that although monastic life was maintained at Whithorn, its sphere of influence contracted to the Machars area alone.[8] While a bishop might be expected to command a wider authority than the monastic community within which he was based, there are strong indications that the pattern of political power within tenth- and eleventh-century Galloway produced a polarisation in ecclesiastical alignments.

The political fragmentation of Galloway between c.900 and c.1100 did not provide the circumstances for a unitary episcopal authority that embraced the region from the Rhinns to Nithsdale. If there were bishops in Whithorn after Heathored, it is unlikely that their see extended beyond the Machars. The establishment of a kingdom in the Rhinns which expanded and contracted to embrace at times at least the southern Hebrides, Mann and Dublin, resulted in the forging of strong ecclesiastical bonds between western Galloway and the Hiberno-Norse world. The monastery at Whithorn, although preserving traditions of its Northumbrian past, looked south and west for its spiritual inspiration and, possibly, for its episcopal services. This orientation and the underlying internal cleavage in Galloway can be seen clearly in saints' dedications, with a strongly Hebridean, or more particularly Ionan, tradition west of the Cree.[9] Indeed, it is quite striking that while there are dedications to important Anglian saints such as Oswald and Cuthbert in Carrick and eastern Galloway, there are none around Whithorn, the supposed centre of Anglian political and religious culture in the region. The political integration of western Galloway into a Manx–Hebridean realm reinforced these divisions in the later eleventh century, at which time a Manx bishop, Gamaliel, was, according to a confused twelfth-century source, also serving the church of Whithorn.[10] Further support for such may lie in the equally confused account of the activities of Wimund, bishop of the Isles, in the late 1140s. In William of Newburgh's record of Wimund's bid for political power in Scotland, an attack is described on another bishop from whom Wimund had attempted to extort tribute.[11] This un-named bishop has been identified with Gilla-Aldan of Whithorn,[12] an identification made more plausible both by the suggested range of Wimund's activities – from Skye to Amounderness – and by local tradition which preserved a memory of warrior-bishops joining battle near the episcopal manor-house of Penninghame.[13] The attack's purposes, other than as a failed attempt at extortion, have never been examined. If Whithorn and Gilla-Aldan were his targets, it may have been a response to the erosion of the sphere of his see that the revival of Whithorn had entailed. Warfare between ecclesiastics where spheres of influence and authority were at stake was not uncommon in this period or region, as is demonstrated by the case of the militant Irish clergy who in 1204 destroyed the monastery established by Cellach, in violation of the rights of the community of Colum-Cille, on Iona.[14]

A connection with Mann would have facilitated the inclusion of Whithorn and its hinterland within the sphere of the bishops of Dublin in the eleventh century. The see of Dublin had been created in c.1028, with its first bishop, Dunan (1028–74), being the appointee of King Sigtryggr Silkiskegg, ruler of the city until 1036. Dunan and his successor, Gilla Pátraic (1074–85), had strong connections with the English Church, in particular with Canterbury, where certainly Gilla Pátraic was consecrated: he and his two successors were former Benedictine monks, Gilla Pátraic at Worcester, Donngus (1085–96) at Christchurch Canterbury and Samuel ua hAingliu (1096–1121) at St Albans.[15] From the time of Gilla Pátraic, if not from Dunan, whose appointment coincided with the intensification of King Knútr's claims of overlordship in the north and west of the British Isles,[16] the bishops of Dublin professed obedience to the archbishops of Canterbury, a relationship which became a major determinant in the direction of religious politics in the Irish Sea–Galloway zone in the late eleventh and early twelfth centuries.

Intermittent joint rule of Dublin and Mann by both Irish-based and Isles-based kings through the eleventh century saw the spread of the spiritual authority of the bishops of Dublin into Mann and, presumably, into the other island and mainland British territories of the kings of Mann. Indeed, the first Dublin bishops, it has been suggested, were drawn from the Dublin–Isles community rather than from amongst the native Irish.[17] The reign of Echmarcach, who was established in Dublin from 1036 to 1038 and from 1046 to 1052; who ruled Mann for at least part of that time and was still in control there in 1060–61; and who possessed western Galloway down to 1064,[18] may have seen that ecclesiastical influence stimulate a radical re-structuring of the religious politics of the region. Again, this should be considered in the context of his recorded submission to Knútr in 1031.[19] The joint rule of Dublin and Mann by Echmarcach down to 1052 had, presumably, seen the confirmation of ecclesiastical bonds that may already have been established during the episcopate of Dunan. The bond was re-affirmed in the 1060s, when Murchaid, king of Leinster, son of

Diarmait mac Maíl na mBó who had driven Echmarcach from Dublin in 1052, invaded Mann, defeated and expelled Echmarcach, and ruled over Leinster, Dublin and Mann down to his death in 1070. The 1070s saw various Irish and Dublin dynasts attempt to establish control over Mann, clearly as an extension of Leinster or Munster influence from the Irish mainland. Around this period, a distinct Manx bishopric – as opposed to earlier bishoprics within the Isles generally – emerged in the person of Bishop Roolwer, who was already in place before Gofraid Crobán established his rule in Mann in 1079.[20] Gofraid's political ambitions followed what had become the established pattern and in 1091 he captured Dublin and assumed the kingship, which he was to hold until his expulsion from the city by Muirchertach ua Briain in 1094.[21]

These developments occurred against the background of Canterbury's strengthening influence in Ireland and it is probable that Roolwer had looked to Dublin and, ultimately, to Canterbury for spiritual leadership. Gofraid and his successors maintained and developed that connection. The spread of Dublin's influence into the Isles and possibly into Galloway, was of major concern to the archbishops of York, especially after 1070 when Archbishop Lanfranc of Canterbury began to challenge the status of the northern metropolitan. Through its spreading connections with the Irish Church, Canterbury was advancing its claim to primacy over the British Isles.[22] Although this threat diminished during the episcopate of Archbishop Anselm of Canterbury, when, with the canonical episcopal consecration of the *comarba* of Armagh in 1106, independently of Canterbury, a native episcopate over which hung no taint of irregular consecration began to emerge.[23] With the Synod of Raith Bressail in 1111 and the resultant scheme for a national system of territorial dioceses throughout Ireland, in which Canterbury's pretensions were clearly rejected by both political and ecclesiastical powers, the door had been closed.[24] Dublin, however, stood apart from the rest of the Irish Church and, for local political reasons, maintained its obedience to Canterbury.[25]

Although Canterbury's ambitions in Ireland generally had been baulked after 1106 by the revived authority of the *comarba* of Armagh, who had won the backing of the formerly pro-Canterbury Muirchertach ua Briain, the threat to York's status from the southern British province remained potent. The Welsh church was set fair for absorption into the province of Canterbury in 1107 when Anselm consecrated the Bishop of Llandaff and extracted his oath of obedience, and through Dublin and the Isles, and in Scotland, Canterbury's influence remained strong. The consecration of Thurstan as Archbishop of York at the hands of Pope Calixtus II in 1119, and the papal judgement of 1120 in favour of the independent status of his see, however, drew a line under the issue. Thurstan, nevertheless, faced a mountainous task in guaranteeing the future security and status of his see, not least since he had only one regular suffragan – Durham – and still faced the influence of Canterbury within the Irish Sea zone.

If western Galloway was integrated into and being served by the bishopric of Mann, what was the position with regard to the remainder of the region? The probable contraction of Whithorn's sphere of authority to the territories of Echmarcach and his successors begs the question of how the Church in eastern Galloway continued to function at even the most basic of levels. Bishops were essential providers of key spiritual services: consecration of churches and graveyards; ordination of priests and consecration of other bishops; and provision of chrism, the sacred oil used in certain sacraments. Some alternative source must have been found which satisfied the needs of the local clergy and people, but where was it? It is not simply a question of supply or convenience but one of political acceptability. Whithorn's probable political and spiritual affiliations at this time may have ruled out Mann, Dublin and, possibly, other Irish sees as the source of episcopal services in eastern Galloway, particularly once Fergus had emerged to power in the Kirkcudbright area. The source must, therefore, have lain within the British mainland.

Traditionally, the Church of Strathclyde has been regarded as the most likely provider of such services throughout Galloway in the period down to c.1128. Certainly, when Strathclyde was territorially resurgent in the tenth century, its bishop presumably enjoyed an extended sphere of influence. But did that influence extend beyond the limits of the kingdom to embrace Galloway? It is unlikely that it did, for the evidence of the inquest carried out on the instructions of the future David I, which mapped the properties associated with the Church of Glasgow and which reflected the eleventh- if not tenth-century pattern of endowments, indicates that its sphere, shorn in the 1090s of the north Cumberland district acquired in the 900s, was limited to Clydesdale, upper Tweeddale and Annandale.[26] The inclusion of Desnes Ioan within Glasgow diocese in the later twelfth century has, in the past, been interpreted as a residual trace of a once more extensive jurisdiction, but that argument hinges on the question of the territorial extent of Fergus's lordship.

It is possible that the spiritual jurisdiction of Strathclyde had been extended greatly in the eleventh century as Máel Coluim mac Donnchada exerted his lordship over the former kingdom. If so, however, it failed to attract any endowments within the wider south-west. It was Skene's contention that prior to the revival of Whithorn, all of Galloway had fallen under Glasgow's jurisdiction in an ecclesiastical reflection of the political authority of David as 'prince of the Cumbrian region', which certainly included the Clyde estuary districts from Carrick to Renfrewshire described as constituting that part of Galloway which he controlled in the reign of Alexander I, and that Desnes Ioan was retained by Glasgow after the reconstitution of the Galwegian see.[27] Some support for this view has been drawn from the mention of lands at 'Edyngaheym' in the Davidian inquest as pertaining to the Church of Glasgow by ancient right.[28] This property is usually identified with Edingham near Dalbeattie, where Daphne Brooke

1. Whithorn School Cross, Whithorn Priory Museum

2. Whithorn Cathedral Priory, re-set twelfth-century doorway at western end of the nave

3. Dundrennan Abbey. The transepts of the twelfth-century church were remodelled in the early twelfth century.

4. Rievaulx Abbey, North Yorkshire

5. Boreland of Borgue, caput of the Morville lordship of Borgue

6. Dundrennan Abbey. The early thirteenth-century effigy of knight identified as the grave monument of Alan of Galloway.

7. Buittle Castle, caput of the Balliol lordship in Galloway

8. Buittle Kirk. Late thirteenth- and fourteenth-century parish church.

9. Sweetheart Abbey, interior of the church looking east

10. Barnard Castle, County Durham. Here Thomas, son of Alan, was 'shut up until decrepit old age' in the custody of his half-sister.

11. Dunrod, deserted medieval village, looking north over the site of the 'manor house' to the churchyard

proposed the former existence of an early monastic community.[29] If correct, this establishes Glasgow with an interest west of Nithsdale, in which territory it had no mensal properties, before *c*.1120. 'Edyngaheym' in the Inquest text, however, lies in a list of places located firmly in Annandale – Hoddom, 'Edyngaheym', Abermilk, Dryfesdale etc. – and an alternative identification with a now lost 'Ednemland' in Annadale has been suggested.[30] Despite such uncertainties, Skene's thesis prevailed until the 1950s when Reid offered a new interpretation. It was his contention that the diocese of Whithorn had extended originally to the Nith but that Desnes Ioan had been detatched from it, most probably by William the Lion during the 1186–89 vacancy at Whithorn. This dismemberment, he argued, was consequent on the political situation in 1174–85, a view which finds more recent support in Scott's hypothesis of an administrative partition instituted by William the Lion in a bid to enhance royal controls west of the Nith after the collapse of the Galwegian rebellion.[31]

Both hypotheses assume the existence of Galloway as a monolithic power-bloc in the tenth and eleventh centuries, either integral to Strathclyde or as an independent kingdom. Neither, furthermore, considered the possibility that Desnes Ioan was a late acquisition by the lords of Galloway. It is evident that the Galloway of Fergus ended originally at the Urr – co-terminous with the twelfth-century bishopric – and that this eastern district formed part of the lordship of Nithsdale which had been confirmed to Uhtred soon after 1160. By Uhtred's time, the diocesan boundaries had crystallised in the pattern which prevailed until the Reformation. Desnes Ioan had been part of Nithsdale and therefore fell with the rest of that district within the spirituality of Glasgow, but that jurisdiction ended at the Urr.

There are, moreover, practical difficulties with arguments in favour of a Strathclyde source for episcopal services in eastern Galloway, not least the prolonged breaks in the episcopal succession in the former. The status of the recorded eleventh-century bishops of Cumbria/Strathclyde/Glasgow is also open to question and it is possible that they never functioned within their nominal see.[32] Indeed, it has been argued that they served rather as suffragans of York in that portion of Strathclyde–Cumbria which was later erected into the see of Carlisle.

If Strathclyde was an unlikely provider of the requisite services, what alternatives offer themselves? The alignment of Whithorn with the Irish or Hebridean Church makes it likely that eastern Galloway looked to Northumbria. Certainly, there is no reason to believe that communication between Galloway and the Northumbrian Church ended with the fall of York to the Danes in 867. Indeed, Anglian monastic communities in the district west of the Pennines continued to function as both political and ecclesiastical centres into the early 900s and were in communication with the Church in Anglian Northumbria north of the Tees.[33] Furthermore, the spread of Danish colonists north-westwards from the Vale of York across

Stainmore into Cumbria and Annandale preserved a corridor of contact between York and the Solway.[34] The York–Dublin axis of the tenth century presumably strengthened this line of communication. York, reinforced by Pope Gregory I's late sixth-century award of metropolitan authority over Britain north of the Humber, and its suffragan see at Durham, which itself possessed strong claims to episcopal authority over the territory of its precursor diocese of Lindisfarne, continued to play an active ecclesiastical role within the Southern Uplands of Scotland and possibly Cumbria, throughout the eleventh century.[35] In the course of vacancies in the see of Strathclyde, for example, it appears that the clergy of that diocese looked to these two Anglian sees to meet their needs, particularly for chrism.[36]

Although the political implications of this arrangement had lasting repercussions for the question of the independence of the Scottish Church, in ecclesiastical terms it underscores the continuing orientation of clerical allegiances at the close of the eleventh century. English royal confirmation of the ecclesiastical subjection of the Carlisle area to the jurisdiction of the archdeacon of Durham in the mid 1090s, moreover, evidently affirmed claims to earlier episcopal authority over that district rather than simply a recent development to reflect the post-1093 political reality of English control over Cumbria.[37] The strong links with York forged in the seventh and eighth centuries, coupled with lingering political and cultural ties, make it highly likely that eastern Galloway, like Strathclyde, was served from York or Durham. If it was acceptable for York to sanction Durham's provision of chrism to Glasgow in the early 1100s, there was little to prevent an identical source of supply for eastern Galloway.

Ties with Durham, or more particularly a strong attachment to the cult of St Cuthbert, are evident in later eleventh- and early twelfth-century eastern Galloway. The continuing vitality of the community at Kirk-cudbright into the 1160s is one dimension of this link, but perhaps more significant is the name of the first historically attested bishop of Whithorn since Heathored in the early ninth century. Gilla-Aldan's name has attracted little comment other than that its Gaelic form probably identifies him as a native cleric,[38] but that is, quite literally, only half the story. The second element of the name, 'Aldan', is Anglian rather than Gaelic. It is not a common personal name, but its use as the specific element in a Galwegian ecclesiastic's name suggests that the original was himself a prominent ecclesiastic. The only obvious candidate is Bishop Aldhan (990–c.1018), who moved the Cuthbertine community from its brief resting place at Chester-le-Street to Durham in 995 and fixed his episcopal see there.[39] Although hardly an outstanding example of abstinence and celibacy – his daughter, Ecgfrytha, liberally dowered with Church properties, married Earl Uhtred of Northumbria[40] – he played a central part in the revival of St Cuthbert's community and held a key place in the political life of Northumbria until his death in 1018. As discussed in Chapter 1, his descendants through Ecgfrytha played a prominent role in the stormy politics of Northumbria and York for the remainder of the eleventh and into the twelfth century and were deeply embedded into the pattern of lordship in Cumberland by the 1050s. In this they had been aided by the spreading power of Earl Siward, husband of Ecgfrytha's granddaughter, Ælffleda, who had asserted his lordship over the Danish colonised zone extending north-west from York to the Solway.[41]

Both the Durham connection and the strong cross-Solway political links which had been re-affirmed by the Danish colonisation of parts of Cumberland, southern Dumfriesshire and south-eastern Kirkcudbright-shire, offer media through which his cult or memory could have reached Galloway. If Gilla-Aldan himself was not drawn from the remarkably hybrid noble strata of Northumbria,[42] it is most likely that he was connected in some way with a Cuthbertine community within Galloway. The most obvious candidate here is Kirkcudbright where, although the community appears to have been thoroughly Gaelicised in its character, the veneration of Cuthbert continued to play a key part in its spiritual life.[43] Although it cannot be proven, there is a strong possibility that Gilla-Aldan was head of the Kirkcudbright community and, presumably, would have stood in a close personal relationship with Fergus, whose seat of power lay adjacent.

The sudden emergence of Gilla-Aldan as bishop of Whithorn has occasioned debate as to his origins and the implications of this apparent revival of the see. The historical record is singularly uninformative, comprising only a mandate of Pope Honorius II, dated to December 1128, which instructs an un-named bishop-elect of Whithorn to present himself to his 'appropriate metropolitan', Archbishop Thurstan of York, for consecration.[44] This is followed by an oath of obedience sworn by Gilla-Aldan, elect of Whithorn, to Thurstan at York some time thereafter, presumably before the outbreak of war between David I and Stephen in 1137.[45] These tersely worded documents mask the tortuous complexity of the political and ecclesiastical manoeuvering of which the election of Gilla-Aldan was only part. His appointment was no simple local issue but was embedded at the heart of the conflict surrounding Thurstan's claims to metropolitan supremacy over the Scottish sees, and also the three-cornered political relationship of Galloway, England and Scotland.

The two documents themselves provide few answers and raise many more questions. Most contentious is the identity of the agency responsible for Gilla-Aldan's election, with David I and Fergus standing as rivals for that distinction. David's role in the re-construction of the Scottish diocesan structure has led some historians to regard the revival at Whithorn as his achievement,[46] while those who would minimise Scottish influence within Galloway at this date favour an independent action on the part of Fergus.[47] Arguments in favour of David centre on the non-coincidence between the boundaries of the twelfth-century secular and ecclesiastical Galloways. Since the diocese was not co-extensive with the lordship, it has been suggested, Fergus cannot have been the organising agent. But since the smaller see of Whithorn can be shown to have marched with the bounds of Fergus's pre-1160 lordship, such arguments lose their validity. The early twelfth-century diocese marched with the boundaries of Fergus's lordship and David's principality of Cumbria and by the time that Desnes Ioan was acquired by Uhtred in the 1160s, the spiritual boundaries had crystallised. This, however, does not establish Fergus's candidacy as the secular agent responsible for the revival of Whithorn, for, as the case of the see of Caithness demonstrates, while the bishopric there was co-extensive with the mainland Scottish domain of the earl of Orkney and Caithness, it was the creation of David I, not the earl.[48]

Scottish concerns with episcopal re-organisation had as many political and secular considerations behind them as religious ones. David's personal familiarity with the pattern of territorial dioceses in England and its uses in reinforcing royal authority, and the political implications for secular power which had arisen from the moves towards such a system in Ireland in the Synod of Raith Bressail, provided a strong incentive for the Scots to pursue similar directions. A policy of using bishops as royal agents can be seen in Moray, Ross and Caithness, where secular political influence otherwise depended on the crown's fragile relationships with the native powers.[49] An appointment at Whithorn and the physical reconstruction of the see could represent a precursor of that northern policy, with Gilla-Aldan, like Andrew at Caithness in the 1140s, being a reliable servant intruded into a position of local power. Furthermore, like Bishop John at Glasgow, the installation of a royal servant in the see would have circumvented the unwelcome influences of Archbishop Thurstan, whom David was seeking to exclude from any role in the government of the Scottish Church.[50] Pope Honorius's instruction to the elect of Whithorn to go to York for consecration and the resulting profession of obedience to Thurstan, however, would have been the total failure of such a hypothetical policy.

Most telling against Gilla-Aldan's appointment as a Scottish act is the divergence from David I's preference for a non-native episcopate. Gilla-Aldan was probably of Gaelic stock. Furthermore, his name indicates associations with the Cuthbert cult in Galloway and connections with the centre of that cult at Kirkcudbright. If this was the case, not only was he probably a native Galwegian but he was also associated with the Church centre at the heart of Fergus's territorial power. The contrast with David's policy at Glasgow and St Andrews, or at Dunkeld, Aberdeen and Ross where native incumbents were succeeded by non-Gaelic clerics as vacancies arose, could not be sharper.[51] This is unlikely to have been an expedient forced on David as a consequence of the weakness of Scottish influence in Galloway, for in similar political circumstances he was able to intrude a Scottish cleric to the see of Caithness. Scottish involvement in the process at Whithorn, therefore, seems unlikely.

Fergus stands as the only viable alternative secular agent through whom the see was revived. He holds a central place in the development of the Galwegian Church in the first half of the twelfth century and is linked inseparably with the foundation of Whithorn Priory.[52] His possible establishment of Augustinian canons there has given rise to a tradition of earlier involvement in the revival of the see. There is strong inferential evidence for this, not least the probability that Gilla-Aldan was an east Galloway cleric, head of the Kirkcudbright community. The evidence for Fergus's state-building activities, discussed in Chapter 2, raises the possibility that he had imposed his man on the territorially influential and economically powerful monastery at Whithorn in an ultimately successful bid to control the spiritual focus of western Galloway. The pre-existing affiliations of Whithorn through Mann were with Canterbury, but Fergus's own pro-York leanings ensured that the new bishopric was subject to York.

The parallels with thirteenth-century efforts to consolidate Scottish control in Galloway, discussed below, are striking. For Fergus, the Church of Whithorn was central to his efforts to forge a unitary lordship from the patchwork of territories over which he had established mastery. The creation of a single ecclesiastical authority to march with his temporal domain, moreover, may have been seen by him as bolstering his royal pretensions. A single Galwegian diocese emphasised both Galloway's political unity and its physical separation from neighbouring kingdoms, as the precedent of David's see of Glasgow demonstrated. Just as the alignment of the Ostmen dioceses in Ireland with the Church of Canterbury had been a political development intended to underscore their distinctiveness from the secular Irish polity, so was Whithorn's alignment with York a declaration of Galloway's status *vis-à-vis* Scotland. While the revival of the see constituted an overt assertion of his political independence and a clear rejection of any threat of absorption into the see of Glasgow, with all the political implications involved in that, its primary objective was to provide substance to his kingdom and to enhance his personal prestige through association with the premier regional cult.

Political opportunism underlay Fergus's actions at Whithorn and political convenience ensured that he turned to York for support in his efforts. For both Fergus and Thurstan, the creation of a Galwegian diocese free from the claims of rival metropolitan churches or their political counterparts was a matter of expediency. It is the immediate forging of the Whithorn–York bond that argues decisively against David I's role in the process as anything other than a bystander.[53] At this juncture, David was seeking the creation of a Scottish province free from subjection to York or Canterbury.[54] His ambition was complicated by the fact that his preferred location for the Scottish metropolitan see, St Andrews, was vacant and that he was reluctant to compromise the status of either the bishop-elect, Robert of Scone, or the Scottish Church generally, by seeking his consecration from Thurstan, who was demanding his submission and obedience. Thurstan, however, was eventually obliged to suspend his claims temporarily under pressure from both David I and Henry I, and consecrated Robert without prejudice. Against this background, it is unlikely that had David played any part in the revival of Whithorn he would have countenanced Gilla-Aldan's acceptance of York's metropolitan supremacy. Gilla-Aldan's submission strengthened Thurstan's general claims.

David's role must, at most, have been a passive one. I have argued elsewhere that David's acquiesence may have been the price for Thurstan's temporary relaxation of his demands concerning Robert and the Scottish Church generally,[55] but this depends heavily upon modern notions of the geographical extent of what David regarded as the kingdom of the Scots. Nevertheless, there are some attractions in the hypothesis, not least that David must have conceded something to gain Robert's consecration. Certainly, he halted his efforts to secure archiepiscopal status for St Andrews, a move guaranteed to mollify Thurstan. Acceptance of York's claims over Whithorn may have been a further concession. David's lordship over the region was tenuous and it could be argued that it would have cost him little to yield on this point. Such a hypothetical deal would have held great attractions for Thurstan, who, as set out above, was in desperate need of additional suffragans for both spiritual and political reasons. The importance of the revived see of Whithorn to him should not be understated.

Counter to the above is the extent to which Thurstan's success in establishing his supremacy over Whithorn reinforced his claims towards the Scottish Church. Irrespective of David's role in the revival of Whithorn, his aggressively anti-York stance with regard to Glasgow and St Andrews would have ruled out any concession in respect of Galloway. To yield there would have effectively undermined his efforts to deny York's metropolitan supremacy over his national Church. This fact alone underscores that it was more than royal indifference which secured Whithorn's acceptance of Thurstan's claims: Galloway was clearly not regarded as an integral part of either the secular or ecclesiastical manifestations of the kingdom of the Scots.

As discussed above, Gilla-Aldan's election came at a critical moment for the province of York in its current struggle with Canterbury. So convenient was the timing that it is difficult not to see Thurstan's hand in the business. His concern was not so much to secure a nominally Scottish suffragan before re-asserting his claim to be the proper northern metropolitan but to strengthen his rebuttal of Canterbury's claims of primacy over his province, where papal support had only recently swung behind York. Gilla-Aldan's profession of obedience gave Thurstan his third territorial suffragan diocese which, together with Durham and the see of Mann, provided York with the necessary number of bishops for the canonical consecration of his successors and removed his dependence on the titular bishop of Orkney, whom he maintained in his household. For Thurstan as much as Fergus, therefore, the revival of Whithorn was a declaration of independence.

THE LOYAL SUFFRAGAN

Gilla-Aldan's profession of obedience to Thurstan confirmed in ecclesiastical terms the political alignment of Galloway up to 1135. Just as Fergus looked to Henry I of England for support and protection, so the see of Whithorn, alone among all the northern British dioceses outwith the direct lordship of the English crown, accepted its status as a suffragan of York. This bond was strained to breaking point in the turbulent political climate that followed Henry's death, when Fergus was faced with the growing power of David I in Cumberland and Northumbria. By 1136, Fergus had fallen under David's shadow and allied with him in his campaigns into northern England in support of the Empress Matilda. As a consequence, he found himself facing his spiritual superior, Archbishop Thurstan, on the battlefield. Spiritual censure may have followed as a result of the un-Christian behaviour of the men of Galloway during that campaign, but worse was to follow.

Thurstan's death in 1140 came at a critical juncture in the political conflict. King Stephen moved swiftly to secure the election of a loyalist to this politically sensitive and highly symbolic see, putting pressure on the chapter of York to elect his nephew, William FitzHerbert. Stephen's manipulation of the election was blatant and provoked a storm of criticism not just within the province of York but within the Church generally. Questions over the legitimacy of FitzHerbert's election were growing in strength and soon gained the backing of the Cistercian Order, who had a powerful, but hardly disinterested, political supporter in David I, and a still more influential spiritual weapon in the form of Bernard of Clairvaux. At the hands of Bernard and the Cistercians in general, FitzHerbert was subjected to a storm of denunciation and abuse which fatally undermined his authority within his province.[56] Deputations to Rome led by Ailred of Rievaulx and Walter of London, archdeacon of York, highlighted the divisions within the see of York itself. Nevertheless, he maintained some control over his see until 1147, when the new Cistercian pope, Eugenius III, responding to news of the violence of FitzHerbert's supporters against his opponents and attacks on Fountains Abbey, and having failed to get evidence on oath from William of St Barbe, the new bishop of Durham, that FitzHerbert's election had not been obtained by pressure, declared him deposed and ordered a new election. Unsurprisingly, the result was the election of Bernard of Clairvaux's former pupil and fellow religious of Pope Eugenius, Henry Murdac, abbot of Fountains. FitzHerbert's deposition did not end the matter, for Stephen and the majority of the English clergy refused to recognise Murdac's election until January 1151. For a decade, then, the spiritual life of the province of York was poisoned by this bitter and protracted dispute.

Galloway was not immune to the polarisation of opinion within the province and, despite the continuing political alignment of Fergus with his all-powerful neighbour, David, the Church in Galloway appears in general to have offered its support to FitzHerbert. The evidence for this is largely circumstantial but a strong case can be argued in the light of what appears to be a distancing from the Cistercians on the part of Fergus and, presumably, Gilla-Aldan, soon after the founding of the first Cistercian colony in Galloway in 1142.[57]

It is not known when Gilla-Aldan died. He was evidently still alive in June 1151 when, named simply as G, he was instructed by Eugenius III to offer his obedience to Henry Murdac.[58] His year of death is normally given as 1154, as it was in December of that year that his successor, Christian, was consecrated.[59] Christian, however, was possibly a Cistercian monk himself,[60] or was in sympathy with that Order, which might suggest that he was elected with the support of Murdac and/or David I, both of whom died in 1153. On Murdac's death, William FitzHerbert was re-instated as archbishop by the new pope, Anastasius IV, and returned in triumph to York in May 1154 but was himself to die, by poison it was rumoured, only seven weeks' later on 8 June.[61] A Cistercian supporter of Henry Murdac is unlikely to have sought consecration at the hands of the man whom his Order had so vilified and discredited, and the vacancy at York which followed FitzHerbert's death would have further delayed his consecration. To avoid the implications of consecration other than by his metropolitan, Hugh de Puiset, elect of Durham, had travelled to Rome for consecration,[62] but Christian appears to have awaited the rapidly unfolding course of events in England. A swift election of a new archbishop was instituted by Archbishop Theobald of Canterbury, who had wisely distanced himself from the previous decade of acrimony at York, and on 10 October 1154 his archdeacon, Roger of Pont-l'Evêque, was consecrated. Two months later, on the same day as the coronation of Henry II of England, Christian was consecrated bishop by Archbishop Hugh of Rouen.[63] Archbishop Roger was, evidently, present at the consecration of his suffragan but, as he had not yet received his pallium from the pope, had not officiated.[64]

While there is no surviving record of an oath of obedience made by Christian to his metropolitan, subsequent events make such a submission definite. In consequence, Christian alone among the 'Scottish' bishops named in Pope Adrian IV's mandate of 27 February 1155, which enjoined them to obey Archbishop Roger as their legitimate metropolitan, would have encountered no difficulties in compliance.[65] Indeed, throughout his thirty-two-year episcopate, Christian was to display consistent loyalty to York, in sharp contrast to the Scottish bishops.

Christian's relations with Fergus are unknown but he appears to have forged close ties with his son, Uhtred. The bishop was a regular witness to Uhtred's charters and confirmed a number of his grants of land and churches in eastern Galloway.[66] Significantly, most of the surviving documents concern subjects within Desnes Ioan, which Uhtred acquired soon after 1160, and make no reference to the bishop of Glasgow. Indeed,

Uhtred's grants of property at Troqueer to the hospital of St Peter at York and of Kirkgunzeon to the Cistercian abbey of Holm Cultram in Cumberland are couched in language which makes clear both his and Christian's obedience to York, a declaration diametrically opposed to the stance of the bishops of Glasgow. It would seem, then, that Uhtred, with the active support of his bishop, was seeking, and to some degree succeeding, in bringing the enlarged lordship of eastern Galloway under the sole episcopal superiority of the see of Whithorn. This ambition was to rebound, with near disastrous consequences, in the early 1180s.

In contrast with the apparent closeness of Christian to Uhtred, there are no signs of a similarly warm relationship with Gillebrigte, in whose lands west of the Cree the bishop's cathedral church was located. Reginald of Durham in his *Vita Godrici* describes the persecution of Christian by 'a certain powerful man'[67] usually identified as Gillebrigte, although there is no corroborating evidence for this.[68] The breakdown, when it came, occurred in the later 1170s, for in 1176–77 Christian was still evidently in place within Galloway. In 1176, the papal legate, Cardinal Vivian, who had been despatched by the pope on a mission to Scotland, Ireland, the Isles and Norway, entered Galloway and, presumably having met with Christian, sailed at Christmas to Mann and Ireland.[69] In June 1177 he returned to Britain and, on 1 August, held a council at Edinburgh.[70] There, he suspended Christian for his failure to attend but, as he had probably already met the bishop at Whithorn the previous winter and must have been well aware of Christian's ready acceptance of York's metropolitian supremacy, his actions may have been little more than shadow boxing. Indeed, Christian, who had in March 1176-77 been the only 'Scottish' bishop to attend a council of the English Church in London – the Scottish episcopate having been released from any obligation to attend after 30 July 1176 by the bull *Super anxietatibus*, which effectively freed the Scottish Church from subjection to English metropolitan supremacy – used this as an opportunity to confirm the status of the bishops of Whithorn as suffragans of York. Christian rejected the authority of Cardinal Vivian, claiming that his bishopric lay within the province of York, over which Archbishop Roger held a legatine commission.[71] The consequence of this action was the effective separation of Galloway from the body of the emergent *ecclesia Scoticana* and its subsequent confirmation as a member of the province of York.

The crisis in Christian's episcopate followed swiftly upon the conclusion of Cardinal Vivian's legation in 1177. Its cause was not the sentence of suspension pronounced against him by Vivian for, as Howden indicated, Christian sheltered behind his obedience to Archbishop Roger of York and his legatine status and continued in office.[72] The roots of his difficulties extended back to the 1160s and his closeness to Uhtred but may have had a more immediate origin in any part he played in 1175–76 in bringing Gillebrigte to heel: he has been identified as one of the bishops who secured

Gillebrigte's negotiated surrender to William and subsequent submission to Henry II.[73] His evident alignment with Uhtred's son, Roland, for whom he was witnessing charters soon after 1174,[74] presumably aggravated his already strained relationship with Gillebrigte. There is no firm evidence for his expulsion from Whithorn, but it appears that before c.1180 he was largely resident in Cumberland.

Christian had long-standing links with the see of Carlisle. From as early as 1159–60, he had evidently been providing episcopal services within that see during the prolonged vacancy that followed the death of Bishop Æthelwold. Payments to him out of the noutgeld receipts from the sheriffdom of Carlisle[75] suggest that his visits were of quite long duration and might indicate that the political climate of Galloway in the late 1150s had seen him forced out of his bishopric. Certainly, Walter Daniel noted with a certain satisfaction that Christian had been unable to settle the struggle between Fergus and his sons, in which Ailred of Rievaulx had sought the role of peacemaker in 1159.[76] Perhaps significantly, it was at this time that Christian witnessed his one act of Malcolm IV,[77] issued in a major assembly of the Scottish clergy and nobility, possibly at Dunfermline. Importantly, Uhtred too was to be found at the Scottish royal court at this time, and it is possible that the bishop's later association with him had developed as early as the late 1150s and that his alignment with Uhtred had forced his withdrawal from Galloway in the face of the hostility of Fergus and, presumably, Gillebrigte.

Even after Malcolm IV's campaign of 1160 and the establishment in power over eastern Galloway of Uhtred, Christian maintained his links with Carlisle diocese. In c.1166, for example, possibly around the same time that he attended a court of William the Lion at Lochmaben in the company of both Uhtred and Gillebrigte, he witnessed the foundation charter of Lanercost priory (1165–74), in which he took precedence over the local Carlisle clergy and had earlier been involved in the endowment of the planned community,[78] while in c.1175 he was the only bishop to witness an act in favour of the cell of St Mary's Abbey, York, at Wetheral, a community over which the bishop of Carlisle exercised supervision.[79] After 1176–77 and Cardinal Vivian's visit to Whithorn, the general dearth of *acta* from Galloway renders it impossible to locate Christian with certainty within his see.[80] He can, however, be traced outside Galloway, and it is possible that the final years of his life were spent acting as a suffragan bishop within York and Lincoln dioceses. His estrangement from Galloway was proclaimed in a confirmation in favour of Holm Cultram abbey, probably dating from c.1185, in which he declared his intention to be buried there rather than at Whithorn.[81] In a clear statement of his continued adherence to Cistercian principles and, presumably, a reaffirmation of his origins, it was at Holm Cultram that he took up residence in his last days, dying there on 7 October 1186.[82]

Christian's prolonged absence from his see after c.1177 had serious implications for the diocese of Whithorn. Cobbled together only in 1128 out of territories with differing recent ecclesiastical allegiances as part of Fergus's empire building, it, like the lordship itself, risked cleavage along the imperfectly welded internal divisions which had re-appeared by 1160. Christian's active involvement in Uhtred's ecclesiastical policies in Desnes Ioan, clearly without any acknowledgement of the rights of the bishops of Glasgow over this area, must have infuriated the Church of Glasgow. Glasgow's and, consequently, the king of Scots' hostility was presumably further fuelled by Christian's unswerving recognition of York's metropolitan supremacy. These factors had combined by 1181 when Bishop Jocelin appealed to Rome and received a confirmation from Pope Lucius III of the lands, properties and rights of his Church. Included in the list of 'partes et parochie' of his diocese were Glenken and Desnes and 'whatever is your right in Galloway'.[83] Jocelin's letter to the pope has not survived, but prima facie this represents an attempt to dismember the see of Whithorn. The motivation was primarily political and may have originated with the crown, for it can be assumed that these districts corresponded with the territories secured by Roland after 1174. With Gillebrigte sheltering behind Henry II's overlordship and with every prospect of that situation continuing indefinitely, Roland's dependence on the Scots was being used as a tool to erode York's influence within Galloway. Had political events not overtaken ecclesiastical developments in 1185, it is likely that the see of Whithorn would have been reduced to the territories west of the Cree.

MAINTAINING THE BOND: WHITHORN AND YORK IN THE LATER TWELFTH AND EARLY THIRTEENTH CENTURIES

Christian's confrontation with Cardinal Vivian was the last occasion for over a century on which Whithorn's ties with York were seriously threatened. The death of the bishop in October 1186, close on the heels of Roland's successful occupation of Gillebrigte's lands in 1185, provided a set of superficial circumstances through which the ties could be severed but Henry II of England's firm re-assertion of his rights over Galloway at Carlisle in August 1186 had precluded this possibility. Roland's submission to Henry was explicit: he held Galloway from the English crown 'against all men', a relationship which gave Henry significant rights within the region. Henry chose to exploit those rights, this being most evident in the three-year vacancy which followed Christian's death. Indeed, it is likely that the bishop's death had been anticipated, it being probable that Henry had been made fully aware of Christian's circumstances at nearby Holm Cultram while he was at Carlisle in August. The prolonging of episcopal vacancies was a deliberate act of policy on Henry II's part and, while the extended vacancy at York which followed the death of Archbishop Roger in 1181 provided the immediate cause for the delay in providing a new bishop for its suffragan see, as had happened with the suffragan sees of the province of Canterbury during the exile of Archbishop Thomas Becket, Whithorn fits clearly into this policy.[84] This is supported by the speed with which a candidate was provided after Henry's death in July 1189, before the consecration of the archbishop-elect of York, Geoffrey Plantagenet. Richard I's policy of filling episcopal vacancies was clearly being extended to include Whithorn.

It appears that Bishop John was elected to the see in late summer 1189, most likely through the exercise of patronage of the see by the English crown. He first appeared, as bishop-elect, at the coronation of Richard I at Westminster on 3 September 1189, less than three months after King Henry's death.[85] His consecration followed on 17 September in Pipewell Abbey in Northamptonshire, with the archbishops of Dublin and Trier and the bishop of Annaghdown officiating as proxies for Geoffrey Plantagenet.[86] John immediately demonstrated the focus of his spiritual loyalties, ordaining Geoffrey a priest on 23 September at Southwell, just within the see of York.[87] Archbishop Baldwin of Canterbury, in a bid to enforce his primacy over York by obliging Geoffrey to seek ordination and consecration from his hands, had earlier prohibited any other bishops from officiating. His prohibition, however, had neglected to name the elect of Whithorn, who seized the opportunity to proclaim his obedience to York through his actions.

It is clear from the inaction of either King William or Roland during this period that the inclusion of Whithorn within the province of York and the wider English Church had become firmly established in the period after 1177. This was confirmed by the omission of Whithorn from the constituent sees of the Scottish Church set out in the bull *Cum universi* of March 1189 or March 1192.[88] Continuing English political domination of the lordship and the clearly pro-York stance of the incumbent ensured that there was no political will to secure the separation of Whithorn from the English Church. As a consequence, Whithorn remained, at least nominally, suffragan of York into the fifteenth century, although the upheavals of war after 1296 and schism from 1378 had severed any active relationship long before.

Throughout his episcopate, John can be glimpsed primarily in a York or Galloway context: his back was turned firmly on Scotland. Despite the prominence of Roland and Alan in Scottish politics, there is no indication that John ever attended King William's court: he witnessed no royal *acta*; did not attend legatine councils of the Scottish Church; and only once acted as a judge-delegate in a Scottish case, and that in neighbouring Glasgow diocese.[89] By way of contrast, throughout his twenty-year episcopate, he maintained the bonds with York that had been formed in 1189. He, along with the bishops of Durham and Glasgow, had received a papal mandate to consecrate Geoffrey in 1190, but the ceremony was delayed until August 1191 and was finally performed at Tours without the involvement of any of York's suffragans.[90] After this point, his relationship with Archbishop Geoffrey does not appear to have been a close personal one but clearly that of metropolitan and suffragan. Indeed, surviving evidence for personal attendance on his archbishop is limited to his witnessing of one charter by him in favour of the canons of Welford in Northamptonshire, dated 1190–94, and accompanying him to Richard I's great council at Nottingham in March 1194.[91] His was, however, an uneventful episcopate and provided ideal circumstances for the cementing of the bonds that had been strained over the previous half century.

Throughout the thirteenth century the link remained strong, with successive archbishops of York exercising active roles in the elections of 1235, 1253 and 1293.[92] During the last, Archbishop John le Romeyn secured administrative control of the see for the duration of the vacancy and appointed an official, despite the hostility of both the canons of Whithorn and the archdeacon of Galloway.[93] Whereas metropolitan supremacy and affiliation had been the dominant issue of the twelfth century, the see was dogged in the thirteenth century by the question of patronage, particularly once Scottish political control had been established over Galloway after 1234. While there was no question of detaching Whithorn from York at this stage, indeed the links to York were strengthened despite Scottish domination, it was of paramount importance for the secular controllers of Galloway to secure their influence over the regional Church.

Control of patronage or influence over elections to the see is inseparable from the issue of its twelfth-century revival. Little detail survives until the contentious election of 1235 but evidence for a prolonged struggle between 'clergy and people' and the canons of Whithorn, who claimed to constitute the chapter of the diocese, suggests that election may have lain originally, at least nominally, with the former. Fergus's domination of this group, particularly of the irregular clerics who comprised the Whithorn community, may have secured the election of Gilla-Aldan. The Whithorn clergy may have exercised considerable influence in the process, perhaps claiming a right with Northumbrian precedent. Replacement of these secular clerics by canons regular in the later twelfth century perhaps added to the conflict between the proponents of the two forms of election, with the canons claiming any rights formerly vested in their predecessors.

In whose hands lay the patronage of the see is a matter of debate. Gilla-Aldan's associations appear wholly local and his apparent ties to Fergus suggest that he was nominated by him. For Christian, matters are less clear-cut. His consecration at Bermondsey on the same day as Henry II's coronation points towards his being an English nominee, but his personal affiliation with Holm Cultram, a monastery founded by David I and Earl Henry in 1150, and possible association with Henry Murdac, could indicate that he was originally a Scottish candidate. This would fit comfortably with the evidence for David I's extended personal influence over the Solway region and northern Irish Sea zone down to his death in 1153. Whichever is the case, it is difficult to see the hand of Fergus in his appointment and it appears that he and his successors lost control over nominations to the see at this stage, although they were to retain great influence in the election process. Certainly, there is no evidence for their exercising control of the patronage of Whithorn in the fashion of the earls of Strathearn at Dunblane.[94] Indeed, the 1189 election of Bishop John points to continuing English influence, presumably derived from Henry II and Richard I's overlordship of Galloway and the maintenance of the political and religious ties with York.

The Quitclaim of Canterbury would not have ended this position, as it dealt with secular matters and the see of Whithorn had been confirmed as a suffragan of York in the 1170s. As a diocese within an English province, elections at Whithorn would have remained subject to English royal intervention. The election in 1209 of Alan's chamberlain, Walter,[95] has been taken as evidence for an assertion of local control over appointments but circumstances indicate otherwise. Walter's election coincided with King John's northern expedition that secured William the Lion's submission to his overlordship.[96] Alan of Galloway was closely involved in negotiations between the kings, being one of the two oath-takers swearing to uphold the treaty that set out their new relationship. Alan had private meetings with John at Carlisle, from which stemmed his participation in the English king's Irish campaigns. Walter's election, then, was probably a sign of favour by John towards a man whose military and naval power would provide a vital element in his plans for the rigorous assertion of his lordship in Ulster. This was, however, to be the last demonstration of English royal control over the patronage of the see.

The contentious double election of 1235, while continuing to highlight the influence and role of York at Whithorn, underscored a shift in favour of Scottish interest. Set against a backdrop of political disturbance in England, which probably diverted Henry III's attention to more pressing secular business, and the growing authority of Alexander II in Scotland and his recent military conquest of Galloway, the election was a highly charged and intensely politicised affair. The death of Bishop Walter was followed by the presentation of two rival candidates claiming election by two opposed bodies: the prior and canons of Whithorn acting as the cathedral chapter on the one hand and the 'clergy and people of the diocese on the other, the latter clearly acting in accord with the wishes of Alexander II. *Prima facie*, this affair illustrated the rearguard action of the traditional rights of 'clergy and people' against the papal innovation of investing cathedral chapters with electoral rights.[97] No record survives of procedures or the identity of the electors on previous occasions, but the 1235 situation suggests that elections had been attributed to 'clergy and people'.

In 1235, Gilbert, novice-master of Melrose, was elected to the vacant see by 'clergy and people'. A Cistercian monk drawn from the monastery most favoured by the Scottish king, whose monks were also to provide him with bishops in Caithness and other politically 'frontier' sees,[98] his appointment was clearly part of Alexander II's political settlement of Galloway following Alan's death. The local influence of the bishop of Whithorn made control of that office by a man closely allied to the Scottish crown an imperative as Alexander struggled to enforce his will on the region. Indeed, the speed with which Gilbert was nominated on the death of Walter indicates the king's anxiety to secure the election of a pro-Scottish cleric to an office that could easily have become a major focus of opposition to crown policy. Gilbert, however, was not a complete outsider, for he had formerly been abbot of Glenluce,[99] which indicates Alexander's awareness of the need to impose a man who was at least familiar with local politics.

Native opposition to Alexander's plans was not slow to emerge. Three weeks later, the prior and canons of Whithorn elected Odo Ydonc, former abbot of Premonstratensian Holywood in Nithsdale and a fellow canon at Whithorn.[100] His electors considered themselves to constitute the cathedral chapter and, as such and in accordance with papal policy, their claim carried weight in Church circles. Despite appearances, it is unlikely that the canons' actions were motivated by primarily political considerations. Foreign intrusion in the election process had been commonplace down to 1209 and it is more likely that the canons were using the local hostility to Alexander II's heavy-handed policies as a vehicle to cover their own self-interested actions. Determination to secure the election of one of their own number to the bishopric and so end the tensions that had previously soured the relationship between the canons and the bishops was paramount.[101]

The background and progress of this hotly contested election have been researched in detail and need not be rehearsed in full here.[102] All studies reach the same general conclusion and emphasise the role of lay interests in the process. Alexander II claimed that Gilbert was the unanimously elected candidate of clergy and people,[103] resorting to a formula already rejected in his own kingdom in favour of capitular election. Made a month after the election of Odo, this was patently untrue. Odo's counterclaim denied the right of anyone other than the chapter to elect bishops and stated that unspecified foreign clerics and secular powers had been instrumental in Gilbert's appointment.[104] Further references to the king of Scots 'who now holds Galloway', and to 'the war being waged in Galloway' by him, leave no doubt as to the identity of the secular powers in question.[105] This conveys the impression that the Whithorn clergy had associated themselves with the rebellion against Alexander II and Ashley goes so far as to suggest that they were working in association with Thomas, the favoured native candidate for the lordship.[106] There is no evidence to support this view, which fails to recognise that the primary aim of the canons was to secure recognition of their right to elect bishops.

The canons' claim hinged ultimately upon their role as the chapter of the cathedral. This was not without precedent for, while colleges of secular canons constituted the cathedral chapters in most Scottish dioceses,[107] the Augustinian communities attached to the cathedrals at St Andrews and Carlisle were in the process of securing that role for themselves, while in several English sees, such as Durham, Winchester and Canterbury, convents of Benedictine monks had long held the position of cathedral chapters.[108] The length of the litigation and Odo's success in his appeals to York and Rome, which stressed the illegality of Gilbert's election, indicates the strength of his case in terms of current canon law. His ultimate failure to secure consecration cannot, therefore, be attributed to the weakness of his canonical position but to the diplomatic abilities of Alexander II.

Gilbert's consecration at York in September 1235[109] temporarily ended the issue of control of the elections. The only matter that had been settled, however, was that rights of patronage were vested henceforth in the Scottish crown, ending a century of English domination. This was confirmed in 1253–54 when the Comyn-dominated royal council secured the election of Henry of Holyrood.[110] Capitular involvement in the process is suggested by John Balliol's protest, which challenged the election in defence of the rights of the people of Galloway,[111] a protest that probably reflected more the disappointment of an influential local lord than a principled defence of ancient popular rights. Balliol's appeal may have been concerned with rights of patronage,[112] as suggested by the *Chronicle of Lanercost* account, but the same chronicle describes the new bishop, Henry's, election in ambiguous terms that raise the possibility that Balliol was fighting a rearguard action to maintain the form of the 1235 election. In one sense, this was a question of patronage, for Balliol could have held a highly influential role in elections by 'clergy and people'. His objections, however, proved fruitless and Bishop Henry was duly consecrated at York, thus ending the role of 'clergy and people' in future elections. By the time of the next election, in 1293, the rights of the chapter had been confirmed and they were maintained into the fourteenth century when direct presentation gradually supplanted capitular independence.

SCOTTISH BISHOPS

The death of Bishop Walter in 1235 brought a significant change to the role of the bishops of Whithorn and to the Church in Galloway in general. For Alexander II, the death of a bishop associated closely with the native ruling house was entirely fortuitous and too good an opportunity to be let slip. A consummate politician and astute governor, Alexander had forged a close relationship with the Church in Scotland and was to use bishops as frontline agents of royal power. In Ross, Caithness and Argyll, he was to use clerics drawn from abbeys and orders with which he enjoyed a close personal relationship as his representatives. Through them, he could exercise a close supervision over regional affairs even when the local secular powers may have been hostile to his will. In Galloway, identical considerations underlay his determination to appoint Gilbert, master of the novices at Melrose, the monastery with which he enjoyed a unique personal bond.

The intrusion of Gilbert into Whithorn represented only part of a more general attack on what may have been hostile elements within the native Church in Galloway. A raid on Tongland, Alan's own personal foundation, left the prior and sacristan of the house dead.[113] Although committed by what are described as renegade elements in the army left by Alexander to suppress resistance in the lordship, the chronicle accounts of the affair seek to exonerate the king from any complicity in the deaths, perhaps suggesting that there was some contemporary suspicion. Alexander, certainly, was keen to remove from positions of influence any clerics who could provide inspirational leadership to those opposed to his settlement of Galloway, although elsewhere he resorted to less violent means. At Dundrennan and Glenluce, the deposition of abbots Jordan and Robert on the instructions of the general chapter of the Cistercian order and their replacement by Leonius and Michael, both monks of Melrose, was unmistakably an act of royal policy.[114] Royal anxiety to maintain control over the head of the Cistercian filiation in Galloway was confirmed in 1239 when Leonius was elected to the abbacy of Rievaulx. His replacement at Dundrennan was another Melrose monk, Richard, prior of that house.[115] It was only in 1250, by which time Alexander II was dead and Galloway had been more firmly integrated into the kingdom that a Dundrennan monk succeeded to the abbacy of his house.[116]

While Alexander was prepared to interfere in the episcopal elections and secure the deposition of the heads of the chief monasteries and their replacement by suitably loyal candidates, he could not pursue this course to its logical conclusion: the separation of Whithorn from the metropolitan authority of York and its addition to the body of the *ecclesia Scoticana*. As recently as 1218, Pope Honorius III, in the bull *Filia specialis* had confirmed the independent status of the Scottish Church and listed its component sees.[117] Alexander was not going to seek to overturn that settlement at a time when he was moving towards a conclusion of the long-running contest with England over the issue of the northern counties. Gilbert, therefore, although his primary loyalties can be assumed to have lain with Alexander, maintained his predecessors' obedience to York and acted as a loyal suffragan.

Fuller evidence survives for Gilbert's episcopal role than for any of his predecessors at Whithorn and, while still a fragmentary record, it reveals a conscientious diocesan at work and confronting the current ills of the Church. He is to be seen in particular attempting to ensure that the spiritual welfare of his flock at parish level was safeguarded in the face of the growing problem of parish appropriations by religious corporations.[118] This, interestingly, was a greater problem in Scotland than in England, with around 75 per cent of all Scottish parishes appropriated to some monastery or collegiate foundation before 1296 – rising to about 86 per cent by 1560 – as against some 37 per cent south of the border. The see of Whithorn differs markedly from the general English pattern, indicating that while it fell under the metropolitan jurisdiction of York, in its traditions of religious patronage and secular affiliations to particular religious houses it was fully integrated into the Scottish sphere. Although the fourth Lateran Council of 1215 had recently enacted canons intended to curb abuse of the process of appropriation and to ensure that suitable parish clergy were maintained on an adequate stipend,[119] the provisions were regularly flouted and diocesans recognised that they were fighting a losing battle. In common with the bishops of the *ecclesia Scoticana*, therefore, Gilbert sought to regulate rather than overturn the process. In particular, he attempted to place controls and safeguards on the appointment of curates. At Borgue, for example, where the right of patronage of the parish church had been granted *c*.1230 to the canons of distant Dryburgh Abbey,[120] in *c*.1240 he agreed to the appropriation of the revenues of the parish following the death of the incumbent, with the proviso that ten merks, six acres of arable and one of pasture be set aside for the support of succeeding vicars.[121] At Dryburgh's other Galloway parishes, Sorbie Major and Sorbie Minor in the Machars, economic realities brought Gilbert to concede an amalgamation which was financially advantageous to the canons, who consequently had only one stipend rather than two to meet from the parish revenues.[122] Although this arrangement benefited Dryburgh, Gilbert's primary concern appears to have been to rationalise the parish structure where unviably small economic units had been developed into parishes by the secular landholders in the later twelfth century. In addition to the internal affairs of his diocese, however, Gilbert was to maintain an active role within the province of York. He was especially active at Durham during episcopal vacancies there, dedicating altars and granting indulgences, the last occasion, in July 1253, occurring shortly before his death.[123]

Gilbert's episcopate set the pattern for the future. His successor, Henry, the former abbot of Holyrood, was chosen probably both for his connections with Scottish government and his knowledge of Galloway where his abbey was a major landholder.[124] Like his predecessor, he was a Scot in his political allegiance but moved easily into the English ecclesiastical hierarchy as a suffragan of York. His forty-year tenure of the see confirmed this notional duality but also cemented the trends evident by the time of Gilbert, which showed the character of the Church in Whithorn diocese to be closer to the Scottish pattern than to that of the rest of its province. This process may have been accelerated by the continuing importation of Scottish clerics, noted above in respect of Dundrennan and Glenluce, but evidence for this is less clear-cut. By the time of his death,

Galloway had been politically integrated into the kingdom of the Scots, a process that had seen the authority of the crown reinforced by its control over the senior ecclesiastical offices of the former lordship. This centrality of the Church to the mechanisms of political control in Galloway was confirmed in the course of the sixty years of intermittent warfare that broke over the region after 1296, warfare that confirmed the 'Scottishness' of the diocese and hastened the severing of the link with York.[125]

Notes

1 Duncan, *Making of the Kingdom*, 256–80.
2 Donaldson, *Scottish Church History*, 11–24; see, for example, the case of St Andrews in Watt, *Fasti*, 289–90.
3 Watt, *Series Episcoporum*, i, 24.
4 Hill, *Whithorn*, 21–23.
5 Symeon of Durham, ii, 115 and note.
6 Midmer, *English Medieval Monasteries*, 164.
7 Oram, 'Whithorn and York'; Brooke, *Wild Men*, 69, 78; Hill, *Whithorn*, 23-24.
8 See, for example, Craig, 'Pre-Norman sculpture'.
9 Brooke, *Wild Men*, 75–76. In the vicinity of Whithorn, the churches of St Fillan at Sorbie and St Comgan at Kirkcowan, a pairing of saints which was very popular in the Gaelic west, may further indicate strong Norse–Gaelic influence in this period.
10 'Chronicon Metricum Ecclesiae Eboracensis' in *Historians of York*, ii, 461–62.
11 William of Newburgh, 75.
12 Anderson, *Early Sources*, ii, 97.
13 M'Kerlie, *Lands and Their Owners*, ii, 160.
14 *AU*, ii, 240-42.
15 M. T. Flanagan, *Irish Society, Anglo-Norman Settlers, Angevin Kingship* (Oxford, 1989), 15–20.
16 Smyth, *York and Dublin*, ii, 310; Hudson, 'Knútr and Viking Dublin', 325–27.
17 Ibid., ii, 311.
18 See, Anderson, *Early Sources*, i, 591–92.
19 *ASC*, 159.
20 *Chron. Mann*, 40.
21 Anderson, *Early Sources*, 48, 93–94.
22 Flanagan, *Irish Society*, Chapter 1.
23 Ibid., 23.
24 Ibid., 25–26.
25 Ibid., 30–31.
26 *Glasgow Registrum*, no. 1.
27 Skene, *Celtic Scotland*, ii, 375.
28 *Glasgow Registrum*, no. 1, 5.
29 Brooke, 'Desnes Cro and Edingham'.
30 Nicolaisen, *Scottish Place-Names*, 73.
31 Reid, 'Feudalisation of lower Nithsdale', 108–09; Scott, 'Early sheriff', 90–91.
32 Shead, 'Origins', 220–25.
33 Wainwright, 'Submission to Edward the Elder', 330–31.
34 Fellows-Jensen, *Scandinavian Settlement Names in the North-West*, 5–7.
35 See Historia Regum, 101, for the early twelfth-century view of Lindisfarne's sphere of authority in the mid-ninth century. This embraced Carlisle in the west and spread as far as the failed seventh-century see of Abercorn on the

Forth. Carlisle had evidently been granted to Cuthbert by King Ecgfrith in 685 and the bishop had used the property to endow a nunnery. This had been destroyed in the Viking raids of the 900s and later Durham tradition saw this as marking the reversion of the property to the Cuthbert community. 'Symeon' was at pains to emphasise this point at several places in his writings, stressing, for example, that Abbot Eadred of Lindisfarne in the 880s bore the cognomen 'Lulisc' because he had dwelt at Carlisle (ibid., 114) and that 'Luel, which is now called Carluel, was not only St Cuthbert's property of right, but was also adjunct to his see from the times of King Ecgfrith' (HDE in *Symeon of Durham*, i, 53 and note). His stress on this issue reflects Durham's opposition to the proposed creation of a new see of Carlisle by Henry I.

36 H. H. E. Craster, 'A contemporary record of the pontificate of Ranulf Flambard', *Archaeologia Aelieana*, vii (1930), 39.

37 Barlow, *William Rufus*, 206.

38 Hill, *Whithorn*, 23; Oram, 'In obedience and reverence', 87.

39 For the career of Aldhun see *De Obsessione Dunelmi*.

40 Ibid., 215.

41 Stenton, *Anglo-Saxon England*, 419.

42 The case of 'Gillomichael', described by Symeon of Durham as 'quidam ultra amnem Tinam praepotens', illustrates the more general presence of Gaelic name forms amongst the upper strata of Northumbrian society. Symeon of Durham, i, 102.

43 Reginald of Durham,177–79.

44 *Historians of York*, ii, 48–49.

45 Ibid., ii, 60.

46 E.g. M'Kerlie, *Lands and Their Owners*, ii, 423–24.

47 Cowan and Easson, *Religious Houses*, 212; Radford and Donaldson, *Whithorn and Kirkmadrine*, 15; Sprott, 'Ancient cathedrals', 2.

48 Crawford, 'Earldom of Caithness', 99–101.

49 See e.g. Oram, 'David I'.

50 Duncan, *Making of the Kingdom*, 256–61.

51 Watt, *Fasti*, 28; Donaldson, *Church History*, 23; Barrow, *Kingship and Unity*, 67–68.

52 Brooke, *Wild Men*, 88; Backmund, 'Premonstratensian order', 38.

53 If the Kirkcudbright community had continued to recognise the spiritual leadership of the successor of St Cuthbert – in Gaelic terms his *comarb* – then it is likely that eastern Galloway had remained in York's sphere through the eleventh century. The possible extension of Kirkcudbright's influence to Whithorn would have had the effect of re-establishing the York affiliations of the old episcopal centre.

54 Duncan, *Making of the Kingdom*, 259–60.

55 Oram, 'In obedience and reverence', 89.

56 See, for example, *Letters of St Bernard*, nos 187–88. He describes FitzHerbert as 'a man who puts not his trust in God his helper, but hopes in the abundance of his riches.' He continues that 'he is rotten from the soles of his feet to the crown of his head.' He is, furthermore, 'an unrighteous man' who may attempt to 'swallow up righteousness in the Curia, even as he has done in England'.

57 Brooke, *Wild Men*, 90–92. For an alternative hypothesis concerning the dating and development of the earliest Cistercian community in Galloway, see J. G. Scott, 'The origins of Dundrennan and Soulseat Abbeys', *TDGNHAS*, lxiii (1988), 35–44.

58 Watt, *Series Episcoporum*, 24.

59 *Chron. Holyrood*, 127.

60 His later strong ties with Holm Cultram might indicate that he had earlier been

professed of that house, the foundation of David I and Earl Henry in 1150.

61 *Chron. Holyrood*, 125; Warren, *Henry II*, 425.
62 *Chron. Holyrood*, 125.
63 Ibid., 127–28.
64 *Benedict of Peterborough*, i, 166–67; *Chron. Holyrood*, 127 note 7.
65 *SAEC*, 238.
66 See: *Holyrood Liber*, no. 25 (datable *c.*1167–86); *Holm Cultram Register*, nos 120, 120a; *CDS*, ii, no. 1606(6).
67 Reginald of Durham, *Vita Godrici Heremitae*, (Surtees Society, 1848), 258–59. Reginald uses the adjective *dives*, normally translated as wealthy or rich, but in this context carrying the medieval meaning of possessing the power and influence of wealth.
68 Brooke, *Wild Men*, 115.
69 Howden, *Gesta*, i, 136. For a general discussion of Vivian's legation, see Fergusson, *Medieval Papal Representatives in Scotland*, 53–55. For his activities in Mann, see *Chron. Mann*, s.a 1176.
70 *Chron. Holyrood*, 162; *Chron. Melrose*, 42.
71 *Benedict of Peterborugh*, i, 166–67.
72 *Chron. Howden*, ii, 135.
73 *AMW*, 191–92; Bower, *Scotichronicon*, vol. 4, 323; Watt, *Series Episcoporum*, 26.
74 *Holm Cultram Register*, no. 121. This charter is normally dated to 1185–86, based on the assumption that Roland did not hold any of the lordship of Galloway before Gillebrigte's death in January 1185.
75 *CDS*, i, nos 67, 72.
76 Walter Daniel, *Life of Ailred*, 46.
77 *RRS*, i, no. 118.
78 *RRS*, ii, no. 80; Watt, *Series Episcoporum*, 25; *Lanercost Cartulary*, nos. 1 and 180. In similar fashion he witnessed a grant to Lanercost by Ada Engain, dated 1167–1174, *Lanercost Cartulary*, no. 37.
79 *Wetheral Register*, 85.
80 See Watt, *Series Episcoporum*, 26–27 for his subsequent career.
81 *Holm Cultram Register*, no. 141.
82 *Chron. Melrose*, 95.
83 *Glasgow Registrum*, no. 57.
84 Warren, *Henry II*, 385; Howell, *Regalian Rights*, appendix A.
85 *Benedict of Peterborough*, ii, 79.
86 Ibid., ii, 87.
87 Ibid., ii, 88.
88 Duncan, *Making of the Kingdom*, 275; Barrell, 'Background to Cum universi'; Ferguson, *Medieval Papal Representatives*, 25.
89 Watt, *Series Episcoporum*, 27; Ferguson, *Medieval Papal Representatives*, 212, no. 11.
90 Watt, *Series Episcoporum*, 27.
91 *Reg. Romeyn*, i, 227; *Chron. Howden*, iii, 241.
92 *Reg. Gray*, 120-22; *Reg. Romeyn*, i, nos. 1286, 1388–89, 1390–92, 1396.
93 Brentano, 'Redating a Whithorn document', 192–93; Brentano, 'The Whithorn vacancy', 71–83.
94 J. H. Cockburn, *The Medieval Bishops of Dunblane and their Church* (Edinburgh, 1959), 3–4. For an opposing view see Donaldson, 'Bishops and priors', 135–36.
95 *Chron. Melrose*, 54.
96 Duncan, *Making of the Kingdom*, 242–51; Warren, *King John*, 193–94
97 Donaldson, *Church History*, 25–30.

 98 Oram, 'Prayer, property and profit', 84–85.
 99 *Chron. Melrose*, 111.
100 Ibid., 113.
101 Donaldson, 'Bishops and priors', 136 and note 17a.
102 Dowden, *Bishops of Scotland*, 356–57; Donaldson, 'Bishops and priors', 136–37; Ashley, 'Odo, elect of Whithorn', 62–69.
103 *Historians of York*, iii, 148–49.
104 *CPL*, i, 193.
105 *Reg. Grey*, 170, 171.
106 Ashley, 'Odo, elect of Whithorn', 66–67.
107 Cowan, 'The organisation of secular cathedral chapters'.
108 Barrow, *The Kingdom of the Scots*, Chapter 7.
109 *Chron. Melrose*, 83.
110 Watt, *Fasti*, 129.
111 *Chron. Lanercost*, 59–62.
112 Ibid., 62; Donaldson, 'Bishops and priors', 137.
113 *Chron. Melrose*, s.a. 1235.
114 Ibid.
115 Ibid.
116 Ibid.
117 Donaldson, *Historical Documents*, 30–32.
118 For a detailed discussion of this issue, see Cowan, 'Appropriation of parish churches', and idem, 'Vicarages and the cure of souls'.
119 See, *Hartridge Vicarages in the Middle Ages*, where the canons of the Council concerned with appropriation, vicarages etc., are cited in full.
120 *Dryburgh Liber*, no. 65.
121 Ibid., no. 66.
122 Ibid., no. 82.
123 *Finchale Charters*, 169, 172, 175, 177; *Rites of Durham*, app. vi, nos vi, viii.
124 For his career, see Oram, 'Heirs of Ninian', 64–66. He was active in northern England by 1260 (*Finchale Charters*, 179–80). In 1286, Archbishop John le Romeyn excused him from his annual visits to York on account of his old age (*Reg. Romeyn*, ii, 85) but in 1291 he was given a commission to perform pontifical duties in York diocese during the archbishop's absence (*Reg. Romeyn*, ii, 100). He died on 1 November 1293.
125 Oram, 'Heirs of Ninian', 66–69.

7

COLONISATION, INTEGRATION AND ACCULTURATION
c.1160–*c*.1300

COLONISATION AND CONTINUITY[1]

In common with the mainstream of the traditional interpretation of the relationship between so-called 'Anglo-Norman' culture and the largely Gaelic societies encountered along the peripheries of its main zone of penetration, the history of Galloway has been presented in the past as characterised by a cultural clash. Here, Gaelic conservatism, represented by the native dynasty and its kindred branches, was confronted by the Brave New World of north-western European Frankish culture, and despite a long rearguard action was progressively supplanted by this more dynamic international tradition. Survival there may have been, but it was at a low level, politically submerged under a tide of aggressive colonisation which underpinned the imposition of a 'feudal' settlement on the lordship by the king of Scots, cowed by a succession of savage police actions in the wake of native rebellions, and swamped by the acculturation of its own social elite into the cultural milieu of a dominant colonial aristocracy. It is a powerful image, one well in tune with most modern colonial and post-colonial perceptions of the nature and effect of colonial plantation into regions of already well-defined native culture. At a superficial level, the medieval narrative accounts of the relationship between Galloway and the Scots support such perceptions, presenting an apparently incontrovertible record of a highly political conflict between a colonising crown and a resistant local power, to which heightened colour is given by the persistent undercurrents of cultural confrontation which run through the record.

This traditional narrative of conquest and colonisation, throughout the whole of the highland zone of mainland Britain and in Ireland, went largely unchallenged until the late 1980s when the dynamics of the processes of conquest, colonisation and cultural change received a radical reassessment.[2] Central to this re-evaluation is criticism for historians' perceived 'soft spot for conquest',[3] a wholly justified view, for any survey of historical texts or handbooks reveals that the chronology of change is punctuated by reference to invasions, battles, or sieges.[4] At both national and local level, change is associated most commonly with a cataclysmic political event or violent social upheaval. As we are now becoming increasingly aware, however, physical invasion constitutes but one plane in the dynamics of 'conquest', and could indeed represent a comparatively minor stage in an extended process. Military invasion was often the culmination of decades – if not centuries – of increasing cultural or economic domination, as in the English relationship with the native princes of north Wales. Conversely, initial attempts at outright military conquest might fail to achieve concrete results, with more lasting success attained through more subtle methods. In Wales and in Ireland, economic dependence, progressive acculturation achieved through colonial infiltration and the absorption of native elites into the political and cultural nexus of the dominating society, played a greater part in engendering change than our war-fixated sources indicate.

This new model for domination and conquest is particularly well suited to the history of Galloway. The traditional narrative of Scottish invasions and native rebellions between 1160 and 1247 is the product both of the bias within the surviving annalistic evidence for the politics of the region, and of the 'spin' which modern scholars have placed on their interpretation of these same records. The medieval sources, none of which represent a native account, focus on five main episodes of war or rebellion in 1160, 1174, 1185, 1235 and 1247.[5] Beyond details of those years, Galwegian affairs are dominated by reference to involvement in wars in England, Ireland and Mann, a concentration on military matters which distorts interpretations of Galwegian society and obscures the motives of the region's rulers and their relationship with foreign powers. More particularly, the emphasis on war, invasion, rebellion and conquest has generated a negative view of the colonial settlement within Galloway and the formulation of a 'cataclysmic' interpretation of the evidence for such settlement. Indeed, the focus has lain on the military and aristocratic aspects of the 'conquest' of Galloway, to the neglect of the ecclesiastical, economic and administrative elements within the process. But even aristocratic colonisers and their residences, when freed from the more pejorative overtones implicit in the term conquest, can be viewed in a much less sinister light, their presence in Galloway uncoupled from a traditional portrayal as consequent on invasion and subjugation. When regarded as an element in the unspectacular processes of cultural assimilation, development of economic, political and ecclesiastical ties with adjoining territories, and the progressive integration of the lordly dynasty into the ranks of the emergent Anglo-Scottish nobility of the later twelfth and thirteenth centuries, the presence of foreign settlers in the lordship becomes less sinister.

Later twelfth-century Galloway has long been labelled as the last bastion of Gaelic conservatism and violent 'anti-feudal' sentiment in southern mainland Scotland. It has been represented as a region where the spread of 'feudal' settlement had to 'creep tentatively along the shores' of the Solway[6] under constant threat of violent native reaction. This reputation derives principally from the perceived late importation into Galloway of classically 'feudal' institutions – the knight and his feu – and the violent anti-foreign reaction that met their arrival in the period 1174–85. This anti-foreign reaction, though patently directed at the Scottish crown and the visible symbols of its domination of Galloway, has been represented as an anti-feudal movement.[7] It is, however, difficult to comfortably reconcile that anti-feudal labelling with the fact that during this same period Gillebrigte entered a relationship with Henry II of England that was more overtly feudal than any aspect of the Scottish overlordship which he was seeking to escape. Certainly, such violent and widespread reaction against the supposed introduction of Anglo-Norman settlers and their influences is unique in Scotland south of the Forth, and does not even bear close comparison with the other main centres of resistance to increasing royal authority, such as Moray and the far north of the mainland.[8] The historiographical bias, however, demands a re-alignment: the reaction in Galloway was a backlash against Scottish – royal – domination, not against introduction of new-fangled institutions, such as knight service.

A multi-aspect process of 'conquest' had been at work in Galloway since the early decades of the twelfth century, with ecclesiastical influences and the beginnings of the integration of the native social elite into the Anglo-Scottish nobility at the forefront of the process. Of particular importance were the re-forging of political ties between Galloway and the English crown, at first on a personal level between Fergus and Henry I. This bond had a profound impact on the political evolution of the lordship and moulded its political alignments into the thirteenth century and beyond. From as early as c.1120 Henry I was extending his authority into Cumbria and the adjacent northern sector of the Irish Sea, in parallel with the establishment of David as 'prince of the Cumbrian region'. Among a range of mechanisms employed by Henry to promote stability on his northern frontier was the marriage of one of his brood of illegitimate daughters to Fergus, so establishing a kinship tie with a powerful regional lord. It was this personal bond, as we have seen, which went furthest towards opening up Galloway to foreign influences in the course of the twelfth century. It must be stressed, however, that this was a personal bond and that its impact was most apparent in the actions of Galloway's native rulers. What it did not do was immediately open up the lordship to a flood of foreign colonists or alien cultural imports, but it did change the social and cultural perspectives of Fergus's younger son. The clearest implication of the marriage was that Galloway's lord gained access to the mainstream of mainland British power-politics, and that through him the English crown had gained an additional and highly influential means of entry into the northern Irish and Hebridean political zone.

Fergus, of course, continued to function as an essentially free agent in this western maritime world, strengthening and maintaining ties with the Manx kings in particular. Nevertheless, while Mann remained of central importance to Fergus and his heirs, it was to their English kin that they turned increasingly as the twelfth century progressed. Indeed, it was the tie with the Norman dynasty as much as Scottish political domination that lay behind Fergus's involvement in David I's intervention in the English civil war. Certainly, English weakness from c.1136 until c.1154 brought no lessening of influence within Galloway. For example, the appointment of Bishop Christian in 1154 was an act of Angevin royal policy:[9] the tie with York was strengthened rather than diminished during the years of David's annexation of northern England, despite control of the archiepiscopal see by the hostile Cistercian Henry Murdac. The Scots' occupation of Carlisle, however, must have increased their political influence within Galloway, and it is likely that the long-established ties with Cumbria facilitated this process. This trans-Solway connection had a profound impact on the development of the lordship.

At the heart of the connection stood Uhtred. As a kinsman of David I, being descended from Maldred, younger brother of Donnchad mac Crinain, Uhtred's father-in-law Waltheof was an important figure in the political structure of the English north-west, inclining towards the Scots but Anglian and Anglicised in his background. Marriage into this family established Uhtred's place in David I's new Anglo-Scottish establishment, its success being marked by the pro-Scottish stance adopted by his segment of the Galloway dynasty after at least c.1160. It was, of course, a two-way mechanism, for through it, while Uhtred gained access to the tightly knit world of the Cumbrian nobility and possession of his family's first non-Galloway estate at Torpenhow, foreigners also gained access to Galloway.

With the Allerdale marriage came the interlinked issues of colonisation and conquest as media for change in later twelfth-century Galloway, for from this point the structure of power within the lordship was refashioned at an accelerating rate. Gunnilda of Allerdale brought Uhtred into contact with the changing world across the Solway, enmeshing him in a new social circle that coloured his perspectives profoundly. In return, it was this new Cumberland and Westmorland society that provided Uhtred and his son with the body of colonists that they introduced into their territories. This, of course, begs the question of why Uhtred and Roland chose to introduce a colonial nobility. Was it a matter of choice, done in emulation of the policies that had brought a vast access of power to the king of Scots, or was it a consequence of the turbulent relationship between Galloway and the crown for the quarter century after 1160?

One view of the colonising venture in Galloway has dominated the traditional historiography for over a century. This, a cataclysmic interpretation, regarded it as the hostile act of Máel Coluim IV, who was viewed as having imposed the settlement of knights loyal to him on the lordship in the aftermath of his 1160 campaigns.[10] The presence of Anglo-Scottish settlers apparently confirmed a traditional narrative that presented the forcible implanting of foreigners to act as crown agents as a mechanism through which the security of the south-western regions of the kingdom could be assured, and by whom the assimilation of Galloway into the kingdom could be expedited. That the crown itself did not retain any properties as part of this colonising programme and, indeed, alienated a large portion of recently acquired land in southern Nithsdale to Uhtred, in stark contrast to its policy in contemporary Moray, sits awkwardly with an interpretation of this colonisation as part of a considered scheme of occupation and domination. Indeed, the failure of the crown to retain any land for itself in Galloway until after 1234 is usually glossed over in the conventional narratives. The inconsistencies in this thesis of conquest-driven settlement beg an alternative interpretation, and from this has developed a thesis which views the growth of 'feudalism' within Galloway as a gradual programme, encouraged and supported by the Scottish crown, but not imposed on the lordship as an instrument of conquest.[11]

It is in the aftermath of Fergus's overthrow in 1160 that the first documentary evidence for the establishment of Anglo-Norman colonists emerges. The sudden appearance of a colonial settlement in what, it must be stressed, is a highly fragmented historical record that represents only a fraction of the whole, has seen this development identified as an inseparable consequence of Máel Coluim IV's military conquest of Galloway. An early indication of change is preserved in a fifteenth-century transumpt in the cartulary of Dryburgh Abbey of a charter to the canons given by a Hugh de Morville recording his gift to them of the church of Borgue.[12] The transumpt, shorn of its witness list, lies out of sequence in what is otherwise a block of thirteenth-century documents. Its fifteenth-century heading 'Prima donatio super ecclesiam de Worgis', and the assumption that the titleless Hugh de Morville in question was the king's constable, led Fraser in his 1847 edition of the cartulary for the Bannatyne Club to propose a date of c.1150 for this 'first gift'. Rather than see 'Prima donatio' as simply indicating the first grant concerned with Borgue, Fraser interpreted this as signifying the first gift made to the abbey after its foundation in 1150. Such a date, however, would require Hugh de Morville to have possessed Borgue over a decade earlier than the next surviving record of colonising landownership in Galloway. In an endeavour to fit what is known of the burst of infeftments which followed 1160, Duncan, accepting the traditional identification of the granter as Hugh de Morville, lord of Lauderdale, conjectured that the estate had been given to the constable as part of an otherwise unknown settlement imposed on Fergus by David I.[13] There are, however, too many leaps of faith in that argument for it to be easily accepted. Indeed, the inescapable conclusion is that Fraser dated the charter too early, that the identification of the granter with David I's constable is incorrect, and that some other Hugh de Morville was responsible. Alternative Hughs are easy to find; indeed, Uhtred's marital ties with Cumbria suggest immediately that the man in question was the elder son and namesake of the constable, who entered the service of Henry II after 1157 (in 1170 acquiring lasting infamy as one of the four king's knights who assassinated Becket) and who received the lordship of north Westmorland which his father had held previously as a vassal of David I.[14] A second alternative is the son of Simon de Morville who held the lordship of Burgh-by-Sands in Cumberland in right of his wife. This Hugh was a household knight of Henry II and came into his inheritance in 1167; as lord of Burgh-by-Sands he was a near neighbour of Uhtred's Torpenhow properties and, as Henry II's protégé, a natural candidate for advancement by a man whose kinship with the English king was a matter of personal pride.[15]

If re-dated to the 1160s, Borgue's grant to Hugh de Morville fits into the recognised programme of progressive colonisation underway in the aftermath of Fergus's overthrow. Victory in 1160 gave the Scots an unprecedented opportunity to break the unpredictable independence of Galloway's rulers and impose a favourable re-definition of their relationship with the Scottish crown. It is implicit in Howden's account of the 1174 rising that Malcolm IV had established mechanisms for the supervision of the lordship,[16] but it is equally clear that he sought to conciliate Fergus's sons. Uhtred's accommodation with Malcolm in the late 1150s and contribution to his father's downfall probably lie behind the king's apparent failure to define the relationship between the lordship of Galloway and the crown in explicit terms; the relationship remained purely personal. The success of this rapport with Malcolm was underscored by Uhtred's acquisition of new territories by gift of the king.[17] But the crown also benefited, for the lordship had been significantly weakened by division between Uhtred and Gillebrigte. Furthermore, it appears that Uhtred's new lands entailed entry into a relationship with the crown that defined his service dues from this acquired property in overtly 'feudal' terms. Desnes Ioan had not been part of Fergus's domain. Here Malcolm could impose what conditions of tenure he wished. Malcolm may simply have intended Uhtred's inclusion in the dismemberment of Nithsdale to facilitate the enforcement of royal rights; for instance the collection of cain in Desnes Ioan may have been eased. But the consequences went far beyond mere improvement of the mechanisms for revenue collection, for the military aspects of tenure emerge as the key element in crown interests in the region. Although no charter granting Desnes Ioan to Uhtred survives, his efforts to introduce colonists into that district leaves little doubt as to the basis on which it had been granted.

Whatever the detail of this defined relationship, it is clear that as part of his obligations to the crown Uhtred was responsible for providing military service for Desnes Ioan. Furthermore, it is evident that it was Uhtred and not the crown who had the responsibility for producing the men who would perform that service. As it is implicit that it was the service of men accoutred as knights that was required by the king, Uhtred was faced with the task of finding suitable colonists on whom to settle portions of his new territories. Scott argued that soon after 1165 a permanent royal presence was established in Dumfries with the installation of a 'proto-sheriff' in the person of Roger de Minto.[18] He suggests that Roger's authority extended to the Urr, embracing Desnes Ioan, and that he was based at the expropriated seat of lordship of Radulf son of Dunegal at Dumfries. Defence of this new royal stronghold was provided by castleguard service drawn from men settled on Radulf's former properties. Reid, in an analysis of garrison provision at Dumfries in the fourteenth century, demonstrated that less than half of the requirement was provided by tenancies lying to the north and east of the burgh.[19] Scott built from these findings to propose that the remainder were provided from Desnes Ioan. This, then, may have been a further spur for Uhtred to find settlers.

While Uhtred was generous in his disposal of his newly acquired estates, it was not a generosity restricted exclusively to secular colonists, nor did he prodigally grant away his gains. The dearth of primary source material renders impossible the reconstruction of the full tenurial pattern created by Uhtred in Desnes Ioan. Nevertheless, it can be shown that a substantial portion of his acquisition was retained as demesne, while further elements formed the early endowments of the nunnery founded by him at Lincluden and for Holm Cultram Abbey in Cumberland. The extent of Lincluden's properties cannot be determined, since, like all other south-western communities, its cartulary has been lost. However, the suppression of the nunnery in 1389 and its immediate re-foundation as a collegiate church[20] saw its properties re-utilised as the new community's endowment. From the evidence of the collegiate church's lands, part of the parish of Terregles around the confluence of the rivers Cluden and Nith, slightly upstream on the west bank from Dumfries, formed the core of the nunnery properties. The disposition of Holm Cultram's lands in Desnes Ioan is better recorded. To the abbey, Uhtred granted in feu-ferme the lands of Kirkgunzeon in central Desnes Ioan,[21] bordered to the north and west by Walter de Berkeley's lordship of Urr, to the south by Colvend, the estate from at least 1185 of the family of Cospatric of Workington, and to the south-east by Richard fitz Troite's lands of Lochkindeloch. Consisting mainly of scrubby moorland and bog, Kirkgunzeon was not the kind of land sought by aspiring colonial lords, but Holm Cultram recognised its potential as a valuable addition to its acres of sheep pasture.[22] That the grant was made in feu-ferme rather than in free alms is surely significant in view of Uhtred's service dues owed to the crown for Desnes Ioan.

Most of the remainder of Desnes Ioan may at first have been retained by Uhtred as demesne. Kirkpatrick Durham in the hilly north-west of the district was described as a 'tenement' in Dervorgilla's foundation charter of Sweetheart Abbey in 1273, presumably already the holding of the Durand family from whom it received its secondary designation to distinguish it from neighbouring Kirkpatrick Irongray, which was held by the de Valognes family from the time of Roland.[23] The remainder of Kirkpatrick Durham formed a grange of Dundrennan Abbey.[24] It would appear that it, together with Kirkpatrick Irongray before 1174, the remainder of Terregles and the low-lying lands of Troqueer, formed a chain of lordship demesne along the boundary with Nithsdale and Glencairn. Terregles certainly descended through Uhtred's heirs down to the fourteenth century, when it passed to the Herries family.[25] Troqueer, likewise, formed a discrete block within the lordship demesne until its partition between the heirs of Alan after 1234.[26] On their forfeiture in the early fourteenth century the lands were re-united and fell eventually to the Douglases, Archibald Douglas granting them to the hospital of Holywood in 1372.[27] And the final component, Kirkbean at the south-eastern extremity of Desnes Ioan, comprising mainly the later barony of Preston, was certainly under Douglas superiority in the later fourteenth century; within it, the land of Airdrie was held by Gilbert 'the dispenser' from Uhtred's son Roland.[28]

But what of the secular colonisation of this district? Of the four men known or implied from surviving sources to have been settled by Uhtred on his lands, two received properties in Desnes Ioan. These men both had kinship ties with Uhtred and one held primary estates in Cumberland, it being these factors that helped bring them their acquisitions in Galloway. The men in question were Richard fitz Troite, who held land near Carlisle, and Walter de Berkeley, chamberlain to William the Lion and probably brother-in-law of Uhtred. The others, David fitz Terrus, recipient of the lordship of Anwoth to the west of the River Fleet, and Hugh de Morville, lord of Borgue, were also significant landlords in Cumberland and Westmorland. While Uhtred's family connection with Cumberland may have facilitated the forging of bonds with David, Hugh and Richard, other factors may also have contributed. Hugh and Richard, for example, enjoyed the favour of Henry II and occupied important roles in his administration of the region. Uhtred placed great store in his kinship with the king, who may have exploited the connection to re-establish the English influence that had died with Henry I.

The most substantial of the new holdings carved out of Desnes Ioan in the later 1160s was that created for Walter de Berkeley. The exact boundaries of this lordship are now lost, but the medieval parishes of Urr and possibly Blaiket, a portion of Kirkgunzeon and at least part of Lochrutton lay within it.[29] Most of the holdings created by Uhtred comprised compact blocks that came to be equated with a single parish, but Walter's sprawling lordship was on an altogether different scale. The reasons for this may lie in Walter's already prominent social position – he was William the Lion's chamberlain and councillor – but more probably derives from his personal relationship with Uhtred. Here, provision was perhaps being made for a potential cadet branch of the lordly family. No charter survives to give details of either Walter's lordship or the service dues attached to it, but the requirement to provide half a knight's service placed on the lands of Corswadda, a portion of Lochrutton parish which he granted to one William son of Richard, may indicate a heavy burden.[30]

Certainly, Walter's was clearly a major lordship that comprised some of the best land within Desnes Ioan, and the massive motte that he constructed at Mote of Urr is an outspoken proclamation of the power and status of its new lord.

While we can only assume that the conditions of tenure demanded from Walter were commensurate with the scale of the holding granted to him, some more general idea of the burdens imposed on Uhtred's tenants can be obtained from his one surviving charter of infeftment, that recording the grant to Richard fitz Troite, brother of the sheriff of Carlisle, of the lands of Lochkindeloch (i.e. New Abbey parish).[31] The survival in isolation of this document poses several dangers, not least the assumption that it is typical of Uhtred's grants. It records the grant to Richard of 'the whole land of Lochenelo to be held by fee and heritage for the service of one knight'. In addition, Richard received a broad range of privileges, from the right to have the only mill in his new lordship and control of the pannage in the woods of his estate (important in a region where the keeping of large herds of pigs played a major part in the rural economy), through to exclusive deer-hunting rights and the sole entitlement to keep hawks and to take the eggs of birds of prey. In this general array of economic rights the charter is little different from, although perhaps more detailed than, other con-temporary grants to private individuals. The charter's chief value is as a demonstration of the still fluid state of the tenurial relationship between lords and vassals in the mid-twelfth century. As Keith Stringer has pointed out, although granted for the service of one knight, Uhtred took instead an annual rent of eight pounds in silver for so long as he had to pay cain to the king from the districts of Cro and Desnes Ioan, in which latter district Lochkindeloch lay. Once he was quit of the obligation to pay cain, the money payment would cease.[32] This money-rent compares favourably with the sum of ten pounds paid by the monks of Holm Cultram from the lands of Kirkgunzeon, which Uhtred had granted to them in feu-ferme, not in free alms.[33] This reference to an obligation to pay cain from the whole district between the rivers Urr and Nith confirms that service dues were owed to the crown by Uhtred from Desnes Ioan in general.

Alongside these obligations to the crown, Richard's lordship was burdened with dues owed to Uhtred as overlord. These are not detailed in the original charter, but in the later thirteenth century, the estate having reverted to its superior lord's control, additional demands were recorded in the grant of Lochkindeloch as the basis of the monastic estate of Dervorgilla's abbey of Sweetheart. The foundation charter of 1273 reveals that traditional Gaelic renders, such as sorran, as well as innovatory 'feudal' obligations like customs, aids, assizes and gelds, were drawn until its grant in free alms to the Cistercian community.[34] By this date, however, cain had disappeared from the formula of lordly perquisites recited in the charter text, most probably translated into the legal semi-fiction of knight service and converted in reality into a money payment, although certain of the 'feudal' casualties undoubtedly incorporated some such ancient rights of overlordship dressed up in new clothes. The survival of these rights indicates continuity of practice rather than the wholesale replacement of native systems by an imported structure. That such survival of Gaelic practice was more widespread, at least within the eastern segment of the lordship between the Nith and Urr, and in the case of the Sweetheart foundation charter was something more than simple antiquarianism on the part of the clerk who drafted the text, can be inferred from a charter of 1365 granting the lands of Terregles to Sir John Herries.[35] In this, traditional rights such as sorran and 'fathalos' are juxtaposed with feudal terminology in such a way as to indicate that these were still functional dues that required detailed legal definition of the circumstances in which they could be called into operation. Elsewhere, older rights may have been re-defined to meet new circumstances, but little other than terminology relating to the more general aspects of lordship was actually changed.

Thus, in light of the limited nature of the colonial venture in Galloway after 1160, and the original limitation of its impact on native society, arguments that the rebellion of 1174 was a conservative backlash against 'the feudalising tendencies'[36] of the Scottish crown are no longer tenable. The violence that erupted in July 1174 was directed against the visible symbols of Scottish control, of which colonising lords were only one manifestation. Anti-foreign sentiment does not equate with 'anti-feudal' feelings, as it is evident that Uhtred and Gillebrigte were not averse to the enhancement of their own authority that accrued from the changes in the structure of lordship and service that accompanied the colonists.

The anti-foreign aspect of the rising is at once apparent in the language of the chronicles that record the events. These recount acts of particular hostility towards men who could be regarded as crown agents. Howden narrates the expulsion of royal officers, attacks on foreigners and the storming of strongholds held by royal servants,[37] while the Benedict of Peterborough's version of his account highlights assaults on Scottish 'bailiffs and wardens'.[38] Limited archaeological work, discussed below (Chapter 8), has yielded no substantial evidence for the targets of this violence, but at Urr the excavator identified a phase of destruction and subsequent short-term dereliction at the motte.[39] Urr's lord, Walter de Berkeley, was detained in England after the settlement of the Treaty of Falaise as a hostage to ensure William the Lion's good behaviour,[40] and was thus in no position to either defend or re-fortify his stronghold. Walter's closeness to the Scottish king may have singled him out uniquely for the attentions of this xenophobic backlash, for he could easily be labelled as a royal agent implanted into the local power structure. There is, however, no clear evidence within Galloway for any more extensive network of supervision that could have provoked such a violent reaction. Indeed, the main evidence for a programme of crown-directed colonisation with a probable supervisorial function lies well beyond the recognised political frontiers of the twelfth-century lordship, for example in upper Clydesdale.[41] Dumfries may have functioned as the closest centre of royal authority to Galloway, possibly as the base for the bailiffs and wardens mentioned by Howden. An early royal stronghold there may have been the target for hostile attack, its importance to Scottish interests in the region underscored by the rapid construction of a new castle there soon after William's release from captivity in December 1174.[42]

From the initial revolt of 1176 Gillebrigte enjoyed the support of Henry II, and sheltered behind the provisions of the Treaty of Falaise which placed him in a direct vassalic relationship with the English crown and which prevented William from moving against him without Henry's permission. Hostilities between Gillebrigte and his estranged overlord broke out in the early 1180s, possibly provoked by William's building of the new castle at Dumfries or by Roland's consolidation of his position in Desnes Ioan, but Gillebrigte held both threats at bay. His death in 1185, however, brought this Indian Summer of native Galwegian power to an abrupt end. With his legitimate heir, Donnchad, a hostage in England, his supporters were left without a rallying point; that enabled Roland to conquer his uncle's former domain. Contemporary accounts presented him as holding Galloway both by right of inheritance and by right of conquest,[43] having overcome Donnchad's adherents and planted his own followers on their forfeited lands.

The traditional view of Roland's conquest is that he was heavily dependent on Anglo-Norman adventurers drawn from south-eastern Scotland and northern England, as he had spent much of the time since his father's murder in exile at King William's court or with families such as the Morvilles.[44] The ease and rapidity with which he overran Gillebrigte's lordship, however, suggests that he had significant resources upon which to draw within Galloway itself. These were probably largely obtained from those parts of his father's lands – principally in Desnes Ioan – that he controlled in the period 1174–85. As a consequence, any 'foreign' component in his army may have been smaller than the traditional accounts imply. This tallies well with the limited infeftment of colonising Anglo-Norman families by Roland after 1185. Indeed, Roland's power was probably most dependent on the support of his father's former following east of the Cree, the very men whom William of Newburgh names as supporting him against his uncle a decade earlier,[45] and from newcomers established by Roland himself after 1176.

The identity of Roland's native supporters cannot be established but members of the group of Anglo-Norman knights who joined his campaign have made a more lasting imprint on the historical record. Indeed, the prominence of most families of Anglo-Norman origin in Galloway is ascribed to his generosity born of gratitude for their aid in 1185.[46] Among them were men who had been infefted by Uhtred but who may have lost their lands in the turmoil that followed his death. Others, such as Gilbert son of Richer, Philip de Valognes and Thomas fitz Cospatric, may have arrived in the decade after the 1176 settlement between Gillebrigte and Henry II. Evidence for a widespread policy of infeftment post-1185 is scarce but a pattern that parallels closely the distribution evident under Uhtred, with most colonists being introduced on to lands between the Urr and the Nith, is unmistakable. Urr, the lordship of Walter de Berkeley, Roland's uncle by marriage, again formed the centrepiece of the network of 'feudalised' estates in this area. To its south lay Colvend, the possession of Roland's second cousin, Thomas fitz Cospatric, lord of Workington in Cumberland:[47] his family later acquired the designation of 'de Culwen'. To his younger brother, Gilbert, came the lordship of the neighbouring lands of Southwick,[48] which marked the start of his career as one of the most prominent members of the inner circle of men around Roland and his son, Alan. As a result of his closeness to the lords of Galloway, Gilbert occurs most frequently in a Galwegian rather than a Cumberland context, while Thomas's succession to their English patrimony established him as a predominantly Cumberland figure. To the east of Colvend and Southwick lay the lands of Airdrie in Kirkbean parish, granted by Roland to Gilbert son of Richer,[49] completing the evidence for his pattern of infeftments in Desnes Ioan.

The background of Gilbert son of Richer, Philip de Valognes, Walter de Berkeley and the sons of Cospatric stresses the Scottish connections forged by Uhtred and his son. While Walter was brother-in-law of Uhtred, both he and Philip held the office of chamberlain to William the Lion, and Gilbert son of Richer may have been his dispenser.[50] For Thomas and Gilbert fitz Cospatric, although kinship may again have played an important part in their relationship with Roland, their close connections with the Morvilles may have been the catalyst that brought their entry into his service. This Morville link is further emphasised by the arrival in Galloway of a cadet of one of their Lauderdale tenant families, Roger Masculus, who received the moiety of Colvend from Roland.[51] With the exception of Walter, whose tenure of Urr ante-dates 1174, the location of their lands indicates that all these men entered Roland's service before 1185. This is underscored by the fact that none were established on estates seized from the demesne of either Gillebrigte or his vassals. All remained exclusively eastern Galloway in their landed interests. It can be established with some confidence, furthermore, that their failure to capitalise on their earlier connections with Roland and his father to establish a more widespread network of estates was not a consequence of Roland's having to provide for a larger group of men from a finite resource in Gillebrigte's former possessions.

Howden is our chief source for claims that Roland seized Gillebrigte's estates and those of the native lords in western Galloway who had supported him,[52] but there is otherwise little documentary evidence to support claims that he established his own men on these lands. Indeed, there is only one substantiable case for a wholly new family, the de Vieuxponts, being introduced into western Galloway by him. Without doubt, the loss of the cartularies of the Galwegian monasteries has distorted this picture, but even so the fragmentary image which remains scarcely constitutes strong evidence for the subjugation of western Galloway through the efforts of an army of aspiring 'feudal' colonists based on fortified strongpoints. Proponents of this cataclysmic thesis of conquest and colonisation draw strength from the evident plethora of mottes throughout the lordship, taking these as an indication of the sudden and dramatic imposition of a hostile and alien elite.[53] But, as is discussed in detail below in chapter 8, the chronology of motte-building and the issues of building and ownership are more complex than this simplistic proposition allows.

An absence of concrete evidence for large-scale colonisation implies an exaggeration of the traditional Anglo-Norman role in Roland's conquest. The converse of this is that the native Gaelic nobility of the lordship survived the upheavals of 1174–85 and remained the dominant factor in the landholding pattern of central and western Galloway. Substantiation of this contention is difficult, however, for, while the records of Anglo-Norman settlement in Galloway are slight, documentation relating to the native nobility is entirely lacking before the middle of the thirteenth century, and any extrapolation back is made on the basis of the damning silence of negative evidence. Some native families may have suffered social degradation rather than extinction under Roland's regime – but if this were the case they were resurgent in the later thirteenth century when they headed the knightly class. Such a renaissance is unlikely to have happened had the old nobility been entirely displaced or submerged beneath an incoming elite. It is, therefore, preferable to see Roland's colonists as a thin veneer over the existing native aristocracy, who slotted into gaps within that group of families linked to him by bonds of kinship.

This was clearly the case with the de Vieuxponts.[54] In common with most of the colonising families, they were prominent in north-west English elite society. Significantly, they too had risen in the service of Henry II and were also related closely by marriage to Roland's wife, Helen de Morville. They eventually acquired the barony of north Westmorland as a result of Henry II's patronage; William de Vieuxpont received the king's permission to marry Matilda de Morville (daughter of the younger Hugh de Morville and aunt of Helen).[55] The couple's youngest son, Ivo, received the lordship of Sorbie in the Machars from his cousin's husband, Roland.[56] Sorbie consisted of the parishes of St Fillan and St Michael (known as Sorbie Major and Sorbie Minor in the later twelfth century) and lay adjacent to Roland's stronghold and demesne estate at Cruggleton. On Ivo's death the estate was split between his sons, Robert and Alan.[57] Robert lost his inheritance by the mid-thirteenth century, possibly as a consequence of a mortgage,[58] while Alan's portion descended to his son, Robert, from whom there is no sign of further descent. In neither case did the estates escheat through failure of heirs or forfeiture, yet, in less than a century of their introduction as colonists, the de Vieuxponts had vanished from the social landscape as effectively as if they had never existed.

When considered as a whole, the evidence for the colonising movement directed by Roland highlights the importance of his familial links with Cumberland and with the Morvilles. Where settlement can be attributed to Roland one deciding factor was kinship: the de Vieuxponts, de Berkeleys, de Colvends and de Southwicks were all related to him in varying degrees. Those families with no such personal relationship, such as the fitz Troites or fitz Terruses, had arrived under Uhtred, or had perhaps used connections with the Morvilles to gain entry to the inner circle of vassals of the lords of Galloway. No less significant, however, was the increasingly strong bond between Roland and the Scottish crown, a bond established during Uhtred's lifetime and confirmed in the aftermath of Henry II's failure, in Roland's eyes, to deliver justice for the death of his father.[59] While the impact of the incomer on the settlement pattern of the lordship appears less profound than previously supposed, their impact on the lord's household was major. This is immediately apparent in the personnel who regularly witness lordly acts and who can be taken to represent their intimates. Here, a clear dichotomy emerges between Uhtred and his successors in terms of the cultural background of the men involved. Uhtred drew on Anglo-Scandinavians as well as the Gaelic aristocracy:[60] natives such as Gillemore Albanach, Gillecrist MacGillwinin and Uhtred's foster brother, Gillecatfar, regularly witnessed his charters. Men of Anglo-Norman background first appear in connection with grants pertaining to the Allerdale properties, or where one of their own close circle was involved.[61] The character of a witness list reflects the men present at the time of the document's preparation, and would comprise largely of those commonly in attendance on the lord. Uhtred's charters thus proclaim the eclectic nature of his following; under Roland and Alan, on the other hand, there has been a sea-change in the character of the inner group of supporters. Men with Gaelic names almost disappear from the charters, replaced by men bearing Anglo-Norman ones; but whether this was conscious policy, evidence for the adoption of Anglo-Norman names by the Celtic nobility, or the result of a growing involvement with affairs outside Galloway is open to question.[62]

Charters issued by Roland that deal solely with Galloway are rare,[63] rendering it dangerous to state categorically that he consciously turned to foreigners in preference to natives. Uhtred may have deliberately thrust him into the Frenchified court of the kings of Scots and he was clearly at ease in an Anglo-Norman milieu; he is, indeed, better known by his French alternative name, Roland, than by the Gaelic Lachlan of his youth,[64] and in this we may catch a glimpse of the psyche at work within the man. With Roland, unfortunately, we receive only one side of the picture, but it is one which shows a man who by taste and inclination was settled in the world of Frankish culture and society and Anglo-Norman politics: the lords of Galloway were outgrowing their cultural roots. And yet it has to be emphasised: this is only one side of the coin.

Thus far the argument has dwelt on the limited nature of Anglo-Norman colonisation in Galloway and underscored the control over it exercised by Uhtred and Roland. The few charters of Alan lend further support to the image of the Frenchified lord surrounding himself with foreign dependants.[65] Keith Stringer, however, in his analysis of Alan's political career,[66] has drawn attention to his Janus-like personality, underscoring the hybridity in Alan's political personality. As Stringer puts it, 'Alan, though the son of a Norman mother, a great feudal magnate, and the constable of Scotland, was also the hereditary chieftain of a semi-independent Celtic province on Scotland's western fringe'.[67] It is certainly clear from Alan's behaviour in the 1220s that he was acutely conscious of his status as a Gaelic warlord of the western seaboard, but what Stringer's essay brings out is Alan's Anglo-Norman urbanity, his elevated social position within the Scottish aristocracy, and the significance of his dealings with the Scottish crown. Alan himself attached a striking importance to his title and office of constable of Scotland, which takes precedence in charter formulae over his hereditary title of lord of Galloway.[68] This suggests that however important his Gaelic lordship was in terms of his personal authority and military might, Alan entertained no conflicting ideas in his own mind about his social and cultural preferences.

Alan's entourage is, of course, a key source for our understanding of him. In his charters, men of identifiably native stock are conspicuous by their absence; Stringer, indeed, speaks of 'social exclusivity' among those regularly in attendance on Alan.[69] It is difficult to evaluate the significance of this evidence, for does it indicate the social and cultural separation of the lord from his native supporters and people, who are relegated to subsidiary roles in the pursuit and execution of his wishes; or was the support of 'invisible' native landlords an essential prerequisite for Alan's far-flung activities? One insurmountable problem is that the surviving parchment record for the Galloways is primarily non-Galwegian in origin and character – of the thirty-five of Alan's *acta* which survive, only nine involve Galloway business and only two of them were to lay beneficiaries, both of whom received land in Desnes Ioan outwith the ancestral lordship.[70] This renders identification of any differentials in the disposal of property between the lordship inherited from Fergus and the territories acquired by Uhtred impossible. Of the nine Galloway-related items, moreover, only two are preserved with full witness lists and one of these is purely ecclesiastical in content.[71] The one secular act, in favour of Adam, son of Gilbert son of Richer, however, appears to have been issued in the context of a meeting of Alan's court in Galloway. If the witness list is representative of the composition of that court, not one Gaelic lord can be seen to move within Alan's circle.[72] But this was business that did not impinge on the original patrimony west of the Urr. Did Alan operate there without reference to his kinsmen or the native elite? Carrick, where the charters of the earls relate exclusively to the earldom, provides a useful comparison.[73] Witness lists there are dominated by the Gaelic aristocracy, and reveal the inclusion of the earls' kindred in business where the disposal of comital property was involved. Similar circumstances perhaps prevailed in the intensely Gaelic lordship of Roland and Alan; where the patrimony of the lords of Galloway was involved, the interests of the kindred and the native aristocracy must have been considered.

As an alternative to the above, it may be that the kindred was ignored by Roland and his successors and that the Gaelic aristocracy of Galloway was extinguished as a social or political group whose sensibilities required due consideration. It is possible to read Alan's *acta* in that light. Nevertheless, even allowing for the inadequacies of the surviving documentation, there is no indication that colonisation occurred west of the Urr with such great intensity as to permit such a situation as the social elimination of the native nobility and its replacement by an alien elite. And the necessary concomitant of this is that the native aristocracy maintained its social significance after the upheavals of 1185. To take the witness lists of the acts of Roland and Alan as demonstrating its extinction is to distort their testimony, by argument from negative evidence: the absence of men of demonstrably Gaelic origins in the household or curia of the lords, or among the land-holding elite who witnessed their charters, is not proof of non-existence. A more likely scenario is that, as Stringer remarks, 'for all Alan's familiarity with feudal practices, the support of Galloway's native community was crucial to his personal supremacy'.[74]

Such a contention rests on slender documentary foundations, but later thirteenth- and fourteenth-century sources permit retrospective comment on the underlying character of the Galwegian nobility. The twenty years after 1234 constitute a clear break in the documentary record for Galloway and offer a sharp contrast between the evidence pointing *prima facie* to the domination of Galloway by, or reliance of the lords on, an alien elite in the time of Roland and Alan, and quite different evidence pointing to the prominence of native landholders during the time of Dervorgilla and her descendants. This contrast cannot be overstated, and it throws further doubts upon the traditional interpretation of the pre-1234 material.

That no major influx of fresh colonists and dependants occurred after 1234 is manifest from the limited documentary record, but there *is* an unmistakable change in the personnel who witness the acts of Alan's heirs. Old colonist families such as the de Cardoness descendants of David fitz Terrus, or the de Twynholms, are well represented,[75] but new families such as the de Mundevilles from Nithsdale and the de Stobhills from Liddel,[76] members of the wider familial and tenurial circle of the Balliols, also register a presence. Alan's sons-in-law must have introduced a new administrative element, as evidenced by the case of Philip Lovel, who functioned as steward on Roger de Quincy's Galloway estates in the 1240s.[77] Lovel, however, was no landless knight aspiring to propertied success through service to a great magnate such as Earl Roger, and thus put down no roots. The extinction of the Aumale line of Alan's heirs in 1246 and the partition of the de Quincy inheritance in 1263–64, led to Balliol domination among the lordly kin. This position was reflected in reference to them by external and later observers as 'lords of Galloway', a title to which they themselves made no claim. Dervorgilla represented continuity of lordship from the past, in contrast to the de Quincys, who experienced progressively reduced landholding, loss of the leadership of Galloway's political society and diminution of personal links with Galloway. Dervorgilla consequently secured the leadership of the local elite, but as it emerges in the mid-thirteenth century this was a body radically different in composition from that visible before 1234.

Documents relating to Balliol Galloway are few, but they provide insights on the political elite that recognised Dervorgilla's status. The earliest, a witnessed debenture of c.1251, dates from the return of stability after the upheavals that followed Alan's death.[78] It narrates terms for repayment of cash borrowed from Dervorgilla's husband by Maurice Acarsan, a man of Gaelic lineage, and is witnessed by members of the Galwegian nobility. Adam de Twynholm, for example, was a member of a Cumberland family which held the lands of Twynholm to the north of Kirkcudbright and which extended its influence in Galloway in the course of the thirteenth century.[79] Andrew de Kirkconnel was tenant of Kirkconnel in Troqueer.[80] Both represent colonist families who appeared in the earlier thirteenth century on the fringes of Alan's court, but who never enjoyed the prominence of, say, Gilbert fitz Cospatric.[81] Their arrival signals a change in the relationship between Alan's heirs and their principal tenants, as personal bonds beween the original grantors and grantees of land faded. Further change is represented by a third witness, Gillespoc son of Gilbothyn, a man of undoubtedly native stock. Later sources indicate that his family were Balliol tenants in Buittle.[82] Too much can be read into the significance of this one man of clearly Gaelic origin, but here, after three-quarters of a century of silence in the written record, is the first unequivocal evidence for the continued existence of a native landholding class.

More comprehensive evidence for the inner circle around Dervorgilla emerges in the 1270s. Her curia, dominated by descendants of twelfth-century colonial families, can be glimpsed in the witness list to the foundation charter of Sweetheart Abbey.[83] Five knights head the secular witnesses: David and Robert Marshall, Balliol tenants in Wigtownshire,[84] John Carlisle, Cane MacGillolane and John de Grannsard. The knights are followed by Walter de Twynholm, Bertram de Cardoness and Michael son of Durand, this last possibly already tenant of Kirkpatrick Durham and sub-tenant of the Kirkconnels for Mabie in Troqueer.[85] All are of colonial origin, with the exception of one knight: Cane MacGillolane, probable head of the Maclellan kindred.[86] The Maclellans were entrenched in the landholding pattern of the northern Galloway uplands. Through him, contact is established with a world far removed from the close circle of colonists visible before 1234. The Maclellans were one of the extensive 'lineage-based power-groups identifiable in Galloway and Carrick from the end of the thirteenth century'.[87] The existence of a specifically Maclellan lineage cannot be established until the reign of David II, when David McGillolane received the captaincy of the kindred of 'Clenconnon',[88] but members of this powerful kin-group figure prominently in the records of the period 1273–1352 as among the most active Balliol partisans in Galloway. Sir Donald MacCan, Cane MacGillolane's son, emerges in a Balliol context in 1285.[89] He subsequently became a key figure in the native party which supported first the Comyn–Balliol nexus then the English crown in the pre-Bannockburn stage of the Wars of Independence, his former Balliol connection being confirmed by the pension awarded to him by Edward I in compensation for land granted to him by King John Balliol in lieu of a pension previously granted to him by Dervorgilla.[90] He was an active military commander after 1297 and fought against the Bruces until his capture in 1308.[91] The re-opening of the conflict in the 1330s saw the affirmation of Maclellan–Balliol ties. Sir Matthew Maclellan and his son, John, maintained their support for Edward Balliol until the mid-1350s,[92] long after it had become evident that the Balliol cause elsewhere in Scotland was effectively dead. Nevertheless, they submitted to David II and survived to become a major feature in the power structure of the new lordship established in Galloway by the Black Douglases.

The Maclellan/MacCan kindred was not alone in the political culture of later thirteenth-century Galloway, nor was it unique amongst native families in its support for the Balliols. A memorandum of April 1285 recording an action in the law courts at Wigtown reveals further native families active on Balliol business.[93] On this occasion no colonial families are represented, the lay nobility instead being represented by Sir Donald MacCan, Thomas McCulloch and Roland Askeloc. Askeloc, or McGachen as he appears also to have been known,[94] led a Wigtownshire family that had connections with both the de Quincy heirs and the Balliols. From Dervorgilla Roland had apparently received Borgue in Kirkcudbrightshire,[95] which he forfeited in 1306 for his support of Robert Bruce.[96] This connection with the Balliols' rivals was confirmed in February 1302 when Robert Bruce secured a pardon for Roland's son, Hector, for murder and other crimes committed by him. Flirtation with the Bruce cause, however, was short-lived, if the Roland named as a casualty fighting with Donald MacCan against Edward Bruce in 1308 can be identified as Roland Askeloc.[97] Greater steadfastness was displayed by the McCullochs. Sir Thomas, his brother Michael, and a William McCulloch, all of the county of Wigtown, submitted to Edward I at Berwick in 1296.[98] Loyalty to Edward had its rewards, with Thomas being one of the beneficiaries of the Ordinance for the Government of Scotland in 1305, when he received the sheriffship of Wigtown.[99] Like the Maclellans, they preserved their land and status through submission to the Bruces, but adherence to Edward Balliol after 1332 led to forfeiture and poverty-stricken exile.[100]

The greatest native kindred in Galloway were the MacDowells, who occupied a central role in the wars against the Bruces in the period 1306–12 and 1332–54 and were clearly the leaders of native society. Strong popular traditions accord them a blood link with the lordly dynasty,[101] a suggestion strengthened by the existence of junior male segments of the Galloways from whom no definite descent can be traced. They may descend from Fergus, son of Uhtred, some support for this being drawn from the frequency with which the Christian names Uhtred and Fergus occur within the MacDowell family in the fourteenth century.[102] Although there is no articulation of any such claims to kinship, it provides the simplest explanation for their leadership of native society after 1296. Indeed, it is highly likely that the MacDowells held the status of 'kenkynnol' of the Galloway kindred after the senior branch ended in heiresses in 1234, which would accord well with their close association with the Balliols. From the deposition of John Balliol in 1296 until the establishment of Douglas power in the 1360s, the MacDowells were the single most important family in the region, and this position was recognised by both Scotish and English efforts to win or preserve their allegiance.[103] No record survives of the Mac-Dowell's landholding pattern before c.1300, but the leading involvement of Dougal MacDowell in the capture of Alexander and Neil Bruce at Loch Ryan in 1307 might imply that their properties lay mainly in Wigtownshire. This is supported by the *Chronicle of Lanercost* in 1334, where MacDowell raised Galloway 'beyond the Cree', i.e. to its west, against Balliol's supporters in eastern Galloway.[104] Both Bruce and Balliol parties contended for the support of rival segments within the MacDowell kindred, and by the 1350s branches of the family held land and offices scattered throughout the lordship.[105]

From the above, it can be seen that traditional interpretations of the relationship between native and settler in Galloway, the nature of the processes of colonisation, and the implications of such settlement, require re-appraisal. Historians, moreover, must reconsider their previously uncritical acceptance of the principal source for the history of Galloway in the twelfth century, Roger of Howden. Because of his personal involvement in the affairs of the lordship after 1174 and standing in the administration of Henry II, Howden has gained the status of unimpeachable authority for all things Galwegian, but this blind faith has compromised historical interpretation. Can we on the one hand question his motives in reporting affairs as he did, while continuing on the other to accept his narrative as the basis for interpretation of the three-cornered relationship of Galloway, Scotland and England in the reign of Henry II? At a primary level, his presentation of the revolt of Gillebrigte and Uhtred and the triumph of Roland must be regarded as hyperbolic. Archaeologists, too, must confront the questionable reliability of Howden's narrative, or more correctly of modern interpretations of that narrative. Without Howden there are no convenient *termini post* or *ante quem* for the dating of mottes, while the naïve social re-constructionalism that portrayed the relationship between native and colonist as one of confrontation and domination of the former by the latter is revealed as a chimera. Freed from interpretations that dictate that all mottes are the products of the 'conquests' of 1160 or 1185, the straitjacket that forces definition of the relationship between motte-builders and natives in conventional black-and-white terms of a clash of cultures evaporates. As studies elsewhere in Scotland have demonstrated, attention has been focused on the processes of change, or the degree of change, without a balancing recognition of the levels of continuity that underlie the evidence of the documentary record.[106]

Clearly there is great change in Galloway in the century after 1136, but it must be projected against underlying continuity. The survival of native laws, for example, demonstrates that the lords of Galloway could not ride roughshod over tradition or replace all native institutions with Anglo-Norman innovations, and signals where real power in the lordship lay.[107] The maintenance of this lawcode as late as the fifteenth century implies that the society living under that code drew its traditions largely from its earlier medieval ancestors. That such a code could and did survive is, furthermore, an indication of the shallowness of any 'conquest' of Galloway by Anglo-Normans. As Rees Davies pointed out, 'the imposition of peace and good order and the establishment of sound laws'[108] was the justification used by the Anglo-Normans for conquest and were its more obvious results; the examples of the introduction of English law into Wales and Ireland and of Edward I's plans for Scotland in 1305 need only to be considered. For a supposedly dominant Anglo-Norman aristocratic elite to have lived and functioned under a native lawcode without engineering its replacement or radical restructuring is without parallel.

Keyhole history, typified by the traditional interpretations of the Galloway material, has produced a distorted picture of local relationships, or the dynamics of change and, especially, of the attitudes of Gaelic lords to the innovations of the twelfth century: we have taken positive evidence and produced a negative image. The greatest failure of this approach, however, is in its neglect of the counter-evidence that has always been available to redress the imbalances. Apparently contradictory later thirteenth- and fourteenth-century material has usually been presented in terms of a late Gaelic revival that happened only because the Anglo-Norman families either turned native or were uprooted in the course of the Wars of Independence. This, however, cannot be reconciled with the assertion that the native nobles who dominated Galloway in the 1300s were the successors of those destroyed over a century earlier by their own social leader, who had then introduced a wholly alien aristocracy.

Colonisation did occur. What must be re-considered – and it is a subject which the evidence from both here and from other regions, such as Strathearn, Mar or Moray, has shown to have profound implications for our whole traditional historiography of the relationship between the Gaelic 'fringes' and the 'feudalised' core of the medieval kingdom – is the direction and motivation of the movement. Much can be learned from the Galwegian example. Its most striking feature, if any weight is to be placed at all on the surviving documentary evidence for colonisation in the period 1160–1234, is the distribution of the estates granted to the colonists. The bulk of these were in the 'acquired land' of Desnes Ioan, outwith the patrimonial lands west of the Urr. The reasons for this have already been set out in part above, but there are deeper aspects that require attention, especially in the distinction between inherited and acquired land. Similar attitudes to the treatment of land can be detected in Scottish rulers from David I to Alexander II, who took different approaches to properties within the heartland of Scotia between the Forth and the Mounth and to those outwith that core: Lothian, the central and western Southern Uplands, and Moray and Ross witnessed the chief drive towards colonisation - which was not necessarily a colonisation dictated by the military realities of 'conquest-driven' expansion of the sphere of Scottish royal authority. Further parallels can be drawn, particularly with regard to the mechanics of royal control in frontier zones. The settlement of Moray after 1130, for example, used dynastic links with native powers in Atholl, Ross and Caithness rather than intensive infeftment as the chief mechanism for control over the Spey basin and its hinterland.[109] Comparisons can be made between the position of Inverness as hub of a supervisory system for the inner Moray Firth zone and the identical role for Dumfries over Galloway and the Solway Firth in the 1160s. As with Galloway, moreover, it was initially *behind* these supervisory systems that the bulk of colonisation took place – largely restricted to the coastal plain between Inverness and the Spey – until William the Lion pushed the effective reach of crown authority southwards into Badenoch and northwards beyond the Cromarty Firth after 1179. The parallels with Máel Coluim IV's policies in upper Clydesdale are obvious.

Similar attitudes towards the introduction of foreign colonists have been identified in the earldoms of Mar and Strathearn in the twelfth and thirteenth centuries,[110] and may be detected also in Lennox. In Mar, despite the close family links of the native lineages with major Anglo-Norman families such as the de Warennes and the strong relationship between the earls and the crown, there was no introduction of colonising families into the earldom. In Strathearn, the earls likewise introduced no foreign colonists into the heartland of their earldom nor involved themselves in a policy of sub-infeftment.[111] Indeed, in these cases, as with Galloway, there was evidently no attempt made by the crown nor any move by the earls to re-define their relationship, thereby obviating any necessity for such a policy. In a quite striking parallel with Galloway, in Strathearn, where men of Anglo-Norman background can be seen to establish footholds within the comital lands, they are men whose relationship with the earls stemmed from ties of marriage. Significantly, such infeftments also took place on lands peripheral to the core of comital power in central and western Strathearn, mainly on the southern and western fringes of the earldom. As with the policy of the lords of Galloway whereby control was maintained over the extensive uplands of northern Galloway, upper Strathearn, especially around Loch Earn, was retained in the hands of the Gaelic earls – a split pattern of landholding that survived to the mid-fifteenth century.[112] This phenomenon can be recognised in the Lennox, but is even more strikingly manifest in Mar, where the thirteenth-century partition of the earldom between Earl Duncan, son of Morgrund, and the Durward descendants of Earl Gilchrist, saw Duncan retain the upper straths of the Dee and Don in western Aberdeenshire, while the lowland east of the earldom passed to his rivals.[113] Clearly, modern economic perspectives, moulded by the post-eighteenth-century re-shaping of the rural landscape and demographic patterns, have distorted current views on what constituted valuable property.[114] The key factor identified in Mar, and in Cynthia Neville's arguments concerning Strathearn, however, is in the underscoring of the essential role played by the earls in determining the nature of colonisation in their lands: the crown may have wished to see greater foreign influence in such strategic power-blocks, or the accommodation of alien social and cultural practices which would have facilitated their more rapid integration into the framework of more extensive and intensive royal authority, but without the co-operation of the earls the means of extending that influence was denied. In Strathearn, only in territories outwith the earldom proper, acquired in the later twelfth century, can crown influence over service dues and tenure be detected.[115] The similarities to the situation obtaining in the acquired lands of Desnes Ioan under Uhtred are immediately striking.

What, then, of the heartland of the old lordship? The lack of documentation handicaps discussion, especially with regard to the native families and the estates retained by Uhtred and Roland during the main phase of colonisation. Nevertheless, using the sources considered above, together with late records such as the chamberlain of Galloway's 1456 accounts, which list the demesne of the forfeited Black Douglases,[116] a partial reconstruction of the position in the pre-1234 period can be made. This establishes that all documented instances of colonisation occur in the low-lying districts of Galloway, especially around the estuaries of the Urr, Dee and Fleet and, while the lords retained some demesne in these lowland areas, the bulk of their property lay in the uplands. Where there is evidence for the possessions of native landholders, such as Gylbycht McMalene who held lands in the Glenkens,[117] or the Maclellan lords of Balmaclellan,[118] these also are concentrated in the upland zone. This tallies strikingly with the pattern of medieval lordship and settlement in the English Lake District depicted by Angus Winchester,[119] or Carrick, where an extent of the earldom estates prepared in c.1260, when two-thirds of the demesne was in royal hands during the wardship of Countess Marjory, shows a similar concentration of demesne in the hilly areas of Carrick, including Straiton, Glengennet and Bennan, but with other major estates in the more fertile zones such as Dalquharran in the Girvan valley and Turnberry on the coast.[120] In Carrick, too, colonists received land in the more fertile – and peripheral – arable lowlands of the lordship, such as the feu granted to Roger de Skelbrooke at Greenan, south of Ayr.[121] Here, however, Anglo-Norman colonisation was on a minor scale and the essentially Gaelic nature of Carrick society remained undisturbed. But Carrick was a poor earldom and the earls could afford to alienate neither substantial portions of their demesne nor key members of their own kindred and the native elite, to provide estates for incoming foreigners.

Any lingering doubts concerning the essentially Gaelic nature of the families holding significant estates in Galloway in the Middle Ages can be dispelled by the steadily increasing volume of documentation available from the second half of the fourteenth century onwards.[122] Such families surface as the long-established leaders of society, not as a resurgent Gaelic underclass. What is displayed, underscored by the events of the Wars of Independence, is the continuing identification of leading native families with the dynasty founded by Fergus, and especially with Dervorgilla's line which was dominant in Galloway from the mid-1260s. Through her, some semblance of the old lordship was preserved to serve as the focus for a society left leaderless by Alan's death and the failure of Thomas's rebellion in 1235. Dervorgilla offered continuity from the great days of the lordship and inherited the loyalty of her ancestors' native supporters. Her curia, and the background of the men who were prepared to fight in defence of the rights of her son and grandson, demonstrate that the Anglo-Scottish conquest of Galloway is a figment of the febrile imaginations of modern historians, founded on the dramatic prose of Roger of Howden and his copiers, a smokescreen that has obscured the underlying character of Galwegian society. Despite the 'Normanised' aspects of their characters, the lords of Galloway were Gaelic lords, and it was from their Gaelic aristocracy and people that Dervorgilla, like Alan, Roland and Uhtred before her, drew power and position.

Notes

1 This chapter is a developed version of the argument presented in 'A family business. Colonisation and settlement in twelfth- and thirteenth-century Galloway'.

2 See Davies, *Domination and Conquest*. For a re-interpretation of these processes on a European-wide level, see Bartlett, *The Making of Europe*.

3 Davies, *Domination and Conquest*, 1.

4 See, for example, R. L. Storey, *Chronology of World History: The Medieval World 800–1491* (Oxford, 1973).

5 See e.g.: *Chron. Holyrood*, 136–37; *Chron. Howden*, ii, 57, 60, 63, 299, 309; Matthew Paris, *Chron. Majora*, iii, 364–66, iv, 653; *Chron. Lanercost*, 42; *Chron. Melrose*, 77, 94, 144–47.

6 Barrow, *Kingship and Unity*, 47.

7 The anti-feudal aspect runs strongest through the work of M'Kerlie, *Lands and Their Owners*, and re-surfaces more recently in the work of Professor Geoffrey Barrow.

8 See e.g. B. E. Crawford, 'The earldom of Caithness and the kingdom of Scotland 1150-1266', *Northern Scotland*, ii (1974–77); also (revised) in Stringer (ed.), *Nobility of Medieval Scotland*; Oram, 'David I'.

9 Watt (ed.), *Series Episcoporum*, i, 25; Oram, 'In obedience and reverence', 90–91.

10 E.g. Wigtownshire Charters, pp. xvi–xix; Barrow, *Kingship and Unity*, 45, 47–50; Duncan, *Making of the Kingdom*, 182–83.

11 E.g. Oram, 'Lordship of Galloway', 189-200; Brooke, *Wild Men*, 101–04; Brooke, 'Fergus of Galloway'.

12 *Dryburgh Liber*, no. 68.

13 Duncan, *Making of the Kingdom*, 136, 164.

14 Barrow, *Anglo-Norman Era*, 31, n. 3, 74–76; but see also 81–82.

15 F. Barlow, *Thomas Becket* (London, 1986), 236, 258. Barlow, however, has confused this Hugh de Morville with the constable's son, wrongly attributing him a part in the archbishop's murder; cf. Barrow, *Anglo-Norman Era*, 74–76. I am indebted to Dr Keith Stringer for his help in untangling this knotty problem of too many Hughs.

16 *Benedict of Peterborough*, i, 67.

17 Stringer, 'Records', no. 3.

18 Scott, 'An early sheriff?', 90–91.

19 Reid, 'Feudalisation of lower Nithsdale', 104–05.

20 *CPL*, Clement VII, 145.

21 *Holm Cultram Register*, no. 120.

22 Ibid., no. 133.

23 See above p. 98.

24 *RRS*, vi, no. 235.

25 *RRS*, vi, no. 210; *RMS*, i, no. 193; cf. ibid., i, App. 1, no. 123.

26 *CDS*, ii, no. 824 pt. 4. For a discussion of this document, see above p. 148.

27 *RMS*, i, no. 483.

28 Stringer, 'Periphery and core', App. (A), no. 1.

29 Urr and Blaiket descended to Walter's son-in-law, Enguerrand Balliol; *Holyrood Liber*, no. 81. Walter himself was in dispute with Holm Cultram over the marches between his properties and their grange of Kirkgunzeon; *Holm Cultram Register*, nos 120a, 122, 123. Corswadda in south-east Lochrutton was granted by Walter to William, son of Richard; *Wigtownshire Charters*, pp. xxiv–xxv.

30 *Wigtownshire Charters*, pp. xxiv–xxv.

31 Cumbria Record Office, Lowther Archive, D/Lons/L5/1/S1. For a full text with comments, see Stringer 'Records', no. 9.

32 Stringer, 'Records', no. 9 and note. I accept that this is the more probable interpretation than that of the money being an additional burden imposed by Uhtred, as suggested in 'A family business?', 125–26.

33 *Holm Cultram Register*, no. 121.

34 *RRS*, vi, no. 235.

35 *RMS*, i, no. 192.

36 *Wigtownshire Chrs*, p. xxi.

37 *Chron. Howden*, ii, 57.

38 *Benedict of Peterborough*, i, 67–68.

39 Hope-Taylor, 'Mote of Urr', 167–72.

40 *Benedict of Peterborough*, i, 97–98.

41 Tabraham, 'Norman settlement in Upper Clydesdale', 114–28.

42 Reference to an 'old fortification' at Dumfries in *Glasgow Registrum*, no. 50 may be to the stronghold of Radulf, lord of lower Nithsdale, which had been taken over by the crown after *c*.1165. It may, however, refer to a much older and abandoned site, possibly a hill-fort.

43 William of Newburgh, i, 237.

44 Roland's presence in the household of the Morvilles is attested by his appearance as a witness to several of their acts, e.g. *RRS*, ii, no. 236; *Melrose Liber*, i, nos 94, 108, 111.

45 William of Newburgh, i, 186–87.

46 *Wigtownshire Charters*, pp. xxi–xxix.

47 Stringer, 'Records', no. 18; *St Bees Register*, no. 92.

48 *Holm Cultram Register*, no. 131.

49 Stringer, 'Records', no. 35.

50 See Stringer, 'Records', no. 35. Gilbert was a regular witness to acts of William the Lion: *RRS*, ii, nos 45, 48, 62, 79, 80 etc.

51 *St Bees Register*, no. 60.

52 *Benedict of Peterborough*, ii, 339, 349.

53 *Wigtownshire Charters*, pp. xxii–xxiii.

54 Reid, 'De Veteripont', 96–106.

55 Ibid., 91.

56 *Dryburgh Liber*, nos 75–77, where Ivo grants the church of Sorbie Major to the canons of Dryburgh.

57 Ibid., nos 72–73; nos 71–73 place Sorbie Minor in the hands of Robert de Vieuxpont, while no. 75 records possession of Sorbie Major by his brother.

58 *CDS*, i, no. 1808.

59 I acknowledge and accept Keith Stringer's gentle chiding of my failure elsewhere to give due recognition to the importance of the relationship in which most of Roland's tenants stood with the Scottish crown.

60 See for example, the witness lists to *Holyrood Liber*, nos 23, 24, or Ragg, 'Five Strathclyde and Galloway charters', no. 2.

61 Ragg, 'Five Strathclyde and Galloway charters', no. 2.

62 For the issue of cultural and political influences and the naming fashions of 'native' aristocracies, see Bartlett, *The Making of Europe*, 270–80.

63 Stringer, 'Records', nos 16–26.

64 Cf. *Holyrood Liber*, no. 24, and *Holm Cultram Register*, no. 120 for Lachlan alias Roland. Barrow raises the same point: *RRS*, ii, 13–14. While Roland is standardly accepted as representing the commonly used Latinised form of Lachlan, it is probable that this was the form of name used in everyday life by the lord of Galloway. Where he is mentioned by name in that most Gaelic of chronicles, the *Annals of Ulster*, he is referred to as 'Rolant mac Uchtraigh': *AU*, ii, 235.

65 See, for example, the witness list to *CDS*, i, no. 553; Stringer, 'Periphery and core', Appendix (A), no. 1; *St Bees Register*, no. 42.

66 Stringer, 'Periphery and core', especially 98–99.

67 Ibid., 82.

68 Ibid., 101.

69 Ibid., 98, where the quotation is taken from R. Bartlett, 'Colonial societies of the High Middle Ages', in *Medieval Frontier Societies*, eds R. Bartlett and A. MacKay (Oxford, 1989), 29.

70 Stringer, 'Records', nos 31, 33, 34, 41 47, 50, 54, 62, 63.

71 Stringer, 'Records', nos 35 and 54.

72 This is underscored by comparison with the evidence for the men attending his courts in Cunninghame and Lauderdale and for the composition of his mobile retinue. All are dominated by Anglo-Normans. See: Stringer, 'Periphery and

core' and idem, 'Records'.

73 E.g. *Melrose Liber*, i, nos 29, 32, 36, 189; *North Berwick Carte*, nos 1, 13–15.

74 Stringer, 'Periphery and core', 83–84.

75 *RRS*, vi, no. 235; *CDS*, ii, no. 212.

76 *Oxford Balliol Deeds*, no. 592.

77 Matthew Paris, *Chron. Maj.*, v, 270–72.

78 *Oxford Balliol Deeds*, no. 592.

79 William son of Gamell of Twynholm granted the advowson of the church of Twynholm to the canons of Holyrood before 1234: *Holyrood Liber*, no. 67. Walter of Twynholm was keeper of the sheriffdom of Wigtown for Edward I in 1296: *CDS*, ii, no. 824.

80 *Holm Cultram Register*, nos 116–19, 148–55.

81 Gilbert fitz Cospatric, Lord of Southwick, witnesses: *CDS*, i, no. 553; Stringer, 'Early lords of Lauderdale', Appendix, no. 7; *St Bees Register*, nos 42, 60, 62; Stringer, 'Periphery and core', Appendix (A), nos 1–3.

82 *CDS*, ii, nos 824, 1588, for Patrick M'Gilbochyn. Bain suggested that the 'Patrick de Botel' who submitted to Edward I at Berwick on 28 August 1296 (*CDS*, ii, no. 823) may be the same man. He may be a son of Gillespoc.

83 *RRS*, vi, no. 235.

84 *CDS*, iii, no. 258, records the lands of Tocstruther (Toskerton in the parish of Stoneykirk), held by the Marshalls in the early fourteenth century.

85 *Holm Cultram Register*, nos 144–46, 148, 151–54.

86 Brooke, 'The Glenkens', 49–50.

87 See *CDS*, i, no. 253, for 'the chief men of the lineage of Clenafren' in Galloway; and, for discussions of the office of 'kenkynnol', H. L. MacQueen, 'The laws of Galloway: a preliminary survey', in Galloway: *Land and Lordship*, eds. Oram and Stell, and H. L. MacQueen, 'The kin of Kennedy: "kenkynnol" and the common law', in *Medieval Scotland*, eds Grant and Stringer.

88 *RMS*, i, app. ii, no. 913, dated to *c*.1344.

89 *Oxford Balliol Deeds*, no. 601.

90 *CDS*, ii, no. 1712.

91 For the career of Donald MacCan see Bower, *Scotichronicon*, vi, 444, n. 54.

92 *CDS*, iii, no. 1578 (3).

93 *Oxford Balliol Deeds*, no. 601.

94 For Askeloc/McGachen see: *CDS*, ii, nos 823, 824 (1).

95 Barrow, *Robert Bruce*, 381, n. 8.

96 Ibid., 326.

97 Bower, *Scotichronicon*, vi, 445, n. 58.

98 *CDS*, ii, nos 823, 824 (1).

99 Ibid., ii, no. 1691.

100 *RMS*, i, app. ii, no. 1114; *CDS*, iii, nos 1390–92, 1412.

101 See, for example, Agnew, *Hereditary Sheriffs*, 613.

102 *RMS*, i, no. 722 and app. ii, nos 835, 1007.

103 Reid, 'Edward Balliol', 52–59.

104 *Chron. Lanercost*, 286–87.

105 *RMS*, i, app. ii, nos 835, 1006, 1007, 1147 and 1176.

106 See, for example, Oram, 'Accommodation, adaptation and integration', or Watson, 'Adapting tradition'.

107 For the laws of Galloway see MacQueen, 'Laws of Galloway: a preliminary survey'. The longevity of Gaelic legal traditions in the south-west is discussed by MacQueen, 'The kin of Kennedy'.

108 Davies, *Domination and Conquest*, 114.

109 Oram, 'David I', 1–19.

110 Oram, 'Accommodation, adaptation and integration'; C. J. Neville, 'The earls of Strathearn from the twelfth to the mid-fourteenth century' (Aberdeen University PhD thesis, 1983) 30, 63; Watson, 'Adapting tradition'.
111 Neville, 'A Celtic enclave', particularly 81–92.
112 A. Grant, 'The higher nobility and their estates in Scotland, c.1371–1424' (Oxford University D Phil Thesis, 1975), 232–39.
113 Oram, 'Accommodation, adaptation and integration'.
114 For the value of upland territory to medieval landlords see A. J. L. Winchester, *Landscape and Society in Medieval Cumbria* (Edinburgh, 1987), 19–22.
115 Neville, 'A Celtic enclave', 76–79.
116 *Exchequer Rolls*, vi, 191–210; *Atlas of Scottish History to 1707*, eds P. G. B. McNeill and H. L. MacQueen (Edinburgh, 1996), 446.
117 *RMS*, i, app. ii, no. 316.
118 Scottish Record Office, Register House Charters, MS.RH.6/219: *RMS*, ii, 907.
119 Winchester, *Landscape and Society in Medieval Cumbria*, 19–22, 81–85.
120 I. A. Milne, 'An extent of Carrick in 1260', *SHR*, xliv (1955); J. Fergusson, 'An extent of Carrick in 1260', *SHR*, xliv (1955), 190–92.
121 E.g. *Melrose Liber*, i, nos 31–36.
122 E.g. *RMS*, ii, no. 907; *Morton Registrum*, i, pp. lix–lxi, 'Rentale Quarundam Baroniarum Dominorum de Dalkeith, 1376'.

8

'AND HE BUILT CASTLES AND VERY MANY FORTRESSES': THE PHYSICAL EVIDENCE

Within Scotland, Galloway possesses the single greatest concentration of earthwork remains – generically labelled mottes – commonly assigned to twelfth- or thirteenth-century 'Anglo-Norman' aristocratic colonisation. Since Frederick Coles first drew the attention of his contemporaries to this class of monument over a century ago,[1] the mottes of Galloway have featured prominently in studies of this form of defensive site.[2] The coincidental survival of Roger of Howden's narrative account of events in the period 1174 to 1186 has added weight to such studies, for his chronicles appear to fossilise in their report of the rebellion of Uhtred and Gillebrigte, and the activities after 1185 of Roland, a chronology of motte-building in Galloway. As a consequence of this, research into mottes and 'Anglo-Norman' settlement in Galloway in general has been moulded by the historical sources to fit a traditional historiography which interprets the introduction of such fortifications as a two-phase operation carried out under the direction of a hostile external agency.[3] Such mottes, it has been claimed, represent 'the spread of the feudal system'[4] and there is, as a result, a tendency to view their development as the product of an alien elite working under the aegis of the crown and in confrontation with the native Gaelic population and traditional forces of lordship.

As discussed in the preceding chapter, the confrontational interpretation runs strongly throughout the traditional narrative of the politics of the lordship from 1160 onwards. The conquest of Galloway in 1160 by Máel Coluim IV and the enforced retirement of Fergus to Holyrood Abbey are taken commonly as the point of departure in the process of colonisation. The partitioning of the lordship between Uhtred and Gillebrigte was accompanied, it is argued, by an 'enforced infeudation' spearheaded by 'Anglo-Norman' colonists.[5] As part of this programme the first mottes were constructed in the lordship. Following the capture of William the Lion at Alnwick in 1174, the brothers rebelled and:

> expelled from Galloway all the bailiffs and guards whom the king of Scotland had set over them; and all the English and French whom they could seize they slew; and all the defences and castles which the king of Scotland had established in their land they besieged, captured and destroyed . . .[6]

Gillebrigte then had his brother murdered and, fighting a rearguard action of Celtic chauvinism against the innovations of feudalism and knight-service, kept the 'Anglo-Norman' colonisation of Galloway at bay until his death in January 1185. Immediately after Gillebrigte's death, Roland invaded Galloway:

> and slew all who would oppose him, and reduced all that land to himself. Moreover, he slew also the most powerful and richest men in all Galloway, and occupied their lands. And in them he built castles and very many fortresses, establishing his rule.[7]

Roland's success was achieved with the connivance of William the Lion and his new regime was founded on the settlement of 'Anglo-Norman' knights throughout Galloway, infefted with lands seized from the former supporters of Gillebrigte. It was these incomers who undertook the second major phase of motte-building, and the widespread distribution of their strongholds in the lordship is viewed as testimony to the scale of the colonisation and to the continued hostility of the subjugated Galwegians.

The standard interpretation, then, is that two main phases of construction are represented in the physical remains. The earlier is assigned to the period between 1160 and 1174, when Galloway was seen as 'being held within the Scottish kingdom only by means of incoming feudal settlement'.[8] However, only four mottes can be assigned firmly to this period on the basis of the charter evidence alone: Anwoth, Borgue, Ingleston and Urr.[9] The violent upheavals of 1174 supposedly resulted in the destruction of these strongholds, but the limited amount of excavation undertaken on any of these sites does not permit such a claim to be advanced with security: Brian Hope-Taylor's excavation at Urr – which still awaits final publication – produced inconclusive evidence for the dereliction of the site;[10] at Balgreggan fragments of carbonised wood and burnt daub exposed in the eroded sides of the mound have been interpreted as possible evidence for its destruction by fire,[11] but this has not been tested by excavation and there is no documentary evidence for 'Anglo-Norman' penetration so far west before the proposed second phase of colonisation initiated by Roland after 1185.

It is to this second phase that the majority of mottes in Galloway are attributed normally,[12] marking the influx of colonising families into the lordship under Roland's direction. Stewart Cruden has no doubt that mottes are generally markers of the spread of feudalism and symbols of subjugation. R. C. Reid, too, saw the earth and timber castles as the epitome of feudalism and the product of the conquest of Galloway by foreigners.[13] The number of these alien monuments and their widespread distribution do seem to indicate that a comprehensive conquest and colonisation did occur. Certainly, if the chronicle references to Roland's re-conquest of his lost patrimony are taken at face value, the thirty-three mottes and related sites identified within the pre-1996 Stewartry District alone constitute cogent reasons for accepting the standard account of invasion, subjugation and enforced infeudation.

The density of mottes in Galloway is exceeded in mainland Britain only by that in the Welsh March. There, the extraordinary concentration of such sites is attributed to the fluidity of the frontier with the Welsh principalities and the turbulence of a region in which Norman earls had succeeded in gaining and preserving an unparalleled degree of freedom from crown interference.[14] The apparent similarities between Norman and Angevin policies towards Wales and Scottish penetration of Galloway has seen the Welsh situation be adopted as the exemplar of the nature and scale of the colonisation in Galloway: military conquest and subsequent control by an alien elite based on fortified strongpoints. This contention, typified by Reid,[15] is based solely on the numbers and distribution of the type of monument represented, and, as has been argued above, does not stand up to detailed scrutiny of the charter evidence for the colonisation of Galloway, as opposed to the chronicle accounts. All that can be stated with certainty is that the earth and timber castles of motte type were an innovation introduced into the lordship in the course of the twelfth century.

The re-appraisal of the historical evidence offered above does not seek to deny that there was an influx of colonists into Galloway after c.1160, rather it challenges the mechanics and circumstances of the movement. As already discussed, the chronicle and charter evidence fall into two discrete sections: that relating to Uhtred and that concerned with Roland. It needs to be stressed once more, however, that what survives is probably a remnant of a much more substantial body of *acta* of the lords of Galloway and that the marked bias in the spatial distribution of the lands and individuals involved is more apparent than real. Nevertheless, there are indications that while the image that can be reconstructed is but a disarticulated portion of the whole, a faithful representation of the wider picture can be recovered from its shards.

How, though, does the re-interpretation of the documentary sources offered above affect the interpretation of the physical remains? In the first place, it suggests that too great an emphasis has been placed on the notion of 'enforced infeudation'. This has caused a disproportionate focus on the physical remains which appear to support the tradition of intrusive colonisation under the aegis of an aggressively interventionist Scottish crown, while the native involvement in the process has been played down or ignored. Secondly, it outlines the dangers inherent in too rigid an adherence to a framework derived from uncritical acceptance of the contemporary record. The break in colonisation that supposedly occurred between 1174 and 1185 can be shown to be a fiction, at least in an ill-defined region of eastern Galloway which had come under the rule of Roland soon after his father's murder. Rather than two phases of motte construction throughout Galloway in general, we should rather be looking at a steady spread of the building tradition within the territories of Uhtred and his son after 1160, with slower growth west of the Cree possibly followed by an acceleration after 1185. There may be destruction evident at some sites, but any resulting dereliction should probably be seen as short-lived rather than lasting over a decade until Roland's conquest of his uncle's domain. Finally, there is a need to re-assess the criteria on which motte building to a 'classic' model is ascribed to colonists, while non-standard or 'anomalous' sites are viewed as the product of native builders who lacked the understanding or ability to imitate the imported tradition.

Until the 1980s, archaeological and historical research in Galloway shied away from the pre-lordship era of the eleventh and early twelfth centuries. The total absence of native documentation for this period has rendered it a barren zone for historians, and, without a convenient historical schema within which to operate on sites other than Whithorn, no archaeologist has stepped confidently or intentionally where the historians fear to tread. In common with the rest of mainland Scotland, therefore, our knowledge of the form taken by centres of lordly power before the 'Anglo-Norman' era – after the possible demise of centres of Northumbrian lordship – is sketchy.[16] In Galloway, modern excavation of a pre-twelfth-century seat of secular lordship is restricted to the earliest phases of occupation on the later castle site at Cruggleton in the Machars, and to the current programme of excavation at Buittle.[17] There are, however, many other lines of enquiry that might bear fruit, should we build on the few tantalising fragments which appear in later documentation, or in the place-name record.

One important step forward would be to identify sites associated with the lords of Galloway themselves, and then, working by analogy, to earmark similar sites which may represent the seats of the native nobility. Locations associated with Fergus are few in number and are generally encumbered with later work, but what may have been his chief seat, Castle Fergus in the high ground immediately east of Kirkcudbright,[18] is free of post-medieval development. This earthwork site comprises two oval mounds, one called Palace Isle and the other Stable Isle, which rise from the bed of a now-drained lochan. Heavily eroded by modern agricultural action, but of still considerable extent, the larger mound is defended by a denuded earthen rampart. From the surviving remains, it was clearly approached by a causeway from the north-east and depended on the surrounding waters and marsh for protection rather than on the seemingly light defences which enclosed it. No indication of the internal arrangements of the twelfth-century complex is discernible; the traces of a masonry building within the enclosure are believed to be the footings of a later medieval residence.

A number of presumed medieval defended island sites of this general form have been identified elsewhere in Galloway,[19] but potentially one of the most important of these, Burned Island in Loch Ken, escaped the attention of Curle and the Royal Commission surveyors of the Stewartry in the early 1910s. The island, which may in fact be a crannog, has now been partly submerged by the raising of the loch level in the 1930s as a consequence of the Ken–Dee hydro-electric system. This strategic site was probably the chief seat of the lords of Galloway in Glenken, and its medieval name, Erysbutil, suggest earlier origins as a centre of power in the Anglian period.[20] It remained important into the fourteenth century, when it was held by Edward Balliol during the 1330s and 1340s; according to Wyntoun, Balliol was there in 1346 while the pro-Bruce Kennedies ravaged the south-west.[21] Balliol granted the castle of Burned Island in 1352 to his faithful supporter, William de Aldeburgh, his charter conveying the barony of Kells in Glenken together with 'Insula Arsa', and the adjoining barony of Crossmichael to the south.[22] This charter implies that Burned Island should be regarded as the caput of the barony of Kells, rather than Kenmure Castle at the northern end of Loch Ken, which was developed by the Gordon family in the later Middle Ages. Here, then, we have the continued use of an ancient seat of lordship utilising a native building tradition, with occupation lasting into the mid-fourteenth century.

Burned Island finds its closest parallels in sites like Castle Loch, Mochrum,[23] the 'old castle' on its island at Lochnaw in the Rhinns, and the most potently symbolic of all lordship sites in Galloway, Threave Castle. The castle on Threave Island in the River Dee some 12km south-east of Burned Island is a product of the late fourteenth- and early fifteenth-century Black Douglas possession of the lordship of Galloway, its massive centrepiece, a stark late fourteenth-century towerhouse, being the work of the founder of their fortunes in the Scottish south-west, Archibald the Grim. Although all the visible remains date from the Douglas period, the place-name indicates greater antiquity as a centre of lordship. Threave is derived from the Brittonic *tref* (a farm, a homestead),[24] but its simplex form, stressed in the Middle Ages by the use of the specific *le Treffe*,[25] may point towards a lordly residence of greater social status. This, indeed, may be the 'insulam de' or 'Island of Dee' where Uhtred met his end in 1174,[26] and it may be the island referred to as being burned in 1308 by Edward Bruce during his campaign against the English and their sympathisers in Galloway.[27] Excavation of the fourteenth-century castle in the 1970s produced only fragmentary evidence for pre-Douglas occupation of the island, but there are indications that an earlier complex of buildings stood to the south of the Douglases' work.[28]

One step further down the social ladder and we enter a landscape where crannogs and island sites emerge as important elements in the patterns of local power. In Wigtownshire alone there are at least thirty-four identified crannog sites, plus a similar number of natural island sites or isolated outcrops in boggy ground that have been utilised for both residence and defence. The majority of such sites have not been explored archaeologically, but most are probably of Iron Age or earlier origin. A substantial number, however, are medieval or at least remained in occupation into the Middle Ages. There has been a general assumption that these crannogs formed part of the vocabulary of native lordly architecture, but, as Christopher Tabraham points out, 'an alien landlord's concern for his family's safety may well have been solved in other ways, and what better than a fortified island or indeed and artificially constructed one – a crannog?'[29] The longevity of the crannog as a lordly setting is well attested in Scotland, with the Burnetts of Leys in Kincardineshire, who lived on their artificial island in the Loch of Leys into the mid-sixteenth century, being just one of the better documented instances. In Galloway, the clearest example of the use of a crannog as a seat of lordship is Lochrutton.[30] This was excavated in the early 1900s and material which pointed to a medieval occupation recovered.[31] Recent radiocarbon dating of timbers recovered from the submerged portion of the crannog places its construction in the period 1175–1270[32] and re-examination of the ceramic material recovered in Barbour's original excavation indicated a later medieval date rather than the thirteenth-century provenance which he had proposed, underscoring the continuity of use at this site into the late Middle Ages.[33]

Other early sites associated with the lords of Galloway take quite different forms. Of these, Buittle and Cruggleton are obscured by later stone structures, but both have been the subjects of excavation in recent years. In its general form, Buittle is a promontory fortification carved out of the gravel terrace on the west side of the Water of Urr. A broad ditch of as yet unknown date cuts off a headland of the terrace to form the northern and western sides off a large outer enclosure. The apex of the headland is separated from this main enclosure by a second broad ditch and the smaller, detached portion was the site of the later thirteenth-century stone castle. A twelfth-century date has been postulated for the construction of the main earthwork defences, and the suggestion has also been made that the bipartite division of the site may reflect its development into a motte-and-bailey format.[34] The Anglian origin of the place-name (botl, a lordly hall[35]), however, suggests that some portion of the defences might be considerably older.

A similar interpretation and physical layout obtains at the clifftop promontory site of Cruggleton in the Machars. Excavation revealed a major phase of development in the twelfth century, with the formation of what has been interpreted as a motte-and-bailey on the headland, utilising the natural topography of the site.[36] As at Buittle, a large outer enclosure – the 'bailey' – is separated from the adjoining fields by a broad ditch, now eroded by ploughing. At the southern extremity of the enclosed area lies a higher, subsidiary peninsula of the headland, to which the label 'motte' has been attached.[37] At Cruggleton, however, the excavation demonstrated the development of the site from the late Iron Age onwards, and again it is possible that the substantial defences represented by the unexcavated landward ditch are of prehistoric or early historic origin.

At Buittle certainly, and to a lesser extent at Cruggleton where there was the raising of an artificial clay and shale-chipping platform above the level of the earlier remains,[38] the labelling of the constituent components as 'bailey' and 'motte' appears disingenuous and based on relative layout, for the scale of these sites far outstrips that of other motte-and-bailey fortifications in Galloway. At Buittle, the summit area is approximately 50m by 30m, or over a third again larger than the Morville's motte at Boreland of Borgue and more than twice the area of Walter de Berkeley's Mote of Urr. The accommodation provided by the massive bailey at Mote of Urr, however, brings that site up to a comparable scale with Buittle, but it is probable that the extensive enclosure – entirely within which the motte is sited – represents the re-use of an Iron Age defensive work rather than a medieval build which reflects the status of its owner.[39] Urr apart, therefore, Buittle and Cruggleton are divided significantly from the remainder of the Galloway motte-and-baileys by their monumental scale. While this may reflect the pretensions of the twelfth-century lords of Galloway, constructing fortifications which quite literally set them head and shoulders above their vassals, is it not more simply a question of modern application of ill-defined terminology to monuments which bear a superficial similarity to the supposed 'classic' motte-and-bailey form?

As a specific class of fortification mottes lack the homogeneity of form that the all-embracing generic implies. Interpretations of the variations in form that are evident throughout Scotland are loaded with cultural determinism. There is general agreement that they are the product of foreign influences, but that is not to say that 'classic' forms, i.e., the inverted 'pudding-basin' or truncated cone with surrounding ditch, possibly with a basal court, as at Balmaclellan for instance, are exclusively the product of incoming colonists conversant with that building technique, while variants which depart from this 'classic' form should be seen as native attempts to copy superior military engineering.[40] The suggestion that sites which depart from the supposedly pure form of the motte represent native anomalies built in imitation of nearby 'Anglo-Norman' forms sit awkwardly with the suggestion that an incoming colonist could satisfactorily adopt a native settlement form – the crannog – for his residence.[41] Indeed, as has been noted in England, 'there is no blueprint' for mottes, and 'excavation is beginning to show that they were the results of innumerable experiments, each adapted to its surroundings'.[42]

Galloway mottes show clear experimentation in the forms adopted by their builders. The greater proportion of the sites fall into the rough category of 'classic' forms, mostly of freestanding inverted pudding-basin type without evident basal courts. Apart from ringworks, a class of monument only recently recognised in Galloway,[43] the remainder of the sites fall under the category of 'anomalies'. Of the classic form, only four in the Stewartry possess obvious baileys enclosed by earthwork defences, that is, Boreland of Borgue, Southwick, Kirkcarsewell and Mote of Urr, this last possibly representing the re-use of a prehistoric fortification, while in Wigtownshire only one site, High Drummore, conforms to this type. At

Boreland of Borgue, Southwick and Kirkcarsewell, the baileys are reduced to either vestigial bumps or appear as cropmarks only, which raises the possibility that some now freestanding mottes have had baileys obliterated through ploughing. Two other mottes in the Stewartry, at Boreland of Anwoth and Kirkclaugh, possess baileys but diverge from the 'classic' format. Both utilise natural features. At Anwoth a long alluvial ridge has been scarped and cut in two to form a 'motte' and a 'bailey', but there has been no attempt to raise the height of the former above the latter. Kirkclaugh makes a more radical departure from classic form, its cliff-edge motte being surrounded on two landward sides by an unusually narrow L-shaped bailey between the ditch on the landward arc of the motte and the outer ditch which cuts off the neck of the headland on which it stands.

The general absence of baileys at most of the Galwegian sites may be one of the clearest indicators of the nature of the colonising ventures in Galloway after 1160. In Ireland, Dr Tom McNeill has highlighted the proliferation of mottes in the primary areas of Anglo-Norman colonisation after 1166 and their particular density in the frontier zones of the great lordships carved out by the colonising lords in, for example, Meath, Oriel and Ulster. Within these frontier zones he has identified a significant density of mottes with baileys, while in the hinterlands of the lordships bailey-less mottes predominate. He argues that mottes with baileys represent the militarisation of the frontier zones, being the sites at which military forces would congregate in troubled times, or where garrisons would be stationed. In Ulster, this garrison capacity is a feature of sites associated with the early colonisation of that lordship after 1177 by the de Courcys.[44] Similar dates can be assigned to Urr, Borgue and Anwoth, where Walter de Berkeley, Hugh de Morville and David fitz Terrus were Uhtred's tenants, but no firm date can be assigned to the remaining mottes with baileys. If McNeill's interpretation of Irish motte-and-bailey sites is accepted, and extended to Galloway, here on the one hand appears to be the physical evidence for the garrisoning and military supervision described by Howden, but on the other the numbers and distribution of such sites hardly constitute compelling grounds for acceptance of the cataclysmic interpretation of dominance and conquest by an alien elite based on fortified garrison-posts.

This comparative rarity of baileys as a feature of the military architecture of the Scottish south-west suggests that other forces were at work. Clearly, if baileys indicate the presence of a garrison, the absence of such enclosures at most Galwegian sites must surely argue strongly against the tradition of an army of occupation led by colonists imposed on the lordship by the Scottish crown. Indeed, the absence of baileys might indicate an essentially non-military aspect to the colonising process. With Walter de Berkeley and Hugh de Morville, status may have been the determining factor as much as any other reason, the one being chamberlain to the king of Scots and possibly a brother-in-law of Uhtred, the other a knight prominent in the service of Henry II and a major landholder in northern England. The extended households that were a reflection of the exalted status of some such lords may have required the provision of additional accommodation in the baileys. This, however, does not necessarily imply that bailey-less mottes were regarded as socially inferior.

Mottes standing in isolation form the most substantial group in Galloway. Eleven out of the eighteen in the Stewartry ascribed to the twelfth or thirteenth centuries by Tabraham fall into this category, while at least thirteen more lie in those parts of Galloway outwith his survey area. It is possible that as at Borgue and Southwick the baileys have been all but obliterated by ploughing, or were simple palisaded enclosures without substantial ditches or ramparts which would leave prominent traces of their existence. A considerable (but without individual geophysical or invasive investigation, indeterminate) number, however, appear never to have possessed a permanent outer enclosure. Probable examples of this type are Balmaclellan, Kirkland Motte at Parton, and where the only visible outer defence is a heavily silted ditch encircling the upcast mound. Such sites are by far the most prevalent form found in Scotland, but few have received detailed examination in recent years. In Galloway, the only freestanding motte to have been the subject of modern excavation is Sorbie in Wigtownshire, the seat of the Vieuxponts after 1185. Unfortunately, however, the excavation of this site was left uncompleted and no final report on the work undertaken has been produced.

The final group, the supposed 'native anomalies', defy attempts to categorise them more specifically. These include such oddities as Lochrinnie and Trostrie, where the 'mottes' take the form of massively elongated mounds with substantial summit platforms. Lochrinnie also has a 'bailey' raised on a smaller version of the adjoining motte. As at Boreland of Anwoth, the natural configurations of these sites appear to have been the main determinants of layout. Lochrinnie is scarped from an alluvial mound on the north side of the Cairn valley, while at Trostrie an isolated rock outcrop has been utilised as the core of the motte. A second form, epitomised by Roberton in Borgue parish, represented an adaptation of the bailey-less motte formed by digging away a deep ditch around a small platform at the edge of a steep natural drop, rather than constructing a mound from the upcast soil. It is accepted in England and Wales that there is no reason to view such utilisation of natural features as in any way representing inferiority of design,[45] or to stigmatise them as feeble native attempts to copy 'Anglo-Norman' models. After all, flexibility of approach and an ability to adapt to local circumstances was one of the great characteristics of the culture responsible for the introduction of the motte-and-bailey castle throughout Europe. It is a design, moreover, which readily lends itself to adaptation and modification to suit the lie of the land.[46]

While it is fairly clear that motte-and-bailey sites in Galloway belong generally to the period from 1160 to 1174–85 – a chronology that neatly parallels that postulated for similar sites in Ulster – it is impossible to offer such precise parameters for a chronology of bailey-less mottes of all forms. Both groups are certainly not mutually exclusive chronologically. Bailey-less Ingleston in New Abbey parish,[47] for example, the caput of the lordship of Lochkindeloch granted to Richard fitz Troite by Uhtred, was contemporary with the motte-and-bailey sites of Urr, Borgue and Anwoth. It is evident, however, that while mottes with baileys continued in use after 1185,[48] no new sites of this form were constructed. Even less precision can be offered with regard to bailey-less mottes, especially since none in this category in Galloway have been excavated in recent years. Despite this dearth of dating evidence, however, there has been an almost unconscious tendency to assume that the majority must date from Roland's solo rule between 1185 and 1200, for Howden did recount how Roland 'built castles and very many fortresses'.

Without an extensive programme of excavation of the Galloway mottes no precise timespan can be offered for their use as a favoured form of construction for new centres of power. We can say, however, that some functioned as power centres for a considerable period after their construction. Hope-Taylor's excavations at Urr and, outwith Galloway, Peter Yeoman's excavations at Strachan in Kincardineshire, point to continuity of high-status function at these sites into the fourteenth century.[49] This should act as a caveat against the automatic tendency to label mottes in Scotland as a twelfth- or early thirteenth-century phenomenon, for continuity of occupation at some sites points to continued acceptance of this form of defensive residence long after the style had been superseded elsewhere in Britain. The rarity of thirteenth-century stone castles in Scotland, while attributable in part to the ravages of the Wars of Independence, is more a symbol of the prodigality of a few *nouveaux riches* of Alexander III's reign rather than the parsimony of the wider Scottish nobility. Castles such as Bothwell, Dirleton or Caerlaverock serve only to distract from a landscape that is otherwise largely free of major stone-built fortifications outwith royal hands, a sharp contrast with the contemporary scene elsewhere in Britain and Ireland. Indeed, castle building in stone as an expression of wealth and power does not seem to have been a characteristic of most of the established Scottish higher nobility in the pre-Wars of Independence era, and, it should be added, was a characteristic acquired quite late thereafter by several prominent families. The probable continued use of the earth and timber defences of Huntly by the Gordons into the mid-fifteenth century should warn us of the pitfalls of the simplistic schemes of development which present a chronological flow from mottes, to enceintes, to towerhouses, each style neatly pigeon-holed in discrete temporal blocks.

In Galloway, with the exception of the major stone castles built by the lords of Galloway and their direct successors in the thirteenth century, there is a striking dearth of recognisable medieval defensive sites to which a later thirteenth- or earlier fourteenth-century date can be assigned. The building of Threave shortly after 1369 marked a watershed in castle building in the region, that much is accepted. What followed from the development of Threave is generally understood, but the earlier traditions that it supplanted are largely ignored. Hall-houses, such as those recognised at Hestan Island, Ardwall Island, Luce Sands and, possibly, Castle Loch, Mochrum,[50] offer only a partial solution to the problem. Many more would have to be identified before it could be argued with confidence that a tradition of hall-house building – in timber or stone – developed in Galloway in the politically stable and apparently prosperous years post-1250. The abundance of mottes and related sites, however, presents a more obvious possibility, particularly in light of the evidence for continuity of occupation at some mottes into the fourteenth century, if not indeed into the fifteenth century. There are certainly pointers in this direction: Pulcree in Anwoth parish, Little Duchrae in Balmaghie and Little Richorn in Urr,[51] none of classic motte form, indicate a continuing tradition of earth and timber fortification into the fifteenth century, documentarily attestable at Little Duchrae to 1455.[52]

Potentially the clearest evidence for the longevity of mottes and related earthwork forms, and some indication of dating, lies in lordships or parishes with more than one medieval lordly centre. A good example is Borgue. Here the pre-1974 civil parish represented the post-Reformation amalgamation of three medieval units – Borgue, Kirkandrews and Senwick – and there are three medieval earthwork sites: Boreland of Borgue, Roberton and Barmagachan.[53] This is not a case of one motte per pre-Reformation parish, for, of these, none lies in Senwick, which was a demesne estate of the lords of Galloway and partitioned between Alan's daughters after 1234. Roberton lies in the former Kirkandrews parish, a separate lordship held by the Ripley family by c.1234–42,[54] but by reason of its non-classic format has been labelled as a native product.[55] Boreland motte is commonly recognised as the caput of the lordship held by Hugh de Morville in the late twelfth century and which passed to Ralph de Campania in the early thirteenth century.[56] Held by Ralph's heirs until 1282, when it was quitclaimed to their superior, Dervorgilla,[57] this motte survived as a functioning seat of lordship into the late thirteenth century: there are no grounds for inference of dereliction at the time of its reversion to Dervorgilla.[58] Nor can it be taken as read that it was abandoned after 1282, for Dervorgilla granted Borgue to the native Askeloc or MacGachen kindred,[59] for whom no other lordship centre within Borgue can be recognised. Boreland, however, cannot be the 'Castleton de Borg in Galwythia' held in 1260 by Robert de Campania, son of Ralph's brother, Robert de Campania, and younger brother and heir of William de Campania, lord of Stokes in Leicestershire, where he issued a charter confirming an annual rent owed to Lindores Abbey from his newly inherited properties,[60] for 'Borgue' was then held by Ralph's grandson, Nicholas, and passed subsequently to his son, Robert.[61]

Where then is Robert de Campania's Castleton of Borgue? Barmagachan is the obvious candidate and stylistically meets the criteria demanded for identification as the seat of a colonising lord,[62] but the earthwork lies in the medieval Kirkandrews parish. We have, then, two medieval earthworks within the one lordship, one supposedly the product of an English incomer and the other a native-built emulation of it, and can provide lords for both. Rather than the acceptably 'Anglo-Norman' Barmagachan being the caput of Robert de Campania's lordship, however, it is more likely that 'native' Roberton is the probable site, for Robert, after all, was the name of lords of Castleton of Borgue in two successive generations at least. By extension, Barmagachan should be the seat of Bernard de Ripley, lord of Kirkandrews, and was possibly built following a division of Castleton of Borgue following the death of Robert's elder brother, William. Margaret, the surnameless heiress through whom Bernard acquired his properties, may have been the daughter of William,[63] or indeed of the original Robert. If this interpretation is correct, the construction of a second power centre within a partitioned lordship of Castleton of Borgue/Kirkandrews cannot be dated any earlier than the death of Alan of Galloway in 1234, as his widow, Rose de Lacy, witnessed the charter of Bernard and Margaret to St Bees Priory, and probably nearer to 1240, and Roberton, as the seat of Robert II de Campania, was still in occupation after 1260.

In Borgue, then, we have a trio of lordships where mottes not only function as the seats of power into the later thirteenth century – and beyond – but where they were constructed as late as the end of the second quarter of the thirteenth century, over half a century after the end of what is seen traditionally as the second phase of motte building under Roland. Furthermore, the construction of Barmagachan does not represent the product of an outmoded tradition adopted by a conservative and culturally backward native nobility, but was the product of a northern English knight with connections at the Scottish court.[64] To Bernard de Ripley, an earth and timber residence of motte type still conveyed an acceptable statement of his status in society.

Borgue/Barmagachan is one situation where the documentation allows speculation on dating and longevity of site function. The mid-thirteenth century, then, on the basis of the documentary evidence represents a *terminus ante quem* for most building in this tradition in Galloway. Excavation outwith Galloway, however, at Roberton in Clydesdale, has indicated that mottes were still being constructed in the politically volatile climate of the early fourteenth century,[65] and raises the possibility that many of the Galloway sites were constructed during the savage warfare in the lordship in the 1300s. Can a similar line be drawn under probable periods of occupation? The answer is a tentative yes, for it can be inferred that the Wars of Independence and the forfeiture of families who had held land in Galloway from at least the 1180s marked the end of the functioning life of several mottes. It is likely that these fell victim to the devastating raids of Edward Bruce before 1312, in much the same way as Strachan in

Kincardineshire was destroyed by his elder brother during his north-eastern campaigns.[66] The mottes at Colvend and Southwick, held before 1314 by branches of the same family, are good examples here. At Colvend, although the pre-1314 lords briefly regained tenure,[67] the lordship was granted to Alexander Bruce, bastard son of Edward Bruce,[68] the first in a succession of fourteenth-century lords for whom this property was simply one, and not a particularly important, component in a complex of scattered estates. Effectively, it ceased to be the centrepiece of the possessions of a family of knightly rank and passed into the hands of a magnate for whom it was simply a source of revenue to be exploited and rarely, if ever, visited. As at Strachan, its fourteenth-century lords had no requirement for a permanent residence at the old motte site.

It is a pattern that appears, too, at Anwoth. There, David fitz Terrus's motte continued as the seat of his successors and probable descendants, the de Cardonesses. The last identified members of that line, John and Michael de Cardoness, were active in 1296,[69] while their immediate predecessor and probable father, Bertram de Cardoness, had been a member of Dervorgilla's curia.[70] Association with the Balliol family and opposition to the Bruces after 1306, probably accounted for their disappearance as landholders in Galloway. The lands, described as in royal hands through forfeiture, were granted in 1342 to Malcolm Fleming, Earl of Wigtown.[71] As with Colvend, a previously important estate had passed to a largely absentee lord, whose chief political and territorial interests were, despite his title, concentrated in Dunbartonshire and northern Lanarkshire. This grant confirmed the abandonment of the old motte, and when a new resident power in the form of the McCullochs gained possession in the fifteenth century, a new lordship centre was constructed: Cardoness Castle. The equation of forfeiture or extinction of the ancient lords and resultant abandonment of the traditional seats of lordship by absentee successors is one that can be charted across Galloway.

In the absence of more general documentation, it is still a long step in the dark from the dating of the construction of Barmagachan to the building of Threave, but by the time of Bernard de Ripley's arrival at Kirkandrews the pattern of medieval lordship in Galloway that survived even the traumas of the early fourteenth century had largely crystallised. What evidence we do have points to the continued function of the established centres of lordship rather than the construction of new ones, a level of stability that survived the brief upheaval which followed Alan's death in 1234, and lasted until the Bruce campaigns in Galloway after 1307, and in some cases well beyond that. The continuing use of the mottes established in the later twelfth and thirteenth centuries into the fourteenth century is, in itself, prima facie evidence for the underlying stability of Galwegian society and the continuity of landholding patterns. Where the parvenus of later thirteenth-century Scotland marked their social arrival with the construction of sophisticated and expensive castles of stone, the old established families needed to make no such public statements of their political status and economic power. It is, moreover, indicative of confidence in the continuity of stability, where the provision of advanced military technology was not regarded as a priority in aristocratic budgets. It cannot, however, simply be a question of economic determinants: the comparative richness of Galloway's thirteenth-century ecclesiastical architecture is testimony to general local affluence in the pre-Wars of Independence era, not just the wealth of the Church. Such survival, at its most basic level, must bear witness to the inherent social conservatism of the south-western Scottish nobility: it is certainly evidence for the continued acceptability of earth and timber fortifications as symbols of lordship in an age where advances in military engineering had long rendered any primary defensive function redundant.

Notes

1 F. R. Coles, 'The Motes, Forts and Doons of Stewartry of Kirkcudbright', *PSAS*, xxv (1890–91), 352–96; F. R. Coles, 'The Motes, Forts and Doons of the Stewartry of Kirkcudbright', *PSAS* (1891–92), 117–70; F. R. Coles 'The Motes, Forts and Doons of the East and West Divisions of the Stewartry of Kirkcudbright', *PSAS*, xxvii (1892–3), 98–182.

2 E.g. C. J. Tabraham, 'Norman settlement in Galloway: recent fieldwork in the Stewartry', in D. Breeze, *Studies in Scottish Antiquity Presented to Stewart Cruden* (Edinburgh, 1984); G. G. Simpson and B. Webster, 'Charter evidence and the distribution of mottes in Scotland', in Stringer (ed.), *Nobility of Medieval Scotland*, 1–24.

3 *RRS*, i, 12–13; *RRS*, ii, 7–8, 13–14; Barrow, *Kingship and Unity*, 47–49; Duncan, *Making of the Kingdom*, 181–85; Tabraham, 'Norman settlement in Galloway', 121–22; Simpson and Webster, 'Charter evidence', 9–10.

4 S. Cruden, *The Scottish Castle* (Edinburgh, 1981), 10.

5 Tabraham, 'Norman settlement in Galloway', 122.

6 Benedict of Peterborough, i, 67–68.

7 Ibid., i, 339–40.

8 *RRS*, ii, 8.

9 Simpson and Webster, 'Charter evidence', 9–10; Tabraham, 'Norman settlement in Galloway', 100, 120, table 2.

10 B. Hope-Taylor, 'Excavations at Mote of Urr, interim report, 1951 season', *TDGAS*, xxix (1950–51), 167–72.

11 RCAHMS, *The Archaeological Sites and Monuments of Scotland*, xxiv, *West Rhins* (Edinburgh, 1985), 185.

12 Simpson and Webster, 'Charter evidence', 10; Tabraham, 'Norman settlement in Galloway', 122.

13 *Wigtownshire Charters*, xxii–xxiii.

14 F. Barlow, *The Feudal Kingdom of England 1042–1216*, 3rd edition (London, 1971), 90, 161–65.

15 E.g. *Wigtownshire Charters*, xxii–xxiii.

16 See S. Driscoll, 'Formalising the mechanisms of state control', in Foster, Macinnes and MacInnes, *Scottish Power Centres*.

17 G. Ewart, *Cruggleton Castle. Report of Excavations 1978–81* (Dumfries, 1985); for Buittle, see A. Penman, *Botel Bailey Excavation. Interim Report 1992–1994 and 1996* (Castle Douglas 1995 and 1997).

18 RCAHMS, *Kirkcudbright*, no. 263.

19 E.g. RCAHMS, *Wigtownshire*, no. 98.
20 *ER*, vi, 262–63; Brooke, 'Northumbrian settlement', 302.
21 *Chron. Wyntoun*, ii, 477.
22 *CDS*, iii, no. 1578 (3).
23 C. A. R. Radford, 'Castle Loch, Mochrum', *TDGAS*, xxviii (1949–50), 41–63.
24 Brooke, 'Northumbrian settlement', 303.
25 *RMS*, ii, nos 86, 133, 383.
26 *Benedict of Peterborough*, i, 79.
27 Bower, *Scotichronicon*, vi, 345, 445 n. 73.
28 G. Good and C. J. Tabraham, 'Excavations at Threave Castle, Galloway, 1974–78', *Medieval Archaeology*, 25 (1981), 136.
29 Tabraham, 'Norman settlement in Galloway', 110.
30 Ibid.
31 J. Barbour, 'An account of excavations at Lochrutton lake-dwelling', *TDGNGAS*, 2nd series xvii (1902–03), 246–54.
32 B. A. Crone, 'Crannogs and chronologies', *PSAS*, 123 (1993), 245–54.
33 Tabraham, 'Norman settlement in Galloway', 110.
34 A. M. T. Maxwell-Irving, 'The castles of Buittle', *TDGNHAS*, lxvi (1991), 59–66 at 59–60, plans 60 and 62; Coles, 'Motes, forts and doons', *PSAS*, 26 (1892), 132–35; Tabraham, 'Norman settlement in Galloway', 99.
35 Nicholson, *Scottish Place-Names*, 77.
36 Ewart, *Cruggleton Castle*, 18–22.
37 Ibid., 4.
38 Ibid., 18.
39 Stell, 'Medieval buildings and secular lordship', 146.
40 Tabraham, 'Norman settlement in Galloway', 121.
41 Ibid., 118–19.
42 J. Steane, *The Archaeology of Medieval England and Wales* (London, 1984), 38.
43 Tabraham, 'Norman settlement in Galloway', 118.
44 T. E. McNeill, *Castles in Ireland. Feudal Power in a Gaelic World* (London, 1997), 66–70; McNeill, *Anglo-Norman Ulster*, 65–68, 85–87.
45 Steane, *Archaeology of Medieval England and Wales*, 38.
46 P. Yeoman, *Medieval Scotland: an Archeaological Perspective* (London, 1995), 95.
47 RCAHMS, *Galloway*, ii, no. 385.
48 Hope-Taylor, 'Excavations at Mote of Urr', 171.
49 Ibid.; P. Yeoman and others, 'Excavation at Castlehill of Strachan, 1980–81', *PSAS*, 114 (1984), 315–64.
50 C. A. R. Radford, 'Castle Loch, Mochrum', *TDGNHAS*, xxviii (1949–50), 41–63; C. A. R. Radford, 'Balliol's manor house on Hestan Island', *TDGNHAS*, xxxv (1956–57), 33–37; C. Thomas, 'Ardwall Island: the excavation of an early Christian site of Irish type', *TDGNHAS*, xliii (1966), 84–116.
51 Tabraham, 'Norman settlement in Galloway', 92, 95, 117.
52 *ER*, vi, 199, 347.
53 Tabraham, 'Norman settlement in Galloway', 96–98.
54 *St Bees Register*, no. 67.
55 Tabraham, 'Norman settlement in Galloway', 121.
56 *Dryburgh Liber*, nos 64–65, 68; Tabraham, 'Norman settlement in Galloway', 98.
57 *CDS*, ii, no. 212.
58 Tabraham, 'Norman settlement in Galloway', 98.
59 Oram, 'A family business?', 138–39.

60 *Lindores Chartulary*, no. CXIII.
61 *Dryburgh Liber*, no. 65; *CDS*, ii, no. 212.
62 Tabraham, 'Norman settlement in Galloway', 121.
63 Barrow, *Anglo-Norman Era*, 113–14.
64 Ibid., 192.
65 G. Haggarty and C. J. Tabraham, 'Excavation of a motte near Roberton, Clydesdale, 1979', *TDGNHAS*, lvii (1982), 51–64.
66 Yeoman, 'Castlehill of Strachan', 345.
67 *CDS*, iii, no. 1428.
68 *RMS*, i, app. ii, no. 319.
69 *CDS*, ii, no. 823.
70 *CDS*, ii, no. 212; *RRS*, vi, no. 235.
71 *RRS*, vi, no. 52.

9

LAND AND SOCIETY

Thus far, the argument has focused primarily upon the native and colonial ruling elites of medieval Galloway. The economic and social structures that supported those elites, and the mechanisms upon which were founded their status and authority, however, have scarcely been glimpsed, yet it is from the lower orders of native society that the lords of Galloway drew their military and naval power and upon whom their personal wealth was founded. Furthermore, while the structure of tenures and patterns of estates that supported the incoming 'feudal' nobility of the later twelfth and thirteenth centuries can be recovered in some detail, the nature of the pre-feudal structures makes little positive impact on the written record. The role of knight service and the feu or fief, as the basic elements in the relationship between lords and vassals in medieval north-western European culture, have come to dominate most interpretations of the re-structuring of elite social bonds in those parts of the British Isles into which continental Frankish culture percolated or was thrust in the eleventh and twelfth centuries.[1] Yet, it is evident that any re-structuring that took place was neither total nor exclusive, for it accommodated much of the pre-existing mechanisms into what became a hybridised construct and functioned alongside native systems with no clear evidence for conflict, confrontation or collision. Indeed, the careers of men such as Roland and Alan indicate how smoothly the two traditions could interlock, for while they stood clearly at the apex of a 'feudal pyramid' and moved in a world dominated by Frankish cultural norms, they were equally at home in the Norse–Gaelic society of the maritime west. While they introduced many of the new forms into Galloway, primarily through the personnel whom they implanted within the lordship, it is evident that they made no effort to re-define their relationships with the native nobility, nor attempt to undertake a wholesale re-ordering of the fiscal mechanisms upon which those relationships were based. Duality characterised Galwegian society before 1300.

Documentary evidence detailing the workings of native society, its administrative structure and its fiscal functions, is scanty in the extreme, and in the following much will be built from place-name evidence and from the data fossilised within the records of the ruling classes. The highly complex society that had evolved by the end of the eleventh century had its traceable origins in the pre-Roman Iron Age and its underlying Bronze Age antecedents. But those formative years spanning the era of people movements that followed the Roman withdrawal from Britain remain an area of uncertainty and debate, with recent archaeological work only now beginning to offer insights on this period and adding to our limited knowledge and understanding of it.[2] The great complexity of the population make-up of the south-western peninsula is, however, certain and elements from all the major racial or cultural groups common to Dark Age Britain are represented.[3]

THE LAND: UNITS OF ASSESSMENT

The cultural complexity of medieval Galwegian society is revealed by the evidently conflicting systems upon which the social and economic framework of the lordship was based. In particular, the units of assessment used in land valuation and from which the lords drew their military service and revenues, that can traced through place-name evidence and limited documentary records, show the presence of an array of forms that can be assigned sequentially in either chronological terms, or in terms of the dominance of a particular cultural group. It must be stressed, however, that the record is fragmentary, and that no overall pattern can be determined, although some hints of a system may be traceable in western Galloway, the region most exposed pre-1100 to influences from the Norse–Gaelic world of Mann and the Isles. The fragments that survive from these earlier systems, moreover, are largely submerged in the pattern of assessments that was developed post-1300. This system, based on merkland units, apparently bears little relation to the earlier systems.

The variety of valuation units in Galloway speaks of an eclecticism that may not have been solely the result of its cultural composition. Indeed, it is possible that different elements were drawn from a number of systems and adapted to suit local requirements. Thus, elements more common to north-eastern Scotland, such as *davochs* (literally a 'seed vat'), are found alongside those common in the western Highlands and Islands, for instance the *pennyland*, while in conjunction with these fiscal measures the Anglian *carucate* is found used as a measure of extent or capacity.[4] It is not the intention here to embark upon an extended analysis of the development of these normally opposed systems, but it is necessary in the present context to provide some background.

Two main systems of assessment predominated in northern and western Scotland before the thirteenth century, namely those based on either the davoch or the ounceland (*terra unciata*): a unit of land valuation used for the levying of taxation.[5] Neither system is strictly mutually exclusive, except in Caithness and the Northern Isles where the davoch is not found, and Galloway where the ounceland is absent but its sub-divisions are present. Both systems are based on a graded scheme of smaller elements that possibly developed from an original levy based on households. The ounceland in particular, with its sub-division into twenty pennylands, shows the full development of this graded scale. It is found mainly in areas of Scandinavian settlement, where it is assumed to represent the adaptation of a pre-existing structure to suit the administrative needs of the colonists. The davoch, by contrast, is regarded as a Celtic phenomenon, and appears to be more closely associated with agrarian production than the ounceland, which is more difficult to associate with measures of productivity.[6]

The association of the davoch with agricultural production can be seen mainly in a north-east Scottish context, the bulk of the evidence linking it with the former Pictish heartland.[7] It was believed formerly that its distribution was confined to the region north of the Forth–Clyde isthmus, but place-name research has revealed its presence in Galloway and Carrick.[8] The apparent close link with arable production led McKerral to argue originally that it was specifically an arable measure, but of variable extent in acreage.[9] Such variation was interpreted as a reflection of the quality of the land and the level of advancement of its arable development. The crux of his view was that the davoch represented the collective productive acreage of the arable community. In a later development of his argument, McKerral accepted an administrative function for the davoch, but retained his interpretation of it as primarily a measure of production. He did, however, change his views concerning how it was structured, regarding it instead as a collective entity assessed on a set number of households and forming the basis of liability to certain dues and renders.[10] To facilitate the operation of this scheme, each davoch was divided into *ceathramh* (quarterlands) not necessarily comprising a quarter of its total acreage, but responsible for a quarter of its taxation. This fiscal role for the davoch was later rejected, most notably by Geoffrey Barrow, who instead favoured a strict role as a measure of capacity with a possibility of a set acreage.[11] This is supported by documentary sources from the north-east, in which it is implied that a davoch could be made up of a set number of carucates. Geographical variations in the davoch's acreage have been identified, which range from 416 acres in the north and east of Scotland, down to forty-eight acres in parts of the west.[12] The greater variation in extent apparent in the west might imply that the davoch there was less firmly tied to the concept of a fixed measure and that it held more of a function as a fiscal unit.

The regional variations in size and mode of sub-division point to major differences in the purpose and organisation of the systems. In the west it followed the structure of the ounceland, with sub-divisions into *ceathramh* or individual *pheighinn* (pennyland), themselves lesser fiscal units. The Anglian carucate was unknown in the Gaelic west, but is common throughout eastern Scotland, where Northumbrian influence was strongest. The Gaelic origins of the name davoch, and its easy equation with the ounceland in the west, point to its early development in that region, from whence it may have been brought east by Gaelic-speaking colonists.

Certainly, its application in the north-east in conjunction with non-Gaelic sub-divisions, suggests an adaptation to meet an agricultural organisation radically different from that for which it was originally devised. It is possible, then, that the davoch only gained dominance in the east after the mid-ninth century, when its original homeland was coming under Scandinavian influence. In the former Pictish territories the fiscal davoch underwent metamorphosis to meet the problems posed by a system based on substantial arable districts rather than a notional grouping based on households. This could explain the dual character that the davoch displays, both as a unit of fixed extent and as an expression of the render from that unit.

It is with the fiscal role of the davoch that studies into its development in western Scotland have been concerned. John Bannerman's work on the *Senchus Fer nAlban* has stressed the unit's probable Argyll origins.[13] There, expressed in a somewhat idealised form in the *Senchus*, households were grouped into twenties for the purposes of naval assessment and levies, and it is argued that these units, although never so designated in the text, formed the progenitors of the davoch/ounceland system. The association between the twenty household and twenty pennyland structures appears inescapable.[14] The equation of household and pennyland is strengthened by later charter evidence, as in the grant made *c.*1200 by Raonall mac Somairle to Paisley Abbey of the annual render of one penny from every house in his territories that had a hearth.[15]

The link between the davoch/ounceland systems and naval levies has been questioned in recent research,[16] but there are some pieces of evidence to support the connection. The link may be seen in a letter dated to *c.*1304, from John, earl of Atholl, to Edward I that stated that a certain 'Lochlann' was to raise a galley of twenty oars from every davoch in his possession,[17] with the oarsmen presumably raised from each pennyland. This western and Gaelic character of the davoch, and its probable use as a means of military assessment, may serve to explain its presence in Galloway. The cultural and political relationships between Galloway and the Scandinavian colonies in Ireland, Mann and the Isles established in the tenth century, coupled with evidence for early Gaelic colonisation in Galloway and Carrick, may have provided the means for the transmission of the system into south-west mainland Scotland.

The nature of the Galwegian davoch remains open to question. The sub-divisions into *ceathramh* and *pheighinn* are present, but the dating of their introduction is subject to debate. A later date seems most likely, probably at a time when familiarity with its uses elsewhere had demonstrated the administrative value of such sub-units.[18] The complicating factor in Galloway is the use and existence of carucates, which could date from the period of Anglian domination in the eighth and ninth centuries rather than being introduced with Anglo-Norman colonists in the twelfth century. There must remain a question, moreover, of whether the carucate ever possessed any physical reality in Galloway or if it was simply a scribal fiction created to allow unfamiliar Gaelic land denominational units to be expressed in a form familiar to both clerks and the recipients of the property grants. The presence of *ceathramh* and *pheighinn* in both charters and place-name forms points towards the western-style davoch with its primarily fiscal role, but the fourteenth-century evidence is in direct contradiction of this. Robert I's grant of property in Claunch and Kilsture in the Machars to Richard McGuffog included an award of eight bovates,[19] which represent one carucate or one quarter of a north-eastern davoch of 416 acres. It is possible, however, that exotic nomenclature has been applied to the Gaelic system, or that the king was introducing new methods of land division and assessment into Galloway as part of his radical re-distribution of territory following the victory over the Balliol–Comyn party in the lordship.

This apparently contradictory evidence may point to a blend of systems, with the purely fictional and notional on the one hand and the practical on the other. There is circumstantial evidence for the equation of the Galwegian with the western davoch in the records of the naval power of the lords of Galloway in the twelfth and thirteenth centuries, but the basis on which the fleets were levied and manned is unknown. The presence of davochs, however, may point to a structure akin to that recorded in the *Senchus*, while the geographical proximity of Galloway to Argyll might provide the context for the transmission of the system between these areas.

Place-names containing the davoch generic are restricted mainly to the southern part of the Stewartry, with a small group in Carrick. Only one example is known from Wigtownshire (Map 3). The noun has been corrupted to *doach* or *doch* and figures as both prefix and suffix. It is most frequently found as a farm name; those surviving as topographical elements only may represent its application to a topographical feature rather than its former use in association with a unit of land assessment on the ground locally. The main distribution of davoch names in the south-east of the Stewartry preserves the association of the davoch with arable cultivation. There is only one clear instance in surviving documentation of the grant of a davoch, expressed as a named estate composed of four quarterlands. This was the grant by Dervorgilla Balliol of the four quarterlands of Outon in the Machars to the canons of Whithorn.[20] Lying immediately to the north of Whithorn, this is an area of good mixed agricultural land and in 1473 two of these quarterlands, transmogrified into merklands and supporting touns, still formed important elements within the economic resources of the priory.[21]

LESSER UNITS

The proliferation of place-names in the south-west that relate to sub-divisions of the davoch lends support to the equation of the Dalriadic and

Galwegian units. The main sub-unit is the quarterland or *ceathramh*, which is restricted almost exclusively to the bounds of the lordship (see Map 4). Five-pennyland groupings, equal to a *ceathramh*, also occur in Carrick, such as the lands of 'Donarchualfe' and Beath granted to Whithorn Priory by Duncan fitz Gilbert.[22] The place-name form survives, generally as a prefix in *Kirrie-*, *Kir-* or *Cor-*, very occasionally corrupted to *Kil-* (for example, Killantrae NX 350451, is Kerintray in 1494).[23] Its distribution is mainly in lower lying agricultural districts. The name today is linked primarily with some of the larger farms.

Quarterland divisions are common to both the davoch and ounceland systems, and also to the later Irish equivalent, the *baile-biataigh*. At Outon in the Machars, each quarterland appears to have supported a single toun by the later fifteenth century.[24] Bannerman has shown that the minimum number of households held by the head of a *cenél* was five, and that the household groupings of the *Senchus* are expressed as multiples of that figure.[25] It is noticeable that among Robert I's grants quarterlands or five-pennyland groupings formed the largest single awards to secular beneficiaries made in Galloway.[26] This may imply the survival of some residual notion of status attached to the holders of such units. Even the grant to Richard McGuffog, expressed in terms of bovates, represents a holding of a quarter davoch in its north-eastern form.

The most common unit found in charters and place-names is the single pennyland or *pheighinn*. These have their greatest density in central Carrick and more thinly throughout the lordship proper (Map 5). In place-names it is represented by the prefix *pen-* or *pin-*, and occasionally by the suffix *-fin* or *-phin*.[27] Grants of single pennylands are common from the earlier thirteenth century onwards.[28] The pennyland's prominence as a landholding of men of substance makes its relative lowliness in the scale of fiscal units difficult to accept. Later Highland and Hebridean evidence shows it as a unit of perhaps no more than four acres extent. This contrasts with the thirteenth-century material from Carrick, where the pennyland occurs as a clearly valuable and extensive holding. In the 'extent' of the earldom of Carrick demesne drawn up in 1260, estates such as the fourteen pennyland of Straiton, or the ten pennyland of Drumfad and Glen App were valued at seventy-six marks annually for the former and forty marks for the latter, which gives and annual value of from four to six marks per pennyland.[29] McKerral pointed out that this gave in turn an annual value to the davoch in Carrick of nearly ten times the maximum found in the west Highlands and Islands.[30] This implies, as he went on to argue, that the pennyland in Carrick had lost its purely fiscal meaning by the mid-thirteenth century and had become a vague term applied to blocks of land of varying worth.

As with the davoch, the pennyland in its fiscal sense had apparently no fixed acreage. If it can be equated with the 'household' of the *Senchus*, then presumably it comprised sufficient arable and pasture to support a substantial population. This argues against it being a small unit, and that its

Hebridean transformation into a tiny area paying a fixed rent must be a late development. In some parts of the Isles, it evidently acquired the meaning of a penny-*worth* of land, but in Galloway it preserved its former importance. Certainly, there it came to form named units of apparently variable extent, which contained differing proportions of good and bad land. This probably accounts for the widely ranging values of the Carrick extent. In no instance in Galloway or Carrick can the pennyland be seen to take on the meaning of land of the annual value of one penny of rent.

Where pennylands survive in Galloway and Carrick as place-names, it is mainly as farms in the mixed-farming hill districts. This distribution may reflect recognition, made at the time of their establishment as pennylands, of the unsuitability of such terrain for easy division into larger quarterland units. Individual pennylands may have stood in isolation within the landscape and expanded gradually through assarts into the surrounding marginal, or through acquisition of grazing rights on upland pastures. Through such processes, some pennylands evidently grew into large estates, probably the property of men of some substance in native society, and many times greater in extent than the original pennyland assessment.

A few place-names preserve the memory of smaller units, but such sub-divisions are recorded very rarely in medieval documentation. The two divisions that occur are the half-pennyland (*leathpheighinn*) and the farthingland (*fàirdean*), but their occurrence as place-names is restricted solely to Carrick and Nithsdale (Map 5). The half-pennyland is unknown in Galwegian charter sources, but there is a fourteenth-century record of the grant of a farthingland. This was part of a grant by Robert I to John McNeil of Carrick, of the pennyland of Craigcaffie (Killichaffie in the charter) and the farthingland of Beoch on the eastern shore of Loch Ryan.[31] This rarity in charter sources probably reflects the insignificance of the quarter pennyland in terms of the general land-holding pattern, an eightieth of a davoch being a fairly minor unit. In the Highlands and Islands the *fàirdean* became associated with single acres of land.[32] The one farthingland in Galloway, being a piece of named property – clearly a freestanding unit of some antiquity at the time of its grant by Robert I – that now forms a farm, suggests that like the pennyland in the south-west these fractions had lost their original fiscal role by the end of the thirteenth century and came to possess a far greater value than their original assessed level.

What meaning and interpretation can be placed on this fragmentary evidence is far from clear. It can be seen that the south-western davoch and its pennyland components represented the blending of two systems, probably a reflection of a fairly late date of introduction and development when both the davoch and ounceland systems were fully evolved elsewhere in Scotland. The distribution of the surviving place-names in Galloway and Carrick, with their strongly western bias, may be simply an accident of survival, but it offers alternatively evidence – albeit circumstantial – for close contacts with and integration into the world of the Norse–Gaelic colonies of the west. It is probably no accident that this constitutes the zone of Galloway with clearest contacts with this western maritime world before the 1100s, falling within the sphere of greatest Gall-Gaidhel influence, and forming part of the Manx and Isles-based dominion of Echmarcach in the eleventh century. There is also some indication of Northumbrian influence on the system, with the Galloway davochs being measured also in terms of carucates and oxgangs or bovates, in common with the north-eastern Scottish examples, for which Anglian influence can also be postulated. In both cases, the davoch is linked primarily to arable land.

It would appear that the fragmentary system that can be traced in Galloway represented the fiscal structure upon which the wealth of the lords of Galloway and their immediate predecessors was founded. The use of the pennyland in particular points towards a taxation system akin to that used within the territories of the earls of Orkney or kings of Mann. In Galloway, however, there also appears to be some affinity with the earlier Dál Riatan ship-levy system, with the Galwegian davoch fulfilling the role that the ounceland came to occupy in the Gaelic west. There is, however, no clear link to the *leidanger* system of naval assessment and levy that was developed by the Norwegian crown. The davoch in Galloway, with its basis in twenty pennyland groupings, can be equated with the ounceland elsewhere. It is possible that the pennyland system was grafted on to an older, underlying pattern of davochs, possibly as late as the twelfth century, when Galwegian naval power began to emerge as a major force in the Irish Sea world. Certainly, it had been adopted as the principal fiscal mechanism in Galloway by the beginning of the thirteenth century.

STRUCTURES OF SOCIETY

The notional fiscal divisions of the land were of great relevance in the relationship of lords and vassals, for they formed the basis for the assessment and levying of services, dues and renders owed to superior lords. For the bulk of the populace, however, they probably had little meaning or relevance. Certainly, the fiscal impositions that they brought had to be borne alongside cain and, from the twelfth century, teind, but the units themselves were a largely administrative fiction that often lacked reality on the ground. The groups of agricultural communities – the basic elements in Galwegian rural society – from which the fiscal divisions were constructed, represented the reality in which the majority of the population moved.

Any attempt to gain a comprehensive overview of the pattern of estates and their component farm settlements in Galloway is restricted by the highly fragmentary nature of the surviving documentation. Individual units can be traced in isolation, but the charters give little indication of organisational mechanisms or of the social activities of the farmers themselves. Groups of charters, such as those relating to Holyrood Abbey's estate at Dunrod or Holm Cultram's grange at Kirkgunzeon,[33] are rarities in that they give quite extensive information concerning the build-up of the properties, but even these contain little of the minutiae of estate management. In the absence of written sources, therefore, place-name and archaeological evidence represent the principal sources for any examination of Galwegian rural society in the period *c.*1000–1300.

Agricultural activity in Galloway can be traced from the neolithic period, when migrants from continental Europe settled the region. The medieval faming tradition, however, has more recent roots in the practices of the amalgam of Celtic and Germanic peoples established in Galloway in the post-Roman period. The Brythonic roots of much of the early agrarian system are explicit in the place-name forms, still visible through the later Germanic and Gaelic overlay. The Germanic Anglian naming elements are likewise visible, and settlement is recorded by a spread of names across the fertile southern districts. The Scandinavian elements are less clearly associated with the good farming districts, although the concentration of their settlements in the Machars might indicate efforts to acquire good land.[34]

British settlement names have been the subject of a number of studies, which have shown trends of development from forms indicative of defended settlements (e.g. *cair*), through to unenclosed homesteads (e.g. *tref*).[35] These names point towards the development of a dispersed settlement pattern, with the bulk of the population occupying homesteads of a non-defensive nature, rather than an entrenched population clustered in fortified sites. Fieldwork within Galloway, necessary for the establishment of some indication of the distribution of these early sites, has been undertaken to date on only a limited scale, and as yet there is only patchy physical evidence for the shape and density of the post-Roman native British settlement pattern in the region. Clear social stratification, however, such as this place-name hierarchy might reflect, can be identified in the archaeological record. A single example of possibly lower status settlement of apparently second-century date has been excavated at Moss Raploch in the upper Dee valley.[36] The simple unenclosed hut circle there stands in sharp contrast to the contemporary massive rectilinear earthworks at Rispain near Whithorn, which enclosed a substantial and evidently high-status agricultural community, or the as yet enigmatic settlement and possible shrine at Buittle.[37] Much more work needs to be done to build such isolated examples into a meaningful pattern.

Archaeological evidence on post-Roman Iron Age sites in Galloway is severely limited, which prevents the clear establishment of links between earlier centres, such as Rispain, and their apparent successors. Excavation has been largely limited to three sites, the fortified centres at Mote of Mark and Trusty's Hill, both of which were occupied in the sixth century by native British elites, and the major ecclesiastical and possibly commercial centre at Whithorn.[38] The development of fortifications at the two former sites should probably be seen as an indication of their place in the social hierarchy, fortification being one of the most unequivocal symbols of lordly power throughout history, rather than as simply a response to increased raiding. Raids, however, were a feature of sixth- and seventh-century life, as evidenced by the violent ends experienced at both Mote of Mark and Trusty's Hill.

Evidence from these two lordly centres, in the form of Germanic glass and pottery imported from the continent alongside the moulds for casting high-quality metalwork, indicates a high social status. These forts presumably represented the strongholds of a warrior aristocracy, possibly of tribal chieftains, and are thus atypical of the settlements of the majority of the population. Likewise at Whithorn, where there is evidence for the colonisation of the site by a community with strong western Gaulish links, this is a high-status community with a material culture and social organisation unlikely to be characteristic of the native norm. Low status sites of similar date, however, are as yet unknown in Galloway, although fieldwork in Wigtownshire has revealed large numbers of unenclosed huts associated with field systems, some of which must be contemporary with the high-status communities.[39]

Most known examples of hut circles in Galloway survive in marginal districts, a distribution most probably the result of fortuitous survival. Obliteration through modern agricultural and forestry operations does not entirely explain their absence from the Galloway lowlands. This dearth may be explained in part by the use of crannogs rather than land-based dwellings, and, indeed, the former plethora of marshy lochans in Galloway favoured the development of that class of monument. Crannogs in Carlingwark Loch (NX 765615), Milton Loch (NX 839718), Dowalton Loch (NX 4074) and Black Loch (NX 114612), have produced artefactual evidence for occupation into the Roman period, while at Lochrutton (NX 898730), the Iron Age crannog was occupied into at least the thirteenth century.[40]

The nature of the rural economy within which these sites operated is an area of continuing debate. The traditional view up until the 1970s, based on the limited work undertaken in the Scottish uplands, inclined towards a pastoral economy, which practised only limited arable cultivation. This interpretation was characterised at one extreme by Stuart Piggott's description of a socially fragmented culture of 'Celtic cow-boys and shepherds, footloose and unpredictable, moving with their animals over rough pasture and moorland',[41] an image reinforced by the presentation of such a pastoral society in the Irish epic poem *Táin Bó Cuailgne*. The advent of aerial photography as a significant archaeological tool, however, has exploded the myth through demonstration not only of the former intensity of early settlement in what are still the primary agricultural zones of the country but also of the former presence of substantial zones of cultivation in what are now marginal uplands, grasslands and moor. The emphasis is currently directed towards the evidence for arable cultivation, which has drawn further support from the physical remains of ploughs, quernstones and carbonised grain from excavated sites. Pollen analysis, however, has produced no clear picture, as yet, of the nature of the Galwegian landscape and the intensity of agriculture in the early historic period, although in some areas of the Galloway highlands there is evidence for a programme of forest clearance followed by the development of grasslands rather than a shift into cereal cultivation.[42]

Clearer evidence for the development of large-scale arable cultivation in the fifth century AD has been found at Whithorn. There, significant numbers of plough pebbles, used in mouldboard ploughs to prevent the rapid wearing of the wooden foot, have been recovered from securely datable contexts, as have fragments of two millstones from a substantial, probably water-driven, mechanical mill.[43] The practice of intensive arable cultivation at this site, however, might reflect its evidently superior technological development in this phase of its occupation, itself possibly attributable to the presence here of a community of émigrés from western Gaul who introduced late Roman agricultural techniques, building traditions and industrial methods through their monastery. Until Whithorn can be placed into a wider context in the local and regional settlement pattern through large-scale excavation of other sites in Galloway, we are forced to rely upon the limited evidence from field surveys and place-name studies that indicate a largely pastoral economy. The possible uniqueness of Whithorn is underscored by the absence of evidence for the higher altitude cultivation known in the eastern Borders, but the wetter climate of Galloway may always have rendered the local uplands less suitable for arable cultivation. Where there is evidence for human activity in these zones, forest clearance evidently led to the establishment of open grasslands rather than fields of cereals. Such evidence is complemented by the absence of remains of clustered settlements and field systems, which points towards a dispersed society based predominantly on livestock management.[44]

Changes in the basic social and economic structure may have been triggered by the arrival of Gaelic-speaking colonists in the region, possibly as early as the fifth century AD. No settlement types of diagnostically Gaelic form have yet been recognised, and the known early Gaelic place-names are topographical in nature. Nicolaisen has argued for an early spread of Gaelic from early colonies, and proposed that the language and culture had become established throughout the region by c.800.[45] Serious doubts, however, must be cast on his chronology, as two of the generics selected to illustrate his hypothesis, *cill* (a church) and *baile* (village or farm), remained in common usage as name-forming elements throughout the Middle Ages. Irish evidence suggests that *baile* may not have developed as a significant settlement generic until the twelfth century.[46] Certainly, in Galloway, names in *bal-* (the common anglicised contraction of *baile*) continued to be coined in the fifteenth century, e.g. Balmaclellan.[47] It is probable that the chronological position of *baile* and the associated *achadh* (field) elements used to support Nicolaisen's argument, should be pushed forward. A date in the tenth century, which would place these names in the context of both the progressive Gaelicisation of Southern Uplands Scotland and the spread of Gall-Gaidhel influence from Ireland and the Isles into Galloway, would accord better with the chronology offered for these generics in Ireland.

Regardless of dating controversies, these Gaelic generics remain of value as evidence for the development of a Gaelic-speaking culture in Galloway. The density of their distribution, moreover, testifies to the degree of settlement and social domination gained over the underlying British culture. The two elements, *baile* and *achadh*, chart the intensification of settlement, with the former representing primary communities and the latter, a topographic generic that acquired a habitative meaning, representing settlement infill within its bounds. Thus, the formerly non-habitative *achadh*, which referred to the fields associated with the *baile*, came to be applied to new communities that represented sub-divisions of the old. Such a development, however, must surely represent a late stage in the evolution of the Gaelic settlement pattern and is, perhaps, more likely to be a feature of the thirteenth-century population boom and the associated expansion and intensification of arable cultivation which can be recognised throughout the British Isles.

One of the difficulties with the traditional dating of the spread of Gaelic in Galloway is that it appears to have been contemporary with the Northumbrian period of political and ecclesiastical domination of the region. It can no longer be claimed that the Northumbrian colonisation of Galloway was small-scale or superficial, for detailed analysis of the place-name evidence has revealed evidence for administrative structures, ecclesiastical systems and peasant settlement throughout the country west of the Nith.[48] What the distribution of the surviving names demonstrates is a successful cultural domination of the main centres of political, ecclesiastical and economic power in Galloway, concentrated primarily in the lowland districts of southern Kirkcudbrightshire, the Machars and the Rhinns, but spreading also up the major river valleys of the Dee, Ken and Cree. It is a significant feature of the medieval political landscape of Galloway that it was the centres of power established or controlled by the Angles that continued to dominate the region into the fourteenth or fifteenth centuries. Locations such as Buittle (OE *bōtl*, a lordly hall), that came to form the centre of Balliol power in Galloway in the later thirteenth and fourteenth centuries, or Erisbutil on Loch Ken, which formed part of the Douglas demesne in the 1450s: Cruggleton, the seat of political power west of the Cree down to *c.*1300; or Whithorn (OE *Hwiterne*, the White House); all functioned as the nodal points in the Northumbrian power structure. This could be taken as evidence for the imposition of a relatively small elite lording it over a conquered peasantry, but there is also evidence for the establishment of an English-speaking free peasantry in some areas, their presence marked by Carleton place-names (OE *ceorla-tūn*, free-peasant farm). How dense that settlement was, however, remains a moot point, for it is likely that some Anglian settlement names disappeared in the later ninth and tenth centuries.[49]

Physical evidence for Northumbrian secular settlement is extremely scanty, with few sites identified, let alone excavated. At Buittle, little trace of the Anglian presence from which the site derives its name has been recovered in the course of the current excavations.[50] At the Mote of Mark the Anglian occupation formed a brief coda to the Brittonic settlement, while at Cruggleton the possible Anglian hall complex is much disturbed by later medieval structures.[51] Again, it is Whithorn that provides the bulk of the evidence for the Anglian settlement of and economic structures in Galloway. While this was an episcopal and monastic centre, and as such would clearly depart in its physical layout from what might be expected at secular sites, it nevertheless possessed many of the attributes of secular lordship. In particular, it would appear to have lain at the heart of a complex of scattered manors, their location revealed in part through the distribution of the so-called Whithorn School of sculptured stone crosses in the Machars.[52] These crosses are located at or near what may have been Anglian manorial centres, the economic network that supported the high-status community at Whithorn. The dispersed nature of the cross distribution points to a 'multiple estate', a characteristic of Anglian secular and ecclesiastical lordships, where the property of the lord was scattered over a wide geographical area rather than focused on a single centre. The existence of such a support structure at Whithorn can be inferred from what is known of the landed estates of both the later medieval Praemonstratensian priory at Whithorn and the bishops of Whithorn, and also from material recovered during the excavations of the site. Bone remains from the Anglian midden deposits were remarkable for the limited variety of animal species identified and, more strikingly, for the age of the animals and the portions of the anatomy recognised. The skeletal remains showed that the beasts had been butchered into joints, and that young animals in particular had been selected.[53] This may be evidence for the render of foodstuffs and young live animals from the ecclesiastical estates, a form of payment that is known from charter evidence to have occurred at monastic communities in Anglo-Saxon England,[54] and the quantities recovered argue against this being the produce of the immediate environs of the community only. Joints of venison feature prominently in the bone remains, and this might indicate renders in kind from outlying estates, perhaps involving rights to shares in hunting. Grants of such rights to monasteries are recorded locally in the twelfth century, for example Uhtred's gift to Holyrood of the teind of his hunting in Desnes Ioan.[55] At Whithorn, this speaks of highly developed administrative mechanisms and the economic exploitation of an extensive manorial complex. If, as has been argued by Brooke, the later rulers of the region inherited control of significant portions of the Anglian administrative framework within Galloway, then here we can gain some indication of the underlying economic support mechanisms on which the lords of Galloway maintained their household and dependents.[56] Brooke has pointed to the existence of at least two shire units in Anglian Galloway – east and west of the Cree – which, as with their counterparts in the heartlands of Northumbria, would have formed the fiscal entities for the assessment and render of customary dues – military service, food-rents and hospitality – which, in the form of military service, cain and conveth, or 'sorran and fathalos', were still being levied in Galloway into the fourteenth century.[57]

Whithorn's place at the heart of an extensive network of agricultural and pastoral production may have seen it develop a new centrality as a commercial and industrial centre in the tenth and eleventh centuries. On the lower south-facing slopes of the hill occupied by the ecclesiastical complex, fringing the marshy ground that lay between the monastery and the dry ridge later occupied by the medieval burgh, archaeology has identified a localised 'industrial' complex that specialised in the manufacture of combs using bone and antler.[58] Peter Hill has pointed to the traditional identification of comb-making as an urban trade, which at Whithorn might signify the development of the secular community associated with the ecclesiastical complex into a more commercially organised entity. Its main significance, however, is in demonstrating its ability to command and exploit elements of the resources of the established support network of the Anglian community.

This development at Whithorn may be linked to the increasing influence within Galloway of Scandinavian and Norse–Gaelic settlers from the later ninth and through the tenth century.[59] While the material evidence from archaeology for the integration of either Whithorn or the Machars more generally into the commercial nexus of the Dublin-dominated Irish Sea is still slender, strong support for this development is offered by historical sources and place-names. As discussed in Chapter 1, the Scandinavian place-names within Galloway point to a comparatively late – tenth-century – colonisation and one that was strongly localised. There are, however, indications that the hybridised Norse–Gaelic culture imported along with these colonists had a more profound impact on the social and economic structures of the region. The rapid proliferation of Gaelic naming forms from the tenth century onwards suggests quite strongly that the incomers represented a secondary colonisation from primary settlements in the Gaelic west or Ireland, while certain of the generics indicate clearly that they brought with them a system of pastoralism from their primary settlement area. The significance of the key generic *airigh* (a shieling) was outlined in Chapter 1, though its broader importance will be considered here.

Airigh represents the adoption of a Gaelic Irish or Hebridean term by non-Gaelic settlers, and with it the adoption of the dairy-based pastoral economy of the Gaelic west. It has a widespread distribution throughout

Galloway, Mann and the English Lake District, where the common link has been identified as Norse and Norse–Gaelic settlement after *c.*900 as part of the diaspora of colonists attendant on the expulsion of the Scandinavians from Dublin. The origins and growth of the *airigh*/shieling system has been analysed in depth in various regions, but especially in Mann and the Lake District.[60] Eleanor Megaw demonstrated the Gaelic origins of the Manx *eary*, and proposed a pre-Norse origin for the majority of those that developed into permanent settlements. Her early dating for such sites is based on the assumption that Gaelic was already the dominant language in Mann before *c.*900 and that the incoming 'Scandinavian' settlers were Norse speakers rather than already a predominantly Gaelic-speaking group. The absence of *sætr* names (the Old East Norse equivalent term), was used by Megaw to support her theory, who interpreted its non-appearance as evidence for the prior existence of a fully evolved shieling system that the new settlers simply took over absoring the Gaelic terminology with it into their own culture. It is as likely, however, that the new arrivals in the late ninth and tenth centuries were already Gaelic-speaking, and either introduced the Gaelic names to an existing system or developed a transhumance economy along the lines of that which existed in their Hebridean and Irish homelands. Both *sætr* and *eary* occur in the Lake District, which may indicate that the latter had not entirely supplanted its Scandinavian counterpart in the vocabulary of the colonists arriving in that region. *Sætr*, however, is entirely absent from the place-name record of Galloway, which, as in Mann, might indicate a pre-Norse development for the shieling system, or, more probably, emphasises the late arrival of Norse–Gaelic settlers in Galloway and that the Gaelic-speaking character of their hybridised culture was already established early in the tenth century.

Leaving aside the question of dating, Megaw's research produced two distinct groups of evidence. Firstly, there are current *eary* names, now in enclosed farmland, that indicate the prior existence of a shieling, and secondly there are un-named, abandoned sites. The former lie mainly around the 200m contour towards the limits of cultivation, and are generally recorded in the earliest Manx estate records. Many continue to function as hill farms. Manorial records reveal a past existence as upland holdings, commonly linked to a lowland farm. Many *eary* names of this type have personal names as the specific element, which implies individual possession by substantial free landholders. Less can be said about the un-named abandoned sites. These survive mainly as shieling mounds in open moorland – phosphate-rich green hummocks comprising the tumbled remains of drystone and turf huts together with the midden debris associated with human occupation – and lie well beyond the limits of modern enclosed farming, normally between the 300 and 350m contours. None developed into a permanently occupied farm.

Manx documentation showed that the named *earys* developed throughout the Middle Ages, with many having become permanent farms rather than seasonally occupied shielings by *c.*1500. Significantly, some are recorded as *treens* (the local term for an ounceland, representing a corruption of the Gaelicised *tirunga* from the Latin *terra unciata*), which signifies considerable value in their own right. In all cases where the *eary* is valued as a *treen*, the settlement is associated with a *keill* (chapel). There is a clear association between *treens* and *keills*, which may date from the formative years of the valuation system based on ouncelands. Where an *eary* appears as a *treen* and possesses a *keill*, an early date for its development into a permanent settlement can be postulated. Megaw implied that where such transformations had occurred, the origin of the specific *eary* was probably pre-Norse. The development into a permanent settlement may have been triggered by Norse colonisation, which put pressure on the available land and led to an infilling of the settlement pattern and a move to occupation of the lower altitude shielings on a permanent basis. The bulk of these lie near to the primary arable zone, which Megaw compared with the later Norwegian and Scottish 'home-shieling', which was used in spring and autumn when poor weather had stopped grass growth at higher altitudes and rendered the upland shielings unusable for pasturing. The un-named upland sites, therefore, may be the original summer pastures, occupied for only a few months annually.

Galwegian sources lack the detail of the Manx estate records. Documentation concerning the *airie* or *airy*, as the Galwegian sites were known, does not survive before 1500. Most named *airigh* sites in Galloway are now long-established farms, but some are attached to unsettled areas of land. The physical distribution of the Galwegian form is closely similar to its Manx counterpart, with none being sited above the 250m contour and most lying towards the modern limits of arable cultivation on good pasture land. The majority are found in Wigtownshire, particularly in the Machars where areas of arable are interspersed with higher tracts of rocky ground. In the Stewartry, they are restricted to the parishes with a high proportion of mixed agriculture, e.g. Kelton and Rerrick (see Map 6). In both the Machars and the Stewartry, there is a marked correlation between the *airigh* names and the known sphere of Norse settlement. This is clearest in the Machars, where the *airigh* names lie in an arc to the west of the similar arc of Norse settlement names around Whithorn, or along the western fringes of the Bengairn Hills to the east of the area of Norse settlement around Kirkcudbright.[61] In these cases, the modern *airigh* farms may have originated as shielings associated with lowland farms in the Dee valley and the arable lowlands of the Machars. The link between a lowland settlement and hill pasture can be seen most clearly in the parish of Kircolm in the northern arm of the Rhins peninsula. The parish straddles the peninsula, with the higher and exposed western district being predominantly grassland, while the eastern area, from which it is divided by a range of low hills, was chiefly arable. The western area is called Airies, sub-divided in modern times into the farms of Mains of Airies and Little Airies. These must surely have originated as the summer pastures used to keep the dairy herds away from the ripening cereal and hay crops on the east side.[62] Although there is no corresponding Scandinavian settlement name in the east of Kirkcolm parish, the cross-slab from Kilmorie displays some Scandinavian sculptural influences that may represent some level of colonisation of the area.[63] The linguistic structure of the Galloway *airigh*-names is almost exclusively Gaelic, which provides fairly conclusive evidence for the cultural context in which they were formed. This, despite the absence of *sætr* names, is not conclusive evidence for a pre-Norse origin, and may instead reflect name-forming at a time when the Norse population of the Western Isles, Mann and Ireland had lost its distinctive Scandinavian identity and adopted many aspects of Gaelic culture, including the Gaelic language.

TWELFTH- AND THIRTEENTH-CENTURY ECONOMIC DEVELOPMENT

It was from the cultural mix outlined above that the medieval farming society of Galloway evolved. Together with regional topography and the limitations imposed by climate, it produced a complex pattern, where systems of transhumance that supported a pastoral economy geared in some areas principally towards dairying were juxtaposed with zones of intensive arable cultivation. This was a pattern that survived down to the early nineteenth century, but has since been lost in the successive programmes of progressive enclosure of the Galloway landscape and commercial re-afforestation of the uplands. Little detail survives of the local workings and peculiarities of the system, for, other than the charters by which land was granted to secular and ecclesiastical lords, nothing by way of estate records remains from before the later fourteenth century. Nevertheless, even from these rather formulaic documents it is possible to recover a considerable amount of highly illustrative material.

The bulk of the twelfth- and thirteenth-century documentation lies within monastic cartularies, particularly those of Holyrood, Holm Cultram and Melrose abbeys. The surviving Holyrood charters are not greatly informative about the management of the abbey's two main Galwegian estates, Dunrod and Galtway. It appears from the charter evidence that both were co-extensive with the early parishes, which consisted of compact blocks of territory centred on the cultivable areas around nucleated settlements, with extensive upland pasture hinterlands.[64] At both sites the villages' nuclei were abandoned in the late Middle Ages and their former lands given over almost solely to pasture. This has resulted in the survival of considerable earthwork remains at both sites. At Dunrod, most of these are probably late medieval in date, as the village maintained a precarious existence into the seventeenth century.[65] Two key elements in the surviving layout, however, the former parish church and a large ditched earthwork enclosure, certainly belong to the medieval period, the former datable on both charter evidence and the art historical evidence of the style of its late Romanesque font to the mid-twelfth century. The ditched enclosure was excavated in part in the 1960s and was demonstrated by the high quality of the pottery recovered to have been a site of high status, possibly a 'manor-house'.[66] Occupation on the site was shown to commence before the beginning of the thirteenth century and to have continued down to the sixteenth century, when the buildings appear to have been abandoned. The enclosure lies away from the main village area, which is situated immediately adjacent to the west side of the churchyard, and appears to have been inserted into an already established pattern of cultivation. Its date, as indicated by the artefacts from its excavation, together with its comparative remoteness and absence of focality to the village nucleus, suggests its development as a new administrative centre for the former lordly demesne estate after its grant to the canons of Holyrood. As early as 1161–64, Máel Coluim IV extended the protection of the Scottish crown to the canons' men who were being sent out to reside in and develop their recently acquired possession, confirmed their rights to the advowson and lordship of the parish and land, and prohibited anyone to remain on the property against the will of the abbot and canons.[67] This could be read as an attempt to enforce vacant possession, with the canons planning to introduce an agricultural colony onto the land, but it is more probably simply an enforcement of the abbey's rights of lordship, which it may have found difficult to exercise in the disturbed conditions of the early 1160s. That this became an estate centre of some importance to the canons is supported by a mandate of Alexander II, dated 1246, that confirmed the right of the abbot and convent of Holyrood to hear pleas in a court held at Dunrod, and prohibited the 'heirs of Galloway' or their bailiffs from interfering with the holding of that court.[68] Such a privileged franchise ensured the fullest economic exploitation of the property by its lords.

Material concerning Holm Cultram's land at Kirkgunzeon adds detail to this outline image of economic exploitation and exercise of seigneurial rights at Dunrod. While no physical remains have been identified of the grange complex that lay at the core of the property, from Kirkgunzeon some indication can be obtained of the functioning of the rural economy. The estate was a landlocked expanse of mainly upland moor and lowland scrub and, until the draining of the boggy lowlands in the later eighteenth and nineteenth centuries, was primarily pasture. From the outset, pig rearing and sheep farming rather than cereal cultivation was planned, and by the later twelfth century pig herds of up to 500 head were permitted to forage in the demesne woods of the lords of Galloway that lay adjacent to the grange.[69] The importance of pigs to the economy of medieval Galloway is generally overlooked, but their significance is underscored not only by the

Kirkgunzeon example, but also by Gillebrigte's offers to Henry II of tribute in cash and kind, which included the annual render of 500 pigs. Dundrennan Abbey was also involved in pig farming in the twelfth century, and came to an agreement with Holm Cultram over rights to graze on the mast in the demesne woods of the lords in Desnes Ioan.[70] The dispute resolved by this settlement, however, was concerned principally with conflicts over sheep grazing, and it was this form of animal husbandry that can be seen to have developed rapidly in later twelfth- and thirteenth-century Galloway.

Between 1161 and 1174, Holm Cultram was actively seeking to acquire land to the west of the Nith on which to expand its sheep flocks. Its lack of grazing land led to its entry into a feu-ferme arrangement with Uhtred for Kirkgunzeon – this was a commercial lease, not a pious grant by the lord of Galloway.[71] Holm Cultram's opportunism brought it into conflict with Dundrennan, which was also seeking to expand its grazings but which evidently lacked the influence with Uhtred to secure new land. The dispute was settled in a private deal between the abbeys, which permitted Dundrennan alone to acquire new land to the west of the Nith, while both, with the agreement of the other, could seek new properties east of the river. At this time, Dundrennan did not possess a grange outwith its original demesne estate in Rerrick parish, but had acquired one in Kirkpatrick Durham parish, to the north of Kirkgunzeon, before the 1270s.[72] The desire to expand sheep flocks on the parts of these monastic communities may have stemmed originally from domestic demand for sheepskin for the manufacture of parchment and wool for the clothing of the monks, but by the end of the twelfth century was driven largely by the huge profits to be made from wool in the commercial marketplace. Wool production boomed in the thirteenth and fourteenth centuries to meet the demands of the cloth-producing centres of Flanders and Italy, but it was not just monastic suppliers who sought to capitalise on this expanding market, for secular lords and peasant farmers were not slow to recognise the economic potential in sheep farming.

By the mid-thirteenth century, Dundrennan was exporting wool through England, and at the end of the century Sweetheart was similarly engaged, complaining bitterly to the English authorities about the seizure of eight and a half sacks of its wool.[73] It is clear that all three Galwegian Cistercian monasteries were important centres of wool production, although none operated on the scale of Melrose or Newbattle. The accounts of the fourteenth-century Italian merchant Francesco Pegolotti, show Dundrennan and Glenluce as producing fifteen sacks of wool apiece annually, which was half of that produced by Newbattle and just over one-third of Melrose's output.[74] At an estimation of 1000 sheep necessary to produce between four and five sacks of wool, then both Dundrennan and Glenluce were running flocks of at least some 3–4000 head.

The survival of records such as Pegolotti's accounts give a misleading impression of the dominance of the wool production industry by the monasteries. Secular lords and their estate managers were always seeking new ways to maximise the revenue generated on their demesne and were probably equally active from as early – if not earlier – than the monasteries. It is usually assumed that the monastic landlords were the innovators, who developed new forms of economic exploitation, but the monks were themselves largely a product of the secular elites and would have brought their attitudes to estate management and commercialism with them into the monastic communities. No secular estate records survive in Scotland from before the later fourteenth century, but charter evidence makes it clear that the great lords were running significant flocks of their own by the early thirteenth century.[75] Although there is no positive evidence to support this suggestion, it is reasonable to assume that the lords of Galloway were significant figures in the wool-producing economy of Scotland and that wool contributed substantially to the wealth of Roland and Alan in particular. Fourteenth-century evidence, however, makes it clear that the combined clip of the flocks of both secular and ecclesiastical landlords accounted for less than 50 per cent of the total exported, with the majority of sheep and wool being produced by the peasantry.[76] Few indications survive of the scale of the flocks of individual peasants or even of the fermtoun communities that formed the basic unit of peasant economic organisation. Some hints, however, can be extracted from incidental detail in surviving aristocratic charters. For example, in the early 1200s, William son of Gamell, lord of Twynholm, in his grant to the canons of Holyrood of his rights in the church of Twynholm, also gave the canons four acres in the arable of the toun, and one house there with its associated rights of pasture on the common grazing of the community, on which they could graze sixteen sheep and a horse.[77] This did not represent the holding of even a moderately wealthy husbandman, who rented something like fifteen acres, and suggests that flocks of several hundred sheep may have been run by the peasant inhabitants of a toun.

ESTATES AND FERMTOUNS

While individual components of the demesne properties of the lords of Galloway can be identified from the middle of the twelfth century, it is only with the Douglas of Dalkeith rental of 1376 for the barony of Buittle and the accounts of the chamberlain of Galloway for the forfeited Black Douglas estates after 1455 that some idea of the internal structures of these substantial lordly estates can be obtained.[78] Place-names and archaeology, coupled with inferences from the surviving charter sources can, however, again provide some insights on estate organisation before c.1300. The proximity of mottes to early nucleated settlement sites, as at Kelton, Kirkcormack and Twynholm, or the 'manor-house' at Dunrod, indicates that new tiers of lordship were being superimposed upon established agricultural systems and supported by them economically. The Buittle rental reveals that in the later fourteenth century, after the disruptions of half a century of intermittent but savage warfare and the effects of the first great medieval epidemic of bubonic plague, the lands of the barony were divided between some fifteen fermtouns of varying values and extents. Buittle was a large parish, but it is unlikely that this pattern of multiple touns was not replicated throughout Galloway. At Dunrod, for example, while the charter sources speak of only a single 'vill', of which the remains survive around the ruins of the church that formed the nucleus of the parish and estate, it is probable that the nineteenth-century farms that lie scattered around the parish represent the single tenancy units that were constructed from the multiple tenancy touns during the Improvement era in the eighteenth and nineteenth centuries. A similar pattern can be identified in Rerrick, where Dundrennan's demesne estate comprised twelve touns now represented by the main farms of the western half of the former parish.[79] The rents and labour dues of the occupants of these touns would have formed a significant proportion of their lords' revenues, but the landlords also exploited portions of their estate directly for themselves. The main evidence for this lies in the boreland farms, which are the precursors of the 'mains' or home-farms of the post-medieval period. It is generally accepted that the name derives from *bord* or 'table' land, i.e., the mensal lands of the estate. This interpretation has been questioned in England, where it is held by some to refer to land held by bordage tenure, a form of menial tenancy where the lowest class of villein received a cottage from his lord in return for his personal service. Later Scottish evidence, however, supports the first interpretation. For example, an inquest dated 1648 refers to 'the demesne land of Twynholm called Bordland of Cumpstoun', which lies on the west side of the Dee north of Kirkcudbright.[80] The modern farm is Mains of Cumstoun.

In terms of date, the Galloway borelands are probably creations of the twelfth to fourteenth centuries (Map 7). Their close association with the capita of the later twelfth-century lordships suggests their development by the Anglo-Norman knights introduced into Galloway by Uhtred and his heirs. In view of the general trend away from demesne cultivation by the middle of the fourteenth century, and the fragmentation of the early, substantial lordships, it is probable that most were established before *c.*1300.

Angus Winchester's study of bordland/boreland place-names shows that most lay near to the capita of the lordship on good, fertile land.[81] This further clashes with the interpretation of bordland as land held by bordage tenure, which sees such land as frequently comprising assarts from the waste. In general, except where the post-Reformation parish represents an amalgam of pre-Reformation ones, there is only one boreland per parish. Winchester stresses the close relationship between the borelands and the parish nuclei, with the farms in general lying close to the former medieval caput. In such cases as Boreland of Anwoth, Boreland of Borgue and Boreland of Colvend, the mottes themselves lie on the farms of those names, completing the identification between the caput and the mensal lands, which would have formed a discrete block around the lordly residence.

The normal pattern of rural society in Galloway was one of dispersed settlement in a number of small touns spread around the territory of the individual estates. Some of these touns evolved into the larger nucleated settlements of the modern period, but the majority became casualties of the ambitions of improving eighteenth-century landlords, and are now known only from place-names of the successor farms or archaeological remains. Several potentially important archaeological sites are known in Galloway, where the medieval fermtouns were simply abandoned and no single tenancy successor established in their place. The most important are the 'vills' recorded at Dunrod and Galtway in the 1100s, of which the earthworks remains suggest average-sized fermtouns. At Kirkcormack, there is a clear juxtaposition of toun, motte and church, but only slight physical remains survive of the settlement adjacent to the twelfth-century motte. Preston-under-Criffel, the core of a substantial property on the fertile merselands to the west of the Nith estuary, is now marked only by the cross that symbolised its seventeenth-century erection as a burgh of barony with the right to hold a market. Girthon was supplanted in the eighteenth century by the Murrays of Cally's new town of Gatehouse-of-Fleet, while Glasserton was re-located when the Stewart lords of the estate decided to empark the lands around their new mansion, in which the medieval community was located. Twynholm and Sorbie are nowadays the only villages of any significance of earlier medieval origin, the majority of the other small towns and villages of Galloway being of late medieval or modern origin.

The above-mentioned touns came generally to form the central places of compact estates, where the parish and lordship shared the same bounds, and the church or caput in such cases normally lay close to or within the settlement itself. This can be seen at Dunrod, Galtway, Sorbie and Twynholm, where the parish church, the lordship centre, or both, provided a focus for settlement. The physical layout of these settlements themselves, however, is largely unknown. At Twynholm, the medieval settlement lay between the parish church and the motte, probably along the line of what now forms the western end of the main street. William son of Gamell's grant of property to Holyrood gives some indication of the physical division of the fermtoun territory.[82] The land was split between William's demesne, common and land held in severalty. William gave the canons four acres 'in the territory' of the village, meaning within the cultivated land, which he had perambulated and divided from that held by the peasants in the sight of 'responsible men', a house in the village, and a proportionate share in the common pasture and common easements of the community. In a landscape of open rigs, it is unlikely that the canons' land was physically divided from the rigs of the villagers by any substantial barrier, and it is possible that their four acres of arable comprised strips scattered throughout the cultivated area. A holding on this scale was unviable for the canons to run as demesne, even after the development of their cell at Traill to the south of Kirkcudbright, and the property was presumably rented out from an early date.

Divisions between the arable and pasture can still be seen clearly at Dunrod. Most of the earthwork remains here are probably of sixteenth-century date, but there is little reason to believe that they are radically different to the layout of the twelfth-century fermtoun. The focal point, as discussed above, is the twelfth-century church, which occupies a rocky outcrop that rises above the general level of the village area. Surrounding the church is a sub-circular churchyard, bounded on the north and east by a small stream that formed the community's sole source of water. The churchyard is now enclosed by what appears to be a modern boundary wall, but it appears to follow the line of the medieval enclosure. To the west of the churchyard, and running in a broad arc round it, are six artificially levelled platforms that represent the sites of timber-built houses. The platforms average 5m in width by 10m in length, dimensions that suggest a form of longhouse. A second group of three platforms lies roughly 0.5km to the north, on the outer edge of the area of medieval cultivation. There are no traces of tofts or yards at any, but the clustered arrangement of the platforms and the fall of ground away from the broad terrace that they occupy, makes the former existence of such features unlikely. The houses appear to have been unenclosed, although hedge lines or fences may have separated the settled area from the fields and the arable from the adjoining pasture. The rig and furrow lies entirely to the north and east, not around the fermtoun as generally occurs in eastern Scottish examples, and extends up to 1km from the settlement nucleus almost to the boundary with the adjoining parish of Rerrick and Dundrennan's property. The boundary here is formed by a stream, at which was located the post-medieval mill. It is unclear if the medieval mill lay at the same location, for there are some traces of what may have been a milldam and leet on the small watercourse that runs through the village. There are no signs, however, of any substantial mill structure. To the south and west is pasture, with no trace of medieval cultivation, nor any sign of a barrier between it and the adjoining arable. The fermtoun lies between the arable and the pasture, and it is possible that the space formed by the arc of houses and the churchyard wall may have served as a stockyard.

The scale of the settled area at Dunrod does not indicate a substantial population. At most, the surviving late-medieval remains suggest some six to nine households made up the community, which tallies well with evidence from elsewhere in Scotland.[83] The size of the houses, as indicated by the platforms that they once occupied, bears close comparison to the excavated examples from Springwood Park in Roxburghshire, where the later thirteenth-century longhouses averaged 4m by 10m, divided internally into a living area at one end and a byre at the other.[84] Such houses represented the dwellings of the substantial tenant husbandmen of the community, and there would have been smaller, less substantial cottages occupied by the humbler cottars, grassmen (who enjoyed only a share in the common grazing), and landless labourers. With the site at Dunrod providing some idea of the physical form of the Galloway fermtouns, the 1376 rental from the lordship of Buittle offers an insight on the appearance of the rural landscape of the region. This takes shape as an intensively cultivated landscape, broken up into the territories of a series of dispersed fermtouns of some four to eight tenant households. In Buittle, some thirty-eight husbandmen are recorded as renting the fifteen touns, but others may have been sub-tenants of the wealthier and more successful families. Each toun, moreover, would have been supported by a force of smallholders and landless labourers.

In the upland areas, the pattern of settlement is still more dispersed. While touns can be discerned through most of the Glenkens area and in the upper valleys of the rivers Urr, Fleet, Cree, Bladnoch and Luce, the extensive uplands that extended along the border with Carrick were not capable of supporting the forms of husbandry associated with the lowland touns. These, however, were not people-less wastes, for survey work undertaken by the Royal Commission in the west Rhins area has identified various habitation sites of medieval or early post-medieval date located at some remove from the nearest probable fermtoun. These sites range from shieling huts to two or three compartment rectangular and sub-rectangular structures that clearly share a kinship with the longhouse tradition.[85] Few of these structures are recorded as settlements on the earliest detailed maps of the area, dating from the early eighteenth century, which suggests that they were either of very low status – which their scale would otherwise belie – or had been abandoned before that date. None has been excavated and no artefact evidence for dating has been recovered from any of the sites so far recorded. What appear to be isolated farmsteads of this type, however, are on record in the early thirteenth century. For example, Alan of Galloway's confirmation to Durand, son of Cristin, of the grant made to him by Robert, son of Simon of Kirkconnell, of the lands of Mabie and Auchencork in Desnes Ioan, gives a perambulation of the bounds of the property which included such points as 'the path beside the house of Gillek' and the 'stream that runs beside the gate of Gillecoln son of Patin'.[86] These are evidently houses standing apart from the local fermtouns and were clearly of sufficient status to be considered suitable markers on the estate boundary.

The location of properties like these on the peripheries of lordly estates may record the process of expansion of the area under cultivation or grazing. The expansion and contraction of the medieval rural community in this way can be seen in various parts of Galloway in the period down to the early fourteenth century. The most striking evidence relates to the Glenkens, where the campaigns conducted by the Bruce brothers down to *c*.1312 resulted in widespread destruction and de-population. In her examination of the re-colonisation of this district in the later fourteenth and fifteenth centuries, Daphne Brooke has drawn attention to one particular place-name element that apparently charts the process of bringing land from the waste into cultivation or pasture.[87] This is the Gaelic noun *earann* (a share), which survives in the prefixes *arn-*, *ern-*, or *iron-*. The earliest surviving documented mention of an *earann* name dates to 1408, in a charter concerning land in Balmaclellan parish,[88] but the specific elements of several of the names implies the use of the generic at a much earlier period. Certain of the place-names, such as Arnmannoch (the Monks' Share or the Share of the Monks' Vassals, depending on whether the specific is a corruption of *monoch* or *manach*) and Ernespie (the Bishop's Share), point to ecclesiastical involvement in the formation of assarts. Arnmannoch in Kirkgunzeon (NX 858605) lies on land that formed part of the Holm Cultram estate. It is probably to be identified with the 'Clochoc of the Monks' mentioned in a perambulation of the estate in 1289, where it was described as lying across the boundary line from 'Clochoc beg of Culwen'.[89] The modern farms immediately across the old parish boundary from Arnmannoch are Meikle and Little Cloak. A second Arnmannoch lies on the northern edge of Lochrutton parish (NX 888753), and might represent an expansion from Dundrennan's properties centred on Kirkpatrick Durham, immediately to the north. In both cases, the farms lie on marginal grazing land and may represent areas taken out of the waste by monastic estate managers or their tenants.

Evidence from outside Galloway supports the interpretation of *earann* sites as assarted land. In Stirlingshire, in the region of Flanders Moss on the lands of Inchmahome Priory, there is a major concentration of *earann*-names, which include a number that are indicative of ecclesiastical involvement in the reclamation process. Four, Arnprior, Arngibbon, Arnbeg and Arngomerie, lie on the lower slopes the Fintry and Gargunnock Hills, and, with Arntamie in the Menteith Hills, are clearly assarts taken out of the moorland. Arnvicar and Arnclerich, which lie in former marshland on the valley floor, are certainly reclaimed from the Moss.

Moor and woodland reclamation were not the only ways in which land was taken in to cultivation. Inchmahome Priory was reclaiming land from Flanders Moss, and Inchaffray Abbey in Strathearn from the marshes around Madderty. Such ventures reflect in a small way the major programmes of reclamation undertaken by the great East Anglian fenland monasteries, such as Ramsey Abbey.[90] The draining and improvement of estuarine and coastal marshes was another major area of land reclamation. In Scotland, Coupar Angus Abbey's work in the Carse of Gowrie, where they massively expanded the area under cultivation around their grange at Carse Grange, is the best-recorded example of such projects.[91] In Galloway, the work of reclamation was on a much smaller scale, but tracts of coastal saltmarsh were reclaimed. Holm Cultram appears to have deliberately sought possession of areas of saltmarsh, and, using the expertise that it had gained through reclamation of land for grazing from the coastal flats around the abbey, extended its property in Kirkconnel on the Nith through drainage works in the tidal flats.[92] The aim was to gain more pasture, a situation exemplified by the massive works undertaken in Kent and Sussex by the monks of Christchurch Canterbury.[93] The attraction for Holm Cultram in undertaking such work was dual. Land reclaimed in this way, as so-called *novalia*, had been freed from teind by a bull of Pope Innocent II granted to the Cistercian order in general, but it also permitted the expansion of grazing or arable land without having to secure fresh endowments. For the peasantry, assarting was a means of satisfying the increasing demand for holdings, but also offered the opportunity for the maximising of potential profits from the sheep and cattle grazed on this new land, or from the cereal crops cultivated there.

The picture that can be recovered of the rural economy in Galloway in the twelfth and thirteenth centuries is one of steady and unspectacular evolution. The underlying structure of fermtouns grouped into larger economic units appears to have developed largely before 1100 and there is no clear evidence for its substantial development through colonisation after that date. Some internal colonisation through assarting is evident in the thirteenth century, and is probably a local manifestation of the well-recorded Europe-wide expansion of agriculture that resulted from contemporary population and economic pressures. There is more evident change, however, in the basis of the rural economy. From the early 1100s, documentary sources emphasise the importance of animal husbandry throughout the whole of south-west Scotland. Grants such as David I's and Máel Coluim IV's gifts of teinds of their cain of cattle, pigs and cheeses to the church of Glasgow or the monks of Selkirk/Kelso emphasise this pastoral and dairy-based aspect of the economy.[94] This impression is reinforced both through Gillebrigte's offer of cattle and pigs as tribute to Henry II and the table of cattle-based fines for application in Galloway in the aftermath of Roland's takeover.[95] Clearly, cattle formed an important measure of wealth in Galloway, as in Ireland where the size of a man's herd was the chief measure of his social status. By the later twelfth century, sheep were gaining in importance as the trade in wool with Europe developed and, while the main recorded speculators in this lucrative but volatile market appear to have been the monasteries, it is clear that both the secular landlords and the main body of the peasantry were equally enthusiastic participants.

Amid the relative abundance of evidence for the pastoral basis of the Galwegian economy, it is possible to neglect the evidence for a substantial arable element. Here, again, the evidence relating to the main monasteries gives a distorted image, for it would appear from the records of licences granted to the monks of Dundrennan and Glenluce to import grain from Ireland that these abbeys suffered from a dearth of good arable land and lacked access to local supplies of cereals.[96] Thirteenth- and fourteenth-century records, however, demonstrate that wheat, barley and oats were produced on a substantial scale in Galloway's fermtouns,[97] and this monastic trade was probably a consequence of the abbeys' decision to maximise their involvement in the wool trade. A similar course was taken at Melrose, where the arable demesne was run down in favour of increased grazing since the abbey could obtain an abundant supply of grain through the Berwick market. For Dundrennan and Glenluce, the cost of buying wheat through Dublin and Drogheda could easily be offset against the profits from wool.

Fragmentary though the foregoing evidence is, it provides a clear impression of the economic basis for the power of the lords of Galloway in the twelfth and thirteenth centuries. As controllers of the largest complex of estates in Galloway, and with a well-structured fiscal mechanism for its exploitation, Fergus and his heirs, but most particularly Roland and Alan, and ultimately Dervorgilla, commanded wealth that placed them in a league apart from the Scottish nobility. It gave them power and patronage on a quasi-regal level, evident in the surviving buildings of the monasteries that they founded and endowed, and in the scale of the castles that served as their seats of power. Coupled with the military and naval resources at their disposal, it was a wealth that made the lords of Galloway powers to be reckoned with, and as late as the 1450s provided their eventual successors, the Black Douglases, with a formidable foundation for their landed might.

Notes

1 See, for example, Barrow, *Anglo-Norman Era*; McDonald, *Kingdom of the Isles*.
2 E.g., Hill, *Whithorn and St Ninian*.
3 For a discussion of the population make-up, see Oram, thesis, 322–39.
4 Oram, 'Pennyland and davoch', 46–59.
5 Crawford, *Scandinavian Scotland*, 86–91.
6 K. Jackson, *The Gaelic Notes in the Book of Deer* (Cambridge, 1972), 116; R. A. Dodgshon, *Land and Society in Early Scotland* (Oxford, 1981), 75–76.
7 A. C. McKerral, 'Ancient denominations of land in eastern Scotland', *PSAS*, lxxviii (1943–44), 39–80; G. W. S. Barrow, 'Rural settlement in central and eastern Scotland, the medieval evidence', *Scottish Studies*, vi (1962), 123–44; Duncan, *Making of the Kingdom*, 318.
8 J. MacQueen, 'Pennyland and davoch in south-western Scotland', *Scottish Studies*, xxiii (1979), 69–74; B. Megaw, 'A note on "Pennyland and davoch in south-western Scotland"', *Scottish Studies*, xxiii (1979), 75–77.
9 McKerral, 'Ancient denominations', 39–45.
10 A. C. McKerral, 'The lesser land and administrative divisions of Celtic Scotland', *PSAS*, lxxxv (1950–51), 52–64.
11 Barrow, 'Rural settlement', 138–40.

12 Dodgshon, *Land and Society*, 76.
13 J. Bannerman, *Studies in the Early History of Dál Riata* (Edinburgh, 1974), 140–46.
14 W. D. Lamont, '"House" and "pennyland" in the Highlands and Islands', *Scottish Studies*, xxv (1981), 65–76.
15 *Paisley Registrum*, 125.
16 Most notably by D. G. E. Williams, 'Land assessments and military organisation in the Norse settlements in Scotland, *c*.900–1266 AD' (unpublished University of St Andrews PhD thesis, 1996). Williams has postulated links to a system of taxation introduced by the Earls of Orkney, that may have been administered by the Church. This was based on the stable value – one eighth of an ounce of silver – of pennies issued by the Bishops of Cologne.
17 *CDS*, ii, no. 1633; Bannerman, *Dál Riata*, 141.
18 Crawford, *Scandinavian Scotland*, 88–91.
19 *RMS*, i, app. i, no. 101.
20 *RMS*, i, app.i, no. 20.
21 *RMS*, ii, no. 1134. The two touns formed part of a substantial 'golden-handshake' pay-off given to the disgraced former prior, William Douglas.
22 *RMS*, i, app. i, no. 20.
23 MacQueen, 'Pennyland and davoch', 72.
24 *RMS*, ii, no. 1134.
25 Bannerman, *Dál Riata*, 141.
26 *RMS*, i, app. i, nos 20, 102; app. ii, no. 625.
27 MacQueen, 'Pennyland and davoch', 69–70.
28 E.g., *Melrose Liber*, no. 202; *Wigtownshire Charters*, no. 130.
29 I. A. Milne, 'An extent of Carrick in 1260', *SHR*, xxxiv (1955), 46–49.
30 A. C. McKerral, 'An extent of Carrick in 1260', *SHR*, xxxiv (1955), 189–90.
31 MacQueen, 'Pennyland and davoch', 69; *Wigtownshire Charters*, no. 130.
32 Dodgshon, *Land and Society*, 78.
33 *Holyrood Liber*, nos 25, 26, 27, 49, 74; *Holm Cultram Register,* nos 120–41.
34 See Brooke, 'Northumbrian settlements in Galloway and Carrick'; Oram, 'Scandinavian settlement in south-west Scotland'.
35 K. H. Jackson, 'Angles and Britons in Northumbria and Cumbria', in *Angles and Britons*, ed. H. Lewis (Cardiff, 1963), 60–84; W. F. H. Nicolaisen, 'Celts and Anglo-Saxons in the Scottish Border counties. The place-name evidence', *Scottish Studies*, viii (1964), 141–71.
36 J. Condry and M. Ansell, 'The excavation of a hut circle at Moss Raploch, Clatteringshaws', *TDGNHAS*, liii (1977–78), 105–08.
37 A. Haggarty and G. Haggarty, 'Excavations at Rispain Camp, Whithorn, 1978–81', *TDGNHAS*, lviii (1983), 21–51; A. Penman, *Botel Bailey Excavation. Interim Reports* (Castle Douglas, 1994, 1996).
38 A. O. Curle, 'Report on the excavation of a vitrified fort at Rockcliffe known as the Mote of Mark', *PSAS*, xlvii (1913–14), 125–68; A. C. Thomas, 'Excavations at Trusty's Hill, Anwoth, 1960' *TDGNHAS* (1961), 58-70; L. Laing, 'The Angles in Scotland and the Mote of Mark', *TDGNHAS*, 1 (1973), 37–38; Hill, *Whithorn*, Chapter 2.
39 RCAHMS, 'West Rhins', *Archaeological Sites and Monuments of Scotland*, xxiv (Edinburgh, 1985), nos 100–06.
40 RCAHMS, *Galloway*, i, nos 32, 423; idem, ii, no. 201; *PSAS*, lxxxvii (1952–53), 134–52; Tabraham, 'Norman settlement', 87–124; B. A. Crone, 'Crannogs and chronologies', *PSAS*, 123 (1993), 245–54.
41 S. Piggott, 'Native economies and the Roman occupation of North Britain', in I. A. Richmond (ed.), *Roman and Native in North Britain* (London, 1958), 1–27.

42 Cf., Condry and Ansell 'Moss Raploch', 112; J. Jobey, 'Burnswark Hill, Dumfries', *TDGNHAS*, liii (1977–78), Appendix, R. Squires, 'The pollen analysis of a short core from Burnswark Hill', 99–104; H. H. Birks, 'Studies in the vegetational history of Scotland, ii. Two pollen diagrams from the Galloway hills, Kirkcudbrightshire', *Journal of Ecology*, lx (1970), 183–217; H. Nichols, 'Vegetational change, shoreline displacement and the human factor in the late quaternary history of south-west Scotland', *Transactions of the Royal Society of Edinburgh*, lxvii (1968), 145–87.

43 Hill, *Whithorn*, 28–29, 460–61, 464–66.

44 See, Squires, 'Burnswark Hill'; Birks, 'Galloway hills'; Nichols, 'Vegetational change'.

45 W. F. H. Nicolaisen, 'Gaelic place-names in southern Scotland', *Studia Celtica*, v (1970), 15–35; Nicolaisen, *Scottish Place-Names*, 121–48.

46 M. Oftedal, 'Scandinavian place-names in Ireland', in *Proceedings of the Seventh Viking Congress* (Dublin, 1973), 125–33 at 127.

47 Brooke, 'Glenkens', 42; SRO RH6/ii/219.

48 Brooke, 'Northumbrian settlements in Galloway and Carrick'.

49 Ibid., 313–14,

50 Penman, *Botel Bailey. 1997 Interim*, 19.

51 Laing, 'Angles in Scotland', 40-41; Ewart, *Cruggleton Castle*, 14–18.

52 Craig, 'Pre-Norman sculpture in Galloway'.

53 Hill, *Whithorn*, 47, 607–08.

54 Ibid., 608.

55 *Holyrood Liber*, no. 23.

56 Brooke, 'Northumbrian settlements in Galloway and Carrick', 312.

57 Ibid., 312; Barrow, *Kingdom of the Scots*, 7–68. For such renders in action, see *RRS*, vi, no. 235; *RMS*, i, xii-xiv, no. 192.

58 Hill, *Whithorn*, 48–49, 475, 492–93.

59 Ibid., 52.

60 Megaw, 'The Manx "eary" and its significance'; Whyte, 'Shielings and the upland pastoral economy of the Lake District'; Fellows-Jensen, 'Common Gaelic *airge*, Old Scandinavian *aergi* or *erg*?'; Oram, 'Scandinavian settlement names in south-west Scotland'.

61 Oram, 'Scandinavian settlement names in south-west Scotland', figs. 28, 29, 30.

62 MacQueen, 'Gaelic-speakers', 31.

63 Craig, 'Pre-Norman sculpture', 51 and figs 4.3 and 4.5.

64 *Holyrood Liber*, nos. 25, 26, 27, 73.

65 RCAHMS, *Galloway*, ii, no. 217. The font now stands outside the Stewartry Museum in Kirkcudbright.

66 E. F. Burdon-Davies, 'The moated manor at Dunrod, Kirkcudbright', *TDGNHAS*, xliii (1966), 121–36.

67 *RRS*, i, no. 230.

68 *Holyrood Liber*, no. 74.

69 *Holm Cultram Register*, nos 120, 121.

70 Ibid., no. 133.

71 Ibid., no. 120.

72 For Dundrennan's grange, see *RRS*, vi, no. 235.

73 *CDS*, i, no. 2414; idem, ii, no. 1123.

74 Duncan, *Making of the Kingdom*, 230.

75 For the flocks of Patrick, Earl of Dunbar, in 1208 see, for example, *Melrose Liber*, no. 102.

76 Grant, *Independence and Nationhood*, 62–63.

77 *Holyrood Liber*, no. 72.

78 *Morton Registrum*, i, lix–lxi; ER, vi, 191–210.
79 *CDS*, ii, no. 1702.
80 1648 *Inquis. Retorn. Abbrev.*, (Records Commission), Kirkcudbright, no. 250.
81 A. J. L. Winchester, 'The distribution and significance of "bordland" in medieval Britain', *Agricultural History Review*, 34 (1986) pt ii, 129–39.
82 *Holyrood Liber*, no. 72.
83 Yeoman, *Medieval Scotland*, 108.
84 Ibid., 114.
85 RCAHMS, 'West Rhins', nos. 213–29, 231, 233.
86 Stringer, 'Records', no. 47.
87 Brooke, 'Glenkens', 49.
88 SRO RH6/ii/219.
89 *Holm Cultram Register*, no. 255.
90 J. A. Raftis, 'The estates of Ramsey Abbey: a study of economic growth and organisation', *Pontifical Institute of Medieval Studies, Studies and Texts*, 8 (Toronto, 1957).
91 Yeoman, *Medieval Scotland*, 113–14; *Coupar Angus Charters*, i, nos xxxvii, xlvii, lvii.
92 *Holm Cultram Register*, nos 116, 117, 118, 119, 150.
93 R. A. L. Smith, *Canterbury Cathedral Priory: A Study in Monastic Administration* (Cambridge, 1943).
94 *Glasgow Registrum*, no. 9; RRS, i, no. 131.
95 *APS*, i, 378, cc. xxii, xxiii; Duncan, *Making of the Kingdom*, 185–86.
96 *CDS*, i, nos 765, 933, 974, 1891, 2414; idem, ii, no. 182.
97 *ER*, i, 22–23, 151–54.

CONCLUSION: THE FAILED KINGDOM

Myth and tradition play a strong part in modern Galwegian thinking on the history of their land and people. Old ideas die hard, particularly those that paint the story of Galloway in the vibrant but bloody colours of a glorious Gall-Gaidhel heritage, of a mingling of painted Picts and horn-helmeted Viking warriors, and of a magnificent era of power, wealth and independence from the Scots that was ended only through royal deceit and the overwhelming might of Scottish armies. This picture, created over the last 150 years by antiquarian commentators and powerfully reinforced more recently by popular and populist writers, is an attractive but gross distortion of the historical reality. Much of the tradition is spurious, or builds from elaborate hypotheses with little or no basis in fact. Beneath the fiction, however, runs an undercurrent of reality; behind the fables lurk even more colourful facts.

Where tradition and fact run closest is in their agreement on the complexity of the cultural background of the medieval Galwegians and their society. This, however, does not mark out Galloway as a land apart, a unique cultural entity manufactured through a process of hybridisation, but serves rather to set it firmly into a broader context within the multi-cultural world of the northern British mainland and Irish Sea region. Too often in the past, Galloway has been interpreted and presented in a hermetically sealed isolation that seeks to emphasise this sense of difference, a view reinforced by the entrenched particularism of the Galwegians in the later thirteenth and fourteenth centuries, but which proves evanescent when the focus of research is shifted from the narrow bounds of the medieval lordship to the wider political and cultural communities in which it stood. Galloway in the Early and High Middle Ages was never insular or insulated from the world around it, but was a hub, a pivot, and a crossroads that linked the Gaelic north and west to the Anglicised south and east.

In many ways, it was this centrality of Galloway to a region into which greater powers sought to intrude their influence from the early historic period onwards that characterised its history and drove forward its development. From Northumbrians in the seventh and eighth centuries, through the Norse, Irish and Gall-Gaidhel in the tenth and eleventh centuries to English and Scottish kings in the eleventh, twelfth and thirteenth centuries, it was foreign powers that shaped the destiny of the region. Galloway was an area to be controlled, for it dominated the northern Irish Sea, Clyde estuary and southern Hebrides. The ruler of Galloway could control the western sealanes and the trade that flowed along them. It was this potential that led to the creation of the lordship itself in the early twelfth century and gave the lords of Galloway their century of international prominence.

The lateness of Galloway's creation and development, however, may have been the Achilles' Heel that ensured its ultimate failure. By the 1100s, the pattern of political development in the British Isles had begun to crystallise after several centuries of fluidity, and the probable failures and success stories amongst the petty kingdoms and states that had emerged from the chaos of the Viking era can be identified from this point. Indeed, none of the petty, often personal, empires built in the eleventh and twelfth centuries survived as viable, independent powers much beyond 1200. Angevin centralism had moved swiftly to end that threat in its own backyard, curbing the ambitions of Strongbow in Leinster and John de Courcy and Hugh de Lacy in Ulster, and thrusting its lordship into Wales. In Scotland, Somairle's empire had disintegrated on his death and by the 1220s, after decades of debilitating internecine strife and conflict with the Scottish crown and its agents, his brood of sons and their offspring had been sucked into a Scottish orbit. The path taken by the lordship of Galloway had been no less turbulent, the only question had been which of the major political powers in Britain would succeed in drawing it into its embrace.

As the dominant force within the British Isles, England's political, ecclesiastical, cultural and economic influences permeated the archipelago and sucked lesser powers into the vortex of domination. Scotland was still in a fairly embryonic state, despite the comparative antiquity of Gaelic Alba from which the later medieval kingdom was evolving, and only time would tell whether or not it would escape absorption by the English crown. Scotland, though, had several distinguishing features around which an identity could be built, particularly the strong, centralising monarchy that stood at the heart of native and colonial society in the kingdom. The kings of Scots were the founts of a system of laws that gave a sense of identity to the people who lived within its ambit, which, although it drew strongly on the influences of English and French law, was distinctively Scottish. Scotland had, too, a Church with a strong sense of national identity, that the monarchy cultivated and used as a tool to emphasise the unity of people under one king and one spiritual authority. Furthermore, it had a developed and expanding economy that, although linked strongly to that of its southern neighbour, pursued an independent course. Such features, although still developing, gave Scotland the means of establishing its own identity and of maintaining this despite the dominance of England.

The failures in medieval Britain lacked these characteristics. Wales, Mann and Ireland lacked unity and the political and governmental developments attendant on centralising monarchy. All fell under the political domination of the English crown through the twelfth century. All, too, experienced greater or lesser degrees of domination by the English Church, especially by the see of Canterbury. Crucially, all were ultimately dependent on England for their commercial life. Galloway shared this experience. Despite the aspirations of its rulers, it had been drawn into the English political orbit by the 1120s. Its Church was unquestionably suffragan of the see of York; the economic life of the lordship was bound firmly into the zone of English commercial domination in the Irish Sea. From its very origins, Galloway was subject to forces of domination and overlordship that were to ensure ultimate failure. This congenital handicap was compounded by unequal resources, for, although wealthy and powerful in their own right, the lords of Galloway could never command the wealth and manpower at the disposal of the kings of England or Scotland. In a world where might was almost invariably right, this represented a death sentence.

Execution of the sentence, when it came, was at Scottish not English hands. The shifting patterns of power in northern Britain from the later twelfth century had seen Galloway brought increasingly under Scottish domination. Processes of colonisation, by nobles and clerics, had shifted Galloway's traditional pattern of links with northern England to one of alignment with the Scots. The process had been facilitated by the integration of the native ruling house into the ruling elite of Scotland through successive generations of inter-marriage. This reinforced the progressive shift of Galloway's political horizons from an English-dominated south to a Scottish-dominated north and west. Although personal bonds between the nobility of Galloway and England remained strong throughout the thirteenth century and beyond, it was with the Scots that the future for Galloway lay. Once the Scottish crown had consolidated its mastery of the Southern Uplands in the second half of the twelfth century, and had begun to extend its influence into the Clyde estuary lands at the beginning of the thirteenth century, the projection of that influence into the lordship acquired a certain inevitability.

It is easy to lose sight of the encroachment of Scottish domination through the twelfth and thirteenth centuries against the backdrop of the reinforcement of English influence over Galloway from 1174 through to the 1200s, or the glorious Indian Summer of power that marked the apogee of Galloway's greatness under Alan. From the time of Roland, the lords of Galloway were occupying a peculiar position between autonomy and dependence. Except in Irish eyes, they had lost the title and status of kings, and held instead that nebulous catch-all rank of *dominus*. From being masters of their own domain they had become officers of a foreign king, dispensing a foreign justice and fighting for political objectives that were not necessarily their own. Even Alan's final great military adventure, presented in the past as the final flourish of an independent power, was fought in the context of the political ends of the Scottish crown. The processes of integration that turned Galloway into a Scottish province had begun long before 1234.

Perhaps the one surprise is the speed of the end when it came. From the semi-independent status of Alan to the 'feudal' dependence of his successors was just one short step and, although the path between the two was to see one futile rebellion and its heavy-handed suppression, it was a shift that was accomplished with comparative ease. Of course, a king like Alexander II, ruthlessly determined to eliminate all rivals to his power, both dynastic and magnatial, and single-minded in pursuit of his objective of the mastery of north Britain, should not be expected to have shown restraint when such a wonderful opportunity for the extension of his authority was presented to him. Faced with a Scottish king with the resources and the will to end the ambiguity of the century-old relationship between Galloway and Scotland, and having operated already for half a century within the political orbit of the Scottish crown, rebellion was an act of desperation rather than hope in a last-ditch attempt to preserve the integrity and autonomy of the lordship. With hindsight, however, it can be seen that the 1235 rising represented a final act in a process that had begun in the reign of David I and which, despite the bloody intermission of Gillebrigte's ten-year defiance of Scottish authority, had largely been accomplished through peaceful rather than violent means. The very fact that the Galwegians appealed to Alexander II in 1234–35 to provide them with a lord who would preserve the unity of their land gives a graphic confirmation of the degree to which Galloway had been integrated into the Scottish polity by that date. Alan's failure to provide a legitimate male heir in 1234 marked the end, not the beginning, of a process of steady, creeping domination and assimilation that, if anything, had accelerated towards a conclusion during the illusory independence of his reign as lord of Galloway. Alan's personal disappointment was simply a trigger that sprang a long prepared trap.

Table 1: The Lords of Galloway

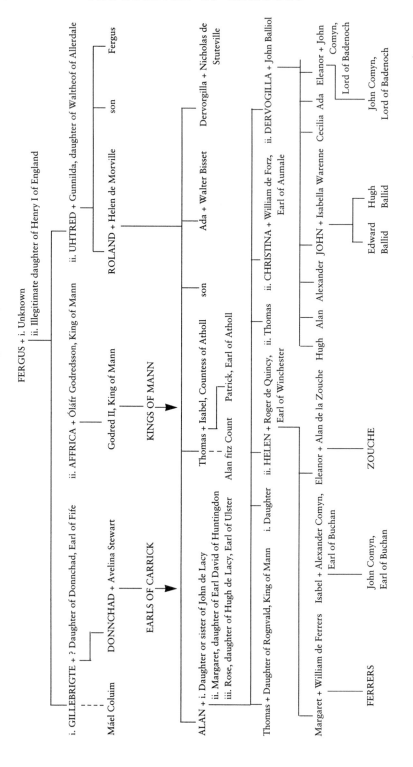

Table 2: Some family connections of Alan of Galloway

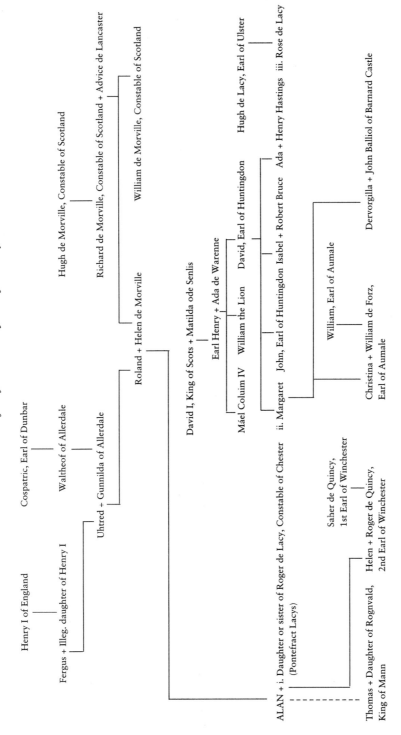

MAPS

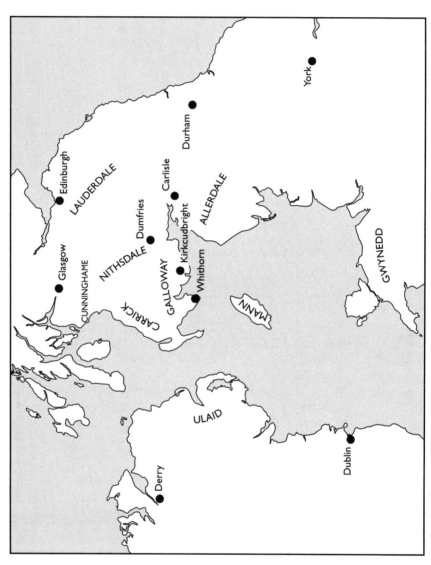

Medieval Galloway and Its Connections

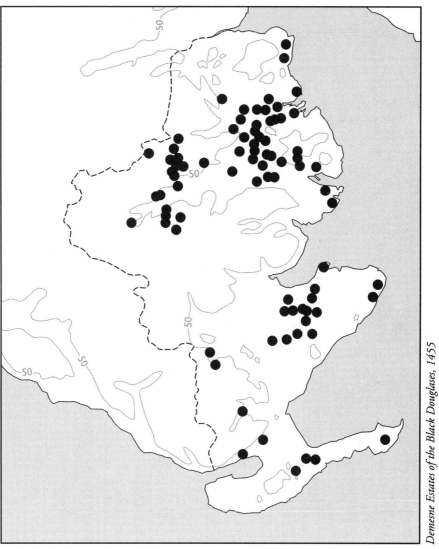

Demesne Estates of the Black Douglases, 1455

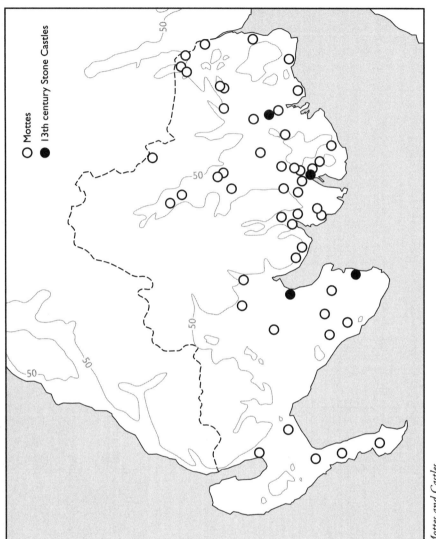

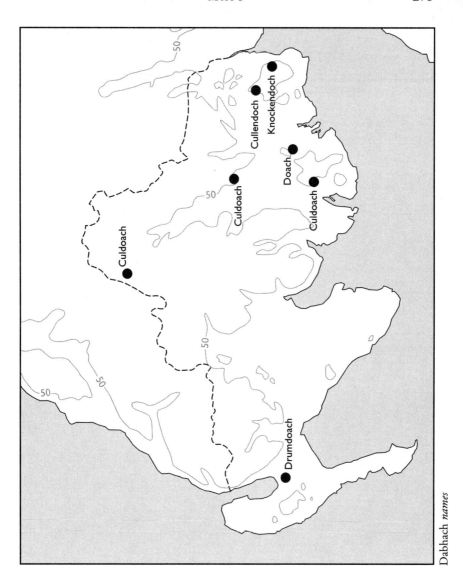

Dabhach *names*

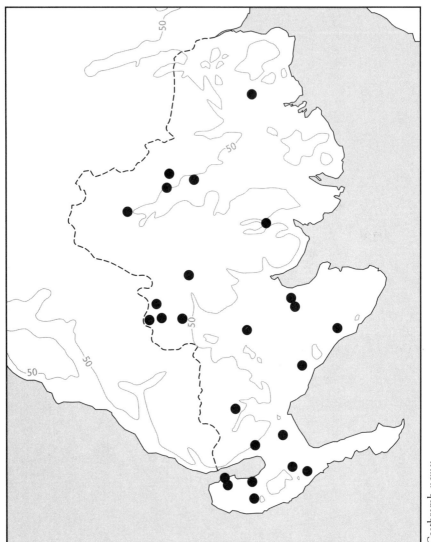

Ceathramh *names*

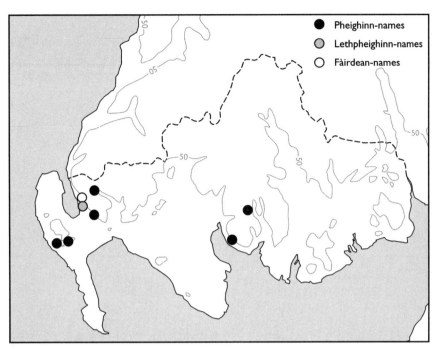

Phaighinn, Lethpheighinn *and* Fàirdean *names*

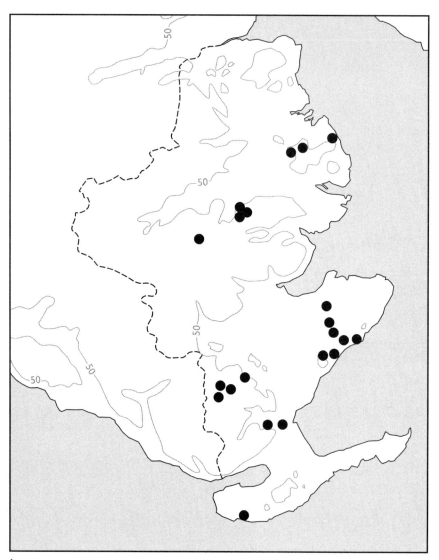

Àirigh *names*

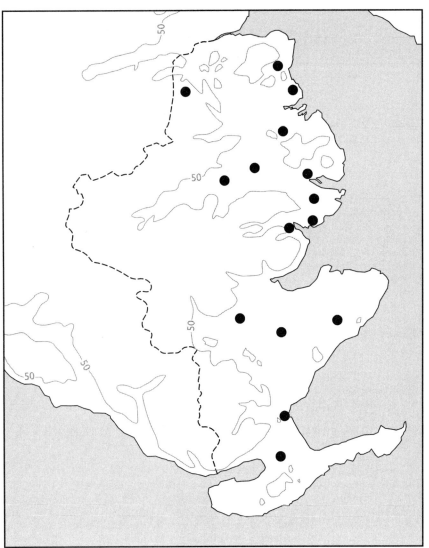

Boreland *names*

BIBLIOGRAPHY

THESES

Grant, A., 'The higher nobility and their estates in Scotland, *c*.1371–1424' (unpublished Oxford University DPhil thesis, 1975).

Neville, C. J., 'The Earls of Strathearn from the twelfth to the mid-fourteenth century', (unpublished Aberdeen University PhD thesis, 1983).

Oram, R. D., 'The lordship of Galloway, *c*.1000–*c*.1250' (unpublished St Andrews University PhD thesis, 1988).

Simpson, G. G., 'An Anglo-Scottish baron of the thirteenth century: the acts of Roger de Quincy, earl of Winchester and constable of Scotland' (unpublished Edinburgh University PhD thesis, 1965).

PUBLISHED SOURCES

A Scottish Chronicle Known as the Chronicle of Holyrood, eds A. O. and M. O. Anderson (Scottish History Society, 1938).

Acts of the Parliaments of Scotland, eds T. Thompson and C. Innes (Edinburgh, 1814–75).

Androw of Wyntoun's Orygynal Cronykil of Scotland, ed. A. Laing (Edinburgh, 1872–79).

Ailred of Rievaulx, *Saints of Hexham*, in *The Priory of Hexham: The History and Annals of the House* (Surtees Society, 1863).

The Anglo-Saxon Chronicle, trans. G. N. Garmonsway (London, 1972).

Annales Prioratus de Dunstaplia, in *Annales Monastici*, ed. R. Luard, iii (London, 1866).

Annals of Furness in Chronicles of Stephen etc., ed. R. Howlett (London, 1884–89).

Annals of Ireland. The Fragments by Dubhaltach MacFirbisigh, ed. J. O'Donovan (Dublin, 1860).

Annals of Loch Cé, ed. and trans. W. Hennessy, i (London, 1871).

Annals of the Reigns of Malcolm and William, Kings of Scotland, ed. A. C. Lawrie (Glasgow, 1910).

Annals of Ulster, ed. and trans. by W. Hennessy and B. MacCarthy (London, 1887–93).

Baedae Continuatio, in *Baedae Opera Historica*, ed. C. Plummer (Oxford, 1896).

Bede, *A History of the English Church and People*, trans. L. Sherley-Price (London, 1896).

Bernard of Clairvaux, *St Bernard's Life of St Malachy of Armagh*, ed. and trans. H. J. Lawlor (London, 1920).

'Brevis Descriptio Regni Scotiae', in *Miscellany of the Maitland Club*, iv (Glasgow, 1847).

Calendar of Documents Relating to Ireland, ed. H. Sweetman (Dublin, 1875–86).

Calendar of Documents Relating to Scotland, ed. J. Bain (Edinburgh, 1881–88).

Calendar of Documents Relating to Scotland, eds G. G. Simpson and J. D. Galbraith, v [supplementary] (Edinburgh, 1986).

Calendar of Entries in the Papal Registers Relating to Great Britain and Ireland: Papal Letters, eds W. H. Bliss and others (London, 1893–).

Calendar of Patent Rolls Preserved in the Public Record Office 1216–1509 (London, 1891–1916).

Carte Monialium de Northberwic (Bannatyne Club, 1847).

Charters of the Abbey of Beauly (Grampian Club, 1877).

Charters of Endowment, Inventories and Ancient Rolls of the Priory of Finchale in the County of Durham (Surtees Society, 1837).

Charters of the Hospital of Soltre, of Trinity College, Edinburgh, and Other Collegiate Churches in Midlothian (Bannatyne Club, 1861).

The Chartulary of Lindores Abbey 1195–1479, ed. J. Dowden (Scottish History Society, 1903).

Chronica Regum Manniae et Insularum. The Chronicle of Man and the Isles. A Facsimile of the Manuscript Codex Julius A. VIII in the British Museum (Douglas, 1924).

Chronica Rogeri de Hovedon, ed. W. Stubbs (London, 1868–71).

Chronicle of Benedict of Peterborough, ed. W. Stubbs (London, 1867).

Chronicon de Lanercost (Bannatyne Club, 1839).

The Chronicle of Man and the Sudreys, eds. P. A. Munch and Rev. Dr Goss (Douglas, 1874).

Chronicle of Melrose (facsimile edition), eds. A. O. Anderson et al. (London, 1936).

Chronicle of Robert of Torigny, in *Chronicles of the Reigns of Stephen, Henry II and Richard I*, ed. R. Howlett, iv (London, 1889).

Chronicle of Walter of Guisborough, ed. H. Rothwell (Camden Society, 1957).

Councils and Ecclesiastical Documents of Great Britain and Ireland, eds A. W. Haddan and W. Stubbs (Oxford, 1869–79).

Documents Illustrative of the History of Scotland, ed. F. Palgrave (London, 1837).

Documents Illustrative of the History of Scotland, ed. J. Stevenson (Edinburgh, 1870).

Early Scottish Charters Prior to AD 1153, ed. A. C. Lawrie (Glasgow, 1905).

Early Sources of Scottish History 500–1286, ed. A. O. Anderson (Edinburgh, 1922).

Eirspennill's Håkon Håkon's son's Saga, in Konunga Sögur, ed. C. R. Unger (Christiania).

English Historical Documents, ed. H. Rothwell, iii (London, 1975).

The Exchequer Rolls of Scotland, eds. J. Stuart, G. Burnetts et al. (Edinburgh, 1878–1908).

Fergus, ed. E. Martin (Halle, 1872).

Flateyiarbok, eds C. R. Unger and G. Vigfusson (Christiania, 1859–68).

Joannis de Fordun, Chronica Gentis Scotorum, ed. W. F. Skene (Edinburgh, 1870–71).

Furness Coucher Book, iii, pt. iii (Chetham Society, 1919).

Guillaume le Clerc, The Romance of Fergus, ed. W. Frescolin (Philadelphia, 1983).

Hacon's Saga, in *Icelandic Sagas*, trans. G. W. Dasent, iv (London, 1894).

Highland Papers, ed. J. R. N. Macphail (Scottish History Society, 1914–34).

Histoire des Ducs de Normandie et des Rois d'Angleterre, ed. F. Michel (Paris, 1840).

'Historia Fundacionis Prioratus Insule de Traile', in *Bannatyne Miscellany*, ii (Bannatyne Club, 1836).

Historians of the Church of York and Its Archbishops, ed. J. Raine (London, 1879–94).

Historical and Municipal Documents of Ireland AD 1172–1320, ed. T. J. Gilbert (London, 1870).

Inquisitionem ad Capellam Domini Regis Retornatum, quae in publicis archivis Scotiae adhuc servantur, Abbreviatio, ed. T. Thomson (Records Commission, 1811–16).

John of Hexham, Historia Regum, continuata per Joannem Hagulstadensem, in Symeonis Monachi Opera Omnia, ed. T. Arnold (London, 1885).

Jordan Fantosme's Chronicle, ed. and trans. R. C. Johnston (Oxford, 1981).

The Knights of St John of Jerusalem in Scotland, eds I. B. Cowan et al. (Scottish History Society, 1983).

The Lanercost Cartulary (Cumbria County Record Office MS DZ/1), ed. J. M. Todd (Surtees Society, 1997).

The Letters of St Bernard of Clairvaux, trans. B. Scott James (Stroud, 1998).

Liber Cartarum Sancte Crucis (Bannatyne Club, 1840).

Liber Sancte Marie de Calchou (Bannatyne Club, 1846).

Liber Sancte Marie de Dryburgh (Bannatyne Club, 1847).

Liber Sancte Marie de Melros (Bannatyne Club, 1837).

Memoriale Fratris Walteri de Coventria, ed. W. Stubbs (London, 1872–73).

Memorials of St Edmund's Abbey, ed. T. Arnold (London, 1890–96).

Njal's Saga, trans. M. Magnusson and H. Pálsson (London, 1960).

Orderic Vitalis, *The Ecclesiastical History of Orderic Vitalis*, ed. and trans. M. Chibnall (Oxford, 1969–)

Orkneyinga Saga, trans. A. B. Taylor (Edinburgh, 1938).

Orkneyinga Saga, trans. H. Pálsson and P. Edwards.

The Oxford Deeds of Balliol College, ed. H. E. Salter (Oxford Historical Society, 1913).

Matthew Paris, *Chronica Majora*, ed. H. R. Luard (London, 1872–83).

Patrologia Latina, ed. J. P. Migne, clix, pt ii (Paris, 1854).

Pont, Timothy, *Galloway Topographised* (no date).

Ralph de Diceto, *Imagines Historiarum*, in *Radulfi de Diceto Decani Lundoniensi Opera Historica*, ed. W. Stubbs (London, 1876).

Regesta Regum Scotorum, eds G. W. S. Barrow et al. (Edinburgh, 1960–).

Reginald Monachi Dunelmensis Libellus de Admirandis Beati Cuthberti Virtutibus (Surtees Society, 1835).

Reginald of Durham, *Libellus de Vita et Miraculis S. Godrici, Heremitae de Finchale*, ed. J. Stevenson (Surtees Society, 1847).

Register and Records of Holm Cultram, eds F. Grainger and W. G. Collingwood (Cumberland and Westmorland Archaeological and Antiquarian Society, 1929).

The Register of the Priory of Wetheral, ed. J. E. Prescott, CWAAS Record Series, i (Kendal, 1897).

Register of William Greenfield, Lord Archbishop of York, eds A. H. Thompson and W. Brown (Surtees Society, 1931–38).

Register of Walter Gray, Lord Archbishop of York, ed. J. Raine (Surtees Society, 1870).

Register of John le Romeyn, Lord Archbishop of York (Surtees Society, 1913–16).

Register of the Priory of St Bees, ed. J. Wilson (Surtees Society, 1915).

Register of the Priory of Wetheral, ed. J. E. Prescott (Cumberland and Westmorland Archaeological and Antiquarian Society, 1897).

Registrum Episcopatus Glasguensis (Bannatyne Club, 1843).

Registrum Episcopatus Moraviensis (Bannatyne Club, 1837).

Registrum Honoris de Morton (Bannatyne Club, 1853).

Registrum Magni Sigilli Regum Scotorum, eds J. M. Thompson et al. (Edinburgh, 1882–1914).

Registrum Monasterii de Passelet (Maitland Club, 1832).

Registrum S. Marie de Neubotle (Bannatyne Club, 1849).

Richard of Hexham, *De Gestis Regis Stephani et de Bello Standardi,* in *Chronicles of Stephen,* etc., ed. R. Howlett, iii (London, 1886).

Rishanger, William, *Cronica et Annales,* ed. M. T. Riley (London, 1865).

Roger of Wendover, *Rogeri de Wendover Chronica sive Flores Historiarum,* ed. H. G. Hewlett (London, 1841).

Rites of Durham, Being a Description or Brief Declaration of All the Ancient Monuments, Rites and Customs Belonging or Being Within the Monastical Church of Durham Before the Suppression. Written 1593 (Surtees Society, 1902).

Rotuli Litterarum Clausarum, ed. T. Duffus-Hardy (Records Commission, 1833).

Rotuli Scotiae in Turri Londiniensi et in Domo Capitulari Westmonasteriensi Asservati, eds D. Macpherson et al. (1814–19).

Scottish Annals from English Chronicles 500 to 1286, ed. A. O. Anderson (London, 1908).

Selectus Diplomatum et Numismatum Scotiae Thesaurus, ed. J. Anderson (Edinburgh, 1739).

Symeonis Monachi Opera Omnia, ed. T. Arnold (London, 1882).

Symson, Andrew, *A Large Description of Galloway* (Edinburgh, 1823).

Two Lives of St Cuthbert, ed. and trans. B. Colgrave (Cambridge, 1940).

Vetera Monumenta Hibernorum et Scotorum Historiam Illustrantia, ed. A. Theiner (Rome, 1864).

Walter Bower, *Scotichronicon,* eds D. E. R. Watt et al. (Aberdeen and Edinburgh, 1987–99).

Walter Daniel, *The Life of Ailred of Rievaulx,* ed. and trans. F. M. Powicke (London, 1950).

Wigtownshire Charters, ed. R. C. Reid (Scottish History Society, 1960).

William of Newburgh, *Historia Rerum Anglicarum,* in *Chronicles of Stephen,* etc., ed. R.Howlett, i–ii (London, 1884–85).

WORKS OF REFERENCE

A Biographical Dictionary of Scottish Graduates to 1410, ed. D. E. R. Watt (Oxford, 1977).

The Complete Peerage, eds. G. Cockayne et al., xi (London, 1949).

Cowan, I. B., *The Parishes of Medieval Scotland* (Scottish Record Society, 1967).

Cowan, I. B. and Easson, D. E., *Medieval Religious Houses. Scotland,* 2nd edition (London, 1976).

Donaldson, G., *Scottish Historical Documents* (Edinburgh, 1970).

Dowden, J. *The Bishops of Scotland* (Glasgow, 1912).

Fasti Ecclesiae Scoticanae Medii Aevi Ad Annum 1638, ed. D. E. R. Watt (Scottish Record Society, 1969).

Ferguson, P. C., *Medieval Papal Representatives in Scotland: Legates, Nuncios, and Judges-Delegate, 1125–1286* (Stair Society, 1997).

Inventories of Ancient Monuments: Royal Commission on the Ancient and Historical Monuments of Scotland, Fourth report and inventory of monuments and constructions in Galloway, i, *County of Wigtown* (Edinburgh, 1912); Fifth report, etc., ii *Stewartry of Kirkcudbright* (Edinburgh, 1914); *County of Dumfries* (Edinburgh, 1920).

Royal Commission on the Ancient and Historical Monuments of Scotland 'West Rhins', *Archaeological Sites and Monuments of Scotland,* xxiv (Edinburgh, 1985).

The Scots Peerage, ed. J. Balfour-Paul (Edinburgh, 1904–14).

Series Episcoporum Ecclesiae Catholicae Occidentalis Ab Initio Usque AD Annum MCXCVIII, Series VI, Britannia, Scotia et Hibernia, Scandinavia, i, Ecclesia Scoticana, ed. D. E. R. Watt (Stuttgart, 1991).

Storey, R. L., *Chronology of the Medieval World 800 to 1491* (Oxford, 1973).

SECONDARY WORKS

1. BOOKS

Agnew, A., *A History of the Hereditary Sheriffs of Galloway* (Edinburgh, 1864).

Anderson, J., *Scotland in Early Christian Times*, 2nd edition (Edinburgh, 1881).

Baldwin, J. and Whyte, I. D. (eds), *The Scandinavians in Cumbria* (Edinburgh, 1981).

Bannerman, J., *Studies in the Early History of Dalriada* (Edinburgh, 1974).

Barlow, F., *Edward the Confessor* (London, 1970).

Barlow, F., *William Rufus* (London, 1983).

Barlow, F., *Thomas Becket* (London, 1986).

Barrow, G. W. S., *Feudal Britain. The Completion of the Medieval Kingdoms 1066–1314* (London, 1956).

Barrow, G. W. S., *The Kingdom of the Scots* (London, 1973).

Barrow, G. W. S., *Kingship and Unity, Scotland 1000–1306* (London, 1981).

Barrow, G. W. S., *David I of Scotland (1124–53), The Balance of New and Old* (Reading, 1985).

Barrow, G. W. S., *Robert Bruce and the Community of the Realm of Scotland*, revised edition (Edinburgh, 1988).

Bartlett, R. and MacKay, A. (eds), *Medieval Frontier Societies* (Oxford, 1989).

Bartlett, R., *The Making of Europe. Conquest, Colonisation and Cultural Change 950–1350* (London, 1993).

Batey, C., Jesch, J. and Morris, C. (eds), *The Viking Age in Caithness, Orkney and the North Atlantic* (Edinburgh, 1993).

Boardman, S. (ed.), *Native Kindreds* (forthcoming).

Breeze, D. (ed.), *Studies in Scottish Antiquity Presented to Stewart Cruden* (Edinburgh, 1984).

Brooke, D., 'Gall-Gaidhil and Galloway', in R. D. Oram and G. P. Stell (eds), *Galloway: Land and Lordship* (Edinburgh, 1991).

Brooke, D., *Wild Men and Holy Places. St Ninian, Whithorn and the Medieval Realm of Galloway* (Edinburgh, 1994).

Brotherstone, T. and Ditchburn, D. (eds), *Freedom and Authority. Historical and Historiographical Essays Presented to Grant G. Simpson* (East Linton, 2000).

Byrne, F. J., *Irish Kings and High Kings* (London, 1973).

Carpenter, D. A., *The Minority of Henry III* (London, 1990).

Chalmers, G., *Caledonia* (Glasgow, 1887–1902).

Cockburn, J. H., *The Medieval Bishops of Dunblane and Their Church* (Edinburgh, 1959).

Cowan, E. J. and McDonald, R.A., (eds), *Alba: Celtic Scotland in the Middle Ages* (East Linton, 2000).

Cowan, I. B., *The Medieval Church in Scotland*, ed. J. Kirk (Edinburgh, 1995).

Crawford, B. E., *Scandinavian Scotland* (Leicester, 1987).

Crawford, B. E. and MacGregor, L. J. (eds), *Pennyland and Ounceland in Norse and Celtic Scotland* (St Andrews, 1987).

Crawford, B. E., *Scandinavian Settlement in Northern Britain* (London, 1995).

Cruden, S., *The Scottish Castle* (Edinburgh, 1960).

Davies, R. R., *Domination and Conquest: the Experience of Ireland, Scotland and Wales, 1100–1300* (Cambridge, 1990).

Dodgshon, R. A., *Land and Society in Early Scotland* (Oxford, 1981).

Donaldson, G., *Scottish Church History* (Edinburgh, 1985).

Douglas, D. C., *William the Conqueror* (London, 1964).

Duffy, S., *Ireland in the Middle Ages* (London, 1997).

Duncan, A. A. M., *Scotland. The Making of the Kingdom* (Edinburgh, 1975).

Ewart, G., *Cruggleton Castle* (Dumfries, 1986).

Fawcett, R. (ed.), *Medieval Art and Architecture in the Diocese of Glasgow, The British Archaeological Association Conference Transactions*, xiii (1998).

Fellows-Jensen, G., *Scandinavan Settlement Names in the North-West* (Copenhagen, 1985).

Flanagan, M. T., *Irish Society, Anglo-Norman Settlers, Angevin Kingship. Interactions in Ireland in the Late Twelfth Century* (Oxford, 1989).

Foster, S., Macinnes A. I. and MacInnes, R. (eds), *Scottish Power Centres from the Early Middle Ages to the Twentieth Century* (Glasgow, 1998).

Frame, R., *The Political Development of the British Isles, 1100–1400* (Oxford, 1990).

Given-Wilson, C. J. and Curteis, A., *The Royal Bastards of Medieval England* (London, 1984).

Gourlay, R. and Turner, A., *Historic Kirkcudbright: The Archaeological Implications of Development* (Glasgow, 1977).

Grant, A., *Independence and Nationhood. Scotland 1306–1469* (London, 1984).

Grant, A. and Stringer, K. J. (eds), *Medieval Scotland. Crown, Lordship and Community* (Edinburgh, 1993).

Hartridge, R. A. R., *A History of Vicarages in the Middle Ages* (Cambridge, 1930).

Hill, P. H., *Whithorn and St. Ninian. The Excavation of a Monastic Town 1984–91* (Stroud, 1997).

Howell, M. E., *Regalian Rights in Medieval England* (London, 1962).

Huyshe, W., *Dervorgilla, Lady of Galloway and Her Abbey of the Sweetheart* (Edinburgh, 1913).

Huyshe, W., *Grey Galloway, Its Lords and Its Saints* (Edinburgh, 1914).

Jackson, K. H., *The Gaelic Notes in the Book of Deer* (Cambridge, 1972).

Kapelle, W. E., *The Norman Conquest of the North: The Region and Its Transformation 1000–1135* (London, 1979).

Laing, L., *The Archaeology of Late Celtic Britain and Ireland c.400–1200 AD* (London, 1975).

Lloyd, A., *King John* (Newton Abbott, 1973).

McCluskey, R. (ed.), *The See of Ninian. A History of the Medieval Diocese of Whithorn and the Diocese of Galloway in Modern Times* (Ayr, 1997).

McDonald, R. A., *The Kingdom of the Isles. Scotland's Western Seaboard c.1100–c.1336* (East Linton, 1997).

MacGibbon, D. and Ross, T., *The Ecclesiastical Architecture of Scotland* (Edinburgh, 1896–7).

Mackenzie, W., *The History of Galloway From the Earliest Period to the Present Time* (Kirkcudbright, 1841).

M'Kerlie, P. H., *The History of the Lands and Their Owners in Galloway*, 1st edition (Paisley, 1877), 2nd edition (Paisley, 1906).

McNeill, T. E., *Anglo-Norman Ulster. The History and Archaeology of an Irish Barony 1177–1400* (Edinburgh, 1980).

McNeill, T. E., *Castles in Ireland. Feudal Power in a Gaelic World* (London, 1997).

Mac Niocaill, G. and Wallace, P. F. (eds), *Keimelia: Studies in Medieval Archaeology and History in Memory of Tom Delaney* (Galway, 1988).

Milis, L. J. R., *Angelic Monks and Earthly Men: Monasticism and Its Meaning to Medieval Society* (Woodbridge, 1992).

Morrison, A., *Rural Settlement Studies* (Glasgow, 1980).

Nicolaisen, W. F., *Scottish Place Names* (London, 1976).

Ó'Corráin, D., *Ireland Before the Normans* (Dublin, 1972).

Oram, R. D. and Stell, G. P. (eds), *Galloway: Land and Lordship* (Edinburgh, 1991).

Oram, R. D. and Stell, G. P. (eds), *Lordship and Architecture in Medieval and Renaissance Scotland* (East Linton, 2000).

Oram, R. D. (ed.), *Scotland in the Reign of Alexander II* (forthcoming).

Orpen, G. H., *Ireland Under the Normans* (Oxford, 1911).

Owen, D. D. R., *William the Lion 1143–1214. Kingship and Culture* (East Linton, 1997).

Penman, A., *Botel Bailey Excavation, Interim Report 1992–4* (Castle Douglas, 1995).

Penman, A., *Botel Bailey Excavation, Interim Report 1996* (Castle Douglas, 1997).

Poole, A. L., *From Domesday Book to Magna Carta 1087–1216* (Oxford, 1955).

Radford, C. A. R. and Donaldson, G., *Whithorn and Kirkmadrine* (Edinburgh, 1953).

Richmond, I. A. (ed.), *Roman and Native in North Britain* (Edinburgh, 1961).

Rivet, A. L. F. and Smith, C., *The Place-Names of Roman Britain* (London, 1979).

Robertson, J., *On Scholastic Offices in The Scottish Church of the 12th and 13th Centuries* (private circulation, 1853).

Robertson, J. F., *The Story of Galloway* (Castle Douglas, 1964).

Robison, J., *Kirkcudbright (St Cuthbert's Town): Its Mote, Castles, Monastery and Parishes Churches* (Dumfries, 1926).

Simpson, W. D., *The Celtic Church in Scotland* (Aberdeen, 1935).

Simpson, W. D., *The Province of Mar* (Aberdeen, 1934).

Skene, W. F., *Celtic Scotland*, 2nd edition (Edinburgh, 1886–90).

Smith, B. (ed.), *Britain and Ireland 900–1300. Insular Responses to Medieval European Change* (Cambridge, 1999).

Smith, R. A. L., *Canterbury Cathedral Priory: A Study in Monastic Administration* (Cambridge, 1943).

Smyth, A. P., *Scandinavian York and Dublin* (Dublin, 1975-79).

Smyth, A. P., *Warlords and Holy Men. Scotland, AD 80–1000* (London, 1984).

Steane, J., *The Archaeology of Medieval England and Wales* (London, 1984).

Stell, G. P., *Dumfries and Galloway* (Edinburgh, 1985).

Stenton, F. M., *Anglo-Saxon England* (Oxford, 1971).

Stones, E. L. G. (ed.), *Anglo-Scottish Relations 1174–1328* (Oxford, 1970).

Stringer, K. J. (ed.), *Essays on the Nobility of Medieval Scotland* (Edinburgh, 1985).

Stringer, K. J., *The Reign of Stephen. Kingship, Warfare and Government in Twelfth-Century England* (London, 1993).

Summerson, H., *Medieval Carlisle: The City and the Borders from the Late Eleventh to the Mid-Sixteenth Century* (Kendal, 1993).

Sumption, J., *Pilgrimage, An Image of Religion* (London, 1975).

Tabraham, C., *Scotland's Castles* (London, 1997).

Turner-Simpson, A. and Stevenson, W., *Historic Wigtown: The Archaeological Implications of Development* (Glasgow, 1981).

Wainwright, F. T., *Scandinavian England*, ed. H. P. R. Finberg (Chichester, 1975).

Watt, J., *The Church in Medieval Ireland* (Dublin, 1972).

Winchester, A. J. L., *Landscape and Society in Medieval Cumbria* (Edinburgh, 1987).

Whyte, I. D., *Scotland Before the Industrial Revolution. An Economic and Social History of Scotland c.1050–c.1750* (Harlow, 1995).

Yeoman, P., *Medieval Scotland: an Archaeological Perspective* (London, 1995).

Young, A., *Robert the Bruce's Rivals. The Comyns c.1212–1314* (East Linton, 1997).

2. ARTICLES, ESSAYS AND SHORTER NOTES

Ashley, A., 'Odo, elect of Whithorn', *TDGNHAS*, xxxvii (1958–59), 62–69.

Backmund, N., 'The Premonstratensian order in Scotland'. *Innes Review*, iv (1952–3), 25–41.

Barbour, J., 'An account of excavations at Lochrutton lake-dwelling', *TDGNHAS*, 2nd series xvii (1902–03), 246–54.

Barrell, A. D. M., 'The background to *Cum universi*: Scoto-papal relations 1159–92', *Innes Review*, 46 (1995), 116–38.

Barrow, G. W. S., 'The beginnings of feudalism in Scotland', *BIHR*, xxix (1956), 1–31.

Barrow, G. W. S., 'Rural settlement in central and eastern Scotland, the medieval evidence', *Scottish Studies*, vi (1963), 123–44.

Barrow, G. W. S., 'The Scottish judex in the 12th and 13th centuries', SHR, xlv (1966), 16–26.

Barrow, G. W. S., 'The pattern of lordship and feudal settlement in Cumbria', *Journal of Medieval History*, I (1975), 117–37.

Barrow, G. W. S. and Royan, A., 'James, fifth Stewart of Scotland 1260(9)–1309', in K. J. Stringer (ed.), *Essays on the Nobility of Medieval Scotland* (Edinburgh, 1985).

Bartlett, R., 'Colonial societies of the High Middle Ages', in R. Bartlett and A. MacKay (eds), *Medieval Frontier Societies* (Oxford, 1989).

Birks, H., 'Studies in the vegetational history of Scotland ii. Two pollen diagrams from the Galloway hills, Kirkcudbrightshire', *Journal of Ecology*, lx (1970), 183–217.

Brentano, R. J., 'Re-dating a Whithorn document', *TDGNHAS*, xxx (1951–52), 192–93.

Brentano, R. J., 'Whithorn and York', *SHR* (1953), 144–46.

Brentano, R. J., 'The Whithorn vacancy', *Innes Review*, iv (1953), 71–83.

Brooke, D., 'Kirk-compound place-names in Galloway and Carrick', *TDGNHAS*, lviii (1983), 56–71.

Brooke, D., 'The Glenkens 1275–1456: snapshots of a medieval countryside', *TDGNHAS*, lix (1984), 41–56.

Brooke, D., 'The deanery of Desnes Cro and the church of Edingham', *TDGNHAS*, lxii (1987), 48–65.

Brooke, D., 'Gall-Gaidhil and Galloway', in R. D. Oram and G. P. Stell (eds), *Galloway: Land and Lordship* (Edinburgh, 1991).

Brooke, D., 'Fergus of Galloway: Miscellaneous notes for a revised portrait', *TDGNHAS*, lxvi (1991), 47–58.

Brooke, D., 'The Northumbrian settlements in Galloway and Carrick: an historical assessment', *PSAS*, 121 (1991), 295–327.

Brooke, D., *The Medieval Lords of Galloway 1. Fergus the King* (Whithorn, 1991).

Burdon-Davies, E.F., 'The moated manor at Dunrod, Kirkcudbright', *TDGNHAS*, xliii (1963), 121–36.

Cameron, A. I., 'Bagimond's roll for the archdeaconry of Teviotdale', *Miscellany of the Scottish History Society*, v (1933), 79–86.

Candon, A., 'Muirchertach Ua Briain and naval activity in the Irish Sea, 1075–1119', in G. Mac Niocaill and P. F. Wallace (eds.), *Keimelia: Studies in Medieval Archaeology and History in Memory of Tom Delaney* (Galway, 1988), 397–415.

Chadwick, N. K., 'St Ninian: a preliminary study of the sources', *TDGNHAS*, xxvii (1948–49), 9–53.

Clay, C. T., 'Two Dervorguillas', *EHR*, lxv (1950), 89–91.

Clough, T. H. McK. and Laing, L., 'Excavations at Kirkconnel, Waterbeck, Dumfriesshire, 1968', *TDGNHAS*, xlvi (1969), 128–39.

Coles, F. R., 'The motes, forts and doons of the Stewartry of Kirkcudbright', *PSAS*, xxv (1890–91), 352–96.

Coles, F. R., 'The motes, forts and doons of the Stewartry of Kirkcudbright', *PSAS*, xxvi (1891–92), 117–70.

Coles, F. R., 'The motes, forts and doons of the east and west divisions of the Stewartry of Kirkcudbright', *PSAS*, xxvii (1892–93), 98–182.

Condry, J. and Ansell, M., 'The excavation of a hut circle at Moss Raploch, Clatteringshaws', *TDGNHAS*, liii (1977–78), 105–13.

Corner, D., 'The Gesta Regis Henrici Secundi and Chronica of Roger, Parson of Howden', *BIHR*, lvi (1983), 126–44.

Cowan, E., 'The Vikings in Galloway: a review of the evidence', in R. D. Oram and G. P. Stell (eds), *Galloway: Land and Lordship* (Edinburgh, 1991).

Cowan, I. B., 'Some aspects of the appropriation of parish churches in medieval Scotland', *Scottish Church History Society Records*, xiii (1957–59), 203–22.

Craig, D. E., 'Pre-Norman sculpture in Galloway: some territorial implications', in R. D. Oram and G. P. Stell (eds), *Galloway: Land and Lordship* (Edinburgh, 1991).

Craster, H. H. E., 'A contemporary record of the pontificate of Ranulf Flambard', *Archaeologia Aeliana*, vii (1930), 33-56.

Crawford, B. E., 'The earldom of Caithness and the kingdom of Scotland, 1150–1266', in K. J. Stringer (ed.), *Essays on the Nobility of Medieval Scotland* (Edinburgh, 1985), 25–43.

Crawford, B. E., 'Norse earls and Scottish bishops in Caithness: a clash of cultures', in C. Batey, J. Jesche and C. Morris (eds), *The Viking Age in Caithness, Orkney and The North Atlantic* (Edinburgh, 1993), 129–47.

Crone, B. A., 'Crannogs and chronologies', *PSAS*, 123 (1993), 245–54.

Crowe, C., 'Excavations at Brydekirk, Annan, 1982–84', *TDGNHAS*, lix (1984), 33–40.

Cruden, S., 'Glenluce Abbey. Finds recovered during excavation', *TDGNHAS*, xxix (1950–51), 177–94 and xxx (1951–52), 179–90.

Curle, A. O., 'Report on excavation of a vitrified fort at Rockcliffe known as the Mote of Mark', *PSAS*, xlviii (1913–14), 125–68.

Dickinson, W. C., 'Surdit de Sergaunt', *SHR*, xxxix (2960), 170–75.

Donaldson, G., 'The bishops and priors of Whithorn', *TDGNHAS*, xxvii (1948–49), 127–54.

Driscoll, S., 'Formalising the mechanisms of state control', in S. Foster, A. I. Macinnes and R. MacInnes, *Scottish Power Centres* (Glasgow, 1998).

Duffy, S., 'Irishmen and Islesmen in the kingdoms of Dublin and Man, 1052–1171', *Eriu*, xliii (1992), 93–133.

Duncan, A. A. M. and Brown, A. L., 'Argyll and the Isles in the earlier Middle Ages', *PSAS*, xc (1956–57), 192–220.

Duncan, A. A. M., 'The earldom of Atholl in the thirteenth century', *Scottish Genealogist*, vii (1960), 2–10.

Duncan, A. A. M., 'Bede, Iona and the Picts', in R. H. C. Davis and J. M. Wallace-Hadrill (eds.), *The Writing of History in the Middle Ages* (Oxford, 1981).

Dunlop, A. I., 'Bagimond's Roll – a statement of the tenths of the kingdom of Scotland', *Miscellany of the Scottish History Society*, vi (1939).

Dunning, G. C., Hodges, H. W. M. and Jope, E. M., 'Kirkcudbright Castle, its pottery and ironwork', *PSAS*, xci (1957–58), 117–38.

Durkan, J., 'The bishop's barony of Glasgow in pre-Reformation times', *RHCHS*, xxii (1986), 277–301.

Fellows-Jensen, G., 'Common Gaelic *airge*, Old Scandinavian *aergi* or *erg*?' *Nomina*, iv (1980), 67–74.

Fellows-Jensen, G., 'Scandinavians in Dumfriesshire and Galloway; the place-name evidence', in R. D. Oram and G. P. Stell (eds), *Galloway: Land and Lordship* (Edinburgh, 1991).

Fergusson, J., 'An extent of Carrick in 1260', *SHR*, xxxiv (1955), 190–92.

Gillingham, J., 'Killing and mutilating political enemies in the British Isles from the late twelfth to the early fourteenth century: a comparative study', In B. Smith (ed.), *Britain and Ireland 900–1300. Insular Responses to Medieval European Change* (Cambridge, 1999).

Good, G. and Tabraham, C. J., 'Excavations at Threave Castle, Galloway, 1974–78', *Medieval Archaeology*, 25 (1981).

Greenberg, J., 'Guillaume le Clerc and Alan of Galloway', *Proceedings of the Modern Language Association*, lxvi (1957), 524–33.

Greeves, R., 'The Galloway lands in Ulster', *TDGNHAS*, xxxvi (1957–58), 115–21.

Haggarty, G. and Tabraham, C. J., 'Excavation of a motte near Roberton, Clydesdale, 1979', *TDGNHAS*, lvii (1982), 51–64.

Haggarty, A. and Haggarty, G., 'Excavations at Rispain Camp, Whithorn, 1978–81', *TDGNHAS*, lviii (1985), 21–51.

Higgitt, J., 'Manuscripts and libraries in the Diocese of Glasgow before the Reformation', in R. Fawcett (ed.), *Medieval Art and Architecture in the Diocese of Glasgow, British Archaeological Association Conference Transactions*, xxiii (1998), 102–110.

Higham, N., 'The Scandinavians in north Cumbria: raids and settlement in the later ninth to mid-tenth centuries', J. Baldwin and I. D. Whyte (eds), *The Scandinavians in Cumbria* (Edinburgh, 1981).

Hope-Taylor, B., 'Excavations at Mote of Urr. Interim report, 1951 season', *TDGNHAS*, xxix (1950–1), 167–72.

Hudson, B., 'Knútr and Viking Dublin', *Scandinavian Studies*, 66 (1994), 319–35.

Hunter-Blair, P., in *Studies in Early British History*, ed. N. K. Chadwick (Cambridge, 1954), 165–68.

Jackson, K. H., 'The Britons in southern Scotland', *Antiquity*, xxix (1955), 77–88.

Jobey, J., 'Burnswark Hill, Dumfriesshire', *TDGNHAS*, liii (1977–78).

Kerr, H. F., 'The priory church of Whithorn', TSES, xi (1934–36).

Kirkby, D. P., 'Strathclyde and Cumbria: a survey of the historical development to 1093', *TCWAAS*, lxxii (1962), 77–94.

Laing, L. R., 'Timber halls in Dark Age Britain, some problems', *TDGNHAS*, xlvi (1969), 110–27.

Laing, L. R., 'Medieval settlement archaeology in Scotland', *Scottish Archaeological Forum*, i, (Glasgow, 1969).

Laing, L. R., 'The Angles in Scotland and the Mote of Mark', *TDGNHAS*, l (1973), 37–52.

Lamont, W. D., '"House" and "Pennyland" in the Highlands and Islands', *Scottish Studies*, xxv (1981), 65–76.

Lawlor, H. C., 'The vassals of the earls of Ulster', *Ulster Journal of Archaeology*, iii (1940), 16–26.

Legge, M. D., 'Some notes on the Roman de Fergus', *TDGNHAS*, xxvii (1948–49), 163–72.

Legge, M. D., 'The father of Fergus of Galloway', SHR, xliii (1964), 86–87.

McDonald, R. A., 'Scoto-Norse kings and the reformed religious orders: patterns of monastic patronage in twelfth-century Galloway and Argyll', *Albion*, xxvii (1995).

McDonald, R. A., '"Treachery in the remotest territories of Scotland:" northern resistance to the Canmore dynasty, 1130–1230', *Canadian Journal of History*, xxxiii (1999), 161–92.

McDonald, R. A., 'Rebels without a cause', in Cowan, E. J. and McDonald, R. A. (eds), *Alba: Celtic Scotland in the Middle Ages* (East Linton, 2000).

McGill, J. M., 'A genealogival survey of the ancient lords of Galloway', *Scottish Genealogist*, ii (1955), 3–6.

McKerral, A., 'Ancient denominations of agricultural land in Scotland', *PSAS*, lxxviii (1943–44), 39–80.

McKerral, A., 'The Kintyre properties of Whithorn Priory and the bishopric of Galloway', *TDGNHAS*, xxvii (1948–49), 183–92.

McKerral, A., 'The lesser land and administrative units of Celtic Scotland', *PSAS*, lxxxv (1950–51), 52–64.

McKerral, A., 'An extent of Carrick in 1260', *SHR*, xxxiv (1955), 189–90.

MacQuarrie, A., 'Kings, lords and abbots: power and patronage at the medieval monastery of Iona', *TGSI*, liv (1984–86), 355–75.

MacQuarrie, A., 'The kings of Strathclyde *c*.400–1018', in A. Grant and K. J. Stringer (eds), *Medieval Scotland. Crown, Lordship and Community* (Edinburgh, 1993), 1–19.

MacQueen, H. L., 'The laws of Galloway: a preliminary survey', in R. D. Oram and G. P. Stell (eds), *Galloway: Land and Lordship* (Edinburgh, 1991).

MacQueen, H. L., 'The kin of Kennedy: "kenkynnol" and the common law', in A. Grant and K. J. Stringer (eds), *Medieval Scotland: Crown, Lordship and community* (Edinburgh, 1993).

MacQueen, J., 'The Picts in Galloway', *TDGNHAS*, xxxix (1960–61), 127–43.

MacQueen, J., 'The Gaelic speakers of Galloway and Carrick', *Scottish Studies*, xvii (1973), 17–33.

MacQueen, J., 'Pennyland and davoch in south-western Scotland', *Scottish Studies*, xxiii (1979), 69–74.

MacQueen, W. W., 'The Miracula Nynie Episcopi', *TDGNHAS*, xxxviii (1959–60), 21–57.

Maxwell-Irving, A. M. T., 'The castles of Buittle', *TDGNHAS*, lxvi (1991), 59–66.

Megaw, B., 'The barony of St Trinians in the Isle of Man', TDGNHAS, xxvii (1948–49), 173–82.

Megaw, B., 'Pennyland and davoch in south-western Scotland', *Scottish Studies,* xxiii (1979), 75–77.

Megaw, E., 'The Manx "eary" and its significance', in P. Davey (ed.), *Man and the Environment in the Isle of Man*, (BAR British Series, liv, pt ii (1978), 327–45.

Milne, I. A., 'An extent of Carrick in 1260', *SHR*, xxxiv (1955) 46–49.

Murray, N., 'Swerving from the path of justice: Alexander II's relations with Argyll and the Western Isles 1214–49', in R. D. Oram (ed.), *Scotland in the Reign of Alexander II* (forthcoming).

Neville, C. J., 'A Celtic enclave in Norman Scotland: Earl Gilbert and the earldom of Strathearn, 1171–1223', in T. Brotherstone and D. Ditchburn (eds), *Freedom and Authority* (East Linton, 2000).

Nichols, H., 'Vegetational change, shoreline displacement and the human factor in the late quaternary history of south-west Scotland', *Transactions of the Royal Society of Edinburgh*, lxvii (1968), 145–87.

Nicolaisen, W. F. H., 'Norse place-names in south-west Scotland', *Scottish Studies*, iv (1960), 49–70.

Nicolaisen, W. F. H., 'Celts and Anglo-Saxons in the Scottish border counties. The place-name evidence', *Scottish Studies*, viii (1964), 141–71.

Nicolaisen, W. F. H., 'Scottish place-names, 24: slew- and sliabh', *Scottish Studies*, ix (1965), 91–106.

Nicolaisen, W. F. H., 'Gaelic place-names in Southern Scotland', *Studia Celtica*, v (1970), 15–35.

Oftedal, M., 'Scandinavian place-names in Ireland', *Proceedings of the Seventh Viking Congress* (Dublin, 1970), 125–33.

Oram, R. D., 'Pennyland and davoch in south-west Scotland: a review of the evidence', in B. E. Crawford and L. J. MacGregor (eds), *Ouncelands and Pennylands in Norse and Celtic Scotland* (St Andrews, 1987), 46–59.

Oram, R. D., 'In obedience and reverence: Whithorn and York *c*.1128–*c*.1250', *The Innes Review*, xlii (1991), 83–100.

Oram, R. D., 'Fergus, Galloway and the Scots', in Oram, R. D. and Stell, G. P. (eds.), *Galloway: Land and Lordship* (Edinburgh, 1991).

Oram, R. D., 'Bruce, Balliol and the lordship of Galloway', *TDGNHAS*, lxvii (1992), 29–47.

Oram, R. D., 'A family business? Colonisation and settlement in twelfth- and thirteenth-century Galloway', *SHR*, lxxii (1993).

Oram, R. D., 'Heirs to Ninian: the medieval bishops of Whithorn (*c*.1100–1560), in R. McCluskey (ed.), *The See of Ninian* (Ayr, 1997), 49–80.

Oram, R. D., 'Prayer, property and profit. scottish monastic power centres in the twelfth and thirteenth centuries', in S. Foster, A. I. Macinnes and R. MacInnes, *Scottish Power Centres* (Glasgow, 1998).

Oram, R. D., 'David I and the conquest and colonisation of Moray', *Northern Scotland*, 19 (1999), 1–19.

Oram, R. D., 'Dervorgilla, the Balliols and Buittle', *TDGNHAS*, lxxiii (1999), 165–81.

Oram, R. D., 'Accommodation, adaptation and integration: the earls and earldom of Mar *c*.1100–*c*.1300', in S. I. Boardman, *Native Kindreds* (forthcoming).

Owen, D. D. R., 'The craft of Guillaume le Clerc's Fergus', in L. Arathoon (ed.), *The Craft of Fiction: Essays in Medieval Poetics* (Rochester, Michigan, 1984), 47–81.

Piggott, S., 'Native economies and the Roman occupation of north Britain', in I. A. Richmond (ed.), *Roman and Native in North Britain* (Edinburgh, 1961).

Pryde, G. S., 'The burghs of Dumfriesshire and Galloway. Their origin and status', *TDGNHAS*, xxix (1950–51), 81–131.

Radford, C. A. R., 'Excavations at Whithorn. First Season, 1949', *TDGNHAS*, xxvii (1948–49), 85–126.

Radford, C. A. R., 'Castle Loch, Mochrum', *TDGNHAS*, xxviii (1949–50), 41–63.

Radford, C. A. R., 'Cruggleton church', *TDGNHAS*, xxviii (1949–50), 92–95.

Radford, C. A. R., 'Excavations at Chapel Finian', *TDGNHAS*, xxviii (1949–50), 28–40.

Radford, C. A. R., 'Excavations at Whithorn (final report)', *TDGNHAS*, xxxiv (1955–56), 131–94.

Radford, C. A. R., 'Balliol's manor house on Hestan Island', *TDGNHAS*, xxxv (1956–57), 33–37.

Radford, C. A. R., 'The churches of Dumfriesshire and Galloway', *TDGNHAS*, xl (1961–62), 102–16.

Raftis, J. A., 'The estates of Ramsey Abbey: a study in economic growth and organisation', *Pontifical Institute of Medieval Studies, Studies and Texts*, vii (Toronto, 1957).

Ragg, W. F., 'Five Strathclyde and Galloway charters – four concerning Cardew and one the Westmorland Newbigging', *TDGNHAS*, v (1916–18), 231–64.

Reid, R. C., 'The early ecclesiastical history of Kirkgunzeon', *TDGNHAS*, xiv (1926–28), 201–18.

Reid, R. C., 'The history of Southwick prior to the Reformation', *TDGNHAS*, xiv (1926–28), 218–23.

Reid, R. C., 'Cruggleton castle', *TDGNHAS*, xvi (1929–30), 152–60.

Reid, R. C., 'The early Kirkpatricks', *TDGNHAS*, xxx (1951–52), 61–84.

Reid, R. C., 'De Veteripont', *TDGNHAS*, xxxiii (1954–55), 96–106.

Reid, R. C., 'The feudalisation of lower Nithsdale', *TDGNHAS*, xxxiv (1955–56), 102–13.

Reid, R. C., 'Edward Balliol', TDGNHAS, xxxv (1956–57), 38–63.

Reid, R. C., The monastery of Applegarth', TDGNHAS, xxxv (1956–57), 14–19.

Reid, R. C., 'The priory of St Mary's Isle', *TDGNHAS*, xxxvi (1957–58), 9–26.

Rusk, J. M., 'The Abbey of Luce', *TSES*, xi (1934–36), 14–30.

Schmolke-Hasselmann, B., 'Der arthurische Versroman, et "Le Roman de Fergus": technique narrative et intention politique', in K. Varty (ed.), *An Arthurian Tapestry: Essays in Memory of Lewis Thorpe* (Glasgow, 1981).

Scott, J. G., 'An early sheriff of Dumfries?', *TDGNHAS*, lvii (1982), 90–91.

Scott, J. G., 'A note on Viking settlement in Galloway', *TDGNHAS*, lviii (1983), 52–55.

Scott, J. G., 'The origins of Dundrennan and Soulseat Abbeys', *TDGNHAS*, lxiii (1988), 35–44.

Scott, J. G., 'Bishop John of Glasgow and the status of Hoddom', *TDGNHAS*, lxvi (1991), 37–45.

Scott, J. G., 'Galloway in the 1100s', *TDGNHAS*, lxviii (1993), 131–33.

Scott, J. G., 'The partition of a kingdom: Strathclyde 1092–1153', TDGNHAS, lxxii (1997), 11–40.

Sellar, W. D. H., 'The origins and ancestry of Somerled', *SHR*, xlv (1966) 123–42.

Sellar, W. D. H., 'Marriage, divorce and concubinage in Gaelic Scotland', *Transactions of the Gaelic Society of Inverness*, li (1978–80), 463–93.

Shead, N. F., 'The origins of the medieval diocese of Glasgow', *SHR*, xlviii (1969), 220–25.

Simpson, G. G. and Webster, B., 'Charter evidence and the distribution of mottes in Scotland', in K. J. Stringer (ed.), *Essays on the Nobility of Medieval Scotland* (Edinburgh, 1985).

Simpson, W. D., 'The Ninianic controversy', *TDGNHAS*, xxvii (1948–49), 155–62.

Sprott, G. W., 'The ancient cathedrals of Scotland', *TSES*, ii (1906–09).

Stell, G. P., 'Medieval buildings and secular lordship', in R. D. Oram and G. P. Stell (eds), *Galloway: Land and Lordship* (Edinburgh, 1991).

Stewart-Brown, R., 'The end of the Norman earldom of Chester', *EHR*, xxv (1920), 26–54.

Stringer, K. J., 'A new wife for Alan of Galloway', *TDGNHAS*, xlix (1972), 49–55.

Stringer, K. J., 'Galloway and the abbeys of Rievaulx and Dundrennan', *TDGNHAS*, liv (1979), 174–77.

Stringer, K. J., 'The early lords of Lauderdale, Dryburgh Abbey and St Andrews Priory at Northampton', in K. J. Stringer (ed.), *Essays on the Nobility of Medieval Scotland* (Edinburgh, 1985).

Stringer, K. J., 'Periphery and core in thirteenth-century Scotland: Alan son of Roland, Lord of Galloway and Constable of Scotland', in A. Grant and K. J. Stringer (eds), *Medieval Scotland: Crown, Lordship and Nobility* (Edinburgh, 1993).

Stringer, K. J., 'Acts of lordship: the records of the Lords of Galloway to 1234', in T. Brotherstone and D. Ditchburn (eds), *Freedom and Authority. Historical and Historiographical Essays Presented to Grant G. Simpson* (East Linton, 2000).

Stringer, K. J., 'Reform monasticism and Celtic Scotland: Galloway *c.*1140–*c.*1240', in Cowan and McDonald, *Alba*.

Tabraham, C. J., 'Norman settlement in upper Clydesdale: recent archaeological fieldwork', *TDGNHAS*, liii (1977–78), 114–28.

Tabraham, C. J., 'Norman settlement in Galloway; recent fieldwork in the Stewartry', in D. Breeze (ed.), Studies in Scottish Antiquity Presented to Stewart

Cruden (Edinburgh, 1984).

Tabraham, C. J., 'Excavations at Whithorn Priory, Wigtown District, 1972 and 1975', *TDGNHAS*, liv (1979–80), 29–38.

Taylor, A. B., 'Karl Hundason, king of Scots', *PSAS*, lxxi (1937).

Thomas, C., 'Two early ecclesiastical sites (Isle of Whithorn and Ardwall Island) and their significance', *TDGNHAS*, xxxviii (1959–60), 71–82.

Thomas, C., 'Excavations at Trusty's Hill, Anwoth, 1960', *TDGNHAS*, xxxviii (1959–60), 58–70.

Thomas, C., 'Ardwall Island, the excavation of an early Christian site of Irish type', *TDGNHAS*, xliii (1966), 84–116.

Thomas, C., 'An early Christian cemetery and chapel site on Ardwall Island, Kirkcudbright, *Medieval Archaeology*, xi (1967), 127–88.

Thornton, D. E., 'The genealogy of Gruffudd ap Cynan', in K. L. Maund (ed.), *Gruffudd ap Cynan: A Collaborative Biography* (Woodbridge, 1996), 79–108.

Topping, P., 'Harald Maddadson, earl of Orkney and Caithness, 1139–1206', *SHR*, lxii (1983), 105–20.

Watson, F., 'Adapting tradition? The earls of Strathearn', in R. D. Oram and G. P. Stell (eds), *Lordship and Architecture in Medieval and Renaissance Scotland* (East Linton, 2000).

Watt, D. E. R., 'The minority of Alexander III of Scotland', *TRHS*, xxi (1971), 1–23.

Webster, K., 'Galloway and the Romances', *Modern Language Notes*, lv (1940), 363–66.

Whyte, I. D., 'Shielings in the upland pastoral economy of the Lake District in medieval and early modern times', in J. Baldwin and I. D. Whyte (eds), *Scandinavians in Cumbria* (Edinburgh, 1981).

Williams, J., 'A crannog at Loch Arthur, New Abbey', *TDGNHAS*, xlviii (1971), 121–24.

Wilson, P. A., 'St Ninian and Candida Casa: literary evidence from Ireland', *TDGNHAS*, xli (1962–63), 156–85.

Winchester, A. L., 'The distribution and significance of the place-name "bordland" in medieval Britain', *Agricultural History Review*, xxxiv (1986), 129–39.

Yeoman, P. and others, 'Excavations at Castlehill of Strachan, 1980–81', *PSAS*, 114 (1984), 315–64.

Young, A., 'The political role of Walter Comyn, earl of Menteith, during the minority of Alexander III of Scotland', *SHR*, lvii (1978), 121–42.

INDEX